MAX-PLANCK-GESELLSCHAFT

Universität Augsburg University

TECHNISCHE UNIVERSITÄT MÜNCHEN

THE GEORGE WASHINGTON UNIVERSITY

WASHINGTON, DC

MIPLC Studies

Volume 37

Eugenio Hoss

Deceptive Conducts before the Patent Office

Challenges for Patent Law and Competition Law

Nomos

MIPLC Munich Intellectual Property Law Center
Augsburg München Washington DC

This publication was supported by the Max Planck Society.

The Deutsche Nationalbibliothek lists this publication in the Deutsche Nationalbibliografie; detailed bibliographic data are available on the Internet at http://dnb.d-nb.de

a.t.: München, LMU, Diss., 2018

ISBN 978-3-8487-6134-0 (Print)
978-3-7489-0257-7 (ePDF)

British Library Cataloguing-in-Publication Data
A catalogue record for this book is available from the British Library.

ISBN 978-3-8487-6134-0 (Print)
978-3-7489-0257-7 (ePDF)

Library of Congress Cataloging-in-Publication Data
Hoss, Eugenio
Deceptive Conducts before the Patent Office
Challenges for Patent Law and Competition Law
Eugenio Hoss
335 pp.
Includes bibliographic references.

ISBN 978-3-8487-6134-0 (Print)
978-3-7489-0257-7 (ePDF)

DOI: https://doi.org/10.5771/9783748902577

Published by Nomos Verlagsgesellschaft, Baden-Baden, Germany 2019.
Printed and bound in Germany.

1st Edition 2019

Table of Contents

List of Abbreviations

AGCM	Autorità Garante della Concorrenza e del Mercato (Italian Competition Agency)
AIA	Leahy-Smith America Invents Act
ANDA	Abbreviated New Drug Application
ATC	WHO's Anatomical Therapeutic Chemical Classification System
BGB	Bürgerliches Gesetzbuch (German Civil Code)
BGH	Bundesgerichtshof (German Federal Supreme Court)
CFR	US Code of Federal Regulations
CJEU	Court of Justice of the European Union
Commission	European Commission
DoJ	United States Department of Justice
DPMA	Deutsches Patent- und Markenamt (German Patent and Trademark Office)
EEA Agreement	Agreement on the European Economic Area
EEC Treaty	Treaty establishing the European Economic Community
EPC	European Patent Convention
EPI	Institute of Professional Representatives before the European Patent Office
EPO	European Patent Office
EPÜ	Europäisches Patentübereinkommen (European Patent Convention)
EU	European Union
FDA	United States Food and Drug Administration
FRAND	Fair, Reasonable, and Non-Discriminatory
FTC	United States Federal Trade Commission
FTC Act	Federal Trade Commission Act
GC	General Court of the European Union
H2 blockers	Histamine Receptor Antagonists
IDS	Information Disclosure Statement
IP	Intellectual Property
IPR	Intellectual Property Right
ITC	United States International Trade Commission
MPEP	Manual of Patent Examining Procedure of the United States Patent and Trademark Office
NCA	National Competition Authority
NDA	New Drug Application
NHS	UK National Health Service
OFT	UK Office of Fair Trading

OLG	Oberlandesgericht (German Higher Regional Court)
PatAnwO	Patentanwaltsordnung (German Patent Attorneys' Regulation)
PatG	Deutsches Patentgesetz (German Patent Act)
PCT	Patent Cooperation Treaty
PPI	Proton Pump Inhibitors
R&D	Research and Development
SPC	Supplementary Protection Certificate
SSO	Standard Setting Organisation
StGB	Strafgesetzbuch (German Criminal Code)
TEU	Treaty on European Union
TFEU	Treaty on the Functioning of the European Union
TRIPS Agreement	Agreement on Trade-Related Aspects of Intellectual Property Rights
UK	United Kingdom
UKIPO	United Kingdom Intellectual Property Office
UPC	Unified Patent Court
US, USA	United States of America
USC	United States Code
USPTO	United States Patent and Trademark Office
UWG	Gesetz gegen den unlauteren Wettbewerb (German Act Against Unfair Competition)
WHO	World Health Organization
WIPO	World Intellectual Property Organization
WTO	World Trade Organization
ZPO	Zivilprozessordnung (German Civil Procedural Rules)

Table of Cases

Argentina

Monsanto Co s/ Apel Resol Comisión Nacional de Defensa de la Competencia (case 13676/07) (decision of the Federal Court of Appeals of 30 Semptember 2008)

Australia

Prestige Group (Australia) v Dart Industries, [1992] FSR 143 (Federal Court of Australia)

Brazil

Eli Lilly do Brasil Ltda (Case 08012.011508/2007-91) (decision of the Conselho Administrativo de Defesa Econόmica of 20 August 2014)

European Patent Organisation

Administrative Agreement/MEDTRONIC (Joined Cases G 5/88, G 7/88 and G 8/88) (decision of the EPO Enlarged Board of Appeal of 16 November 1990)

Rokicki (T 0952/00) (decision of the EPO Boards of Appeal of 27 November 2002)

Samsung Electronics (T 2321/08) (decision of the EPO Technical Board of Appeal of 11 May 2009)

Samsung Electronics (T 1123/09) (decision of the EPO Technical Board of Appeal of 17 December 2009)

European Union

Aalborg Portland A/S v Commission (Joined Cases C-204/00 P, C-205/00 P, C-211/00 P, C-213/00 P, C-217/00 P and C-219/00 P) [2004] ECR I-123

AKZO Chemie BV v Commission (C-62/86) [1991] ECR I-3359

AstraZeneca (C-223/01) [2003] ECR I-11809

AstraZeneca (Case COMP/A.37.507/F3) (Commission Decision 2006/857/CE [2006] OJ L332/24)

AstraZeneca v Commission (T-321/05) [2010] ECR II-2805

AstraZeneca v Commission (C-457/10 P) (CJEU, 6 December 2012, ECLI:EU:C:2012:770)

BBI/Boosey & Hawkes: Interim Measures (Case IV/32.279) (Commission Decision 87/500/EEC [1987] OJ L286/36)

Boehringer Ingelheim (Case COMP/39.246)

British Airways v Commission (C-95/04 P) [2007] ECR I-2331

Bronner, Oscar v Mediaprint Zeitungs- und Zeitschriftenverlag (C-7/97) [1998] ECR I-7791

Bundesanstalt für den Güterfernverkehr v Gebrüder Reiff GmbH & Co KG (C-185/91) [1993] ECR I-5801

Centrafarm BV v Sterling Drug Inc (15/74) [1974] ECR 1147

Compagnie Maritime Belge Transports v Commission (Joined Cases C-395/96 P and C-396/96 P) [2000] ECR I-1365

Consorzio Industrie Fiammiferi (CIF) v AGCM (C-198/01) [2003] ECR I-8055

Consten, Établissements SàRL and Grundig-Verkaufs-GmbH v Commission (Joined Cases 56 and 58/64) [1966] ECR 299

Decca Navigator System (Case IV/30.979 and 31.394) (Commission Decision 89/113/EEC [1989] OJ L43/27)

Deutsche Grammophon GmbH v Metro-SB-Großmärkte GmbH (78/70) [1971] ECR 487

Europemballage Corporation and Continental Can Company Inc v Commission (6/72) [1973] ECR 215

Farmitalia (C-392/97) [1999] ECR I-5553

French-West African Shipowners' Committees (Case IV/32.450) (Commission Decision 92/262/EEC [1992] OJ L134/1)

GB-INNO-BM SA v Association des Détaillants en Tabac (ATAB) (13/77) [1977] ECR 2115

GlaxoSmithKline v Commission (Joined Cases C-501/06 P, C-513/06 P, C-515/06 P and C-519/06 P) [2009] ECR I-9291

Hässle AB v Ratiopharm GmbH (C-127/00) [2003] ECR I-14781

Hilti AG v Commission (T-30/89) [1991] ECR II-1439

Hoffmann-La Roche & Co AG v Commission (85/76) [1979] ECR 461

Huawei Technologies Co. Ltd v ZTE Corp., ZTE Deutschland GmbH (Case C-170/13) (CJEU, 16 July 2015, ECLI:EU:C:2015:477)

IMS Health GmbH & Co OHG v NDC Health GmbH & Co KG (C-418/01) [2004] ECR I-5039

Industrie des Poudres Sphériques (IPS) SA v Commission (T-5/97) [2000] ECR II-3755

Intel (Case COMP/C-3/37.990) (Commission Decision of 13 May 2009 [2009] OJ C227/13)

ITT Promedia NV v Commission (T-111/96) [1998] ECR II 2937

Johnston v Chief Constable of the Royal Ulster Constabulary (C-222/84) [1986] ECR I-1651

Keurkoop BV v Nancy Kean Gifts BV (144/81) [1982] ECR 2853

Konkurrensverket v TeliaSonera Sverige AB (C-52/09) [2011] ECR I-527

Metro SB-Großmärkte GmbH & Co KG v Commission (75/84) [1986] ECR 3021

Microsoft Corp v Commission (T-201/04) [2007] ECR II-3601

Motorola - Enforcement of GPRS standard essential patents (Case AT.39985) (Commission Decision C(2014) 2892 [2014] OJ C344/6)

Nederlandsche Banden-Industrie-Michelin v Commission (322/81) [1983] ECR 3461

Parke, Davis & Co v Probel (24/67) [1968] ECR 55

Post Danmark A/S v Konkurrencerådet (C-209/10) (CJEU, 27 March 2012)

Protégé International Ltd v Commission (T-119/09) [2012] OJ C319/6

Radio Telefis Eireann (RTE) and Independent Television Publications Ltd (ITP) v Commission (Joined Cases C-241/91 P and C-242/91 P) [1995] ECR I-743 (*Magill*)

Rambus (Case COMP/38.636) (Commission Decision 2010/C 30/09 [2010] OJ C30/17)

Samsung - Enforcement of UMTS standard essential patents (Case AT.39939) (Commission Decision C(2014) 2891 [2014] OJ C350/8)

Servier v. Commission (T-691/14) (GC, 12 December 2018, ECLI:EU:T:2018:922)

Sot Lélos kai Sia EE v GlaxoSmithKline (Joined Cases C-468/06 to C-478/06) [2008] ECR I-7139

Synetairismos Farmakopoion Aitolias & Akarnanias (Syfait) v GlaxoSmithKline plc (C-53/03) [2005] ECR I-4609

Tetra Pak Rausing SA v Commission (T-51/89) [1990] ECR II-309 (*Tetra Pak I*)

Tetra Pak International SA v Commission (C-333/94 P) [1996] ECR I-5951 (*Tetra Pak II*)

Thetford Corp v Fiamma SpA (35/87) [1988] ECR 3585

United Brands Co v Commission (27/76) [1978] ECR 207

Van Eycke, Pascal v ASPA NV (267/86) [1988] ECR 4769

Volvo AB v Erik Veng (UK) Ltd (C-238/87) [1988] ECR 6211

France

Dolle v Emsens PIBD [1991] 491 III 2 (CA Paris, 11 October 1990)

Germany

Dermatex BGH [1977] GRUR 494
Kunststoffrohrteil BGH [2002] GRUR 511
Luftabscheider für Milchsammelanlage BGH [2006] GRUR 923
Rechtsmittel BGH [1954] GRUR 107
Zierfalten BGH [1965] GRUR 231
OLG Düsseldorf, decision of 14 June 2007, case I-2 U 135/05
OLG Düsseldorf, decision of 26 June 2008, case I-2 U 130/06
OLG Düsseldorf, decision of 6 June 2013, case I-2 U 60/11

Italy

Pfizer Italia srl (decision of the Tribunale Amministrativo Regionale per il Lazio 7467/2012 of 3 Septeeember 2012)

Pfizer Italia srl (decision of the Consiglio di Stato (Italy) 693/2014 of 12 February 2014)

RATIOPHARM/PFIZER (A431) (Provvedimento n. 23194, Autorità Garante della Concorrenza e del Mercato, 11 January 2012, Bollettino n 2/2012)

Netherlands

Dijkstra v Saier C05/200HR (decision of the Supreme Court of the Netherlands of 22 December 2006)

Spain

Pfizer Health AB (Case S/0441/12) (decision of the Comisión Nacional de los Mercados y la Competencia of 13 February 2014)

United Kingdom

Actavis UK Ltd v Eli Lilly & Co [2014] EWHC 1511 (Pat)

Bristol-Myers Squibb Co v Baker Norton Pharmaceuticals Inc [1998] EWHC Patents 300

Chevron Research Company's Extension, Re [1975] FSR 1 (Chancery Division)
Chocosuisse Union Des Fabricants Suisses De Chocolat v Cadbury Ltd [1997] EWHC 360 (Pat)
Clevite Corporation's Patent, Re [1966] RPC 199
Crawford Adjusters v Sagicor General Insurance (Cayman) Ltd [2013] UKPC 17
Dering v Earl of Winchelsea (1787) 1 Cox 318
General Tire & Rubber Co Ltd v Firestone Tyre & Rubber Co Ltd [1975] RPC 203 (Court of Appeal)
Hoechst Marion Roussel Ltd v Kirin-Amgen Inc [2002] EWHC 471 (Pat)
Hormel Foods Corp v Antilles Landscape Investments NV [2005] EWHC 13 (Ch)
Kirin-Amgen Inc v Hoechst Marion Roussel Ltd [2004] UKHL 46
Laboratoires Servier, Les v Apotex Inc [2008] EWCA Civ 445
Reckitt Benckiser Healthcare (UK) Ltd (CE/8931/08) (OFT Decision of 12 April 2011 CA98/02/2011)
Rohm and Haas Co v Collag Ltd [2001] EWCA Civ 1589
Royal Bank of Scotland, The Plc v Highland Financial Partners LP [2013] EWCA Civ 328
Valensi v British Radio Corp [1973] RPC 337 (Court of Appeal)

United States

Abbott Laboratories v Sandoz Inc 544 F 3d 1341 (Fed Cir 2008)
Akzo, NV v EI DuPont de Nemours 810 F 2d 1148 (Fed Cir 1987)
Allied Tube & Conduit Corp v Indian Head Inc 486 US 492 (1988)
American Hoist & Derrick Co v Sowa & Sons Inc 725 F 2d 1350 (Fed Cir 1984)
American Tobacco Co v United States 328 US 781 (1946)
Argus Chemical Corp v Fibre Glass-Evercoat Co Inc 759 F 2d 10 (Fed Cir 1985)
American Cyanamid Company v FTC 363 F 2d 757 (6th Cir 1966)
Armstrong Surgical Center Inc v Armstrong County Memorial Hospital 185 F 3d 154 (3rd Cir 1999)
Aspen Skiing Co v Aspen Highlands Skiing Corp 472 US 585 (1985)
Atari Games Corp v Nintendo of America Inc 897 F 2d 1572 (Fed Cir 1990)
Aventis Pharma SA v Amphastar Pharmaceuticals Inc 525 F 3d 1334 (Fed Cir 2008)
BE&K Construction Co v National Labor Relations Board 536 US 516 (2002)
Bement v National Harrow Co 186 US 70 (1902)
Blonder-Tongue Laboratories Inc v University of Illinois Foundation 402 US 313 (1971)
BRASSELER, USA I, LP v Stryker Sales Corp 267 F 3d 1370 (Fed Cir 2001)
Braun, B Medical Inc v Abbott Laboratories 124 F 3d 1419, 1427 (Fed Cir 1997)

Broadcast Music Inc (BMI) v Columbia Broadcasting System (CBS) 441 US 1 (1979)
Brooke Group Ltd v Brown & Williamson Tobacco Corp 509 US 209 (1993)
Brown Shoe Co v United States 370 US 294 (1962)
Brulotte v Thys Co 379 US 29 (1964)
Brunswick Corp v Riegel Textile Corp 752 F 2d 261 (7th Cir 1984)
Burlington Industries Inc v Dayco Corp 849 F 2d 1418 (Fed Cir 1988)
Buspirone Patent Litigation, Re 185 F Supp. 2d 363 (SD New York 2002)
California Eastern Laboratories Inc v Gould 896 F 2d 400 (9th Cir 1990)
California Motor Transport Co v Trucking Unlimited 404 US 508 (1972)
California Retail Liquor Dealers Assn v Midcal Aluminum Inc 445 US 97 (1980)
Cheminor Drugs Ltd v Ethyl Corp 168 F 3d 119 (3rd Cir 1999)
City of Columbia v Omni Outdoor Advertising Inc 499 US 365 (1991)
Consolidated Aluminum Corp v Foseco Int'l Ltd 910 F 2d 804 (Fed Cir 1990)
Continental TV Inc v GTE Sylvania Inc 433 US 36 (1977)
Coordinated Pretrial Proceedings in Antibiotic Antitrust Actions, Re 538 F 2d 180 (8th Cir 1976)
CR Bard Inc v M3 Systems Inc 157 F 3d 1340 (Fed Cir 1998)
Critikon Inc v Becton Dickinson Vascular Access Inc 120 F 3d 1253 (Fed Cir 1997)
CVD Inc v Raytheon Co 769 F 2d 842 (1st Cir 1985)
Cygnus Therapeutic Systems v Alza Corp 92 F 3d 1153 (Fed Cir 1996)
Dayco Products Inc v Total Containment Inc 329 F 3d 1358 (Fed Cir 2003)
Delano Farms Co v The California Table Grape Commission 655 F 3d 1337 (Fed Cir 2011)
Dell Computer Corporation (FTC Docket C-3658) 121 FTC 616 (1996)
Dick, AB Co v Burroughs Corp 798 F 2d 1392 (Fed Cir 1986)
Digital Control Inc v Charles Machine Works 437 F 3d 1309 (Fed Cir 2006)
Dippin' Dots Inc v Mosey 476 F 3d 1337 (Fed Cir 2007)
Driscoll v Cebalo 731 F 2d 878 (Fed Cir 1984)
Eastern Railroad Presidents Conference v Noerr Motor Freight Inc 365 US 127 (1961)
Eastman Kodak Co v Image Technical Services Inc 504 US 451 (1992)
Ethyl Gasoline Corp v United States 309 US 436 (1940)
Festo Corp v Shoketsu Kinzoku Kogyo Kabushiki Co Ltd 535 US 722 (2002)
FMC Corp v Hennessy Industries Inc 836 F 2d 521 (Fed Cir 1987)
Food Machinery & Chemical Corp v Walker Process Equipment Inc 335 F 2d 315 (7th Cir 1964)
Frank's Casing Crew & Rental Tools Inc v PMR Technologies Inc 292 F 3d 1363 (Fed Cir 2002)
Frazier v Roessel Cine Photo Tech Inc 417 F 3d 1230 (Fed Cir 2005)

FTC v Actavis Inc 133 S Ct 2223 (2013)
FTC v Superior Court Trial Lawyers Association (SCTLA) 493 US 411 (1990)
Gambro Lundia AB v Baxter Healthcare Corp 110 F 3d 1573 (Fed Cir 1997)
Grip-Pak Inc v Illinois Tool Works Inc 694 F 2d 466 (7th Cir 1982)
Handgards Inc v Ethicon Inc 601 F 2d 986 (9th Cir 1979) (*Handgards I*)
Handgards Inc v Ethicon Inc 743 F 2d 1282 (9th Cir 1984) (*Handgards II*)
Hazel-Atlas Glass Co v Hartford-Empire Co 322 US 238 (1944)
Hotchkiss v Greenwood 52 US 248 (1950)
Hydranautics v FilmTec Corp 70 F 3d 533 (9th Cir 1995)
Hydril Co LP v Grant Prideco LP 474 F 3d 1344 (Fed Cir 2007)
Illinois Tool Works Inc v Independent Ink Inc 547 US 28 (2006)
Independent Service Organizations Antitrust Litigation, Re 203 F 3d 1322 (Fed Cir 2000)
Innogenetics, NV v Abbott Laboratories 512 F 3d 1363 (Fed Cir 2008)
Intel Corporation (FTC Docket 9341) (Statement of Chairman Leibowitz and Commissioner Rosch of 16 December 2009)
International Salt Co Inc v United States 332 US 392 (1947)
Jaskiewicz v Mossinghoff 822 F 2d 1053 (Fed Cir 1987)
Jefferson Parish Hospital District No 2 v Hyde 466 US 2 (1984)
Keystone Driller Co v General Excavator Co 290 US 240 (1933)
Kimble v Marvel Entm't, LLC 135 S Ct 2401 (2015)
Kingsdown Medical Consultants, Ltd v Hollister Inc 863 F 2d 867 (Fed Cir 1988)
Kingsland v Dorsey 338 US 318 (1949)
Kobe Inc v Dempsey Pump Co 198 F 2d 416 (10th Cir 1952)
Kottle v Northwest Kidney Centers 146 F 3d 1056 (9th Cir 1998)
Landmarks Holding Corp v Bermant 664 F 2d 891 (2nd Cir 1981)
Lighting World Inc v Birchwood Lighting Inc 382 F 3d 1354 (Fed Cir 2004)
Litton Systems Inc v American Telephone & Telegraph Co 700 F 2d 785 (2nd Cir 1983)
Loctite Corp v Ultraseal Ltd 781 F 2d 861 (Fed Cir 1985)
Madey v Duke University 307 F 3d 1351 (Fed Cir 2002)
Mallinckrodt Inc v Medipart Inc 976 F 2d 700 (Fed Cir 1992)
Manville Sales Corp v Paramount Systems Inc 917 F 2d 544 (Fed Cir 1990)
Mercoid Corp v Mid-Continent Investment Co 320 US 661 (1944)
Microsoft Corp v i4i Ltd Partnership 131 S Ct 2238 (2011)
Molins PLC v Textron Inc 48 F 3d 1172 (Fed Cir 1995)
Monolith Portland Midwest Co v Kaiser Aluminium & Chemical Corp 407 F 2d 288 (9th Cir 1969)
Monsanto Co v Rohm & Haas Co 456 F 2d 592 (3rd Cir 1972)

Morton Salt Co v G S Suppiger Co 314 US 488 (1942)
Motion Picture Patents Co v Universal Film Manufacturing Co 243 US 502 (1917)
Mueller Brass Co v Reading Industries Inc 352 F Supp. 1357 (ED Pa 1972)
Nilssen v Osram Sylvania Inc 504 F 3d 1223 (Fed Cir 2007)
Nobelpharma AB v Implant Innovations Inc 141 F 3d 1059 (Fed Cir 1998)
Norton v Curtiss 433 F 2d 779 (CCPA 1970)
Norton Co v Carborundum Co 530 F 2d 435 (1st Cir 1976)
Organon Inc v Mylan Pharmaceuticals Inc 293 F Supp 2d 453 (D NJ 2003)
Otter Tail Power Co v United States 410 US 366 (1973)
Parker v Brown 317 US 341 (1943)
Penn Yan Boats Inc v Sea Lark Boats 359 F Supp. 948 (SD Fla 1972)
Phillips v AWH Corp 415 F 3d 1303 (Fed Cir 2005) (en banc)
Plastic Container Corp v Continental Plastics of Oklahoma Inc 607 F 2d 885 (10th Cir 1979)
Precision Instrument Manufacturing Co v Automotive Maintenance Machinery Co 143 F 2d 332 (7th Cir 1944)
Precision Instrument Manufacturing Co v Automotive Maintenance Machinery Co 324 US 806 (1945).
Premier Electrical Construction Co v National Electrical Contractors Assn Inc 814 F 2d 358 (7th Cir 1987)
Primetime 24 Joint Venture v National Broadcasting Co Inc 219 F 3d 92 (2nd Cir 2000)
Princo Corp v International Trade Commission 616 F 3d 1318 (Fed Cir 2010) (en banc)
Professional Real Estate Investors Inc v Columbia Pictures Industries Inc 508 US 49 (1993)
Purdue Pharma LP v Endo Pharmaceuticals Inc 410 F 3d 690 (Fed. Cir. 2005)
Rambus (FTC Docket 9302) (Opinion of the Commission of 2 August 2006)
Rambus Inc v FTC 522 F.3d 456 (DC Cir 2008)
Ritz Camera & Image LLC v SanDisk Corp 700 F 3d 503 (Fed Cir 2012)
Rohm & Haas Co v Crystal Chemical Co 722 F 2d 1556 (Fed Cir 1983)
Scanner Technologies Corp v Icos Vision Systems Corp NV 528 F 3d 1365 (Fed Cir 2008)
SCM Corp v Xerox Corp 645 F 2d 1195 (2nd Cir 1981)
Senza-Gel Corp v Seiffhart 803 F 2d 661 (Fed Cir 1986)
Southern Pacific Communications Co v AT&T Co 740 F 2d 980 (DC Cir 1984)
Spectrum Sports Inc v McQuillan 506 US 447 (1993)
St Joseph's Hospital Inc v Hospital Corp of America 795 F 2d 948 (11th Cir 1986)
Star Scientific Inc v RJ Reynolds Tobacco Co 537 F 3d 1357 (Fed Cir 2008)
Stevens, JP & Co Inc v Lex Tex Ltd 747 F 2d 1553 (Fed Cir 1984)

Swift & Co v United States 196 US 375 (1905)

Therasense Inc v Becton, Dickinson & Co 649 F 3d 1276 (Fed Cir 2011) (en banc)

Times-Picayune Publishing Co v United States 345 US 594 (1953)

Tops Markets Inc v Quality Markets Inc 142 F 3d 90 (2nd Cir 1998)

Toys "R" Us v FTC 221 F 3d 928 (7th Cir 2000)

Transource Int'l Inc v Trinity Industries Inc 725 F 2d 274 (5th Cir 1984)

Twin City Bakery Workers v Astra Aktiebolag 207 F Supp 2d 221 (SD NY 2002)

Tyco Healthcare Group LP v Mutual Pharmaceutical Co Inc 762 F 3d 1338 (Fed Cir 2014)

Union Oil Company of California (FTC Docket 9305) (Opinion of the Commission of 7 July 2004) (*Unocal*)

United Mine Workers of America v Pennington 381 US 657 (1965)

United States v Aluminium Company of America (Alcoa), 148 F 2d 416 (2nd Cir 1945)

United States v Columbia Steel Co 334 US 495 (1948)

United States v EI du Pont de Nemours & Co 351 US 377 (1956)

United States v Grinnell Corp 384 US 563 (1966)

United States v Line Material Co 333 US 287 (1948)

United States v Microsoft Corp 253 F 3d 34 (DC Cir 2001)

United States v Standard Electric Time Co 155 F Supp 949 (D Mass 1957)

United States v Univis Lens Co 316 US 241 (1942)

Unitherm Food Systems Inc v Swift-Eckrich Inc 375 F 3d 1341 (Fed Cir 2004)

USM Corp v SPS Technologies Inc 694 F 2d 505 (7th Cir 1982)

USS-Posco Industries v Contra Costa County Building & Construction Trades Council 31 F 3d 800 (9th Cir 1994)

Verizon Communications Inc v Law Offices of Curtis V Trinko, LLP 540 US 398 (2004)

Walker Process Equipment Inc v Food Machinery & Chemical Corp 382 US 172 (1965)

Whelan v Abell 48 F 3d 1247 (DC Cir 1995)

Windsurfing International Inc v AMF Inc 782 F 2d 995 (Fed Cir 1986)

Woods Exploration & Producing Co Inc v Aluminum Co of America 438 F 2d 1286 (5th Cir, 1971)

Chapter I: Introduction

1. *The Underlying Problem*

In a recent patent infringement case between Servier and Apotex, courts in the UK were asked to look into the validity of a pharmaceutical patent that claimed a particular crystalline form of a compound called perindopril. Perindopril is a pharmaceutical compound essentially used to treat hypertension. Its preparation and use had been disclosed in a prior patent. The patent in the referred case, however, claimed a specific crystalline form of a specific salt of this compound, ie the alpha crystalline form of the tert-butylamine salt of perindopril.[1] The High Court found this patent to be invalid for lack of novelty and obviousness According to the findings of the High Court, the patentee had applied for this patent aware that any known process for producing perindopril would have resulted in the object protected by the new patent. The court further explained that the invalidity of the patent could not be expected to be spotted by the patent office at the examination stage, as some experimental evidence would have been required. The Court of Appeals confirmed the decision of the High Court.

Although these findings have been called into question by the General Court and the invalidity of the patent is in fact far from clear,[2] the judgment of the Court of Appeals, given by LJ Jacob, made in passing a handful of interesting remarks which deserve closer scrutiny.

In the first place, the judgment showed concern about the existence of 'specious' patents[3] and stated that '[t]he only solution to this type of undesirable patent is a rapid and efficient method for obtaining its revocation', so that 'it can be got rid of before it does too much harm to the public

1 *Les Laboratoires Servier v Apotex Inc* [2008] EWCA Civ 445.

2 Case T-691/14 *Servier v. Commission* (GC, 12 December 2018, ECLI:EU:T:2018:922). Indeed, when assessing a settlement agreement between Servier and Krka, the GC clearly stated that both parties had good reasons to believe that the patent was in fact valid (paras 1147-1205). For a closer analysis of the Servier case, see Joseph Straus, 'Can Antitrust Adequately Assess Patent Settlement Agreements Disconnected from Patent Law Relevant Facts? The Servier Case – Its Public Perception and its Underlying Facts' (2016) 38 EIPR 533.

3 *Les Laboratoires Servier v Apotex Inc* (n 1) [9]. The court stated in this regard that it is 'the sort of patent which can give the patent system a bad name.'

interest.'[4] At the most, continued the decision, courts could award costs 'if the patent is defended unreasonably.'[5]

Secondly, the Court of Appeals highlighted that competition law could hypothetically provide an additional remedy against this kind of patents, though it lamented that this area of law 'thus far has had nothing or virtually nothing to say about unmeritorious patents.'[6]

As mentioned above, the 'unmeritoruous' nature of Servier's patent is in fact far from certain.[7] Yet regardless of the merits of that particular case, into which it is not necessary to delve for the purposes of this work, the observations of the Court of Appeals prompt two general and far-reaching questions which do not typically loom among European courts. In the first place, it raises the question of the available remedies under patent law, either *de lege lata* or *de lege ferenda*, for countering situations involving deceptive or in some other way undesirable conducts before the patent office. Is it true, in this regard, that the only solution for patent law is to have those patents promptly revoked—and perhaps award legal costs? Secondly, but no less important, it puts a question mark over the role that competition law could play in addressing conducts taking place before the patent office. The judgment insinuates that this field of law could indeed provide an alternative solution against dishonest strategies, though it seems to bay for clearer standards on the matter.

2. *Deceptive Behaviour in Patent Procedures and Available Remedies under Patent Law*

On the first aspect, and moving on from the particularities of the English lawsuit to the more general questions that it entails, it should be noted at the outset that the current legal situation in most EU Member States does not differ much from the one described by the UK Court of Appeals. Indeed, under the existing patent and procedural laws in these jurisdictions, if an undertaking prosecutes a patent application without good faith or resorts to deceptive manoeuvres, neither the patent offices nor the courts dispose of meaningful remedies other than the rejection of the patent application—or, if granted, its subsequent invalidation—and the award of legal

4 ibid.

5 ibid [10].

6 ibid.

7 In fact, the fraudulent nature of the patent discussed in that case was later called into question by the General Court. See text in n 2.

costs. In exceptional circumstances, disciplinary sanctions may also come into play, but probably not much more.

US courts and legislature, in their turn, have historically adopted a completely different approach. On the one hand, they seem to expect from patent applicants a much more cooperative role during the examination procedure by imposing upon them a strict duty of candour. This burden includes, inter alia, the duty to disclose relevant prior art information of which applicants are aware and which they believe might be relevant for the examination of the patent application. On the other hand, failure from the patent applicants to comply with such stringent duties can have devastating consequences during litigation, as courts may find the patent unenforceable on the basis of inequitable conduct.

The inequitable conduct doctrine, which stems from the long-established doctrine of unclean hands, is a rather unique feature of the American patent litigation system and has been developed throughout decades of case law. Over time, it has become a recurrent component of patent infringement suits and also an object of fierce criticism for its wide scope and for increasing the complexity and costs of litigation. It has even been labelled an 'absolute plague'[8] due to the frequency with which it is unsuccessfully invoked. Be that as it may, few courts or scholars dare to advocate for its complete eradication, most of them rather suggesting amendments to reduce its negative effects or a revamp into an economic tool for attaining optimal information levels at the patent office.

In this light, it seems worth considering whether any of those features present under US patent law deserve consideration by European law—be that the EPO, the EU or the national laws of any of their Member States. This would involve asking, in the first place, whether it would be advisable to widen the range of duties imposed upon patent applicants, eg in order to collect material information on patentability. Secondly, if the patent is ultimately granted, one might wonder whether the hypothetical bad faith of a patent applicant before the patent office should become a relevant issue during patent litigation and, in that case, whether it in fact calls for a distinct set of remedies.

---

8 *Burlington Industries Inc v Dayco Corp* 849 F 2d 1418, 1422 (Fed Cir 1988).

3. The Patenting Procedure under the Spotlight of Competition Law. Yet another Angle for the IP v Competition Law Debate

Irrespective of the way in which patent law regulates the patenting procedure and the extent to which patent courts are entitled to take it into account during litigation, the question also arises whether the behaviour of a patent applicant before the patent office can constitute a relevant conduct from a competition law standpoint. Can the deceitful procurement of a patent configure a case of abuse of a dominant position (within the terms of EU law) or monopolisation (in the terms of US antitrust law)?

If one looks into the concerns that are commonly studied by European courts and scholars, it may be noticed that the question of deceptive conduct before the patent office has not traditionally occupied a central place among the general debate on intellectual property and competition. The question, however, seems to have recently gained more attention and certainly offers another interesting angle from where to explore the general interaction between these two areas of law.

It should be noted that, because of their very nature, every patent—regardless of how it has been obtained—is theoretically capable of imposing restrictions upon competitors. In fact, under general conditions, this constitutes one of the distinctive aspects of the patent system, as it encourages firms to innovate with the perspective that they will later enjoy exclusive rights over the accomplished inventions. Furthermore, because patents also incentivise competition in innovation, they also constitute a valuable tool from a competition law standpoint. However, in the hypothetical case where a patent applicant resorts to deceptive strategies to obtain a patent, the fundamental premises underlying the normal equilibrium between intellectual property and competition are disrupted and the intervention of competition law may thus be justified.

The *Servier v Apotex* decision cited above regretted that competition law had virtually nothing to say on this particular question. Since then, however, the CJEU has passed its seminal *AstraZeneca* judgment which dealt precisely with conducts taking place before a patent office.[9] While it is true that *AstraZeneca* concerned a very specific set of facts, essentially related to SPCs and marketing authorisations for pharmaceutical products, the decision unquestionably sheds some light on the problem and confirms that

9 Case C-457/10 P *AstraZeneca v Commission* (CJEU, 6 December 2012, ECLI:EU:C:2012:770).

the way in which an undertaking conducts its patent application can be a target for competition law scrutiny.

On the other side of the Atlantic, a similar question was posited to the US Supreme Court several decades ago in the *Walker Process* case[10] and since then has been on the table in several court judgments. As a matter of fact, it is a defence not seldom raised by defendants in the course of patent infringement suits. Although those pleas very rarely emerge victorious, US courts broadly recognise that these conducts can be a source for antitrust concern. The standards employed by most of them, though, do not entirely coincide with the CJEU's reading in *AstraZeneca* and their approach tends to focus on the enforcement of the patents obtained through fraudulent means rather than on the fraudulent conduct and following grant of the patent itself.

The differences between both jurisdictions may well originate from divergent underlying approaches, but also from historical circumstances, differences in the legal systems and from nuances in the language of the relevant legal provisions. In any case, it would be important to determine how competition law ought to tackle this kind of behaviour by identifying the appropriate theory of harm and, on that basis, develop corresponding standards for its assessment—logically without forgetting that the particularities of each jurisdiction's legal system may ultimately call for different antidotes.

4. *Scope and Structure of this Work*

In the light of the range of interrogations prompted along the preceding paragraphs, the purpose of this work is broken down into two essential research questions. In the first place, and based on the US experience with a strict duty of candour and a vast application of the inequitable conduct doctrine, this project seeks to determine whether there are any lessons to be learnt for Europe—or any other jurisdiction with similar legal system—on these particular aspects. More specifically, it explores (i) whether it would be advisable to impose stricter duties upon patent applicants, eg by demanding from them the disclosure of relevant prior art, and (ii) regardless of the extent of those duties, whether it would be sensible for

10 *Walker Process Equipment Inc v Food Machinery & Chemical Corp* 382 US 172 (1965).

courts to take into account the hypothetical bad faith of a patent applicant as an autonomous defence during infringement proceedings.

In the second place, but certainly no less important, this project attempts to determine how competition law should apply vis-à-vis scenarios involving deceptive conducts before a patent office. The decisions rendered in the US and the EU certainly provide valuable insights, yet—for different reasons—the theoretical criteria underpinning those judgments are at times ambiguous or imprecise. The aim is, hence, to identify the theory of harm underlying these abuses and, from there, understand how EU and US competition rules may be applied within this particular context.

Towards that end, this work is divided into two basic parts. The first part, which is aimed at exploring the first set of questions, comprises two chapters. Initially, in Chapter II, it provides a brief description of the patenting procedure and of the different steps and requirements that patent applicants must follow, both in the US and in Europe, in order to obtain a patent. Next, Chapter III grapples with the question of the behavioural duties of patent applicants by describing the main features of US patent law's duty of candour and inequitable conduct doctrine and comparing them with the situation in Europe. By way of conclusion, the chapter examines the advantages and drawbacks of both systems and balances whether any of the elements present under US law could or should be transplanted to Europe.

The second part of this work deals with the behaviour of patent applicants from a competition law angle. For this purpose, Chapter IV first briefly introduces the fundamental aims and components of competition law, with a logical emphasis on unilateral behaviours. Later, Chapter V succinctly explains the general interaction between intellectual property rights and competition and comprehensively dissects the existing case law in the EU and in the US on the competitive concerns that may be raised against fraudulently obtained patents. Finally, under Chapter VI, the appropriate theory of harm is explored and basic, across-the-board standards for analysis are sought.

PART I: GENERAL RULES ON THE PATENTING PROCEDURE

Considering that this study mainly focuses on conducts taking place before the patent office, it is imperative in the first place to briefly explain how the procedure at the patent office looks like and, most importantly, analyse what kind of duties and responsibilities the established patent and procedural rules set upon the applicants. This analysis is of vital importance to identify not only what kind of specific abuses might actually come about at the patent office, but also the solutions offered by the patent system in the US and in Europe and the underlying policy considerations that drive said approaches. This should also pave the way for later understanding how competition law may arise as an alternative or additional remedy.

This part of the work, hence, is divided into two chapters. First, in Chapter II, it aims at providing a bird's eye view of the general structure and standard stages that characterise a typical procedure before a patent office. Next, in Chapter III, a detailed description of the duties and obligations of patent applicants is portrayed. In this regard, the legal frameworks of the United States and Europe are compared as representative samples of two diametrically different viewpoints from which the issue can be approached. Considering the particularities of the American approach, the chapter concludes by analysing whether it would be feasible and desirable for the European patent system to adjust the duties that are imposed upon patent applicants or for European courts to embrace an inequitable conduct defence or modify the way in which they should solve disputes involving patents that have been fraudulently obtained.

Chapter II: The Procedure before the Patent Office

1. General Framework

At the outset, it is important to bear in mind that patent protection, in contrast to copyright or other intellectual property rights, is not granted automatically and an inventor must thus formulate a formal application before the patent office in order to obtain protection. In fact, as a general principle, a separate application must be filed before the patent office of every country in which protection is sought and each of those applications has to fulfil a number of formal and language requirements.[11] Furthermore, each of them is thoroughly studied by experts, within an examination process that ordinarily lasts several years, in order to test whether they meet all the substantive patentability requirements and whether their subject-matter is not excluded from patentability. The long and winding road that an inventor is expected to follow before the patent office in order to acquire a patent has become today a quite complex procedure. A quick glance at the Guidelines for Examination of the EPO[12] or at the Manual of Patent Examining Procedure of the USPTO[13] illustrates its complexity and the extent of burdens and details that a patent applicant—and the patent office itself—need to observe.

Much has actually changed since the times when the first patents were granted in Venice and in England, namely, at a time when these exclusive rights for inventions were issued as just one species—and a rather rare one—of the general genus of privileges, licenses and regulations.[14] In the first place, the requisites that an inventor must meet in order to obtain a patent have significantly matured since the early stages of the patent sys-

---

11 It should be borne in mind that more than 150 countries are currently members of the Patent Cooperation Treaty (PCT), which essentially allows inventors to file an international patent application and delay for up to thirty months the decision on whether to continue with the application and, if so, in which countries. See text at nn 146ff.

12 EPO, Guidelines for Examination in the European Patent Office (EPO November 2014) (EPO Guidelines).

13 USPTO, Manual of Patent Examining Procedure (9th edn, 2014) (US MPEP).

14 Neil Davenport, *The United Kingdom Patent System: A Brief History* (Mason 1979) 14.

tem. From a time when patents were synonyms of discretionary concessions from the Crown, passing through a period of heightened controls prompted by the English Statute of Monopolies of 1624,[15] the system has slowly evolved from a discretionary prerogative of the sovereign to a bureaucratic procedure under the now universally recognised principle according to which only true inventors are entitled to get a patent.[16] Furthermore, as the system kept developing, complementary requirements arose. In the eighteenth century, for instance, the courts in England started requiring patentees to make sufficient descriptions of their inventions, which not only helped patent owners to prove infringement but also provided competitors with enough information to attack the validity of the patent.[17] As to the inventive step or non-obviousness requirement, US patent case law has recognised it since at least 1850,[18] although it was only statutorily codified many years later.[19] In any case, despite some minor exceptions,[20] the patentability requirements today are to a large extent harmonised in most parts of the world—particularly after the signing of the TRIPS Agreement, which acknowledged the widely recognised require-

15 William R Cornish, David Llewelyn and Tanya F Aplin, *Intellectual Property: Patents, Copyright, Trade Marks and Allied Rights* (8th edn, Sweet & Maxwell 2013) para 3-05. The Statute of Monopolies was enacted by the English Parliament and imposed a general prohibition on the grant of patents by the Crown, except for those granted to 'a manner of new manufacture'. Lionel Bently and Brad Sherman, *Intellectual Property Law* (4th edn, OUP 2014) 377. The test in place during that period was that the grant should not seek to restrain the public of any freedom or liberty that they had before. E Wyndham Hulme, 'History of the Patent System under the Prerogative and at Common Law' (1896) 12 LQR 141, 153.

16 Fritz Machlup and Edith Penrose, 'The Patent Controversy in the Nineteenth Century' (1950) 10 J Econ Hist 1, 2. It should be borne in mind that, in most countries, the right to the patent lies with the first person to file the patent application, regardless of the date of actual invention.

17 Cornish, Llewelyn and Aplin (n 15) para 3-06.

18 In 1850, the Supreme Court of the US stated that, in order to obtain a patent, the inventor was required to show not only novelty, but also some 'ingenuity and skill'. *Hotchkiss v Greenwood* 52 US 248, 267 (1950).

19 The US Patent Act only included a specific provision on non-obviousness in 1952, under section 103. Janice M Mueller, *Patent Law* (4th edn, Wolters Kluwer 2013) 276.

20 Section 112 of the US Patent Act, for example, requires the patent specification to include a 'best mode' –a requirement which is expressly authorised by art 29(1) of the TRIPS Agreement.

ments of novelty, inventive step, industrial applicability and sufficient disclosure.[21]

As the substantive requirements for obtaining a patent developed, the formal procedure for obtaining it evolved as well and experienced significant reforms and adjustments. In England, eg, the procedure was for a long time perceived as obscure and uncertain, until in the middle of the nineteenth century the patent system was reformed and clearer guidelines were drawn.[22] In order to make the system more approachable for all citizens, the UK experimented for a short period of time with a mere registration regime whereby, upon the mere submission of the specification, a patent was granted without any substantial examination as to the merits of the invention—or lack thereof.[23] In the United States, where the English legal tradition naturally had a particularly strong influence, a radically different approach was preferred since the early days. As early as 1836 the United States Patent Office was already assigned with the task of searching prior art and closely examining patent applications before their grant.[24] This examination regime is the one that, in the end, prevailed in most jurisdictions, including the UK,[25] Germany[26] and the EPO.[27] Such a regime naturally demands rules and guidelines that have gradually rendered the procedure into a tremendously sophisticated system and, as technology evolves, the complexity of the patenting process increases at a comparable pace.[28]

21 TRIPS Agreement, arts 27(1) and 29(1). See also Daniel Gervais, *The TRIPS Agreement: Drafting History and Analysis* (4th edn, Sweet & Maxwell 2012) 428-33.

22 Cornish, Llewelyn and Aplin (n 15) para 3-09. Interestingly, Charles Dickens has demonstrated through parodies the bureaucracy that surrounded the obtaining of a patent in England at that time. See Jeremy Phillips, *Charles Dickens and the 'Poor Man's Tale of a Patent'* (ESC 1984).

23 Cornish, Llewelyn and Aplin (n 15) para 3-09.

24 ibid para 3-10.

25 The Patent Office started performing a similar examination in the beginning of the twentieth century. Davenport (n 14) 48 (a decisive factor for implementing examination was a study by the Fry Committee in 1901, according to which 42 per cent of the patents registered at that time were wholly or partly anticipated).

26 Georg Benkard, *Patentgesetz* (Claus Dietrich Asendorf and others eds, 10th edn, Beck 2006) para 7.

27 Bently and Sherman (n 15) 421.

28 John R Allison and Mark A Lemley, 'The Growing Complexity of the United States Patent System' (2002) 82 Bost U L Rev 77, 134.

2. *Synopsis of the Patent Procedure in the USPTO and the EPO*

The procedure to obtain a patent is in principle a national procedure, meaning that a patent application is to be filed in every single country in which protection is sought.[29] Each nation, hence, has in place its own patent office to independently receive patent applications and grant patents that will only be binding within the boundaries of its territory. In the case of Europe, however, a system exists within the framework of the European Patent Organisation[30] under which one single patent office, the EPO, is responsible for a unified granting procedure. Once a patent is granted by the EPO, it is automatically transformed into a bundle of national patents which will have exactly the same legal effects as those national patents granted by the national patent office of each Contracting State.[31] This system does not affect the simultaneous existence of national patent systems, as the EPO is only intended to supplement rather than replace them,[32] although statistics show that a great portion of the patent applications filed in Europe today are filed through the EPO.[33]

The way in which the examination procedure is conducted in every patent office remains mainly an issue to be defined independently by every jurisdiction, as most aspects have not been internationally harmonised.[34]

---

29 Paris Convention, art 4bis(1).

30 It should be borne in mind that the European Patent Organisation is not legally bound to the EU. All Member States of the EU are members of the European Patent Organisation, but the latter also comprises many other members which are not themselves EU Member states.

31 EPC, arts 2(2) and 64(1).

32 Margarete Singer and Dieter Stauder (eds), *The European Patent Convention: A Commentary* (3rd edn, Sweet & Maxwell 2003) vol 1, 15.

33 In Germany, for example, out of the 569 196 patents that were in force in 2013, only 124 432 (ie, 21.9%) had been granted by the national patent office. Deutsches Patent- und Markenamt, 'Jahresbericht 2013' (Lex Lingua 2014) i. In the UK, out of the 397 100 patents where renewal fees were paid in 2013, only 57 900 (14.6%) corresponded to patents granted by the UKIPO, the national patent office. UKIPO, 'Facts and Figures: 2012 and 2013 Calendar Years' (UKIPO 2014) 18.

34 Efforts have been made to harmonise patent procedures, but so far with only limited success. The Patent Law Treaty, eg, constitutes an attempt to harmonise some very important aspects of the procedure by providing maximum sets of requirements that the patent offices of each member state may demand. It was concluded in 2000 and entered into force in 2005. Issues harmonized by this treaty include, among others, requirements for obtaining a filing date, requirements relating to PCT applications, requirements for submitting evidence, etc. The US and several EU countries have already ratified this treaty, although not yet Germany. For an

In fact, a small number of countries still have in place registration systems and do not perform a substantial examination of the patent applications before their grant. Most countries of the world, however, have adopted examination regimes with a significant number of analogous features. This chapter is devoted to succinctly describe the general aspects that characterise the processes both under the EPO and the USPTO, although patenting procedures in most countries share many of their essential features.

A. *Examination Process: an Ex Parte Procedure*

Broadly speaking, the examination procedure is a procedure initiated by the patent applicant, who needs to fulfil a number of both formal and substantive requisites and often demands a considerable amount of time.[35] It constitutes, in a way, a negotiation between the applicant and the patent office examiner,[36] where the former strives to persuade the latter that all the patentability requirements have been met and that the invention actually deserves protection. Although the procedure is mostly *ex parte*, there are certain stages in which third parties are allowed to intervene.[37]

---

updated list of the member states, see <http://www.wipo.int/treaties/en/ip/plt/> accessed 14 February 2018. The TRIPS Agreement, on the other hand, provides in arts 62(2) and (4) for general conditions that all patent procedures should meet, but mostly leaves the issue to the member states' discretion.

35 In the United States, for example, the USPTO takes, on average, around 3 years to examine each patent application, although in some high technology fields the whole examination proceedings can actually take between 5 and 8 years. Warren K Mabey Jr, 'Deconstructing the Patent Application Backlog' (2010) 92 J Pat & Trademark Off Soc'y 208, 218. In Europe, the EPO takes around 3 years and 3 months to examine each application, but once the patent is granted third parties are entitled to file oppositions which may call for several additional years of procedure. Communication from the Commission, Pharmaceutical Sector Inquiry: Final Report (8 July 2009) paras 270-77 <http://ec.europa.eu/competition/sectors/pharmaceuticals/inquiry> accessed 14 February 2018 (Pharma Sector Inquiry).

36 *Rohm and Haas Co v Collag Ltd* [2001] EWCA Civ 1589, [2002] FSR 28 [42].

37 See text at nn 103ff and 113ff.

B. Filing of a Patent Application. Description, Claims and Priority

A patent application can be filed by any person without restrictions as regards the nationality or residence.[38] Although under US law the applications are often filed in the name of the real inventors,[39] the application can be assigned to any third person (in most cases the employer) and the patent may later issue to the assignee of the inventor.[40] Today, both the EPO and the US operate on a first-to-file system, which essentially means that the patent is granted to the first person to submit the application to the patent office.[41] For many years and until not very long ago, however, the US operated under a first-to-invent system, where patents were granted to the first person to make the invention rather that to the first one to file the application.

As to its formal requirements, a patent application should essentially contain a written description of the invention accompanied by one or more claims which must clearly point out the scope and subject-matter of the invention.[42]

I. Description

The description is a very important part of the patent application. It is where the applicant explains in detail what the invention is about and can play a significant role in patent litigation, since it can be used to interpret the scope of the exclusive right.[43] On a more theoretical level, this is an essential element of the specification as it guarantees the information function of the patent system.[44]

The description of a patent normally begins with a description of the state of the art in the specific field of the invention, based on the relevant background art known to the applicant.[45] In most cases, the description will continue with a disclosure of the invention by explaining the technical aspects in such a clear and complete way as to enable any person skilled

---

38 EPC, art 58; § 111 US Patent Act.
39 See 37 CFR §§ 1.41-1.48.
40 Donald S Chisum, *Chisum on Patents* (LexisNexis) para 11.02[2][a].
41 EPC, art 60(2); § 102(a)(1) US Patent Act.
42 EPC, art 78(1); § 112(a) US Patent Act.
43 EPC, art 69(1); *Phillips v AWH Corp* 415 F 3d 1303, 1313 (Fed Cir 2005) (en banc).
44 Bently and Sherman (n 15) 409.
45 EPC, r 42(1)(b); 37 CFR § 1.71; US MPEP, para 608.01(c).

in the art to replicate it and use it.[46] In the case of the EPO, the patent application is further expected to focus on the problem that the invention is trying to solve and the advantageous effects vis-à-vis the prior art.[47] Additionally, the description normally describes at least one way of carrying out the invention, which is typically done by disclosing and explaining in detail one or more practical examples,[48] and in the case of the US it is also expected to disclose the best mode known by the inventor for carrying out the invention.[49] Finally, the patent specification can contain drawings,[50] which together with the description can be used to interpret the claims.[51]

II. Claims

The claims are the core part of a patent specification, since they are the ones which mark out the exact matter for which protection is sought. They should hence delimitate as precisely as possible the scope of the invention and of the exclusive right.[52] Every patent should contain one or more claims[53] which can be categorised, broadly speaking, depending on whether they refer to products or processes,[54] although a range of hybrids also exist.[55] They must be clear and concise and must find support or antecedent basis in the description so that the meaning of the terms in the claims may be ascertainable by reference to that description.[56]

---

46 EPC, art 83; 37 CFR § 1.71(a); TRIPS Agreement, art 29(1).
47 EPC, r 42(1)(c).
48 EPC, r 42(1)(e); 37 CFR § 1.71(b).
49 § 112(a) US Patent Act. See also TRIPS Agreement, art 29(1). The consequences for an applicant who fails to include the best mode, however, have been strongly mitigated with the passing of the Leahy-Smith America Invents Act (AIA), which amended § 282 to state that 'the failure to disclose the best mode shall not be a basis on which any claim of a patent may be canceled or held invalid or otherwise unenforceable'. See Andrew T Robinson, 'The America Invents Act and the Best Mode Requirement: Where Do We Go From Here? (2012) 20 J Intell Prop L 179.
50 EPC, art 78(d); § 113 US Patent Act.
51 EPC, art 69(1); Chisum (n 40) para 11.02[1][b][iii].
52 EPC, arts 69 and 84; § 112(b) US Patent Act. See also EPC, 'Protocol on the Interpretation of Article 69 EPC'.
53 EPC, art 78(1)(c); § 112(b) US Patent Act.
54 Bently and Sherman (n 15) 412-13; Roger E Schechter and John R Thomas, *Principles of Patent Law* (Thomson/West 2004) 25.
55 See Bently and Sherman (n 15) 412-15.
56 EPC, art 84; 37 CFR § 1.75(d)(1).

III. Other Formal Requirements. Inventors and Priority

Together with the customary information that is expected to be provided in any presentation before a governmental institution, a patent application should include information such as the identity of all the inventors, details of the applicant and, where applicable, the details of the professional legal representative.[57] Furthermore, if applications for the same invention have already been filed in other countries, a patent applicant can also include a priority claim.[58] The subject of priority claiming has been harmonised to a large extent by the Paris Convention,[59] which gives patent applicants twelve months from the filing of the first patent application to file other patent applications in other countries.[60] The main effect of such priority claim is that the subsequent filings cannot be invalidated by reason of any acts accomplished in the interval.[61]

Despite their predominantly formal nature, the requirements that are to accompany a patent application might become an important element in the context of this work, due to the significance of the information therein contained and the risks and easiness with which mistakes or misrepresentations can be made.

C. The Application Process

I. Formal and Substantive Examination, Publication and Office Actions

Once the patent application is filed, the patent office normally performs a prompt examination in order to determine whether it fulfils all formal requirements and whether it can be accorded a date of filing.[62] During the course of this examination, however, the office does not yet make any assessment as to the actual patentability of the invention.

Once it has been verified that all the formal requirements have been met, the patent office will ordinarily proceed to publish the patent application, which as a rule happens 18 months as of the date of filing unless the

57 EPC, r 41; § 115(a) US Patent Act; 37 CFR § 1.31.

58 EPC, art 87; § 119(b)(1) US Patent Act.

59 See Georg H C Bodenhausen, *Guide to the Application of the Paris Convention* (BIRPI 1968) 13-14.

60 Paris Convention, art 4(C)(1) and (2).

61 Bodenhausen (n 59) 41.

62 EPC, art 90(1) and (3) and r 40; 37 CFR § 1.53.

applicant requests an earlier publication.[63] Publication is an important stage in patent prosecution: it not only discloses the invention to the public but also enables third parties to file observations as to its patentability.[64] Moreover, if the patent is finally granted, it is as of the date of publication that the owner is entitled to sue for infringement and claim damages.[65]

In the EPO, a search report—the *European search report*—is generally drawn up before the publication of the patent application.[66] The main aim of this report is to point out the relevant prior art that has been found,[67] and it is further accompanied by a preliminary opinion on whether the application seems to meet the patentability requirements.[68] The European search report is to be transmitted to the applicant immediately after it has been drawn up[69] and also published, if possible together with the patent application.[70]

After the publication of the patent application, the patent office proceeds to what is probably the most important stage of the whole procedure: the substantive examination of the patent application.[71] Such examination is carried out automatically in the case of the USPTO,[72] but in the EPO it must be specifically requested by the applicant within six months after the publication of the application[73] and failure to do so leads to the application being deemed withdrawn.[74] The substantive examination con-

63 EPC, art 93; 37 CFR § 1.211(a). In the USPTO, however, an applicant can request the application not to be published provided that the invention has not been and will not be the subject of an application in another country other than the US. 37 CFR § 1.213(a).

64 EPC, art 115; 37 CFR § 1.291.

65 EPC, art 67; § 154(d) US Patent Act.

66 EPC, art 92.

67 EPC, r 61.

68 EPC, r 62.

69 EPC, r 65.

70 EPC, r 68(1). Such publication, however, should not include the preliminary opinion. EPC, r 62(2).

71 EPC, art 94; § 131 US Patent Act.

72 § 131 US Patent Act.

73 EPC, r 70.

74 EPC, art 94(2). It should be noted that other countries, like Germany, have a more pronounced system of 'deferred examination', where an application can be pending without examination for up to seven years from the filing date until the applicant or a third party asks for it. § 44(2) PatG (*Patentgesetz* or German Patent Act). This system helps filtering away unwanted patents without wasting resources on examination, but might also lead to a prolonged uncertainty. Cornish, Llewelyn and Aplin (n 15) para 4-18.

sists of a thorough scrutiny by technical experts in the specific field of the invention in order to ensure that it fulfils all the patentability requirements.[75] This means in particular that the patent office ensures that the invention comprises patentable subject-matter, that it is new, inventive and industrially applicable, and also that it has been sufficiently disclosed and that its claims are clear and supported by the description.[76]

It should be noted that the prior art search that the patent offices carry out in order to assess the novelty and inventive step of an application is usually performed over large databases of patents and patent applications from major patenting countries and of the most important technical literature.[77] Yet despite its comprehensiveness, it is materially impossible for the search to be entirely exhaustive.[78] There may always be pieces of prior art beyond the reach of the examiners, such as remote publications, prior sales of the invention or oral disclosures at exhibitions or conferences, all of which are more commonly brought up by third parties by submitting observations, in opposition proceedings (in the case of the EPO) or later on by defendants during litigation.[79]

In any case, if the examination reveals that the application does not meet all the patentability requirements, the corresponding objections are submitted to the applicants, who are entitled to present within a certain period of time their own observations and any amendments they might wish to make.[80] This negotiation between the applicants and the examiner often extends for a long period of time, until the examiner arrives to a final opinion on whether all the requirements have been met and, hence, whether the patent is to be granted or rejected.[81]

II. Amendments

Applicants are allowed to amend their applications both before and after grant.[82] Amendments are justified in the belief that it would be unreasonable to expect applicants to be perfectly aware of all the relevant facts and

---

75 EPC, art 94(1); 37 CFR § 1.104.
76 Cornish, Llewelyn and Aplin (n 15) para 4-22.
77 ibid para 4-19; Mueller (n 19) 57.
78 EPO Guidelines (n 12) pt B(III) para 2(1).
79 EPO Guidelines (n 12) pt B(VI) para 2 and pt G(IV) para 7(1).
80 EPC, art 94(3); § 132(a) US Patent Act.
81 EPC, art 97; § 131 US Patent Act.
82 EPC, art 123(1); § 132 US Patent Act; 37 CFR §§ 1.115 and 1.116.

circumstances surrounding the invention at the time of filing,[83] especially considering that a first-to-file system encourages inventors to submit their patent applications as early as possible. Those amendments, hence, are ordinarily made in order to take account of prior art, to better describe the invention or to correct or remove mistakes.[84] The amendments, however, cannot by any circumstance contain subject-matter extending beyond the content of the application as filed and, by the same token, may not extend the protection it confers.[85]

Before grant, the applicant is as a rule free to make amendments any time before the receipt of the first office action from the examiner.[86] After that, amendments are basically submitted in order to overcome the observations raised by the examiner.[87]

Amendments after grant are much less frequent.[88] In the EPO, a patent owner can request the limitation—or even the revocation—of a patent as long as it fulfils the general requirements for amendments, and the amendment applies to all Contracting States where the patent has been validated.[89] In the US, patentees can request a certificate of correction in case of, eg, typographical errors,[90] but if they consider that, because of an error, the patent is inoperative or invalid, they can also request the reissuance of the patent in an amended form.[91]

III. Divisional Applications and Unity of Invention

If a single patent application discloses more than one invention, or different aspects of a single invention, the patent application can be broken up through the filing of divisional patent applications.[92] Divisional patent applications cannot extend beyond the content of the earlier application and they are deemed to have been filed on the date of filing of the earlier application.[93]

---

83 Bently and Sherman (n 15) 431.
84 Cornish, Llewelyn and Aplin (n 15) para 4-30.
85 EPC, art 123(2) and (3); 37 CFR § 1.53(b).
86 EPC, r 137(1), (2) and (3); 37 CFR § 1.115.
87 EPC, r 137(3); 37 CFR § 1.111.
88 Cornish, Llewelyn and Aplin (n 15) para 4-34.
89 EPC, arts 105a and 105b and rr 80 and 138.
90 § 254 US Patent Act.
91 § 251(a) US Patent Act.
92 EPC, r 36; § 121 US Patent Act.
93 EPC, art 76(1); 37 CFR § 1.53(d).

There are two main reasons why a divisional application might be filed. The most common situation is that where the application is divided due to a lack of unity of the invention.[94] In this regard, every patent application must refer to one invention only—or to a group of inventions so linked as to form a single general inventive concept.[95] Therefore, if an application refers to more than one invention, the examiner can require the applicant to restrict the application to only one of the inventions and the applicant can file divisional applications for the rest.[96]

On the other hand, even if the application refers to one single invention, the applicant might have economical, procedural, or other reasons for having different aspects of the application divided.[97] A divisional application might be filed, eg, to exclude problematic aspects of the invention from the main application in order to pave the way for its prompt grant, while leaving the most debatable issues to a separate discussion.[98]

IV. Grant, Publication and National Validation

If after the prior art search, the substantive examination, the exchange of views with the applicant and the possible amendments, the examiners are of the opinion that the application meets all the patentability requirements, they will proceed to inform the applicant that they intend to grant the patent and, upon the payment of the corresponding fees, will proceed to issue and publish it at once.[99]

In the case of the EPO, the patent holders will additionally need to validate their patents in each Contracting State of their interest. Indeed, as the EPC system provides for a unified granting procedure, patent applicants are required to indicate the Contracting States where they would like their patents to be in effect.[100] Afterwards, upon the grant of the patent, the Contracting States that were designated may require from the patentee to

---

94 Singer/Stauder (n 32) vol 1, 285; Schechter and Thomas (n 54) 229.
95 EPC, art 82; 37 CFR § 1.141(a).
96 EPC, r 36(1)(b); § 121 US Patent Act.
97 Singer/Stauder (n 32) vol 1, 285.
98 Richard Hacon, *Concise European Patent Law* (Richard Hacon and Jochen Pagenberg eds, 2nd edn, Wolters Kluwer 2008) 91.
99 EPC, arts 97(1) and 98 and r 71(3) (in the EPO, the applicants are also required to file a translation of the claims into the two other official languages); § 151 US Patent Act.
100 EPC, art 79.

provide a translation of the patent into one of the official languages of that state provided that the patent granted by the EPO was not drawn in one of those languages[101] and will then proceed to the local publication of the patent.[102]

V. *Third Party Observations*

Although the procedure to obtain a patent is mainly an *ex-parte* procedure, there are certain circumstances under which third parties are also entitled to participate in the examination. At the early stages of the procedure, that involvement is often very limited,[103] but later on it can become much broader.[104]

During the on-going examination process and before the grant of the patent, both the EPC and US law only allow third parties to take part in it by filing observations and submitting to the patent office prior art and other references concerning the patentability of a specific invention.[105] These filings have to be duly taken into account by the examiners, but they do not transform those who file them into active parties to the proceedings. In particular, they have no right to appeal if, eg, the observations are ignored or disregarded by the examiners.[106]

D. *Post Grant Procedures*

After the patent is granted, there are still certain situations under which patent holders and third parties are permitted to submit specific pleads before the patent office, which may affect the scope or the term of the patent, or even its validity altogether.

---

101 EPC, art 65(1).
102 EPC, art 65(2).
103 Other countries, however, do provide for the filing of oppositions *before* the patent is granted. See, Indian Patent Act, s 25.
104 See text in nn 112-122.
105 EPC, art 115; 37 CFR § 1.99.
106 EPC, art 115; 37 CFR § 1.99(f).

I. Post-Grant Amendments, Ex Parte Reexamination and Supplemental Examination

Under US law, even after grant the patent holders can themselves cite relevant prior art that had not been considered by the USPTO and request a reexamination of said patent.[107] The USPTO should then determine whether a substantial new question of patentability is raised;[108] if yes, it should proceed to reexamine the patent under the same procedural rules established for initial examination.[109]

With the entering into force of the AIA, however, the patentees will probably be inclined to use alternative procedures.[110] Indeed, the new section 257 of the US Patent Act entitles patentees to request a Supplemental Examination in order to consider, reconsider, or correct information believed to be relevant to the patent, which at first sight appears to be more advantageous for the patent holder.[111]

In the EPO, on the other hand, the office cannot re-examine the patent once it has been granted and the opposition period has expired, although, as mentioned above, the EPC2000 has introduced a set of new provisions that allow patent owners to request for the limitation or revocation of the patent.[112]

II. Third Party Intervention after Grant. Oppositions, Post-Grant Reviews and Inter-Partes Reviews

After the grant of the patent, the EPO has historically permitted third parties to intervene before the patent office in a more active way, in order to get the patent revoked or its scope narrowed down. Under the US system, third party intervention has been traditionally much more limited, but the

---

107 § 302 US Patent Act.

108 § 303(a) US Patent Act.

109 § 305 US Patent Act.

110 Dennis Crouch, 'Is the New Supplemental Examination a Complete Replacement for Owner Initiated Ex Parte Reexamination?' (*Patently-O*, 3 October 2012) <www.patentlyo.com/patent/2012/10/is-the-new-supplemental-examination-a-complete-replacement-for-owner-initiated-ex-parte-reexamination.html> accessed 14 February 2018.

111 ibid. Indeed, under the Supplemental Examination procedure, patentees may 'immunise' their patents against subsequent inequitable conduct attacks. See text at nn 280-281.

112 EPC, arts 105a, 105b and 105c.

scenario seems to be gradually changing with the entering into force of the AIA.

Under the EPC regime, any person can file an opposition before the EPO within nine months of the publication of the mention of the grant of the patent.[113] And even after the opposition period has expired, assumed infringers can intervene in on-going opposition proceedings provided that infringement or non-infringement procedures have already been instituted.[114] Oppositions can be filed on the grounds that the invention is not patentable, or that it has not been disclosed in a sufficiently clear and complete manner, or that the subject-matter extends beyond the content of the application as filed.[115] If, after hearing the patent applicant and considering the possible amendments made, the Opposition Division is of the opinion that the application does not meet all the requirements, it proceeds to revoke the patent.[116] It should be borne in mind that the filing of the opposition does not impede the granted patent from becoming a bundle of national patents, but if the Opposition Division later decides to revoke the patent, such decision will have effects on all countries were that patent had become effective.[117]

Under US law, third parties were in the past permitted to intervene at the patent office after the grant of the patent in a rather limited fashion, under the figure of Inter-partes Re-examination, which has been replaced and expanded with the passing of the AIA with two different alternatives.[118] On the one hand, within the first nine months of grant, third parties are entitled to file a Post Grant Review petition before the patent office, so long as they have not already challenged the validity and enforceability of the patent in court.[119] The decision is appealable to the Federal Circuit[120] and if claims are upheld the third party is estopped from challenging the validity of those claims subsequently.[121] On the other hand, after the first nine months of the grant of the patent, third parties are al-

113 EPC, art 99(1).
114 EPC, art 105.
115 EPC, arts 99 and 100.
116 EPC, art 101.
117 EPC, art 99(2).
118 For a broader description of AIA, see 'Recent Legislation' (2012) 125 Harv L Rev 1290.
119 §§ 321(a) and (c) and 325(a)(1) US Patent Act.
120 § 329 US Patent Act.
121 § 325(e)(2) US Patent Act.

lowed to request an Inter Partes Review, which can only rely on prior patents or printed publications.[122]

In addition to that, it is important to bear in mind that, both under the EPO regime and in the US, once the patent has been granted third parties are also entitled to challenge its validity in court.[123]

III. SPCs and Term Extensions

Although the standard duration of a patent is twenty years counted as of the date of filing of the application,[124] there are exceptional circumstances under which such term can be extended.

a. SPCs in the EU

In Europe, the EPC does not directly provide for any alternative to extend the term of a patent, but it does permit the Contracting States to do so under two specific circumstances: (i) in order to take account of a state of war or similar emergency conditions, or (ii) if the subject-matter of the patent refers to a product which has to undergo an administrative authorisation procedure before it can be put on the market.[125] Under these premises, the European Union has implemented the use of Supplementary Protection Certificates (SPCs), which allow for the extension of the patent term for medicinal and plant protection products as a compensation for delays in authorising the products to enter the market.[126] They were specifically introduced to encourage pharmaceutical and plant protection research, by

122 § 311 US Patent Act.

123 EPC, art 138; § 81 PatG; UK Patents Act, s 72; § 282 US Patent Act. It should be noted that, as a patent granted by the EPO becomes a bundle of national patents, a third party interested in challenging their validity in court should do so separately in every designated Contracting State.

124 TRIPS Agreement, art 33; EPC, art 63; § 154(a)(2) US Patent Act.

125 EPC, art 63(2)(a) and (b).

126 SPCs for medicinal products were introduced by Council Regulation (EEC) 1768/92 of 18 June 1992 concerning the creation of a supplementary protection certificate for medicinal products [1992] OJ L182/1, which was later repealed and replaced with a codified version: Regulation (EC) 469/2009 of 6 May 2009 concerning the supplementary protection certificate for medicinal products [2009] OJ L152/1 (SPC Regulation). SPCs for plant protection products were introduced by Regulation (EC) 1610/96 of 23 July 1996 concerning the creation of

guaranteeing a minimum period of effective protection sufficient to cover the investments made and to generate the resources needed to maintain a high level of research.[127]

SPCs are to be lodged independently before the patent office of every Member State where the patent was granted and the extension is sought.[128] Each patent office shall then proceed to establish whether all the requirements have been met, although Member States are permitted to exempt them from verifying certain conditions.[129] If the certificate is granted, the patent term is extended based on the following formula:

X = date of first market authorisation — patent application filing date — 5 years

where X cannot be higher than 5 years.[130] In principle, the scope of the SPC extends only to the product covered by the authorisation to place the corresponding product on the market and for any use of the product that has been authorised before the expiry of the certificate.[131] The CJEU, however, has interpreted that the SPC is sometimes capable of covering any of the forms enjoying the protection of the basic patent, even if not specifically mentioned in the authorisation.[132]

b. Patent Term Extensions in the US

Under US law, the term of a patent can also be extended for the delays incurred in the regulatory review before the marketing authorisation,[133] although it diverges from EU's SPC system in a number of significant aspects. Term extensions in the US due to delays in marketing authorisation

a supplementary protection certificate for plant protection products [1996] OJ L198/30 (Plant SPC Regulation).

127 See Katarzyna Zbierska, *Application and Importance of Supplementary Protection Certificates for Medicinal Products in the European Union* (Shaker 2012) 27-32.

128 SPC Regulation 469/2009, art 9(1); Plant SPC Regulation 1610/96, art 9(1).

129 SPC Regulation 469/2009, art 10(5); Plant SPC Regulation 1610/96, art 10(5). This circumstance might be a very important factor when analysing the *AstraZeneca* decision and the impact it might have on different procedures before the patent office where a stricter scrutiny is observed.

130 SPC Regulation 469/2009, art 13(1) and (2); Plant SPC Regulation 1610/96, art 13(1) and (2).

131 SPC Regulation 469/2009, art 4; Plant SPC Regulation 1610/96, art 4.

132 Case C-392/97 *Farmitalia* [1999] ECR I-5553.

133 § 156 US Patent Act.

are normally referred to as Patent Term Restorations and were first introduced by the Hatch-Waxman Act in 1984 for drug products, medical devices, food additives and colour additives.[134] A request for a patent term restoration is filed before the patent office, which is to verify—with the assistance of the relevant health and agriculture authorities, predominantly the Food and Drug Administration (FDA)—whether all the legal requirements have been met.[135]

In contrast with the EU, the patent term in the US is extended not only for the period of time required by the regulatory procedure after the filing of the marketing authorisation request (normally referred to as New Drug Application or NDA), but also for the time devoted to clinical trials prior to such filing.[136] Also, the calculation does not take into account the filing date of the patent application. Broadly speaking, the term can be adjusted based on the following formula:

X = [filing date of NDA – starting date of human clinical trials]/2 + date of marketing authorisation – date of NDA

where X cannot be higher than 5 years or extend beyond 14 years from the product's approval date.

In addition to the alternative described above, US patent owners can also see the term of their patents extended as a result of the delays in which the patent office itself could have incurred during the examination of the application.[137] The Patent Term Guarantee Act of 1999 sets a number of deadlines to the USPTO and each day of delay beyond these limits gives rise to one additional day in the term of the patent.[138] The exact determination of the term adjustment is carried out by the USPTO and conceded automatically, without the need of the applicant to make a formal request.[139]

134 § 156(f)(1) US Patent Act. In 1988, a similar system was implemented for animal drugs by the Generic Animal Drug and Patent Term Restoration Act.

135 § 156(d)(1) and (2) US Patent Act.

136 § 156(g)(3)(B) US Patent Act.

137 § 154(b) US Patent Act.

138 Schechter and Thomas (n 54) 241.

139 § 154(b)(3) US Patent Act.

IV. Patent Linkage and the Orange Book

Considering that many products, most importantly pharmaceuticals, need to be thoroughly examined in terms of safety and efficacy before they are able to enter the market, a number of countries around the world have put into practice a system normally referred to as patent linkage, whereby the public authority in charge of granting these permissions is restricted of doing so when the product is covered by a patent owned by a third party. Ordinarily, patent offices are not involved in this process.

In the US, such as system was introduced by the Hatch-Waxman Act in 1984. When applying to the FDA to commercialise a new drug in the country, hence, applicants are required to file information on any patent that might exist protecting the drug.[140] Information submitted by all patentees is then published by the FDA in a list commonly known as Orange Book.[141] If third parties later intend to obtain marketing approval for a drug equivalent to one already authorised, they can only do so if they submit a certification declaring that: (i) no patent information has been filed by the first applicant; (ii) such patent has expired; (iii) the date on which that patent will expire; or (iv) that such patent is invalid or will not be infringed.[142] In the latter case, the patent owner must be informed of such application before its approval and can block such procedure for a period of 30 months if it starts legal actions against the new applicant within 45 days.[143] In practice, it basically equates to obtaining an automatic preliminary injunction, since the administrative procedures at the FDA will be stayed and the new applicants cannot enter the market before getting the final authorisation. The USPTO is not involved in these proceedings, neither when the patentees list their patents in the Orange Book nor when third parties intend to obtain marketing approval for drugs already listed there.

In the case of Europe, no such patent linkage exists. In fact, EU law does not seem to allow it either, neither on a European nor on a national level. Both Regulation 726/2004 and Directive 2001/83/EC provide in this regard that authorisations for medicinal products cannot be refused but on the grounds expressly set out therein, and none of them include the existence

---

140 § 505(b) Federal Food, Drug, and Cosmetic Act.

141 The list is officially entitled Approved Drug Products with Therapeutic Equivalence Evaluations. § 505 Federal Food, Drug, and Cosmetic Act.

142 § 505(b)(2)(A) Federal Food, Drug, and Cosmetic Act.

143 § 505(c)(3)(C) Federal Food, Drug, and Cosmetic Act.

of a patent or any other intellectual property right as a valid motive.[144] That being said, there are a few Member States which do provide for some kind of linkange in their internal laws, particularly Hungary, Italy, Portugal and Slovakia.[145]

E. *Alternative Procedures. PCT, Patent Prosecution Highway and the Use of Results from other Patent Offices*

In addition to the standard proceedings, many countries have in place alternative procedures available for the applicants which might add more complexity to the issue. Most significantly, a very large number of countries including the US and all members of the European Patent Organisation are members of the PCT.[146] This treaty essentially provides for the possibility to file an international application in any of the designated receiving offices,[147] and its main advantage is that it provides applicants the possibility to delay for up to thirty months the decision on whether to continue with the application and, if so, in which countries.

Once the international application is filed, the designated patent office performs an early, non-binding prior art International Search Report and an opinion on the patentability and further proceeds to make an international publication of the application.[148] After this stage, the patent applicant can also request for a nonbinding International Preliminary Examination[149] and should in any case continue with the procedure by entering the national or regional phases in the countries of her choice (as long as they are PCT Contracting States) within 30 months after the date of filing.[150]

---

144 Regulation (EC) 726/2004 of 31 March 2004 laying down Community procedures for the authorisation and supervision of medicinal products for human and veterinary use and establishing a European Medicines Agency [2004] OJ L136/1, art 81(2); Directive 2001/83/EC of of 6 November 2001 on the Community code relating to medicinal products for human use [2001] OJ L 311/67, art 126.

145 Filipe Fischmann, *«Reverse Payments» als Mittel zur Beilegung von Patentstreitigkeiten - Ein Verstoß gegen das Kartellrecht?* (Stämpfli Verlag 2016) 335-339.

146 For an updated list of Contracting States, see <www.wipo.int/pct/en/pct_contracting_states.html> accessed 14 February 2018.

147 PCT, art 10.

148 PCT, arts 15, 17(2) and 21.

149 PCT, arts 31 and 35.

150 PCT, art 22(1).

In addition to the PCT, and in view of the fact that patent applications for the same invention are often filed in a range of different countries,[151] many patent offices have entered into collaboration arrangements with each other, and even mutual recognition systems, in order to save resources and avoid repetition of work.[152] And even in the absence of formal agreements, thanks to the considerable simplifications in communication, many patent offices are able to use the search results and examination reports that other patent offices have already issued for the same invention.[153] Some countries even provide for the use of such results expressly in their national laws, eg by waiving the requirements of novelty, inventive step and industrial application when an equivalent patent has already been granted abroad.[154]

F. *The Role of Patent Agents*

As a general principle, inventors are not required to appoint a professional representative to file the patent application and follow the proceedings before the patent office and can thus act on their own behalf.[155] In the EPO, only persons who are not residents and do not have their principal place of business in a Contracting State are compelled to hire a professional representative, ie a patent attorney duly qualified and admitted to practice before the EPO.[156]

Even if not mandatory, the complexity of the entire patenting process and the high risks that an inadequately drafted or prosecuted patent may entail in the future encourage inventors to hire patent attorneys to file and

151 It is estimated that, within the 10 largest patent offices, around 34% of the applications are duplicate applications. London Economics, 'Economic Study on Patent Backlogs and System of Mutual Recognition: Final Report to the Intellectual Property Office' (2010) 80, available at <www.gov.uk/government/uploads/system/uploads/attachment_data/file/328678/p-backlog-report.pdf> accessed 14 February 2018.

152 Jürgen Schade, 'Synergies created by international cooperation in the patent area' in Wolrad Prinz zu Waldeck und Pyrmont and others (eds), *Patents and Technological Progress in a Globalized World* (Springer 2009) 783.

153 Peter Drahos, '"Trust Me": Patent Offices in Developing Countries' (2008) 34 Am J L & Med 151.

154 Martín Bensadon, *Ley de Patentes Comentada y Concordada con el ADPIC y el Convenio de Paris* (LexisNexis 2007) 252, fn 826.

155 EPC, art 133(1); 37 CFR § 1.31.

156 EPC, art 133(2).

handle their patent applications on a regular basis.[157] Hence, in actual fact, the vast majority of patent applications, both in the US and in the EPO, are filed through patent attorneys or patent agents.

Under the EPC regime, all patent attorneys are bound to be members of the Institute of Professional Representatives before the European Patent Office (EPI) and are subject to the disciplinary rules determined by the Administrative Council.[158] In the case of the US, all patent attorneys engaged in practice before the USPTO are subject to its disciplinary jurisdiction.[159] In this light, the disciplinary frameworks implemented by EPI or the USPTO may also play an important role within the context of the present work.

157 Bently and Sherman (n 15) 418.

158 EPC, art 134(1); Regulation on the establishment of an Institute of professional representatives before the European Patent Office [1997] OJ EPO 350, art 5(1).

159 37 CFR § 11.19.

Chapter III: The Responsibilities of the Patent Applicants before the Patent Office

1. *The Duties of the Patent Applicant under US Law*

As observed in the previous chapter, procedures to obtain patents from the EPO and from the USPTO resemble each other to a large extent. Decades of a mutual mimicry that has soared over the last years have made procedures before the patent offices substantially analogous on both sides of the Atlantic, although a few important differences still remain. One of the aspects in which they most strongly differ is precisely the role that the patent applicants are expected to play during the examination of the invention and the consequences that a lack of sufficient candour can have on the patent.[160] In this regard, patent applicants before the USPTO are expected to get involved and collaborate in the examination in a much more active way than in the EPO and strict duties and responsibilities are imposed upon them. The US Supreme Court long ago stated that 'the relationship of attorneys to the Patent Office requires the highest degree of candor and good faith'[161] and that this requirement comprises the duty to report to it all relevant facts underlying the patent application.[162] This kind of remarks

160 Gina M Bicknell, 'To Disclose or not to Disclose: Duty of Candor Obligations of the United States and Foreign Patent Offices' (2008) 83 Chi-Kent L Rev 425, 460; Jay Erstling, 'Patent Law and the Duty of Candor: Rethinking The Limits of Disclosure' (2011) 44 Creighton L Rev 329, 331 ('the United States is unique in requiring such breadth of candor and in linking failures to disclose with the threat of inequitable conduct and the sanction of unenforceability.'). See also Case T 2321/08 *Samsung Electronics* (decision of the EPO Technical Board of Appeal of 11 May 2009) para 7.3 ('the second part of Rule 27(1)(b) EPC 1973 does not put a stringent obligation on the applicant to cite documents reflecting prior art known to him already at the time of filing the application.').

161 *Kingsland v Dorsey* 338 US 318, 319 (1949).

162 *Precision Instrument Manufacturing Co v Automotive Maintenance Machinery Co* 324 US 806, 818 (1945). The Supreme Court also stated that 'the far reaching social and economic consequences of a patent ... give the public a special interest in seeing that patent monopolies spring from backgrounds free from fraud or other inequitable conduct and that such monopolies are kept within their legitimate scope.' Ibid 816.

lit the fuse to the daunting burden that US case law gradually moulded upon patent applicants.[163]

The rules of conduct that determine US patent applicants' duties and responsibilities have been delineated in the course of several decades on the basis of two main pillars: (i) the inequitable conduct doctrine and (ii) the specific regulations of the USPTO that established the so-called duty of candour. The inequitable conduct doctrine is a judicially developed doctrine which enables a court to declare a patent unenforceable—even if valid—if it finds that the patent holder, when conducting the application procedure before the USTPO, engaged in some kind of improper conduct in order to obtain the patent.[164] The duty of candour, in its turn, finds its origin in specific regulations issued by the USPTO, which in fact have been delineated on the basis of the evolving case law on inequitable conduct in a seeming attempt to codify the duties of the applicants.[165] These regulations are commonly known as 'Rule 56' and expressly state that the patent applicant has a duty of good faith in dealing with the office that includes a duty to disclose all known information which might be relevant for the patentability of the application.[166] Although the inequitable conduct doctrine and the duty of candour imposed by the USPTO have been developed simultaneously and strongly influenced each other, the Federal Circuit has clearly stated that they remain independent sets of rules and that ultimately the inequitable conduct doctrine is not bound by the regulation set by the USPTO.[167] The inequitable conduct doctrine was actually born as an equitable defence[168] that stemmed from the long-established doctrine of unclean hands,[169] an axiom that basically proclaims that 'he

---

163 Erstling (n 160) 330.

164 Janice M Mueller, *Patent Law* (4th edn, Wolters Kluwer 2013) 550-51.

165 Kevin Mack, 'Reforming Inequitable Conduct to Improve Patent Quality: Cleansing Unclean Hands' (2006) 21 Berkeley Tech L J 147, 154.

166 37 CFR § 1.56.

167 *Therasense Inc v Becton, Dickinson & Co* 649 F 3d 1276, 1294 (Fed Cir 2011) (en banc). See also R Carl Moy, 'The Effect of New Rule 56 on the Law of Inequitable Conduct' (1992) 74 J Pat & Trademark Off Soc'y 257, 260.

168 An equitable defence is, in general terms, a defence to an action on grounds which formerly was only available in a court of equity. *Black's Law Dictionary* (9th edn, 2009) 483. However, after the merger of law and equity, most equitable defences were incorporated into the common law. T Leigh Anenson, 'Treating Equity Like Law: A Post-Merger Justification of Unclean Hands' (2008) 45 Am Bus L J 455, 456.

169 *Precision v Automotive* (n 162) 819.

who comes into equity must come with clean hands'.[170] It embodies, in a way, the *tu quoque* fallacy that precludes those guilty of wrongdoing from denouncing others performing similar or related wrongs.[171] In the context of patent litigation, this would imply that patent owners cannot expect to enforce their patent rights if they turn up with unclean hands due to their prior deceptive behaviour before the patent office.

The sternness that has come forth in the American patent system has been explained, in the first place, by the very nature of patents, which are affected with a public interest.[172] Furthermore, the *ex parte* nature of patent prosecution and the lack of sufficient intervention by third parties both during and after the examination process have been indicated as essential factors vindicating the strict behavioural regime.[173] It is also often emphasised that the patent applicant is more knowledgeable in the field of the invention and frequently has more relevant information at hand than the examiner.[174] Be that as it may, the specific scope of the patent applicant's duties under US law and the consequences for contravening them have been the subject of extensive debates among US courts, scholars, legislators and practitioners which still persist today.

In this light, the main purpose of this section is to describe the development and key features of the inequitable conduct doctrine and the duty of candour that patent applicants owe to the USPTO. It first analyses the origin and development of these concepts and subsequently studies the standards that have been established and the types of conducts that can be held inequitable in practice. By way of conclusion, it explores whether said conducts can also have disciplinary or criminal consequences for the appli-

---

170 Zechariah Chafee Jr, 'Coming into Equity with Clean Hands' (1949) 47 Mich L Rev 877. It is generally considered that the doctrine of unclean hands serves two fundamental purposes: protecting judicial integrity and promoting justice. Anenson (n 168) 461.

171 Ori J Herstein, 'A Normative Theory of the Clean Hands Defense (2011) 17 Legal Theory 171, 172.

172 *Precision v Automotive* (n 162) 816 ('a patent is an exception to the general rule against monopolies and to the right to access to a free and open market. The far-reaching social and economic consequences of a patent, therefore, give the public a paramount interest in seeing that patent monopolies spring from backgrounds free from fraud or other inequitable conduct and that such monopolies are kept within their legitimate scope').

173 David O Taylor, 'Patent Fraud' (2010) 83 Temp L Rev 49, 54. See also Thomas F Cotter, 'An Economic Analysis of Patent Law's Inequitable Conduct Doctrine' (2011) 53 Az L Rev 735, 778.

174 *Abbott Laboratories v Sandoz Inc* 544 F 3d 1341, 1357 (Fed Cir 2008).

cants. Successively, the following sections will describe how European patent practice deals with these questions and evaluate whether there are any lessons to be learnt based on the US experience.

A. The Origin of the Inequitable Conduct Doctrine. A Stroll down Memory Lane

Since the very first US Patent Act in 1790, each of the patent statutes passed in the US has always provided for some form of private remedy against the procurement of a patent by fraud.[175] The courts, however, were for a long time rather reluctant to apply them.[176] It was only by the mid-twentieth century that courts reconsidered the importance that they were giving to misleading behaviours at the patent office, a shift that might have occurred more due to a growing hostility to patents than to an authentic re-evaluation of the figure of fraud.[177] In that context, the US Supreme Court delivered a series of unprecedented decisions during the first half of the 20th century where it refused to enforce patents on the basis that the patent holders had engaged in fraud during the examination procedure.

In *Keystone Driller Co v General Excavator Co*, the first of this series of cases, the Supreme Court had to deal with a situation where the patent applicant—who later assigned the patent to a third party—had agreed with a prior user of the invention to keep secret and supress the evidence of the details of such prior use.[178] In *Hazel-Atlas Glass Co v Hartford-Empire Co*, the second of these cases, the patent holder's attorneys had arranged the publication of an article in a journal signed by an ostensibly disinterested expert praising the invention as a remarkable advance. That article had then been introduced into the record in the patent office and in the court proceedings in support of the patentability of the invention.[179] In both cases, the Supreme Court denied relief to the patent owners relying on the doctrine of unclean hands, although it mostly focused on the relevance

175 Mack (n 165) 150.

176 Robert J Goldman, 'Evolution of the Inequitable Conduct Defense in Patent Litigation' (1993) 7 Harv J L & Tech 37, 38.

177 ibid 39.

178 *Keystone Driller Co v General Excavator Co* 290 US 240, 243 (1933).

179 *Hazel-Atlas Glass Co v Hartford-Empire Co* 322 US 238, 240-241 (1944).

that the fraudulent behaviour had had on the judicial proceedings rather than on the fraud to the USPTO itself.[180]

It was in *Precision Instrument Manufacturing Co v Automotive Maintenance Machinery Co*[181] that the Supreme Court focused for the first time on the issue of fraud at the patent office as such and recognised that the nondisclosure of relevant information can act as a bar to the enforcement of a patent, and in that way gave birth to the inequitable conduct doctrine.[182] In this case, Automotive and Mr Larson (officer and founder of Precision) had been involved in interference proceedings at the patent office in order to determine who had been the first inventor in the context of two conflicting patent applications.[183] During the interference procedure, Automotive found out that Larson had filed statements containing false information designed to appear as the first inventor. But instead of disclosing this falsehood, the parties settled the interference proceedings and Larson assigned the patent rights to Automotive without disclosing the inaccuracies that such application contained. Later on, Precision began to manufacture a new product and Automotive attempted to enforce its patents against it. The case made its way to the Supreme Court, where the infringement action was finally dismissed on the grounds that the patentee, by concealing information prejudicial to its patent, had not displayed the standard of conduct required for the maintenance of a suit in equity.[184] In so deciding, the Supreme Court stated that

> those who have applications pending with the Patent Office or who are parties to Patent Office proceedings have an uncompromising duty to report to it all facts concerning possible fraud or inequitableness underlying the applications in issue.[185]

Relying on the doctrine of unclean hands, the Supreme Court highlighted the impact that the prior misleading behaviour shown by Automotive

---

180 Raymond P Niro and J William Wigert Jr, 'Patents, Fraud and the Antitrust Laws' (1968) 37 Geo Wash L Rev 168, 170.

181 *Precision v Automotive* (n 162).

182 Katherine Nolan-Stevaux, 'Inequitable Conduct Claims in the 21st Century: Combating the Plague' (2005) 20 Berkeley Tech L J 147, 150.

183 It should be borne in mind that, under the prior US patent regime, patents were not awarded to the first one to file a patent application but to the first one to make the invention. Standards for determining who had actually been the first inventor were rather complex and were often resolved by the patent office in interference proceedings.

184 *Precision v Automotive* (n 162) 819.

185 ibid 818.

could have in the later enforcement of the patent. The court pointed out in this regard that such doctrine 'closes the doors of a court of equity to one tainted with inequitableness or bad faith relative to the matter in which he seeks relief, however improper may have been the behavior of the defendant.'[186] In the specific context of patents, and considering the public interest at stake, the court emphasised that

> this doctrine assumes even wider and more significant proportions. For if an equity court properly uses the maxim to withhold its assistance in such a case, it not only prevents a wrongdoer from enjoying the fruits of his transgression, but averts an injury to the public.[187]

The court did recognise, however, that this does not require the plaintiffs to have absolutely flawless background or have led blameless lives, though 'it does require that they shall have acted fairly and without fraud or deceit as to the controversy in issue.'[188] The question on whether the patents were actually valid was not even considered.[189]

With this decision, hence, the grounds for the inequitable conduct doctrine were established. Which concrete behaviours could actually amount to inequitable conduct, however, remained an unclear issue, for the decision of the Supreme Court offered little guidance as to the specific scope of the patent applicants' duties.[190] The Patent Act in force at that time was also of little help: among the list of defences available to the defendant against infringement actions, it merely provided for a general defence based on falsehood of the patent document or surreptitious or unjust procurement of the patent right.[191]

---

186 ibid 814.

187 ibid 815.

188 ibid 814-15.

189 *Precision Instrument Manufacturing Co v Automotive Maintenance Machinery Co* 143 F 2d 332, 339 (7th Cir 1944).

190 Sean M O'Connor, 'Defusing the Atomic Bomb of Patent Litigation: Avoiding and Defending Against Allegations of Inequitable Conduct after McKesson *Et Al*' (2009) 9 J Marshall Rev Intell Prop L 330, 339-40.

191 The Patent Statute stated that a defendant in an infringement action 'may prove on trial any one or more of the following special matters: First: That for the purpose of deceiving the public the description and specification filed by the patentee in the patent office was made to contain less than the whole truth relative to his invention or discovery, or more than is necessary to produce the desired effect; or, Second: That he had surreptitiously or unjustly obtained the patent for that which was in fact invented by another…' § 61 US Patent Act (1870).

B. *The Development of the Inequitable Conduct Doctrine and the Duty of Candour*

In 1949, only a few years after the Supreme Court's *Precision v Automotive* decision, the US Patent Office issued the Rules of Practice in Patent Cases, which were incorporated into the Code of Federal Regulations under title 37. These rules simply provided under § 1.56—'Rule 56'—that any application fraudulently filed or in connection with which any fraud was practiced or attempted on the Patent Office could be stricken from the files.[192] What exactly constituted fraud was, again, not specified, and even though the rule was passed after the decisions of the US Supreme Court on inequitable conduct, the way they should interplay was not clarified. In the years that followed, it would become a task for the lower courts to define the exact scope of the inequitable conduct defence and to develop its standards.

The first decisions by the lower courts on inequitable conduct already acknowledged that, in order to successfully raise such a defence, the defendants would have to prove that the misconduct had been both culpable and material to patentability.[193] The exact definition of these requirements became the subject of intense debate and led the courts to experiment with many different standards.[194] Furthermore, as the doctrine evolved, it came to embrace not only flagrant affirmative misconducts clearly intended to deceive the Patent Office, as it did in its origins, but also omissions and concealments of information.[195]

Following this thread of decisions, in 1977 the USPTO amended Rule 56 in an attempt to codify the guidelines that had been drawn by the copious case law. The new version of Rule 56 represented a strong change compared to the earlier version, as it defined in a much more detailed way the scope of the duty of candour and the persons who were actually bound by it.[196] The new version, which preserved the jurisdiction of the USPTO to strike patent applications itself, expressly provided that the duty of candour entails for patent applicants a duty to disclose information they are aware of, which is material to the examination of the application and further offered a definition of materiality. Moreover, it provided that the duty

192 37 CFR (1949) § 1.56. This also entailed that the issue of fraud would not only be discussed in court, but also at the USPTO.

193 Goldman (n 176) 53-54.

194 See text at nn 222ff.

195 Goldman (n 176) 56-58.

196 Donald S Chisum, *Chisum on Patents* (LexisNexis) para 11.03[4][b][i].

of candour not only lied upon the inventor, but also upon the patent attorneys and any other person substantially involved in the procedure. Despite a few succeeding amendments, this version of Rule 56 still constitutes the basic structure of the Rule 56 that is in force today.

In the years that followed, the lower courts interpreted Rule 56 as a mere codification of existing case law,[197] denoting that the same conduct that could prevent the enforcement of a patent due to inequitable conduct allowed the USPTO, if discovered before grant, to deny the issuance of the patent.[198] But regardless of this apparent harmony, headaches would emerge before long. The uncertainty generated by the variety of different standards employed by the courts and the easiness with which such a defence was asserted soon prompted concerns among judges, as they perceived that the focus in patent suits was shifting from core issues like validity or infringement to a secondary question like the morality of the patent owner.[199]

It was precisely during this period of time that the Federal Circuit was created, with the predominant purpose of increasing legal certainty and efficiency.[200] Having a more positive view of the patent system,[201] many expected that this new court would transform the inequitable conduct doctrine into a less reachable defence for the defendants, but this did not happen.[202] Quite on the contrary, the Federal Circuit adopted the inequitable conduct doctrine as a tool for fostering full disclosure to the patent of-

197 ibid para 11.03[4][b][ii].

198 *Norton v Curtiss* 433 F 2d 779, 792 (CCPA 1970).

199 *Re Coordinated Pretrial Proceedings in Antibiotic Antitrust Actions* 538 F 2d 180, 196 (8th Cir 1976). This trend might have also been stimulated by district courts that, feeling uncomfortable with complex technical cases, preferred to solve them based on issues that they could more easily comprehend. Goldman (n 176) 67.

200 Rochelle C Dreyfuss, 'The Federal Circuit: A Case Study in Specialized Courts' (1989) 64 NYU L Rev 1, 3. See also Martin J Adelman, 'The New World of Patents Created by the Court of Appeals for the Federal Circuit' (1987) 20 U Mich J L Refom 979, 982 ('The Federal Circuit was not created solely because the patent system was so important that it merited its own court. Rather, the creation of the Federal Circuit was also an outgrowth of the dissatisfaction with the functioning of both the Supreme Court and the federal appellate courts.').

201 In one of its early decisions, the Federal Circuit acknowledged that the need to discourage dishonest conducts at the patent office needed to be balanced with the basic policies underlying the patent system, like encouraging the disclosure of inventions and stimulating investments on innovation. *Rohm & Haas Co v Crystal Chemical Co* 722 F 2d 1556, 1571 (Fed Cir 1983).

202 Goldman (n 176) 70.

fice[203] and hence relaxed the degree of fault required and adopted a relatively lax definition of materiality.[204] What is more, it corroborated that a finding of inequitable conduct had severe consequences for the patent owner: it not only barred the enforcement of the claim under consideration, but also every other claim in the patent.[205] In fact, the Federal Circuit later extended the effects of unenforceability not only to the patent at issue, but also to other related patents in the same technology family.[206] All in all, the defence became an irresistible tool for defendants in infringement suits[207] due to the relatively low standard of proof and the immense reward in case of success.[208] Not surprisingly, one of the Judges of the Federal Circuit soon declared that 'the habit of charging inequitable conduct in almost every major patent case has become an absolute plague.'[209] The doctrine, indeed, had expanded into a much broader form than the very thin Supreme Court case law on which it was built.[210]

In this light, a few attempts were made to bring some order and control the proliferation of inequitable conduct accusations, like an *en banc* decision in 1988 addressing the intent standard.[211] That same year, the patent office announced that it would no longer investigate or reject patent applications on the basis of fraud,[212] emphasising that it was not the best forum in which to discuss these issues, particularly as to the 'intent to mislead' the examination.[213] Since then, the patent applicant's behaviour became an issue that can only be discussed before the courts. Soon after that, in 1992, the Patent Office also amended Rule 56, basically modifying the ma-

203 *American Hoist & Derrick Co v Sowa & Sons Inc* 725 F 2d 1350, 1363 (Fed Cir 1984).
204 Dreyfuss (n 200) 21-22.
205 *JP Stevens & Co Inc v Lex Tex Ltd* 747 F 2d 1553, 1561 (Fed Cir 1984).
206 *Consolidated Aluminum Corp v Foseco Int'l Ltd* 910 F 2d 804, 808-12 (Fed Cir 1990).
207 Nolan-Stevaux (n 182) 148.
208 Taylor (n 173) 65.
209 *Burlington Industries Inc v Dayco Corp* 849 F 2d 1418, 1422 (Fed Cir 1988).
210 Robert P Merges and John F Duffy, *Patent Law and Policy: Cases and Materials* (6th edn, LexisNexis 2013) 1057.
211 *Kingsdown Medical Consultants, Ltd v Hollister Inc* 863 F 2d 867 (Fed Cir 1988) (deciding that a finding that a particular conduct amounts to gross negligence does not of itself justify an inference of intent to deceive).
212 Notice, Patent and Trademark Office Implementation of 37 CFR 1.56 of 8 September 1988 (1095 USPTO Official Gazette 16, 11 October 1988).
213 Chisum (n 196) para 11.03[4][b][v].

teriality standard, although its effect on the inequitable conduct doctrine remained unclear.[214]

Notwithstanding the above, allegations of inequitable conduct continued to rise in the following decades, albeit very rarely in a successful way.[215] As the number of inequitable conduct allegations increased, so did the concerned voices from courts, practitioners and academics due to the substantial strain it caused on the patent system and the high costs it entailed for the parties.[216] A large number of solutions were suggested, many of which advocated for a more economic or utilitarian approach, ie to use the defence as a tool to optimise the quantity and quality of information available to examiners.[217] In 2011, immersed within this intense debate, the Federal Circuit issued an *en banc* decision in the *Therasense* case with the clear aim of controlling the 'plague' and providing stricter standards of analysis.[218] Almost simultaneously, the US Congress passed the AIA, which included—among other significant amendments to the Patent Act—the introduction of a post grant procedure called 'Supplemental Examination',[219] with the same purpose of reducing the number of inequitable conduct-based challenges.[220] The effects that these new developments will have on future litigation remain to be seen.

---

214 ibid.

215 Mack (n 165) 156 ('from 2000 to 2004, an inequitable conduct adjudication appeared in 16% to 35% of all reported patent opinions'); Christian E Mammen, 'Controlling the "Plague": Reforming the Doctrine of Inequitable Conduct' (2009) 24 Berkeley Tech L J 1329, 1358 (in 2008 inequitable conduct was pled as a defence in 40% of the patent cases litigated in the US, but it was rejected in 99.65% of them).

216 Nolan-Stevaux (n 182) 148.

217 See, among many others, Paul M Janicke, 'Do We Really Need So Many Mental and Emotional States in United States Patent Law?' (2000) 8 Tex Intell Prop L J 279; Mack (n 165); Mammen (n 215); Christopher A Cotropia, 'Modernizing Patent Law's Inequitable Conduct Doctrine' (2009) 24 Berkeley Tech L J 723; Cotter, 'An Economic Analysis of Inequitable Conduct' (n 173).

218 *Therasense* (n 167). Already before the decision, the Federal Circuit had been applying an inequitable conduct standard stricter than that applied by the lower tribunals it reviews. Lee Petherbridge, Jason Rantanen and Ali Mojibi, 'The Federal Circuit and Inequitable Conduct: An Empirical Assessment' (2011) 84 S Cal L Rev 1293, 1349.

219 § 257 US Patent Act. See text at nn 110-111 in ch 1.

220 Lisa A Dolak, 'America Invents the Supplemental Examination, but Retains the Duty of Candor: Questions and Implications' (2012) 6 Akron Intell Prop J 147, 148. This new procedure essentially allows patent owners to 'clean and polish' their patents before they go to court, as their patents may not be held unenforceable due to inequitable conduct if the pertinent information is considered dur-

C. Standards for Finding Inequitable Conduct

Regardless of whether it constitutes an affirmative or a negative conduct, the case law has consistently required defendants to show two essential elements in order to make a case of inequitable conduct in a patent infringement suit, namely materiality and intent.[221] That is, a defendant who raises an inequitable conduct defence should demonstrate both that the patentee's conduct had a significant effect on the decision of the patent office and that the patentee had the specific purpose to mislead the patent office. The precise definition of these elements has been the subject of different interpretations since the very first decisions.

I. Intent

Already in 1945, with its seminal decision in *Precision v Automotive*, the US Supreme Court acknowledged that only wilful misbehaviours could furnish sufficient ground for an inequitable conduct defence,[222] suggesting therefore that the element of intent had a significant role to play. During the first years, this element was interpreted in a rather restrictive fashion and most decisions were inclined to allow good faith as sufficient justification, but in the early 1970s a shift in the overall perception of the public interest surrounding the patent system inspired a number of courts to reconsider this stance.[223] With the purpose of balancing the protection granted by a patent with other public policy considerations, such as the importance of having a patent procedure free from scams, courts began to recognise that gross negligence could in some cases constitute sufficient proof of intent.[224] Over time, most courts accepted gross negligence as the new standard of culpability,[225] some of them explicitly stating that subjective

ing a Supplemental Examination. Dennis Crouch, 'Supplemental Examination: Inequitable Conduct Amnesty and Beyond' (*Patently-O*, 16 September 2012) <www.patentlyo.com/patent/2012/09/supplemental-examination-inequitable-conduct-amnesty-and-beyond.html> accessed 14 February 2018.

221 Roger E Schechter and John R Thomas, *Principles of Patent Law* (Thomson/West 2004) 258.

222 *Precision v Automotive* (n 162) 815.

223 Goldman (n 176) 54.

224 *Norton v Curtiss* (n 198) 796.

225 Chisum (n 196) para 19.03A[4][a].

good faith of the patent counsel does not necessarily immunise the possibility of an inequitable conduct case.[226]

The Federal Circuit later recognised this breadth in the intent requirement as a decisive factor that had contributed to the frenetic proliferation of the defence, and in 1988 rendered an *en banc* decision in *Kingsdown* in an attempt to retrace the lax definition of culpability back to the vogue. In a unanimous decision, the Federal Circuit stated that gross negligence would not suffice and that the involved conduct 'must indicate sufficient culpability to require a finding of intent to deceive'.[227]

From then onwards, courts have consistently applied this standard, but time would show that this tuning on the intent standard alone was not able to reduce the exaggerated number of inequitable conduct allegations and that further adjustments were necessary.[228] The Federal Circuit in *Therasense* thus revised several elements of the inequitable conduct doctrine, although in the area of culpability it simply ratified the narrow definition of intent advocated by *Kingsdown* and clarified that, in case of omissions, the defendants should prove 'that the applicant knew of the reference, knew it was material, and made a deliberate decision to withhold it.'[229]

II. Materiality

Although the Supreme Court did not explicitly include a materiality requirement when it first coined the inequitable conduct defence, courts soon recognised it as an essential factor to take into account.[230] Yet considering the limited guidance offered by the earlier cases, different standards soon emerged.

Over time, courts have in fact developed at least three different criteria: (i) the subjective 'but for' standard; (ii) the objective 'but for' standard; and (iii) the 'but it may have' standard.[231] Under the subjective 'but for' standard, defendants are required to show that the misbehaviour caused the examiner to issue the patent and that she would not have done so other-

226 *Argus Chemical Corp v Fibre Glass-Evercoat Co Inc* 759 F 2d 10, 14 (Fed Cir 1985).
227 *Kingsdown v Hollister* (n 211) 876.
228 *Therasense* (n 167) 1291.
229 ibid 1290.
230 Taylor (n 173) 58.
231 *Am Hoist* (n 203) 1362.

wise.[232] Under the objective 'but for' standard, on the other hand, courts would only find inequitable conduct in those cases where the patent not only *would* not have been issued but also *should* not have been issued.[233] Under this standard, thus, a defendant should not only show that the examiner would have refused the application if it had been aware of the truth, but also that said refusal would have been appropriate and that the application does not objectively meet the patentability requirements.[234] In other words, the inequitable conduct determination would be congruent with the validity determination: inequitable conduct would only exist if the patent can be invalidated by the courts. The 'but it may have' standard, finally, emerged some time later as an additional, more expansive test in search of imposing a higher duty of honesty upon applicants.[235] Based on this test, it would be sufficient for a defendant to demonstrate that the misbehaviour *might* have influenced the decision of the examiner.[236]

In addition to these court-developed criteria, the USPTO has also contributed with two different materiality standards when defining the duty of candour—and both have been occasionally cited by the courts. In 1977, when Rule 56 for the first time included a definition of materiality, it implemented a 'reasonable examiner' standard, albeit very similar to the 'but it may have' standard.[237] Based on that standard, information is material 'where there is a substantial likelihood that a reasonable examiner would consider it important in deciding whether to allow the application to issue as a patent.'[238] But in 1992, when the USPTO amended Rule 56, it adopted yet a different standard, under which information is considered material when it establishes 'a prima facie case of unpatentability'.[239] Courts have recognised the standards given by the USPTO as additional standards for assessing inequitable conduct and considered it an appropriate starting point for any discussion of materiality, [240] which denotes that, altogether, they have dealt throughout time with at least five different criteria to define materiality.

---

232 *Plastic Container Corp v Continental Plastics of Oklahoma Inc* 607 F 2d 885, 899 (10th Cir 1979).
233 ibid.
234 ibid.
235 Goldman (n 176) 60.
236 *Plastic Container* (n 232) 899.
237 *Am Hoist* (n 203) 1362.
238 37 CFR (1977) § 1.56.
239 37 CFR § 1.56(b)(1).
240 *Am Hoist* (n 203) 1362-63; *Digital Control Inc v Charles Machine Works* 437 F 3d 1309, 1316 (Fed Cir 2006).

Whilst most lower court decisions dealing with inequitable conduct ended up adopting either the 'but it may have' standard or the 'reasonable examiner' test,[241] the variety of different standards and their unpredictable outcome led to a high level of legal uncertainty.[242] In 2011, thus, in a new attempt to control the overflow of inequitable conduct accusations, a majority of Federal Circuit judges delivered an *en banc* decision in the *Therasense* case,[243] which shed some light on the doctrine and, among other adjustments, recognised a unique definition of materiality. Not surprisingly, the majority favoured a narrow criterion and opted for the 'but-for' test as the governing materiality standard.[244] Hence, inequitable conduct should only exist if it can be proven that the USPTO would not have granted the patent had it been aware of all the facts. It is not entirely clear whether they intended to adopt an objective or a subjective 'but for' standard, as the judgment includes statements pointing in both directions,[245] but the language of the text seems slightly inclined towards the subjective criterion.[246] In any case, little doubt remains that it leans in the direction of a more restricted yardstick, hoping to result in less baseless inequitable conduct accusations in the future.

It should be noted, finally, that the new definition of materiality recognises one exception in cases of flagrant misbehaviours.[247] Indeed, in order to give more flexibility to the doctrine, and incorporating elements from the unclean hands doctrine from which it stems, the Federal Circuit stated that, in cases of affirmative egregious misconducts, the defendants do not need to show that the misbehaviour was but-for material.[248] Yet because this exception only applies to affirmative conducts, any omission of the applicant to submit information, eg on prior sales or relevant prior art—which represent the vast majority of inequitable conduct cases today—will always be measured under the but-for yardstick.

---

241 Chisum (n 196) para 19.03A[3][a]; Mueller (n 164) 557.

242 Erstling (n 160) 343.

243 *Therasense* (n 167).

244 ibid 1291.

245 Cotter, 'An Economic Analysis of Inequitable Conduct' (n 173) 745.

246 *Therasense* (n 167) 1291 ('… even if a district court does not invalidate a claim based on a deliberately withheld reference, the reference may be material if it would have blocked patent issuance under the PTO's different evidentiary standards.').

247 *Therasense* (n 167) 1292.

248 ibid 1292-93.

III. Burden of Proof and the 'Sliding Scale'

In view of the gravity that a charge for inequitable conduct entails, courts have traditionally imposed defendants a heavy burden of persuasion.[249] In this regard, case law has uniformly required proof of inequitable conduct—ie, proof of materiality and intent—to be clear and convincing.[250] That does not entail, however, that said conduct is to be proved directly and that no inferences can be made. On the contrary, courts have acknowledged that inequitable conduct—and particularly the intent element—is rarely provable by direct evidence and hence that circumstantial or indirect evidence can be equally suitable.[251]

Despite the high burden of proof imposed upon the defendants, courts had historically also recognised that, once both materiality and intent had been proven, it was possible for the judge to weigh these two elements together by performing some kind of 'sliding scale' exercise: the greater the relevance of the misconduct, the lesser the degree of intent that needed to be shown and vice versa.[252] In *Therasense*, however, the Federal Circuit has emphatically rejected the employment of any 'sliding scale' and further emphasised that evidence on intent is to be assessed independently from evidence on materiality.[253]

D. Types of Conducts that can be Held Inequitable

After having analysed the standards for finding inequitable conduct, it is important to examine at this point which of the many actions that the patent applicant carries out—or fails to carry out—during the prosecution of a patent application are the ones that can later render a patent unenforceable in practice. As a general principle, the inequitable conduct defence can be raised against acts executed by any person in any way associated with the filing and prosecution of a patent application.[254] This means that the conducts of inventors, patent attorneys, agents, or any individual

---

249 Chisum (n 196) para 19.03B[5][a].

250 *Norton v Curtiss* (n 198) 797; *Star Scientific Inc v RJ Reynolds Tobacco Co* 537 F 3d 1357, 1365 (Fed Cir 2008).

251 Schechter and Thomas (n 221) 263.

252 *JP Stevens* (n 205) 1560; *NV Akzo v EI DuPont de Nemours* 810 F 2d 1148, 1153 (Fed Cir 1987).

253 *Therasense* (n 167) 1290.

254 37 CFR § 1.56 (a).

involved in the procedure before the patent office can equally become relevant when the inequitable conduct defence is raised.[255] Such conducts can take place either at the time of filing the patent application or in any other subsequent stage.

But which are the specific behaviours that can actually trigger the applicability of the inequitable conduct doctrine? In view of the enormous complexity of the patent procedure, the range of different conducts that can become relevant under this doctrine is extremely broad. Generally speaking, these misbehaviours can emerge by way of either a positive or a negative act (ie, commission or omission) and they are frequently sorted into three basic categories: (i) failure to disclose material information; (ii) submission of false material information, or (iii) affirmative misrepresentation of a material fact.[256] This catalogue might appear somehow arbitrary, as it can be difficult at times to draw a sharp line between them. Concealing material information when responding to an office action, eg, might be difficult to distinguish from an affirmative misrepresentation.[257] There are, in any case, specific scenarios that have traditionally attracted more concern than others and which have been in the eye of the storm in most inequitable conduct lawsuits. In this regard, the failure to disclose a prior public use of the invention, the failure to cite known relevant prior art and the submission of false information are probably the patterns of behaviour most frequently denounced and thus justify a closer glance.

I. Failure to Disclose the Prior Public Use of an Invention

As it was mentioned above, one of the pivotal requirements of patentability is the absolute novelty of the invention. This implies that, in principle, if an inventor or any third party in any way discloses the invention to the public before the date of filing of the application (eg by publishing, selling, or just publicly using it), the patent application must be rejected.[258]

---

255 37 CFR § 1.56 (c). See also Chisum (n 196) para 19.03A[4][e].

256 *Molins PLC v Textron Inc* 48 F 3d 1172, 1178 (Fed Cir 1995); Mueller (n 164) 552-53.

257 Under the Restatement (Second) of Torts, the concealment of information is actually equated with affirmative misrepresentation in terms of common law fraud. *Restatement (2d) of Torts* (1977) para 550. See also *Therasense* (n 167) 1314, fn 3 (dissenting opinion by J Bryson and others).

258 Under US law, an exception exists in circumstances where the prior disclosures are made by the patent applicants themselves: in these cases, applicants are

Applicants are required to file an oath stating that they believe themselves to be the original and first inventors and to disclose any material prior art they are aware of,[259] which evidently includes prior disclosures by the inventors themselves.[260]

Situations in which inventors bring their inventions to the market or present them in a catalogue before deciding to file for a patent are certainly not implausible. The inventor may, eg, realise too late about the value of the invention, or have difficulties procuring sufficient funding, or could just be negligent. Under these circumstances, it is not difficult to conceive a patent applicant attempting to hide the prior disclosure of the application to the patent office. The fact that this kind of public disclosures are less likely to be found by the examiner could act as a further inducement.[261]

It is not surprising, hence, that in a large number of cases courts have found patents unenforceable due to a failure to disclose relevant uses, such as prior sales or prior publications of the invention.[262] These conducts should naturally meet the minimum standards of materiality and intent like any other inequitable conduct case, but in practice that will rarely constitute a major issue once the prior disclosure is discovered. It will often be hard for patentees to argue that they were not aware of their own use or that their concealing did not affect the decision of the examiner. Some other situations, however, might present more controversial questions. An applicant could, eg, fail to disclose a prior use convinced that is was an experimental use which did not affect the patentability of the invention.[263]

awarded a grace period of one year as of the date of said disclosure in order to file the application. § 102(b)(1) US Patent Act. The EPC also provides for an analogous exception, although with a much more limited scope, under art 55(1).

259 37 CFR § 1.63(a)(4) and (b)(3).

260 Chisum (n 196) para 19.03A[2][a].

261 ibid.

262 Joel Davidow, *Patent-Related Misconduct Issues in US Litigation* (OUP 2010) 27-28.

263 *Monolith Portland Midwest Co v Kaiser Aluminium & Chemical Corp* 407 F 2d 288 (9th Cir 1969). In this case, the court rejected the argument on the basis that, whatever beliefs the patentee could have had, it failed to disclose the facts to the patent office. Ibid 295. See also *Manville Sales Corp v Paramount Systems Inc* 917 F 2d 544 (Fed Cir 1990) (concluding that, even if the prior use was indeed experimental, such information should still be considered material and therefore the applicant has an obligation to disclose it).

II. Failure to Cite Known Relevant Prior Art

During the early days of the inequitable conduct doctrine, courts were rather hesitant to admit the defence on the grounds of a mere failure to disclose relevant prior art references proceeding from third parties, such as an article in a scientific journal or someone else's patent application, except in those cases where they clearly and completely anticipated the invention.[264] Instead, the first cases were targeted against more flagrant misbehaviours and the first guidelines of the USPTO remained silent about it. A general understanding appeared to prevail that it was the patent office the one who was mainly responsible for searching prior art and verifying the novelty of the invention.[265]

By the late 1960s and early 1970s, however, courts began to interpret that, in addition to the examiners' duties to search for prior art, applicants' duties also comprised the duty to disclose relevant information of which they could be aware, even if emanating from a third party and even if it did not openly anticipate the invention, provided that it could be relevant for the assessment of non-obviousness.[266] This expanded view of the patent applicant's duties was then confirmed by the Court of Customs and Patent Appeals in *Norton v Curtiss*, where the court recognised the limitations of the patent office to examine the applications and the inescapable need to rely on the applicants, which justified the highest standards of honesty and candour.[267] Consistent with this trend of the courts, the patent office amended its Rule 56 in order to also incorporate the heightened standards,[268] and later on the Federal Circuit endorsed this interpretation as well.[269] Today, the disclosure of relevant prior art by patent applicants is a

---

264 Chisum (n 196) para 19.03A[2][b]. See also Goldman (n 176) 56. In 1957, eg, a court stated that the applicant should disclose prior art that describes the invention or comes so close that it clearly and obviously anticipates it. *United States v Standard Electric Time Co* 155 F Supp 949, 952 (D Mass 1957).

265 Chisum (n 196) para 19.03A[2][b][i].

266 ibid para 19.03(2)(b); Goldman (n 176) 58. This was probably connected to the introduction of the non-obviousness requirement in 1952. Goldman (n 176) 57.

267 *Norton v Curtiss* (n 198) 794.

268 37 CFR (1977) § 1.56.

269 *Am Hoist* (n 203) 1363 ('the PTO "standard" is an appropriate starting point for any discussion of materiality, for it appears to be the broadest, thus encompassing the others, and because that materiality boundary most closely aligns with how one ought to conduct business with the PTO.').

standard step in the patenting procedure and is normally carried out by the submission of an information disclosure statement (IDS).[270]

Over time, failure to cite prior art has become the most recurrent type of behaviour discussed in inequitable conduct cases.[271] The most frequent categories of prior art references that applicants fail to cite are patent documents (which include both granted patents and patent applications) and publications in journals, brochures or other mediums.[272] The applicants, however, are expected to cite not only this 'traditional prior art' but also any other kind of information an examiner could consider relevant to allow a patent. In this regard, the failure to disclose prior art cited by foreign patent offices in parallel proceedings,[273] the submission of untranslated or partially translated foreign references,[274] the failure to disclose on-going litigation involving the patent application,[275] the failure to cite connected, co-pending applications at the USPTO[276] and even the failure to cite information important for enablement or best mode[277] have been considered by courts as relevant behaviours that can render the patents unenforceable. What is more, the concealment of a prior art document could amount to inequitable conduct even if the examiners later on find it by themselves during examination and nevertheless grant the patent.[278]

With regard to the timing of the disclosure, the Federal Circuit first appeared to suggest that the disclosure should be immediate and that any further disclosure, even if done before the patent office started examining the

270 37 CFR §§ 1.97-1.98.

271 Schechter and Thomas (n 221) 258.

272 Davidow (n 262) 28.

273 *Molins v Textron* (n 256); USPTO, Manual of Patent Examining Procedure (9th edn, 2014) (US MPEP) para 2001.06(a).

274 David Hricik, 'Where The Bodies Are: Current Exemplars of Inequitable Conduct and How to Avoid Them' (2004) 12 Tex Intell Prop L J 287, 303-04.

275 *Critikon Inc v Becton Dickinson Vascular Access Inc* 120 F 3d 1253 (Fed Cir 1997); US MPEP, para 2001.06(c)

276 *Dayco Products Inc v Total Containment Inc* 329 F 3d 1358 (Fed Cir 2003); US MPEP, para 2001.06(b).

277 Davidow (n 262) 11-16.

278 *AB Dick Co v Burroughs Corp* 798 F 2d 1392, 1396-98 (Fed Cir 1986). Other decisions, however, have suggested that, when a reference is already before the examiner, a finding of inequitable conduct is improper. *Molins v Textron* (n 256). Along the same lines, see also Edwin S Flores and Sanford E Warren Jr, 'Inequitable Conduct, Fraud, and Your License to Practice before the United States Patent and Trademark Office' (2000) 8 Tex Intell Prop L J 299, 311.

patent application, could not purge the behaviour.[279] With the entering into force of the AIA, however, it is clear that patentees are allowed to bring to the attention of the examiner prior art information even after the grant of the patent, via the Supplemental Examination procedure, that—if successful—immunises the patent against inequitable conduct attacks.[280] In any case, patent owners are not required to disclose information that comes to their attention after the patent issues.[281]

Finally, it should be borne in mind that courts have unanimously stated that patent applicants are not expected to cite prior art of which they have no knowledge, as the duty to disclose relevant prior art does not entail for them a duty to carry out a special prior art search themselves.[282] Furthermore, courts have also refused to find inequitable conduct in cases where the undisclosed prior art reference was merely cumulative to other references already available to the examiner.[283]

III. Submission of False Information

Instead of simply concealing relevant data from the patent office, applicants may also attempt to persuade the examiner of the merits of their inventions through affirmative, deceitful behaviours by, eg, submitting false material information or making misleading statements. The fact that the patent office will not normally have the ability to verify or challenge the data renders these behaviours particularly threatening.[284]

A typical example of such behaviour is the submission of data containing inaccurate results or revealing false benefits of an invention. In *Frazier v Roessel*,[285] eg, the applicant had claimed to have invented a new camera-lens and had submitted to the patent office a video-recording in an attempt to persuade the examiner about the advantages of the invention. The court, however, later learned that the recording had been shot with a different lens. It consequently judged that this behaviour constituted a case of in-

279 *Driscoll v Cebalo* 731 F 2d 878 (Fed Cir 1984); *FMC Corp v Hennessy Industries Inc* 836 F 2d 521 (Fed Cir 1987).

280 § 257(c)(1) US Patent Act.

281 Chisum (n 196) para 19.03A[2][b][iv].

282 See, eg, *Am Hoist* (n 203) 1362.

283 *JP Stevens* (n 205) 1560; See also 37 CFR § 1.56(b) (clarifying that information cumulative to date already available for the examiner is not considered material).

284 Chisum (n 196) para 19.03A[2][d]; Hricik (n 274) 306.

285 *Frazier v Roessel Cine Photo Tech Inc* 417 F 3d 1230 (Fed Cir 2005).

equitable conduct and declared the patent unenforceable. Similarly, courts have also declared the unenforceability of patents in cases where the test data that had been submitted was incomplete and inaccurate,[286] where the conditions of the test had been manipulated[287] and where the provider of an affidavit had deceitfully been presented as independent.[288] In fact, one of the cases that gave birth to the inequitable conduct doctrine concerned a journal publication that had been made by an allegedly independent expert.[289] Even a misleading assertion in the patent specification itself can render the patent unenforceable, eg if it falsely implies that a test has been run showing the invention's increased efficacy or surprising results.[290]

Be that as it may, courts have also often counselled caution when dealing with allegedly misleading behaviours so as not to interfere with the duty of advocacy of the attorneys.[291] Indeed, the line between this duty and a misleading statement is sometimes blurry. Courts have repeatedly stated, eg, that disclosing prior art and then persuading the examiner about the inventiveness of the application, even if that involves mischaracterising the relevance of a prior art reference, should not be considered inequitable conduct as long as it is not misleading.[292]

IV. Other conducts

In addition to the more emblematical patterns of behaviour cited above, there are many other different sets of conducts before the patent office that can later lead to a patent being declared unenforceable. The length and

---

286 *Monsanto Co v Rohm & Haas Co* 456 F 2d 592 (3rd Cir 1972).

287 Davidow (n 262) 39.

288 ibid 40.

289 *Hazel-Atlas Glass v Hartford-Empire* (n 179).

290 *Purdue Pharma LP v Endo Pharmaceuticals Inc* 410 F 3d 690 (Fed. Cir. 2005).

291 *Mueller Brass Co v Reading Industries Inc* 352 F Supp. 1357, 1379-80 (ED Pa 1972) ('two conflicting principles tear at an attorney practicing before the patent office. One is that the proceeding is not adversary, so the attorney therefore owes a high duty of candor to the examiner. The second is that the attorney has a duty of advocacy to his client. One should not forget in this context that the examiner himself is or should be an advocate for the public interest and should not be too easily swayed by the applicant's attorney.').

292 *Gambro Lundia AB v Baxter Healthcare Corp* 110 F 3d 1573, 1581 (Fed Cir 1997); *Innogenetics, NV v Abbott Laboratories* 512 F 3d 1363, 1379 (Fed Cir 2008). See also Hricik (n 274) 302 (arguing that examiners are presumed to have studied the prior art and can decide its relevance for themselves).

complexity of the patent application procedure require from the applicants the performance of an immense range of different acts and any of them can become a ticking bomb.

Courts have found, eg, that omitting an inventor[293] or declaring a false priority date[294] when filing a patent application can also render the patent unenforceable. Furthermore, even if applicants disclose all relevant prior art they are aware of, a court could find inequitable conduct if such disclosure is done in such a way that the relevant piece of prior art is submerged in a long list of less relevant references so that the examiner overlooks it.[295] In those cases, courts have stated, applicants have an additional duty to explain the relevance of the prior art.[296]

Other less significant behaviours have also been considered to render a patent unenforceable, even if they do not have any impact on the grant of the patent. In that sense, misrepresentations in order to pay reduced fees as a small entity[297] or a false statement in a Petition to Make Special[298] have been considered sufficiently material to render the patent unenforceable. It has been argued that even the deliberate delaying of the examination procedure could be considered a case for inequitable conduct.[299]

As a side note, courts in the past have also found inequitable conduct in circumstances where the applicant had failed to disclose the best mode to practice an invention.[300] This situation, however, is not likely to be seen in the future, since the AIA has eliminated the possibility to declare a patent unenforceable on the basis of a failure to disclose the best mode.[301]

Last, but certainly not least, it cannot be overlooked that the vast majority of cases cited in the preceding paragraphs were decided before the *en*

---

293 *Frank's Casing Crew & Rental Tools Inc v PMR Technologies Inc* 292 F 3d 1363 (Fed Cir 2002). See also Davidow (n 262) 1, 4-6.

294 Davidow (n 262) 42.

295 *Penn Yan Boats Inc v Sea Lark Boats* 359 F Supp. 948 (SD Fla 1972), affd 479 F 2d 1328 (5th Cir 1973); *Molins v Textron* (n 256) 1184.

296 Chisum (n 196) para 19.03A[2][b][ii].

297 *Nilssen v Osram Sylvania Inc* 504 F 3d 1223, 1231 (Fed Cir 2007).

298 *Scanner Technologies Corp v Icos Vision Systems Corp NV* 528 F 3d 1365, 1375 (Fed Cir 2008). A Petition to Make Special is a request that an applicant can make to the USPTO to promptly examine the application if special circumstances are revealed. US MPEP, para 708.02.

299 Davidow (n 262) 43.

300 *Consolidated Aluminum* (n 206) 808.

301 Paul M Janicke, 'Overview of the New Patent Law of the United States' (2013) 21 Tex Intell Prop L J 63, 76.

banc decision in *Therasense* and could thus be solved differently should they be referred to the courts today.

E. Disciplinary and Criminal Sanctions

Irrespective of the effects that an inappropriate conduct before the USPTO might have on the enforceability of a patent, such conduct can also have disciplinary or criminal consequences on the patent attorneys or agents—and in some cases even on the applicants themselves.[302]

With regard to the attorneys and agents, the USPTO Rules provide that all practitioners engaged in practice before the Office are subject to the disciplinary jurisdiction of the USPTO,[303] which in practice is predominantly a responsibility of the USPTO's Office of Enrollment and Discipline.[304] The USPTO Rules further provide for a specific set of Rules of Professional Conduct comprising a long list of instructions on how practitioners are expected to conduct themselves before the Office,[305] and contravening any of these can lead to a disciplinary measure.[306] These disciplinary rules include, inter alia, a reminder to comply with the duty of disclosure provisions (ie Rule 56),[307] a prohibition to make false statements[308] or to knowingly offer false evidence[309] and a ban on bringing frivolous claims,[310] as well as numerous other situations traditionally covered by ethical regulations, such as the missing of deadlines or conflicts of interests. The sanctions that the Office can impose upon the practitioners include an exclusion from practice, a suspension from practice and a reprimand or censure.[311]

As it seems that any case of inequitable conduct by a practitioner would also violate the Rules of Professional Conduct,[312] one could assume that every finding of inequitable conducts by the courts entails a disciplinary

302 Chisum (n 196) para 19.03B[6][j].
303 37 CFR § 11.19(a); § 32 US Patent Act.
304 37 CFR § 11.2 (b).
305 ibid §§ 11.100-11.901.
306 ibid § 11.19(b)(1)(4).
307 ibid § 11.303(e).
308 ibid § 11.303(a)(1).
309 ibid § 11.303(a)(3).
310 ibid § 11.301.
311 ibid § 11.20.
312 *Jaskiewicz v Mossinghoff* 822 F 2d 1053, 1057 (Fed Cir 1987). See also Ian G McFarland, 'In the Wake of *Therasense* & *Nisus Corp*.: How Can Patent Attorneys

sanction for the patent attorney. The figures from the Office of Enrollment and Discipline, however, reveal a different story: the disciplinary sanctions are extremely rare and clearly outnumbered by the inequitable conduct cases.[313] Such discrepancy might be explained by the fact that inequitable conduct can also be committed by the applicants themselves or other individuals who are not subject to the USPTO's disciplinary rules,[314] although a more plausible explanation might be that the ominous nature of the disciplinary proceedings has left them as a last resource only.[315]

In addition to the disciplinary sanctions, practitioners and even non-practitioners may also be subject to criminal sanctions for their conduct before the USPTO.[316] The Criminal Code of the US provides that whoever, in any matter within the jurisdiction of the executive, legislative, or judicial branch, knowingly and wilfully (1) falsifies, conceals, or covers up by any trick, scheme, or device a material fact; (2) makes any materially false, fictitious, or fraudulent statement or representation; or (3) makes or uses any false writing or document knowing the same to contain any materially false, fictitious, or fraudulent statement or entry, shall be fined or imprisoned not more than 5 years.[317] In practice, however, criminal prosecution for patent fraud has been extremely rare, and it seems that only egregious cases with outrageous factual misstatements could be the object of a criminal punishment.[318]

2. *The Duties of the Patent Applicant in Europe*

As stated above, although the procedures and requirements to obtain a patent in the EPC and USPTO are relatively similar in many aspects, a number of significant differences still exist between the two jurisdictions and the general legal framework that surrounds the responsibilities of patent applicants vis-à-vis the patent office constitutes one of the most no-

---

Defend Themselves against Allegations of Inequitable Conduct?' (2011) 78 Tenn L Rev 487, 497.

313 See Flores and Warren (n 278) 315. Decisions of the Office of Enrollment and Discipline of the USPTO are available at <http://e-foia.uspto.gov/Foia/OEDReadingRoom.jsp> accessed 14 February 2018.

314 Cotropia (n 217) 765.

315 Flores and Warren (n 278) 315.

316 37 CFR §§ 1.4 and 11.18(b)(1).

317 18 USC § 1001(a).

318 Ralph D Clifford, 'Is it Time for a Rule 11 for the Patent Bar?' (2013) 53 IDEA 351, 360.

table examples. In fact, the EPC itself does not contain any provision laying down general behavioural rules, let alone sanctions for conducting the procedure in a dishonest or deceitful way.[319] It does provide, however, that the whole procedure before the EPO is to be governed by the principles of procedural law generally recognised in the Contracting States,[320] which evidently comprise inter alia the principle of good faith.[321] Be that as it may, there can be little doubt about the strong differences that the United States and Europe show in this regard, particularly in two major points: (i) the extent of the patent applicant's duty to disclose relevant prior art, and (ii) the consequences that any dishonest conduct before the patent office can later have on the validity or enforceability of the patent.

This section, thus, focuses on these two specific facets. In the first place, it analyses the extent of the patent applicants' duties within the EPC regime. Subsequently, it evaluates whether the conduct exhibited by patent applicants during examination can have any effects during the enforcement of the patent. Since this issue is, for the most part, a question of national law, the legal regimes of the United Kingdom and Germany have been chosen as representative examples.

A. *Extent of Patent Applicants' Duties. Is there a Duty of Disclosure under the EPC?*

The way in which the EPO expects patent applicants to conduct their application procedures appears to strongly differ from the system in place in the United States. There are, it is true, a few undisputed bases which are present in every patent system. It is hardly conceivable, for instance, that the EPO could tolerate any affirmative misrepresentation or submission of

319 The Boards of Appeal of the EPO, however, have taken into consideration the behaviour of the applicant, eg, when deciding on apportionment of costs. See Case T 0952/00 *Rokicki* (decision of the EPO Boards of Appeal of 27 November 2002) (where a granted patent was opposed by a third party and, since it was shown that the applicant had concealed evidence of relevant prior use and made false statements during the whole procedure, the Board of Appeal decided that the patentee should bear the costs incurred by the opponent).

320 EPC, art 125.

321 See, eg, Joined Cases G 5/88, G 7/88 and G 8/88 *Administrative Agreement/ MEDTRONIC* (decision of the EPO Enlarged Board of Appeal of 16 November 1990 [1991] EPO OJ 137) para 3.2; Margarete Singer and Dieter Stauder (eds), *The European Patent Convention: A Commentary* (3rd edn, Sweet & Maxwell 2003) vol 2, 525.

false documents on the part of the patent applicants, considering the general principles of procedural law applicable to the EPO proceedings.[322] In the same vein, a duty of good faith presumably also comprises a responsibility to draw the attention of the examiner to own prior acts which may affect the patentability of the invention.[323] Yet other conditions are substantially different. Most importantly, the extent of the patent applicants' duty to disclose surrounding information on patentability, such as relevant patent documents or scientific publications, seems to be considerably narrower than in the United States.

It should be reminded at the outset that, although every patent system inherently requires some amount of disclosure, at least as regards to the substance of the invention,[324] the EPC does not explicitly provide for any affirmative duty to disclose prior art in the sense the US law does under Rule 56. It is generally recognised that, whereas in the US applicants have a stringent duty to collaborate with the examination process,[325] the EPC seems to rely less on the information provided by the applicants and to confer the examiners a more inquisitive role. In what appears to be a clear externalisation of this vision, art 114 (1) EPC stipulates that 'in proceedings before it, the European Patent Office shall examine the facts of its own motion; it shall not be restricted in this examination to the facts, evidence and arguments provided by the parties and the relief sought.'

I. Rule 42(1)(b) EPC as a Duty of Disclosure?

Interestingly, rule 42(1)(b) EPC does compel the applicant, when describing the invention in the patent specification, to 'indicate the background art which, as far as is known to the applicant, can be regarded as useful to understand the invention, draw up the European search report and examine the European patent application, and, preferably, cite the documents reflecting such art.' In view of this language, it would be possible to contend that the rule actually imposes some type of disclosure responsibilities upon the applicants, as it requires them to acknowledge and cite all relevant prior art information of which they could be aware.

---

322 See, eg, § 124 PatG ('Im Verfahren vor dem Patentamt, dem Patentgericht und dem Bundesgerichtshof haben die Beteiligten ihre Erklärungen über tatsächliche Umstände vollständig und der Wahrheit gemäß abzugeben.').

323 *Hoechst Marion Roussel Ltd v Kirin-Amgen Inc* [2002] EWHC 471 (Patents) [134].

324 See, eg, EPC, art 83.

325 *Norton v Curtiss* (n 198) 794.

There have been at least two cases at the EPO where the examining divisions have attempted to refuse patent applications on the grounds that the specifications had not acknowledged relevant prior art.[326] In both cases, relevant pieces of prior art which had not been disclosed by the applicants were found in the European search report. As the prior art references emanated precisely from the applicants themselves, the examining divisions interpreted that the requirements imposed by rule 42(1)(b) EPC had not been fulfilled. One of the examining divisions further pointed out to the fact that the German version of rule 42, unlike the English and French editions, does not include the conditioning term *preferably* when laying down the duty to cite the relevant documents, thus reinforcing the idea of a harsher responsibility upon the applicants.[327]

The Boards of Appeal of the EPO, however, forcefully discouraged such reading in both cases and interpreted instead that applicants of European patents do not have a rigorous duty to disclose relevant prior art.[328] Both Boards of Appeal indeed understood that rule 42(1)(b) EPC 'does not put a stringent obligation on the applicant to cite documents reflecting prior art known to him already at the time of filing the application.'[329] The Boards of Appeal further acknowledged that, in those cases where references to relevant prior art are missing from the specification as filed and only later noted by the examiners, said information can be later included in subsequent amendments without entailing any extension beyond the content of the application as filed, in the terms of art 123(2) EPC.[330] Rather than a duty to collaborate with the examiners in the search for prior art, thus, rule 42(1)(b) seems to be perceived as a tool for the informative purpose of the patent system, aimed at ensuring that patent specifications disclose sufficient information to the public about the invention and the surrounding prior art.

It is thus clear that, under the current legal framework at the EPO as interpreted by the Boards of Appeal, European patent applicants do not have

326 Case T 2321/08 *Samsung Electronics* (decision of the EPO Boards of Appeal of 11 May 2009) (*Samsung I*); Case T 1123/09 *Samsung Electronics* (decision of the EPO Boards of Appeal of 17 December 2009) (*Samsung II*).

327 The German version of rule 42(1)(b) oft he EPC reads, in its relevant part, as follows: '... es sollen auch die Fundstellen angegeben werden, aus denen sich dieser Stand der Technik ergibt.'

328 EPO Board of Appeals, T 2321/08 of 11.5.2009; EPO Board of Appeals, T 1123/09 of 17.12.2009.

329 *Samsung I* (n 326) para 7.3; *Samsung Electronics II* (n 326) para 3.

330 *Samsung I* (n 326) para 8.4; *Samsung Electronics II* (n 326) para 3.

a duty to disclose information on relevant prior art.[331] The same can be said about applicants before the major European national patent offices, like the DPMA (Germany) and the UKIPO (United Kingdom),[332] although the DPMA is entitled to require applicants, under specific circumstances and on a case-by-case basis, to disclose the state of the art to the best of their knowledge and to incorporate it into the specification.[333]

II. The Duty of Disclosure in the Travaux Préparatoires

The negotiations for the EPC took place many years after the duty of candour concerns first arose in the US, and a few decisions by national courts of the negotiating members had actually insinuated in the past that patent applicants' failure to disclose relevant prior art of which they were aware could be contrary to the obligation of good faith.[334] The issue, however, does not appear to have been comprehensively discussed while drafting the EPC. Either way, a glance at the *Travaux Préparatoires* might still offer some guidance for interpreting the convention on this matter.[335]

In the first place, parts of the debate seem to emphasise the active and inquisitive role that the patent office must have when examining the application and disregard any burden to furnish the examiners with general information that would be anyway accessible to them, such as scientific publications or other patent applications. In this regard, the debates in the *Travaux Préparatoires* draw the attention to the fact that, unlike a first-to-invent system, the first-to-file system adopted by the EPC encourages applicants to file their applications without delay. For that reason, the patent office should not expect applicants to be able to detect all the background art

331 In the same lines, see also Nöel J Akers, 'The Referencing of Prior Art Documents in European Patents and Applications' (2000) 22 World Patent Information 309, 310 ('to date, this provision has not been interpreted as placing any obligation on the applicant or his representative to inform the European Patent Office of any prior art believed to be relevant.').

332 Jan Krauß, 'Equitable Doctrines in International Patent Laws' in Toshiki Takenaka (ed), *Intellectual Property in Common Law and Civil Law* (Edward Elgar 2013) 103.

333 § 34(7) PatG. See also Akers (n 331) 310.

334 See, eg, *Re Clevite Corporation's Patent* [1966] RPC 199, 204 (Lloyd-Jacob J)

335 Vienna Convention on the Law of Treaties, art 31(2)(b).

surrounding their inventions; this should rather be the examiners' responsibility when later studying their patentability.[336]

Additionally, it might be interesting to point out that, when the British Delegation discussed the implementation of the opposition proceedings, it suggested that they enable competitors to seek the revocation of a patent on the basis of information which could have been beyond the reach of the examiners during the application proceedings, such as the applicant's own prior use.[337] Such language seems to imply that the delegations were aware that applicants' withholding of relevant information constitutes a concrete risk that can lead to the unjustified grant of a patent. But, at the same time, they appear to suggest that an opposition procedure after the grant of the patent constitutes an adequate remedy thereto.

III. Rule 141 EPC and the Limited Duty of Disclosure

Although it is submitted that the EPC does not provide for a duty of disclosure in the sense the US does, it does envisage a number of circumstances where the applicants might nonetheless be required to submit specific types of information to the examiners, particularly in relation to search reports produced by foreign patent offices.

Firstly, although the general principle is that there is no obligation to inform the EPO about what other patent offices assess in parallel cases,[338] the EPC expressly allows EPO examiners to invite applicants, on a case-by-case basis, to provide information on prior art taken into consideration in

---

336 Travaux Preparatoires EPC 1973, BR/45 e/70 (Brussels, 16 December 1970), Additional Observations on the First Preliminary Draft Convention made by the Non-Governmental Organisations: Report by FICPI of 24 August 1970, para 7.

337 Travaux Préparatoires EPC 1973, BR/89 e/71 (Brussels, 18 March 1971), Reports from the Delegations to Working Party I of the Inter-Governmental Conference on the Activities of that Working Party: Report by the British Delegation, para 74; Travaux Preparatoires EPC 1973 (Luxembourg, 20-28 April 1971), Reports on Amendments and Additions to the First Preliminary Draft of a Convention Appearing in the Second Preliminary Draft: Report by the UK Delegation, para 63.

338 OLG Düsseldorf, decision of 6 June 2013, case I-2 U 60/11 [99] (in reference to European patent applications) ('Eine Verpflichtung zur Vorlage von Stellungnahmen anderer Erteilungsbehörden besteht grundsätzlich nicht, da das vorliegende Patenterteilungsverfahren von den Eintragungs- und Erteilungsverfahren anderer Schutzrechte unabhängig ist.').

national or regional patent proceedings.[339] A failure to reply in due time results in the patent application being deemed withdrawn.[340]

Most importantly, when the Implementing Rules of the EPO were amended in 2009, they introduced for the first time an affirmative duty to spontaneously disclose that information in certain circumstances. Indeed, according to the amended version of rule 141(1) EPC, every patent applicant claiming priority on a foreign application 'shall file a copy of the results of any search carried out by the authority with which the previous application was filed.' In other words, all patent applications claiming priority rights (and there are certainly many of them) have a duty to inform the EPO about what transpired in that first filing, and for that reason some have argued that the amendment has actually introduced a limited duty of candour in the EPO.[341] The information is to be filed together with the European application, or without delay after such results have been made available to the applicant.[342] If applicants fail to do so, they receive an invitation from the EPO to provide them, and if they fail to reply in due time the application is deemed withdrawn.[343]

At first glance, this seems to be a relatively strict duty. According to rule 141(2) EPC, however, applicants can be exempted from such duty if the search results are available to the EPO under certain specified conditions. Several patent offices around the world have committed themselves to automatically make available to the EPO the search reports they prepare and thus applicants do not have a duty to file them if the office of first fil-

339 EPC, art 124(1) and r 141(3).

340 EPC, art 124(2).

341 Bradley W Crawford and James V DeGiulio, 'New (Limited) Duty of Candor in the EPO (Amended European Rule 141)' (2010) 8[4] MBHB Snippets 13 (2010), available at <www.mbhb.com/snippets> accessed 14 February 2018. Practitioners have labelled this rule 'European IDS', after its US' equivalent. Krauß (n 332) 105.

342 EPC, r 141(1).

343 EPC, r 70b.

ing has been the US, the UK, Japan,[344] Austria,[345] South Korea,[346] or in those cases where the EPO itself prepared the search report on behalf of a third country—as is the case with France, Italy or the Netherlands—or in the framework of the PCT.[347] In practice, thus, there is a large number of cases in which applicants are exempted from this duty.

In any case, amended rule 141 does introduce additional responsibilities upon the applicants, even though in most cases the information it relates to would be easily accessible for the EPO through alternative, simpler ways, thanks to the technological developments in communication and the growing cooperation among major patent offices around the world. Furthermore, the language of rule 141(1) EPC and the adoption of different exceptions under rule 141(2) EPC is also likely to bring legal uncertainty among applicants as to the extent of their duty. For this reason, the amendment has been the subject of criticism and accused of making the patent procedure more complex without any apparent benefits.[348] The objective of the amendment, indeed, could probably have been achieved in a more efficient way by further forging the ties between the patent offices rather than creating new duties upon applicants.[349] If in most cases the search results would be easily available for examiners without the assistance of the applicant, it could have been more sensible to approach those specific cases separately rather than to impose an all-embracing duty that will prove superfluous most of the times. For the very rare cases where the search results of the first receiving office are not otherwise available, the

344 Decision of the President of the EPO dated 9 December 2010 exempting applicants claiming the priority of a first filing made in Japan, the United Kingdom or the United States of America from filing a copy of the search results under Rule 141(1) EPC – utilisation scheme [2011] OJ EPO 62.

345 Decision of the President of the EPO dated 19 September 2012 exempting applicants claiming the priority of a first filing made in Austria from filing a copy of the search results under Rule 141(1) EPC – utilisation scheme [2012] OJ EPO 540.

346 Decision of the President of the EPO dated 27 February 2013 exempting applicants claiming the priority of a first filing made in the Republic of Korea from filing a copy of the search results under Rule 141(1) EPC – utilisation scheme [2013] OJ EPO 216.

347 Decision of the President of the EPO dated 5 October 2010 on the filing of copies of search results under Rule 141(1) EPC – utilisation scheme [2010] OJ EPO 600.

348 David Brophy, 'Rule 141 and further EPO obstructions' (*IP Kat*, 12 August 2010) <http://ipkitten.blogspot.de/2010/08/rule-141-and-further-epo-obstructions.html> accessed 14 February 2018.

349 ibid.

mechanism already offered in the past by rule 141(3), whereby the examiners explicitly invite the applicants to submit the information they need, was probably sufficient.

IV. *The impact of AstraZeneca*

Beside the limited disclosure duties that the European patent scheme impels today upon patent applicants, it has been stated that the decision of the CJEU in the *AstraZeneca*[350] case might have as a by-product an amplification of said duties, at least for determined firms enjoying a dominant position in the market.[351] This issue is analysed in depth in part II of this work.

B. Legal Consequences of a Deceitful Conduct before the Patent Office

In addition to the differences as to the scope of duties that rest upon patent applicants, the European patent system also differs from US law on the consequences that an inadmissible behaviour at the patent office can have on the patentees and on the enforceability of the patents that they might have obtained thereby.

In the first place, and unlike US law, a dishonest conduct from the patent applicant before the EPO does not provide sufficient grounds for the examining division to refuse the patent application. According to the text of the EPC, an application can only be rejected when it does not fulfil the patentability requirements,[352] but not merely because the applicant shows a reprehensible behaviour.

Most importantly, once the patent has been granted, the manner in which the patent applicant conducted the procedure before the EPO does not seem to have any impact on the validity or enforceability of the patent either. As to patent validity, it should be noted that the EPC provides a limited list of grounds under which national courts may revoke a European patent.[353] This list does not include fraud or false statements made by the

350 Case C-457/10 P *AstraZeneca v Commission* (CJEU, 6 December 2012, ECLI:EU:C:2012:770).

351 See text at n 1107 in ch 5.

352 EPC, art 97.

353 EPC, art 138.

applicant and does not seem to leave any margin of discretion to the Member States. Hence, it would be difficult for Member States to contend that they can admit said conduct as a further ground for invalidity. With regard to enforceability, it should be reminded at this point that the EPC only constitutes a uniform system for the grant of patents but not for their enforcement, which for the most part remains a national concern.[354] This implies that, in order to analyse the impact that the behaviour of the applicant might have on the later enforcement of the granted patent, it is necessary to look into the practice of the different national courts with jurisdiction on these issues. This section specifically analyses how German and British legislators and courts have dealt with situations of patent fraud, since these two jurisdictions seem to be good representative examples of the two major legal traditions in Europe and both have considerable experience on patent disputes.

Unlike their peers in the US, the national courts of the EU Member States do not seem to have developed an inequitable conduct doctrine or any other doctrine of the sort. In fact, courts in the EU seem to devote little attention to the prosecution history and what the applicants could have said or done in the process for obtaining their patents; they rather adhere to a more straightforward investigation of the core legal issues.[355] This is evidenced, eg, by the fact that most EU courts do not embrace a *file-wrapper estoppel* doctrine to interpret the scope of the patents in the way the US courts do.[356] Courts in Germany, the UK and France have emphatically ad-

---

354 It should be noted, however, that some issues of patent litigation are partly harmonised, either through the EPC itself (which in art 138 provides for the only grounds under which national courts can revoke a European patent) or through EU law, such as Directive 2004/48/EC of 29 April 2004 on the enforcement of intellectual property rights [2004] OJ L 195/16 (Enforcement Directive) with regard to remedies and taking of evidence. It should also be noted that most EU countries signed in 2015 an Agreement on a Unified Patent Court (UPC) which has not yet entered into force. It proposes a common patent court that will hear both infringement and patent revocation cases.

355 Paul Cole, 'Patents and Scientific Integrity' [2008(5)] CIPAJ 2, 10.

356 This doctrine, which derives from the *venire contra factum proprium* principle, refers to a rule of patent construction which requires that the claims of a patent be interpreted in light of the statements or amendments made by the applicant during the application process. *Festo Corp v Shoketsu Kinzoku Kogyo Kabushiki Co Ltd* 535 US 722, 733 (2002).

vised against its use,[357] although a few precedents have admitted its usefulness under limited circumstances.[358]

I. Germany

In the case of Germany, courts in principle do not take into consideration the circumstances under which the patent has been obtained. In this regard, a defence based on surreptitiously obtained patents would only be admissible in extremely exceptional cases, in analogy to the situation where a party obtains a court judgment in a manner contrary to public policy along the lines of § 826 BGB (*Bürgerliches Gesetzbuch* or German Civil Code) and is later impeded to execute it.[359] The defence, which is normally referred to as *Patenterschleichung*, had gained some recognition in the past due to the fact that, before its amendment in 1941, the German Patent Act provided for a statute of limitations of five year for challenging the va-

357 In Germany: BGH [2002] GRUR 511, 513 – *Kunststoffrohrteil* (The BGH stated that, for determining the socpe of a patent, art 69 EPC refers exclusively to the claims, the description and the drawings; it neither refers to the proceedings that preceded the grant of the patent nor is it necessary to revert to them from a practical perspective). In the UK: *Kirin-Amgen Inc v Hoechst Marion Roussel Ltd* [2004] UKHL 46, [2005] RPC 9 [35]-[39] ('The courts of the United Kingdom, the Netherlands and Germany certainly discourage, if they do not actually prohibit, use of the patent office file in aid of construction. There are good reasons: the meaning of the patent should not change according to whether or not the person skilled in the art has access to the file and in any case life is too short for the limited assistance which it can provide.'). In France: CA Paris, 11 October 1990 *Dolle v Emsens*, PIBD [1991] 491 III 2. For a summary of the problems associated with this doctrine, see *Bristol-Myers Squibb Co v Baker Norton Pharmaceuticals Inc* [1998] EWHC Patents 300, [1999] RPC 253 [52].

358 See, in Germany: BGH [2006] GRUR 923 – *Luftabscheider für Milchsammelanlage*. In the UK: *Rohm and Haas Co v Collag Ltd* [2001] EWCA Civ 1589, [2002] FSR 28 [42]; *Actavis UK Ltd v Eli Lilly & Co* [2014] EWHC 1511 (Pat) [108]-[112]. An exception to the general EU trend against the file-wrapper estoppel doctrine can be observed in the Netherlands, where in 2006 the Dutch Supreme Court decided that it can be invoked in order to narrow down the scope of a claim. *Dijkstra v Saier*, decision of the Supreme Court of the Netherlands of 22 December 2006, No. C05/200HR. An unofficial English translation is available at <www.ie-forum.nl/backoffice/uploads/file/IEForum/Book9.nl/Dijkstra%20vs_%20Saier.pdf> accessed 14 February 2018.

359 Peter Mes, *Patentgesetz, Gebrauchmustergesetz* (3rd edn, Beck 2011) para 104; Georg Benkard, *Patentgesetz* (Claus Dietrich Asendorf and others eds, 10th edn, Beck 2006) para 70.

lidity of a patent.[360] Hence, once those five years lapsed, defendants in patent infringement cases found themselves barred from disputing the validity of the patent, which led them to search for alternative defensive strategies such as the allegation of patent fraud.[361] In 1941, however, said limitation period was abolished and the BGH suggested that there was no need to admit the defences based on patent fraud any more,[362] although the predominant legal doctrine still considers that it should remain admissible, albeit for exceptional circumstances.[363]

Germany has in place today a bifurcation system, wherein claims on patent infringement and claims on patent validity follow different paths and are handled by different courts: the former by the Regional Civil Courts (*Zivilkammern der Landgerichte*) and the latter by the Federal Patent Court (*Bundespatentgericht*).[364] As a claim on patent fraud allegation could be attempted, hypothetically, under both scenarios, ie, as a defence in patent infringement cases or as an argument against validity in cases where the patent is challenged, it is interesting to analyse how both courts have handled this issue.

Firstly, courts dealing with infringement cases are inclined to disapprove such defences because of the special features of the bifurcation system itself. In this regard, it has been stated that defences based on patent fraud are inadmissible if the underlying facts are also capable of underpinning an opposition or an invalidity action, because in such cases it would be the DPMA or the Federal Patent Court—who deal with oppositions and validity issues, respectively—who would have jurisdiction over these

---

360 Rudolf Kraßer and Wolfgang Bernhardt, *Patentrecht* (6th edn, Beck 2009) para 35(VII).

361 Benkard (n 359) para 70.

362 BGH [1954] GRUR 107 *Rechtsmittel* [46] ('...der Tatbestand der Erschleichung eines Patents durch bewußtes Verschweigen des Standes der Technik ist nur dann erfüllt, wenn die Offenlegung des Standes der Technik zur Versagung des Patents hätte führen müssen. Aus diesem Grunde ist im übrigen nach Wegfall der Präklusivfrist des früheren § 13 Abs. 3 PatG hinsichtlich der dort behandelten Vorwegnahmen kein Bedürfnis mehr vorhanden, den Tatbestand der Patenterschleichung durch bewußtes Verschweigen des Standes der Technik als besonderen Nichtigkeitsgrund zuzulassen, da bei Neuheitsschädlichkeit des verschwiegenen Standes der Technik schon die sich auf diesen erstreckende Neuheitsprüfung zur Vernichtung des Patents führen muß..').

363 Benkard (n 359) para 70.

364 §§ 65 and 143 PatG.

questions.[365] In those cases, the infringement courts could, at the most, decide to stay the proceedings, but not reject a complaint on these grounds only. On the other hand, in those cases where the misbehaviour would not avail an invalidity action (eg, if the fraud was irrelevant for the examiner in granting the patent, or if it was committed to obtain the reinstatement of a valid patent), it has been argued that such conduct cannot constitute the basis of a defence in a patent infringement suit either, although on different grounds: in those cases, it could be interpreted that the restricted list of grounds for invalidation provided by the law encompasses a decision from the legislator in favour of all other patents, even if theoretically objectionable on different grounds.[366]

As far as the invalidity procedures are concerned, it should be reminded that the EPC does not allow courts to revoke a European patent based on the behaviour of a patent applicant itself.[367] Similarly, the PatG does not provide for such ground of invalidity for national patents.[368] The BGH itself had left the question open in an old decision,[369] but today it is generally understood that the plaintiff challenging the validity of the patent cannot ground its action on omissions or misrepresentations from the patentee during prosecution.[370] The BGH actually suggested in a later decision that it would be hard to imagine a situation where the culpability of the patentee could play any significant role in invalidity proceedings, since a decision on whether a patent meets all the requirements provided by the law does not need to look into the subjective state of its owner.[371]

---

365 OLG Düsseldorf, decision of 14 June 2007, case I-2 U 135/05, [2008] GRUR-RR 333; OLG Düsseldorf, decision of 26 June 2008, case I-2 U 130/06; OLG Düsseldorf, decision of 6 June 2013, case I-2 U 60/11 [67].

366 Benkard (n 359) para 70.

367 EPC, art 138.

368 § 21 PatG.

369 *BGH Rechtsmittel* (n 362) 111 ('Auf die umstrittene Frage, ob überhaupt der Tatbestand der Patenterschleichung einen Nichtigkeitsgrund abgeben kann, braucht daher im vorliegenden Falle nicht eingegangen zu werden.') (citations omitted).

370 Kraßer and Bernhardt (n 360) para 35(VII)(8). In this regard, the Higher Regional Court of Düsseldorf stated that, in invalidity procedures, it is not admissible to argue that the examiner would not have granted the patent if it had been aware of the misconduct, as long as these factors do not objectively invalidate the patent. OLG Düsseldorf, decision of 14 June 2007, case I-2 U 135/05, [2008] GRUR-RR 333.

371 BGH [1965] GRUR 231, 234 *Zierfalten* ('…es ist kaum denkbar, daß die Frage des Verschuldens des Patentinhabers wegen Kennens oder fahrlässigen Nichtkennens schädlicher Entgegenhaltungen in einem Nichtigkeitsstreit

Notwithstanding the above, German scholars have debated whether patentees can be held liable for damages under § 826 BGB if they hold and defend a patent knowing that it is invalid, either because of fraud or because of information they learnt about after grant. There is no case law addressing this issue[372] and it has been argued that, since an invalidity action does not constitute a re-examination of the patent, but only a verification of its validity against the specific arguments raised by the plaintiff, the mere defending of the patent cannot be considered illegal.[373] However, if patentees falsely state or deliberately imply that they are not aware of any relevant prior art, the alleged infringers could later be entitled to claim for compensation from the patentees for the damages they suffered.[374]

II. United Kingdom

In the past, UK law specifically allowed to challenge the validity of an exclusive right based on a deceptive behaviour before the patent office. Indeed, before its last substantial amendment in 1977, the UK Patents Act specifically provided for a ground of objection to the validity of a patent based on the fact that 'the patent was obtained on a false suggestion or representation'.[375] The raison d'être of this ground of objection goes back to the birth of patents as royal grants, which as such were subject to be repealed by the king under specific circumstances. Such circumstances comprised, among others, finding that the grant had been obtained on 'false suggestion'.[376] That notwithstanding, when the Patent Act was amended

überhaupt eine Rolle spielen könnte, weil bei der Entscheidung der Frage der Schutzschädlichkeit von Entgegenhaltungen der subjektive Tatbestand ohne Bedeutung ist. Selbst bei Behauptung einer offenkundigen Vorbenutzung würde im Nichtigkeitsstreit die Frage der Kenntnis oder fahrlässigen Unkenntnis von den sie rechtfertigenden Umständen keine Rolle spielen').

372 Kraßer and Bernhardt (n 360) para 35(VII)(8).

373 Rudolf Kraßer, 'Verpflichtung des Patentanmelders oder –inhabers zu Angaben über den Stand der Technik' in Karl Bruchhausen and others (eds), *Festschrift Für Rudolf Nirk zum 70. Geburtstag* (Beck 1992) 537.

374 Krauß (n 332) 117.

375 UK Patents Act 1949, s 32(1)(j). See also Neil Davenport, *The United Kingdom Patent System: A Brief History* (Mason 1979) 35-36.

376 *Prestige Group (Australia) v Dart Industries*, [1992] FSR 143, 164 (Federal Court of Australia). Indeed, as royal grants, patents had to fulfil a number of fundamental requirements, namely that the grant be: (a) within the law; (b) not to the prejudice of existing rights; (c) certain; (d) not in contradiction of the sovereign's in-

and brought into harmony with the rest of the European patent system, the grounds of revocation were amended and redrafted with a view on the prescriptions of the EPC, which entailed dropping some of the grounds of the previous act.[377]

Before its removal from the Patents Act, courts had interpreted this provision to require the false suggestions or representations to have been material for the granting of the patent, ie of such materiality that it could be said that the Crown had been deceived.[378] The types of cases that courts had to deal with in this regard were basically divided into two groups: those where the false suggestion or representation constituted a promise in the specification—usually by misstating or exaggerating the benefits of an invention—and those where the falsehood was extraneous to the specification.[379] Almost all the cases heard by UK courts concerned exaggerations or false statements in the specification about the alleged advantages of the invention,[380] and in most cases these objections overlapped with challenges on patentability.[381] Other challenges based on, eg, false statements or omissions as to prior art, priority or inventorship—which are the predominant allegations in inequitable conduct cases in the US—have been rarely alleged and there seems to be no instance of patents held invalid on such grounds.[382] Either way, cases dealing with false suggestions in any form were rather unusual,[383] and they are not conceivable in the present context, since neither a European patent nor a national UK patent can be invalidated today on the grounds of fraud or misstatements during the application procedure.[384]

Despite not having the capacity to render the patent invalid, it would be interesting to consider whether the fraud at the patent office could in any way affect the enforceability of the patent in court. It is worth recalling that the inequitable conduct doctrine developed in the US stems from the traditional equitable principle of unclean hands, a concept that actually derives from old English case law and which courts in the UK have historical-

tention; (e) free from any false consideration or suggestion; and (f) free from any false recital. Davenport (n 375) 34.

377 Edward Armitage, 'The New British Patent Legislation' (1978) 9 IIC 207, 213.

378 *Valensi v British Radio Corp* [1973] RPC 337, 381 (Court of Appeal).

379 Thomas A Blanco White, *Patents for Inventions and the Protection of Industrial Designs* (5th edn, Stevens & Sons 1983) para 4-1001.

380 ibid para 4-1002.

381 ibid para 4-1001.

382 ibid para 4-1002.

383 *Re Chevron Research Company's Extension* [1975] FSR 1, 4 (Chancery Division).

384 EPC, art 138; UK Patents Act, s 72.

ly recognised.[385] English courts have indeed applied this principle even when dealing with intellectual property issues, eg by preventing trademark holders from enforcing their right on the grounds that their business was fraudulent.[386] But despite the fact that courts had acknowledged that patent applicants' deliberate withholding prior art could be contrary to the obligation of good faith,[387] no court in the UK seems to have applied the unclean hands maxim as a response against a deceptive behaviour at the patent office. Under current UK law, the only stage where a dishonest behaviour before the patent office might have some relevance in court is probably at the time when the judge has to determine whether to award costs to one of the parties.[388]

III. *Disciplinary and Criminal Sanctions*

In connection to the sanctions that patent attorneys are subjected to for improperly conducting the application procedure entrusted to them, the differences between the US system and the disciplinary framework in force in Europe do not appear to be as sharp. Indeed, both under the structure of the EPO and under national laws, sanctions can be imposed upon patent attorneys for dishonest or misleading behaviour in a similar fashion to the disciplinary procedures before the USPTO.

---

385 *Dering v Earl of Winchelsea* (1787) 1 Cox 318, 319 ('… a man must come into a Court of Equity with clean hands; but when this is said, it does not mean a general depravity; it must have an immediate and necessary relation to the equity sued for …').

386 See, eg, *Chocosuisse Union Des Fabricants Suisses De Chocolat v Cadbury Ltd* [1997] EWHC 360 (Pat) [72]-[75] (Citing *Newman v Pinto* [1887] RPC 508 (Court of Appeals), emphasising that 'a plaintiff should fail in the action only in those cases where the court concludes that, in all the circumstances, it is unconscionable for him to be given the relief he would otherwise be entitled to' and concluding that, where the plaintiff has engaged in misleading activities, the closeness of those activities to the right that is being enforced is an essential factor to consider).

387 *Re Clevite* (n 334) 204 (Lloyd-Jacob J).

388 UK Patents Act, s 106(1). Furthermore, where a patent is declared partially valid or when the patent owner amends the specification and claims damages for infringements that took place before such amendment, courts could not award damages, costs or expenses to the patentee if it is shown that the original specification had not been framed in good faith. UK Patents Act, ss 62(3)(b) and 63(2)(b).

Within the European Patent Organisation, the Administrative Council has adopted a set of rules of professional conduct which governs the disciplinary power of the EPI and of the EPO on professional representatives.[389] Among other duties, patent attorneys are required to 'exercise their profession conscientiously and in a manner appropriate to its dignity', and in particular to 'not knowingly make any false or misleading statement'.[390] If they violate these rules, they are subject to disciplinary sanctions, which comprise warnings, reprimands, fines and a temporary or permanent deletion from the list of professional representatives.[391] These sanctions may be imposed by the Disciplinary Committee of the EPI or by the Disciplinary Board of the EPO,[392] and in both cases the decision is appealable to the Disciplinary Board of Appeal of the EPO.[393] However, the number of disciplinary sanctions appears to be quite low so far. In practice, most of the cases under the jurisdiction of the Disciplinary Board of Appeals relate to disputes over the European qualifying examination—where normally candidates challenge the marks awarded—rather than to matters of professional misconduct.[394]

In a similar way, German patent attorneys are also bound to conduct the application procedures candidly and truthfully before the DPMA,[395] and a violation of their duties can result in a sanction such as a warning, a reprimand, a fine or an exclusion from the register.[396] By the same token, in the UK the Rules of Conduct for Patent Attorneys issued by the Chartered Institute of Patent Attorneys provide for a wide catalogue of duties including integrity and to act in the interest of justice,[397] and a violation of said duties can lead to a great variety of sanctions that go from a public no-

389 Regulation of the Administrative Council of the EPO on discipline for professional representatives [1978] OJ EPO 91, [2008] OJ EPO 14. This regulation was adopted under the power conferred by art 134a(1)(c) of the EPC.

390 ibid art 1(1).

391 ibid art 4(1).

392 ibid arts 6 and 7.

393 ibid art. 8. See also Additional Rules of Procedure of the Disciplinary Board of Appeal [1980] OJ EPO 176 and 188.

394 'EPO Round up: Part 2' (*IP Kat*, 7 June 2005) <http://ipkitten.blogspot.de/2005/06/epo-round-up-part-2.html> accessed 14 February 2018.

395 § 124 PatG.

396 § 96 PatAnwO (*Patentanwaltsordnung* or German Patent Attorneys' Regulation).

397 UK Intellectual Property Regulation Board, Rules of Conduct for Patent Attorneys, Trade Mark Attorneys and Other Regulated Persons, rr 5 and 14.

tice, warning or reprimand to a fine, a suspension or removal from the register and even an order to undertake further training.[398]

On a different note, it should not be overlooked that a wilful misrepresentation to the patent office—or to any other department of the government—could also have criminal consequences under the German Criminal Code,[399] as well as under the UK Perjury Act.[400]

3. *Ruminations on the US Experience. What can European Courts and Legislators Learn from it?*

Ultimately, the strict onus that US courts and legislators impose upon patent applicants seems to derive from a combination of traditional equitable principles and a perception of the applicants and their attorneys as sheer collaborators of the examination process. Both the broad scope of the duties—particularly the duty of disclosure—and the lethal consequences for falling foul of any of them position the US as a rather unique case among the different patent offices around the world.[401] An increasing number of patent offices admittedly require applicants to disclose certain information under specific circumstances, primarily prior art references cited by foreign patent offices in parallel examinations, and nearly always upon a case-by-case request from the examiner.[402] None of them, however, seems to impose such a strict, all-embracing obligation of disclosure as the US does. Moreover, the declaration of unenforceability that US courts have developed as a remedy against improper patent prosecution does not appear to have an equivalent figure among the European patent courts either.[403]

Having described in detail the scenario in the US and contrasted it with the very different state of affairs observed in Europe, there is an interrogative that inescapably arises: are European courts and authorities getting it wrong? Is there anything Europe can learn or replicate from the approach taken in the United States? Or is it rather the other way round?

---

398 UK Intellectual Property Regulation Board, Disciplinary Procedure Rules, rule 14.

399 § 263 StGB (*Strafgesetzbuch* or German Criminal Code).

400 UK Perjury Act 1911, ss 2 and 5.

401 Janicke, 'Mental and Emotional States' (n 217) 291.

402 Bicknell (n 160) 457-63.

403 Janicke, 'Mental and Emotional States' (n 217) 292. See also *Les Laboratoires Servier v Apotex Inc* [2008] EWCA Civ 445 [9]-[10].

The question has not been the object of intensive research yet, although a few voices—the loudest stemming from the generic pharmaceutical industry—have suggested that the European patent system should indeed implement an extended duty of candour resembling the one in place in the United States.[404] A more stringent duty of disclosure, they contend, could contribute to increase the quality of the patents that the EPO and other national patent offices issue. The predominant opinion, however, seems to be diametrically opposed to adjusting the law in this course. On the one hand, it is argued, it could only skyrocket the costs of litigation without any perceptible benefits.[405] On the other hand, certain specific features of the European patent system, such as the existence of a post-grant opposition procedure and the imposition of attorneys' fees to the losing party in litigation, might render unnecessary, or even counter-productive, any amendment of the law.[406] In any case, it is a question certainly worth asking.

At heart, there are seemingly not one but two issues that should be addressed at this point and which, although extremely intertwined and generally treated together, deserve to be broken down into independent questions. The first question refers to the scope of the duties that are laid upon the patent applicants, the role they are expected to play during examination and in particular the extent to which they are required to disclose information relevant to patentability. The second question is concerned with the legal implications that an improper behaviour of the patent applicant could have on the later enforcement of the patent. It seems more sensible, thus, to treat both questions independently, as it is theoretically possible to

404 European Generic Medicines Association, 'Patent-Related Barriers to Market Entry for Generic Medicines in the European Union: A Review of Weaknesses in the Current European Patent System and their Impact on the Market Access of Generic Medicines' (2008) 10 and 27 <www.medicinesforeurope.com/wp-content/uploads/2009/06/EGA-IP_Barriers_web.pdf> accessed 14 February 2018. See also Giuseppe Scellato and others, 'Study on the Quality of the Patent System in Europe' (Report for the European Commission, DG Internal Market, 2011) 91-94 <http://ec.europa.eu/internal_market/indprop/docs/patent/patqual02032011_en.pdf> accessed 14 February 2018 (listing the duty of disclosure as a possible tool for increasing patent quality but also acknowledging that there might be arguments against its implementation).

405 Robin Jacob, 'Patents and Pharmaceuticals: A Paper given on 29th November at the Presentation of the Directorate-General of Competition's Preliminary Report of the Pharma-Sector Inquiry' in Hugh C Hansen (ed), *Intellectual Property Law and Policy: Volume 12* (Hart 2013) 653; Cole (n 355) 6.

406 Cotter, 'An Economic Analysis of Inequitable Conduct' (n 173) 777-78; Janicke, 'Mental and Emotional States' (n 217) 292.

conceive one without the other, eg by broadening the applicant's disclosure duties while at the same time restricting the monitoring of such duties to the jurisdiction of the patent office or by solely imposing disciplinary sanctions.

A. *Extent of Patent Applicants' Duties*

As explained above, patent applicants at the USPTO have a strict duty of candour which derives from both Rule 56 and the case law developed around the inequitable conduct doctrine.[407] Patent applicants in Europe naturally have a duty of good faith as well, which requires from them an honest and transparent conducting of the procedure. The scope of this burden, however, seems to be considerably less harsh, particularly with regard to the prior art information that they are expected to disclose. If the extent of duties in each patent office had to be represented graphically, the graph would probably look like the following:

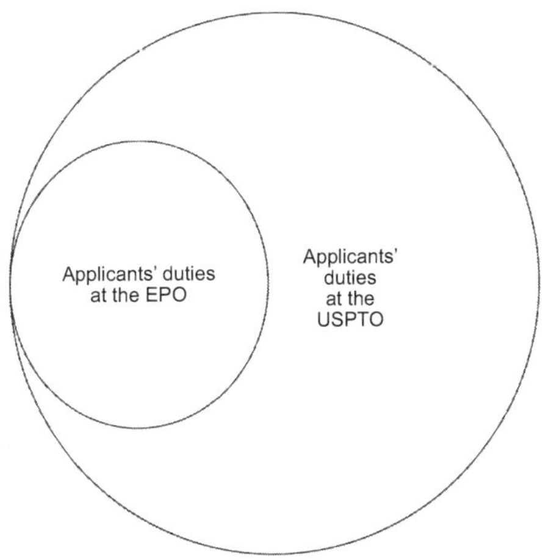

In the first place, thus, it would be opportune to evaluate whether a stricter code of conduct, and particularly an extended duty of disclosure, could deliver any benefits to the European patent system. No one would challenge at this point that, in order to get high quality patents, the examination pro-

407 37 CFR § 1.56; *Therasense* (n 167) 1287.

cedure and the decision to grant should be as transparent and informed as possible. The question is whether an extended duty of candour can contribute in this respect or, to the contrary, whether the remedy would end up being worse than the illness.[408]

From a theoretical point of view, the idea of an extended duty of candour looks quite appealing at first sight. It is submitted that, with today's vast sources of information, the patent office's search for prior art cannot always be 100% complete.[409] In certain cases, applicants may possess more and better information surrounding the invention than the patent office,[410] leading to a situation of information asymmetry.[411] Although competitors or third parties might be equally versed on the subject, their involvement in the examination process is relatively limited until the patent is granted. Moreover, in certain fields of technology the quality of prior art identification by examiners might be particularly vulnerable.[412] Hence, requiring patent applicants to collaborate with the prior art search and examination by furnishing the patent office with all the information they are aware of might seem like a reasonable proposal that could ameliorate the information asymmetry, particularly bearing in mind the far-reaching social and economic impact of patents. This is, indeed, the basic idea behind the stringent duty of disclosure still in force in the United States,[413] and the main argument raised by those advocating the implementation of a similar obligation in Europe.[414] From a practical perspective, however, imposing such a burden on patent applicants might pose a number of unexpected pitfalls, not only due to the complexities in its implementation but also because the benefits for the patent system might be much scarcer than

---

408 Janicke, 'Mental and Emotional States' (n 217) 292. In a similar vein, but with far-reaching conclusions, Mark Lemley argues that strengthening the examination procedure might not always be cost effective, basically arguing that very few patents are actually litigated or licensed. Mark A Lemley, 'Rational Ignorance at the Patent Office' (2001) 95 Northwest U L Rev 1495.

409 EPO, Guidelines for Examination in the European Patent Office (EPO November 2014) (EPO Guidelines) pt B(III) para 2(1).

410 Taylor (n 173) 54.

411 ibid 52.

412 Bhaven N Sampat, 'Examining Patent Examination: An Analysis of Examiner and Applicant Generated Prior Art' (Dphil thesis, University of Michigan 2004) 33-34 ('the quality of issued patents, is likely to be worse in fields where a substantial portion of the relevant prior art is embodied in sources other than U.S. patents, including the scientific and technical literature.').

413 *Norton v Curtiss* (n 198) 794.

414 European Generic Medicines Association (n 404) 10 and 27; Scellato (n 404) 91-94.

imagined,[415] or even backfire and undermine the patent office's examination process altogether. It should not be forgotten, in this regard, that no empirical studies seem to reveal a direct link between increased duties upon the applicants and higher quality of patents. In fact, the prevailing opinion appears to be that the average quality of the patents granted by the EPO is markedly higher than that of the patents granted by the USPTO,[416] and it has been suggested that the existence of a strict duty of disclosure in the latter might in fact be one of the determining factors.[417]

The following paragraphs appraise some of the major concerns that the introduction of such a duty could haul, most of which seem to tip the scales against the implementation of a strict duty of disclosure.

I. Defining the Scope of the Obligation

In the first place, it would be extremely challenging to delineate the duty in a clear way. It should be borne in mind that, based on the general principle of good faith, applicants at the EPO are already expected to reveal information they hold which plainly and unmistakably affects the patentability of their applications, such as their own prior uses or exhibitions. The EPO further requires applicants, under certain circumstances, to submit search reports produced by foreign patent offices, a burden which has already caused some stir among practitioners.[418] But if applicants are expected to put on the table the entirety of the information that the examiner needs for the assessment of the application's inventiveness, such as third parties' patents or scientific publications, severe difficulties could arise.

Firstly, it would be tremendously challenging to delineate the duty in a clear way and to precisely define the range of information that applicants are required to bring forward. In this regard, the legislator should basically

415 Jacob, 'Patents and Pharmaceuticals' (n 405) 653.

416 Bruno van Pottelsberghe de la Potterie, 'The Quality Factor in Patent Systems' (2011) 20 Industrial and Corporate Change 1755. *See also* Susana Borrás, 'The Governance of the European Patent System: Effective and Legitimate?' (2006) 35 Economy and Society 594, 601; Matthis de Saint-Georges and Bruno van Pottelsberghe de la Potterie, 'A Quality Index for Patent Systems' (2013) 42 Research Policy 704, 719 (patents granted by the USPTO are listed among the ones with lowest quality).

417 Bruno van Pottelsberghe de la Potterie (n 416) 1769.

418 Brophy (n 348).

choose between confining the duty to prior art effectively known to the applicants, much like US practice today, or requiring them to disclose the entirety of the existing prior art—regardless of whether they are aware of it or not. In the first case, such a duty could result in applicants adopting an ostrich-like approach,[419] whereby they avoid performing any patentability searches and remain intentionally oblivious, striving to know as little as possible about the surrounding prior art,[420] which could lead to unjustified applications. In the second case, the duty would require applicants to become absolute experts before filing, which seems extremely far-reaching as it would entail immense costs—and delay of applications—that most applicants would not be able to bear.[421] In any case, such a duty would not spare the patent office the need to carry out its own prior art search.

More importantly, if the duty is confined to prior art actually known by applicants, the supervision of such a duty could become a great headache in practice. Indeed, authorities in that event would need determine in every individual case whether the applicants were aware of the relevant-but-undisclosed pieces of prior art—an investigation that has proven to be extremely burdensome in the US.[422]

Finally, it would also be troublesome for applicants to decide which specific pieces of prior art to disclose in each case. Faced with such burden, they would probably be inclined to err on the side of over-disclosure, just to be on the safe side,[423] or in the worst cases even 'bury' highly material references by blurring them inside a long list of less relevant information.[424] Either way, applicant intervention in those cases might thwart rather than ease the job of the examiner.

---

419 Bicknell (n 160) 471.

420 Admittedly, authorities could in that case adopt a 'should have known' approach, although such a solution could result in endless discussions about what the applicants actually should have known, as it would bring negligence issues to the table. Hricik (n 274) 295.

421 Although some have actually argued that in the US the burden on the applicants should be heavier and that they should have a positive duty to search for prior art before filing and submit it to the USPTO. Thomas Schneck, 'The Duty to Search' (2005) 87 J Pat & Trademark Off Soc'y 689, 704.

422 Janicke, 'Mental and Emotional States' (n 217) 292.

423 Bicknell (n 160) 431; Taylor (n 173) 63; Erstling (n 160) 335.

424 Hricik (n 274) 301. It has been suggested that such risk could be alleviated by raising the costs for excessive disclosures. Cotter, 'An Economic Analysis of Inequitable Conduct' (n 173) 775. That proposal, however, might also be difficult to bring into practice.

II. Practical Value

Even if a duty of disclosure were to be successfully implemented in Europe, it is not clear whether the information provided by the applicants would result in practice in higher quality patents,[425] or whether the examiner would take it into consideration at all for that matter. It has been suggested, in this regard, that an extensive duty of disclosure might in fact impede the quality of patent examination instead of furthering it.[426]

As the US has had a duty of disclosure in place for many years, it might be valuable to observe the impact that such duty has had on the examination procedure of the USPTO in practice. In this regard, a number of renowned patent law scholars have carried out an empirical study in order to test whether the USPTO really avails itself of the information submitted by the applicants.[427] The study reveals surprising outcomes, as it shows that patent examiners effectively disregard almost all applicant-submitted prior art, relying almost exclusively on prior art information they find themselves.[428]

The fact that examiners do not take into account prior art submitted by applicants might be explained in some cases by the weakness or irrelevance of the information they submit, although the major factors are probably connected to both information overload[429] and cognitive biases: examiners might just think more highly of their own searches.[430] Moreover, the limited amount of time that examiners can allocate to the study of each application and the large amounts of information that applicants might be inclined to disclose when faced with such a burden could also constitute relevant factors that explain why examiners tend to disregard such information.

---

425 From an innovation policy perspective, a high quality patent should enable those persons having skill in the art to easily understand the invention. From social welfare perspective, a high quality patent would be a patent with little uncertainty over its validity and the breadth of the claims. Bronwyn H Hall and Dietmar Harhoff, 'Post-Grant Reviews in the U.S. Patent System Design Choices and Expected Impact' (2004) 19 Berkeley Tech L J 989, 991.

426 Erstling (n 160) 336.

427 Christopher A Cotropia, Mark A Lemley and Bhaven N Sampat, 'Do Applicant Patent Citations Matter?' (2013) 42 Research Policy 844.

428 ibid 853.

429 Jeffrey M Kuhn, 'Information Overload at the U.S. Patent and Trademark Office: Reframing the Duty of Disclosure in Patent Law as a Search and Filter Problem' (2010) 13 Yale J L and Tech 89, 92.

430 Cotropia, Lemley and Sampat (n 427) 851.

It has further been stated that, even if a duty of disclosure was ever justified, it would not be any more, as the accessibility and power of computer-based prior art searching might render a duty of disclosure not cost-effective.[431] In this vein, it cannot be denied that the circumstances under which the duty of candour was first envisaged in the United States have drastically changed. As a result of the developments in access to information, communications and cooperation between the different patent offices, an obligation to disclose prior art might not make as much sense any longer.[432]

There might still be, it is true, certain situations where information might not be reachable by the examiner, eg in case of limited prior uses or remote and inaccessible public disclosures. Although in some of these cases it could be argued that applicants are already obliged to disclose such information under current laws on the basis of the principle of good faith, it is likely that such information will be known by competitors as well. Hence, EPC regulations on third party observations and oppositions might constitute an effective fall-back remedy. Indeed, under the EPC, third parties are entitled to bring relevant information on patentability to the patent office during the examination of the application via observations,[433] and most importantly, they can file an opposition to the patent within nine months after grant.[434]

---

431 Cole (n 355) 6. See also Erstling (n 160) 357-63 (changes in technology, law and cooperation might make disclosure redundant).

432 As an illustrative example, the FTC carried out in 2003 a thorough evaluation on the duty of candour within the framework of a study on the proper balance of competition and patent law. Despite some voices urging for an expanded duty of candour, the FTC concluded that there is no sufficient evidence indicating that added responsibilities upon patent applicants would actually enrich the patenting procedure. FTC, 'To Promote Innovation: The Proper Balance of Competition and Patent Law and Policy' (October 2003) ch 5, 11.

433 Although third parties do not formally become a party to the examination after submitting observations, examiners have a duty to take said observations into account by if they call into question the patentability of the invention. EPO Guidelines (n 409) pt E(V) para 3.

434 Scholars in the US had actually suggested –before the passing of the AIA– that one of the alternatives to improve the quality of information available to examiners would be to allow greater integration of third parties during prosecution. Robert P Merges, 'As Many as Six Impossible Patents before Breakfast: Property Rights for Business Concepts and Patent System Reform' (1999) 14 Berkeley Tech L J 577, 614; Hall and Harhoff (n 425) 1015. In the same vain, it has been argued that the benefits of an expansive burden upon applicants may be small or negative in a system in which post-grant oppositions are already common. Cotter, 'An Economic Analysis of Inequitable Conduct' (n 173) 778.

III. Interest of Applicants Themselves to have All Prior Art Considered

Either if there is a duty to disclose relevant prior art or not, applicants might nonetheless be interested in having their patents examined against the closest prior art and hence inclined to disclose it on their own initiative, as it could positively affect the quality and value of the patent. In this regard, Caballero and Jaffe argue that 'omission of important references can be grounds for invalidation of the patent, giving the applicant an incentive to make sure that citations appear.'[435] Thus, applicants might be personally interested in disclosing themselves relevant prior art, because the more prior art references are considered and rejected by the examiner, the less likely it is that the patent will be later invalidated during litigation.[436] And even if the patent is not involved in litigation, a higher quality can give the owner a stronger bargaining position in case of opposition or licensing.[437] The incentive to disclose, however, might not be as strong in certain fields of technology where the number of patents of a determined portfolio matters much more than their quality.[438]

IV. Duty of Advocacy

Finally, it is also important to consider that patent attorneys have a duty to defend their clients' inventions and, therefore, should not be expected to provide every single argument to the examiners, who should reach their own conclusions.[439] An extensive duty of disclosure could thus fly on the face of the patent attorneys' duty of advocacy, especially if they are also required to opine on the relevance of every prior art reference, as it would place them in the uncomfortable position of having to first reveal a list of

---

435 Ricardo J Caballero and Adam B Jaffe, 'How High Are the Giants' Shoulders: An Empirical Assessment of Knowledge Spillovers and Creative Destruction in a Model of Economic Growth' in Olivier Blanchard and Stanley Fischer (eds), *NBER Macroeconomics Annual 1993: Volume 8* (MIT Press 1993) 32, fn 22.

436 Erstling (n 160) 334, fn 36. See also Cotropia, Lemley and Sampat (n 427) 845 ('disclosure of prior art to the PTO can help "bulletproof" a patent in later litigation.').

437 Akers (n 331) 310.

438 Bhaven N Sampat, 'When Do Applicants Search for Prior Art?' (2010) 53 J L & Econ 399, 413 (in certain product fields, eg complex-product industries, where many patents cover a given product and the validity of any given patent is not as important, applicants are significantly less likely to contribute prior art).

439 Bicknell (n 160) 445.

prior art and then rebut arguments that perhaps not even the examiner or competitors would have thought of.[440]

B. Legal Consequences of a Deceitful Conduct before the Patent Office

In addition to the question on the ideal breadth of the patent applicants' disclosure duties, a second, closely connected issue deserves to be tackled at this point, namely the legal implications that patent applicants' failure to comply with those duties could have on the later enforcement of the patent. It goes without saying that the relevance of this issue is strongly tied to the breadth of these duties. Yet even if the law of the EPC today, with its less stringent duties, were to remain the same, it is worth considering whether the patent applicants' failure to comply with their duties in the midst of examination, eg by making egregiously false statements, should have any impact at the enforcement stage.

As described above, US courts can hold a patent unenforceable if they find that the patent has been obtained through inequitable conduct—which traditionally consists of a failure to disclose relevant prior art or prior uses but can also occur when submitting false information or making misleading statements. The question at this point, hence, is whether European courts should adopt a similar approach and whether they would actually be enabled to do so by current EU and national laws.

I. Evaluation of the inequitable conduct doctrine in the US

Probably few American legal doctrines have been jeered and condemned as fiercely and passionately as the inequitable conduct defence. It has been called an 'absolute plague',[441] a 'formless liability',[442] the 'atomic bomb'

---

440 Goldman (n 176) 95. See also *General Tire & Rubber Co Ltd v Firestone Tyre & Rubber Co Ltd* [1975] RPC 203, 269 (Court of Appeal) ('It is, after all, the function of a patent agent to argue in honesty for the width of the application.'); *Hoechst v Kirin-Amgen* (n 323) [135] ('while the duty of candour on an applicant for a patent and its patent agent is undoubted and important, one should not carry it too far.').

441 *Burlington Ind* (n 209) 1422.

442 John F Lynch, 'An Argument for Eliminating the Defense of Patent Unenforceability Based on Inequitable Conduct' (1988) 16 Am Intell Prop L Asso Q J 7, 8.

against patent enforcement,[443] and has been likened to enforcing traffic lights with nuclear weapons,[444] or to a death sentence for minor offences.[445] Surprisingly, however, the vast majority of the scholarship and courts seem to nevertheless endorse the underlying justifications of the doctrine and hardly any voice dares to censure its existence as such,[446] albeit the need for major or minor tweaks and adjustments is widely recognised.[447]

In should be reminded that the doctrine in the United States was originally born as a natural reaction to safeguard the transparency of the examining process,[448] strongly impregnated with ethical considerations.[449] It took the form of an unclean hands remedy, reinforced and tailored in consideration of the particular nature of the patent rights and its bearings on society. Without disparaging this moral trait, today many appear to behold it from a more utilitarian perspective, as a potentially valuable tool to induce efficient disclosure of information among patent applicants,[450] yet others are much more hesitant to see any practical benefits,[451] and some go as far as to say that the doctrine is not only failing to achieve its purpose but might even have a backfire effect, hampering rather than enhancing patent quality.[452]

---

443 *Aventis Pharma SA v Amphastar Pharmaceuticals Inc* 525 F 3d 1334, 1349 (Fed Cir 2008) (Rader J, dissenting).

444 Joseph Farrell and Robert P Merges, 'Incentives to Challenge and Defend Patents: Why Litigation Won't Reliably Fix Patent Office Errors and Why Administrative Patent Review Might Help' (2004) 19 Berkeley Tech L J 943, 962.

445 Nicole M Murphy, 'Inequitable-Conduct Doctrine Reform: Is the Death Penalty for Patents Still Appropriate?' (2009) 93 Minn L Rev 2274.

446 See, eg, Merges and Duffy (n 210) 1065 ('a bitter pill indeed … but a necessary tonic in a system where applicants carry so much of the burden of disclosure'). Exceptions can be found in Lynch (n 442); National Research Council of the National Academies, *A Patent System for the 21st Century* (Stephen A Merrill, Richard C Levin and Mark B Myers eds, National Academies Press 2004) 121-23.

447 Lisa A Dolak, 'Inequitable Conduct: A Flawed Doctrine Worth Saving' (2010) 11 Wake Forest Intell Prop L J 1, 12.

448 *Precision v Automotive* (n 162) 816.

449 *Therasense* (n 167) 1285.

450 See, among many others, Cotter, 'An Economic Analysis of Inequitable Conduct' (n 173); Cotropia (n 217); Mack (n 165); Mammen (n 215).

451 Lynch (n 442) 9; Arti K Rai, 'Growing Pains in the Administrative State: The Patent Office's Troubled Quest for Managerial Control' (2009) 157 U Pa L Rev 2051, 2074-77; Janicke, 'Mental and Emotional States' (n 217) 292; Bicknell (n 160) 466.

452 Erstling (n 160) 365.

The grounds on which the doctrine has been criticised are ostensibly heterogeneous. It is often stated, firstly, that the sanction it imposes is extremely severe and disproportionate, for if the court finds anything inappropriate in the conduct of the patentee during prosecution, there is only one remedy: unenforceability.[453] Furthermore, it might be a little unsettling that not only the claims to which the inequitable conduct relates are struck down, but rather the entire patent and potentially even further patents belonging to the same family—even if some of the claims were absolutely unrelated to the alleged fraud.[454]

Disapproving voices have also called the attention to the increased costs and complexity that disputes over inequitable conduct entail, as well as to the way they diverge attention from core issues like infringement and validity.[455] Moreover, the fact that the defence is raised excessively often—and in most cases frivolously—only exacerbates the problem.[456] The largest share of the high costs appear to derive from the subjective element, as it requires courts to dive into the internal sphere of every individual intervening in the process, making discovery proceedings particularly expensive[457] and often requiring attorney depositions with complex attorney-client privilege issues.[458]

Maybe more significantly, concerns have also pointed to the fact that the doctrine is applied at times with absolute disregard for the validity of the patent.[459] Indeed, a patent can be knocked down irrespective of whether it protects genuine—or even revolutionary—inventions, ie, even if all their claims are entirely valid and comply with all the patentability

453 Tun-Jen Chiang, 'The Upside Down Inequitable Conduct Defense' (2013) 107 Northwest U L Rev 1243, 1250-51.

454 Cotropia (n 217) 774-75.

455 ibid 740; Melissa Feeney Wasserman, 'Limiting the Inequitable Conduct Defense' (2008) 13(7) Va J L & Tech 14; Lynch (n 442) 16; Taylor (n 173) 65-66 (pointing out that it might even have a negative impact on reputation).

456 Mammen (n 215) 1344; Cotropia (n 217) 739-40; Wasserman (n 455) 14. It has been suggested, however, that imposing attorney fees against parties failing to prove inequitable conduct could somehow hold back the flood of groundless allegations. Mack (n 165) 172; Taylor (n 173) 91.

457 Wasserman (n 455) 14-15; *A Patent System for the 21st Century* (n 446) 122.

458 Cotropia (n 217) 740.

459 Friedrich-Karl Beier, 'Die Rechtsbehelfe des Patentanmelders und seiner Wettbewerber im Vergleich: Eine rechtsvergleichende Untersuchung zur Chancengleichheit im Patentverfahren [1989] GRUR Int 1, 6; Janicke, 'Mental and Emotional States' (n 217) 292.

requirements.[460] This fact alone, it is argued, is sufficient to cast doubt on the overall benefits that an inequitable conduct doctrine can effectively deliver to social welfare.[461]

In view of these numerous concerns, the shrinking trend in which the doctrine is currently immersed—evidenced by the *Therasense* decision and the new Supplemental Examination procedure—does not come as a surprise. In fact, the stricter standard of proof implemented by the Federal Circuit and the decision of the Congress to allow patentees to 'cleanse' their patents before litigation openly speak of a more sceptical view towards inequitable conduct.[462] Yet the defence is far from disappearing and concerns might still endure, since the generous reward for a successful inequitable conduct plea has not been revised and imposing fees to defendants for groundless allegations remains rather exceptional. Therefore, the ultimate fate of this legal doctrine, and particularly whether it will finally be revamped into a more pragmatic instrument, still remains an open question.

II. *Would it be advisable for European courts to implement a similar doctrine?*

As highlighted above—and regardless of the intense critique—the grounds on which the inequitable conduct doctrine are founded are very seldom challenged within the American legal community. It is conventionally argued that the doctrine is in itself valuable and that defendants, in their role of 'watchdogs', in fact contribute to the integrity of patent examination.[463] Apocalyptic warnings are further made in the sense that excessively limiting the defence, or eliminating it altogether, would inevitably result in applicants reducing disclosure,[464] and even encourage them into deceptive conducts.[465] In Europe, however, where courts have not been persuaded into admitting a comparable defence, those threats have not been materi-

460 Considering that the decision of the Federal Circuit in *Therasense* has adopted a 'but-for' standard of materiality, most cases of inequitable conduct should entangle patents that are also invalid. *Therasense* (n 167) 1291. However, the same decision expressly stated that, in case of affirmative egregious misconducts, the question of whether the patent should have been granted or not becomes irrelevant. Ibid 1292-93.

461 Lynch (n 442) 9.

462 Dolak, 'America Invents the Supplemental Examination' (n 220) 164.

463 Merges and Duffy (n 210) 1058.

464 Cotter, 'An Economic Analysis of Inequitable Conduct' (n 173) 771.

465 Dolak (n 447) 17; Petherbridge, Rantanen and Mojibi (n 218) 1351.

alised, as applicants at the EPO and other national patent offices do not seem to be particularly inclined towards dishonest behaviours. Moreover, despite the duty of disclosure in both offices being entirely different, nothing appears to suggest that, when deciding on any given patent application, examiners in the USPTO actually boast more relevant information on their tables in comparison to their EPO peers—or that they produce better quality patents at all for that matter.

Against this background, one is but strained to conjecture either (i) that the EPO has some kind of secret weapon which the USPTO lacks, or (ii) that the benefits that are normally attributed to the inequitable conduct doctrine are not as incontestable as assumed. Some legal authors in the United States who have addressed this question seem to prefer the first explanation, and they specifically draw the attention to the post-grant opposition process as the ace up the sleeve. Such a system, they contend, not only assists in the task of weeding out undesirable patents at an early stage, but also encourage efficient disclosure—both from the applicants themselves and from third parties.[466]

That the post-grant opposition process in place in the EPO—and in many other countries—plays a vital role in controlling patent quality can hardly be questioned.[467] What is yet to be established, though, is whether this process alone constitutes a substitute to the inequitable conduct doctrine as a matter of fact, and most importantly whether the latter really enjoys the prodigious effects that are to be expected from it. In other words, it would be opportune to determine whether—regardless of the positive effects that the post-grant opposition process can have—implementing a similar doctrine has the potential to further improve patent quality and impel more transparency into the European patenting procedure.[468] To explore the question, both the more ethical and the more utilitarian aspects

466 Cotter, 'An Economic Analysis of Inequitable Conduct' (n 173) 777-78 ('The fact that other countries have oppositions and not an inequitable conduct doctrine, as such, suggests the possibility that disclosure is adequate under such a combination...') ('the benefits of an expansive inequitable conduct doctrine may be small or negative in a system in which post-grant oppositions are common…'), Janicke, 'Mental and Emotional States' (n 217) 292; Becknell, at 466-67.

467 See, eg, Bronwyn H Hall and others, 'Prospects for Improving U.S. Patent Quality via Postgrant Opposition' in Adam B Jaffe, Josh Lerner and Scott Stern (eds), Innovation Policy and the Economy: Volume 4 (National Bureau of Economic Research 2004) 115.

468 What is more, considering that the AIA has meanwhile introduced a process that very much resembles the European post-grant oppositions, such line of reasoning could lead to the conclusion that the inequitable conduct doctrine has be-

of the doctrine should be taken into consideration, although the latter is strongly dependant on the width of the applicants' disclosure duties—duties which remain fairly limited within the EPC.

In the main, and from a more ethical perspective, nothing seems to suggest that patent applicants' inadequate behaviour should automatically make their patents unworthy of any kind of legal aid. Admittedly, the unclean hands doctrine—on which the US' inequitable conduct defence is based—is also acknowledged in the United Kingdom,[469] and in a more limited fashion in Germany.[470] Yet such doctrine requires the misconduct to be directly related 'to the controversy immediately involved in the injunction suit' and 'of a character that renders the plaintiff's interests undeserving of injunctive protection'.[471] Hence, particularly if the invention meets all patentability requirements, an inappropriate conduct at the patent office might not necessarily justify ruling out the enforcement of the granted patent. This is not by any means to suggest that the conduct should remain unpunished, but rather that there might be alternative remedies, such as disciplinary or perhaps even criminal sanctions, which can deliver equally satisfactory results without necessarily bringing the discussion into the patent litigation ground.

Then again, even if not demanded by ethical principles—and even if that was not the purpose that the Supreme Court had in mind when giving birth to it—a doctrine of inequitable conduct might look appealing at first glance from a more utilitarian perspective, since it could function as a tool for attaining optimal amounts of information at the patent office—which should thus lead to better quality patents. Upon closer inspection, however, the benefits might be more ostensible than real.

Firstly, it may constitute in practice an inappropriate interference of the courts in the administrative process. In this regard, the patent office—just like any other administrative institution for the procedures under their authority—is probably in a much better position than the courts to regulate the degree of disclosure that should be demanded from applicants and the appropriate punishment, as nobody knows better than the agency what

---

come obsolete. Before the AIA was passed, Cotter had actually warned that a post-grant opposition process coupled with an inequitable conduct doctrine could induce over-disclosure among US patent applicants. Cotter, 'An Economic Analysis of Inequitable Conduct' (n 173) 777.

469 *The Royal Bank of Scotland Plc v Highland Financial Partners LP* [2013] EWCA Civ 328, [2013] 1 CLC 596 [158].

470 BGH [1977] GRUR 494, 497 – *Dermatex*.

471 *Restatement (2d) of Torts* (1977) para 940.

kind of information they need.[472] In this regard, the US Supreme Court had long ago suggested that the patent office should be the main responsible for supervising the behavioural duties of the patent applicants,[473] although the inequitable conduct doctrine as developed by the case law in that country rather conveys that authority to the courts. The introduction of the Supplemental Examination procedure by the AIA may thus represent an attempt from Congress to revert this trend and gradually reduce the role of the courts in this area.[474]

Furthermore, as referred above, the rewards of such a doctrine could be fairly narrow from the specific standpoint of the EPC, as its benefits would be eclipsed by the post-grant opposition procedure and could even result counterproductive.[475] But even in the absence of such an opposition process, the rewards of an inequitable conduct doctrine may be extremely slim.

It might be helpful, at this stage, to hypothetically set apart the two possible scenarios that can be envisaged if an inequitable conduct doctrine were to be implemented. On the one hand, there would be situations where the inappropriate conduct during prosecution misled the examiner into granting a patent which does not meet all patentability requirements, namely an invalid patent. On the other hand, there would be cases where, despite of the deceiving conduct of the applicant (e.g., by submitting a bogus affidavit aimed at reinforcing the inventiveness of the application), the invention meets all legal requisites and the patent that is granted is perfectly valid. In the first case, the patent should never have been granted, and it was only the deceptive behaviour of the applicant which convinced the patent office into allowing it. In the second set of cases, the misleading conduct might have had more or less influence on the decision of the patent office, but the patent nevertheless embodies a legitimate invention and the patent office was not mistaken in granting it.

---

472 Merges and Duffy (n 210) 1058 (emphasising that, in other areas of law, agencies are held masters of their own procedures and courts show deference towards them); Rai (n 451) 2079.

473 *Kingsland v Dorsey* (n 161) 319-20 ('It was the Commissioner, not the courts, that Congress made primarily responsible for protecting the public from the evil consequences that might result if practitioners should betray their high trust.').

474 Merges and Duffy (n 210) 1068. See text at nn 110-111in ch 1.

475 Cotter seems to subscribe this opinion. Cotter, 'An Economic Analysis of Inequitable Conduct' (n 173) 778 ('the benefits of an expansive inequitable conduct doctrine could be small or negative in a system in which post-grant oppositions are common').

In the United States, the overwhelming majority of inequitable conduct cases discussed in court correspond to the first scenario. In fact, according to an empirical study carried out in 2005, in 89% of the cases where inequitable conduct was found, the claims at issue were also found invalid.[476] Since then, the Federal Circuit has hardened the materiality standards in *Therasense*,[477] meaning that this proportion is likely to be even higher today. If this universe of data had to be represented graphically, the result would probably look like the following:

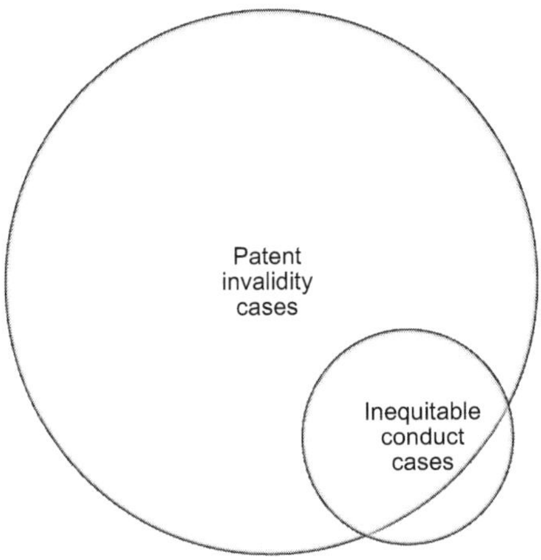

For all those cases described in the first scenario (ie, where not only the patentee has engaged in inequitable conduct during patent prosecution but also the patent is invalid), the existence of a defence based on inequitable conduct seems somehow superfluous, since it would be just overlapping with the traditional invalidity defence. Such redundancy would not be a major concern if it were not because every inequitable conduct allegation exponentially increases the costs of litigation by diverging the discussion to complex and subjective elements, which frequently will have taken place long before and will be very difficult to prove. What is more, at least as it currently exists in the United States, an inequitable conduct defence most times does not relieve the courts from looking into the validity of the patent, since they still have to determine whether the patent could or should have been granted or not when analysing the materiality

476 Nolan-Stevaux (n 182) 163.
477 See text at nn 241-248.

standard. Hence, for the largest part of inequitable conduct cases that can be conceived, the defence would be overlapping with the already existing invalidity defence without delivering any apparent added value. The outcome of those cases would be essentially the same whether the inequitable conduct defence existed or not, but in the latter event entailing much less costs and complications.[478] Perhaps the only differences would reside on the unenforceability 'contamination' of related patent claims (the appropriateness of which is at least debatable) and the award of legal fees—a remedy which is already widely available in Europe.

Be that as it may, the existence of such an inequitable conduct defence could be nevertheless justified for the second scenario, ie in those situations where the patent is valid but improperly procured. In these cases, the defendant would not have other alternative but to allege inequitable conduct, since the invalidity defence would be obviously unavailable. The number of cases where this situation might arise does not seem to be significant, and part of the scholarship has considered this reason enough to veto the doctrine.[479] But even disregarding the frequency with which such circumstances might arise, it is important to ask at this point whether it would be advisable at all to accept an inequitable conduct defence for this sort of cases. In other words: is it reasonable to refuse judicial relief to a patent that shields a legitimate invention for the sole reason that, during the application procedure and for whatever reason, the patentee showed a reproachable behaviour? The Federal Circuit in *Therasense* has expressly replied in the affirmative, stating that if such conduct amounts to affirmative egregious misconduct, inequitable conduct is still applicable, even if the patent is valid.

The approach of the Federal Circuit strikes as highly debatable. It is undisputed that such behaviour should not be tolerated by the law, but it is much less clear whether refusing to enforce the patent constitutes a reasonable remedy, since the invention is in fact new and inventive. Investi-

---

478 See Cole (n 355) (analysing many inequitable conduct cases in the United States, conjecturing how they would have been solved in the United Kingdom and concluding that all those cases would have been solved with an invalidity defence and attorney fees). See also, in the same line, Janicke, 'Mental and Emotional States' (n 217) 292.

479 Janicke, 'Mental and Emotional States' (n 217) 292 ('Under US patent law, it can be said that the inequitable conduct defense truly applies only where the patent is valid but was improperly procured. The number of these instances is bound to be small and does not seem to justify putting every patentee through the cost and jeopardy of a trial on inequitable conduct.').

gating this behaviour is in fact extremely costly and diverts the attention from the core issues like validity and infringement. Most importantly, no matter how disagreeable or immoral the patentee might be, she may have made a valuable technological contribution—precisely what the patent system craves for. And if the conduct at the patent office was improper, it may well be more sensitive to entrust the patrol of that behaviour to spheres which are better prepared for that task, such as the patent office or the bar association through disciplinary sanctions, or even criminal courts in the most severe cases.

In the case of European patent litigation, it should be borne in mind that introducing an inequitable conduct type defence would not only lead to higher costs and longer litigation—a topic that cannot be overlooked—but also might give rise to additional concerns. In Germany and other countries having a bifurcated system in place, for instance, complications would probably emerge in the sense that these pleas would be somewhere halfway between both courts' jurisdiction. If the task were to be assigned to courts dealing with infringement, the whole notion of the bifurcation system would be futile, as those courts would be forced to look closely into validity issues when looking into the materiality of the misconduct. At the same time, it is not clear whether courts dealing with patent validity would have jurisdiction to deal with these pleas, since strictly speaking it would not be an issue of validity. In connection with the latter concern, it is also dubious whether the aggregate of legal instruments in force in the European Member States would permit their national courts to adopt a defence of this sort. Both the EPC and the national patent laws provide for limited lists of grounds under which courts may revoke a patent, and these lists do not include fraud or false statements made by the applicant. And if the patent is declared valid, a court does not seem to enjoy sufficient discretion to refuse its enforcement altogether.[480]

There is a final concern that might also be worth pointing out, not because of the frequency with which it would emerge but rather because it serves to highlight the potential that the inequitable conduct doctrine might have to breed uncertainty among the users of the patent system. An applicant could, in that regard, engage in inequitable conduct and later, after obtaining the patent, assign the right to an innocent third party. In that

480 According to art 13 of the Enforcement Directive, a national court cannot refuse to grant damages in case of infringement. In any event, it should be noted that the implementation by any European court of an inequitable conduct doctrine could have an impact on the whole EPO procedure which, if not followed by the other Member States, could result in a situation of extreme legal uncertainty.

case, it would be necessary to determine whether the patent would remain 'infected' or whether the assignment would instead purge the patent. Either outcome would seem partly flawed. In the first case, which seems to be the solution adopted by US courts,[481] assignees would carry the burden of scrutinising the history of the patent to prevent surprises, and even in that case there might be unveiled risks impossible to detect in the course of standard due diligence searches. The alternative outcome, however, would probably contravene the principle *nemo dat quod non habet*, and the original patentees would find a way to avoid the consequences of their acts. Furthermore, the assignees in that case would have an incentive to bury their heads in the sand in order to know as little as possible about the patent's history so as to reduce risks of liability.

In view of the above considerations, it seems that the implementation of an inequitable conduct doctrine in Europe would be ill-advised. At the end of the day, it constitutes a doctrine whose raison d'être is still debated between pragmatism and an ethical instinct but whose advantages on any of both fronts are questionable at the very least.

In the United States, defendants appear to rely on this defence for a series of different reasons, including its power to tear down otherwise valid and enforceable patents, its impact on all the claims of the patent (and even other patents belonging to the same family) and the fact that it completely inverts the situation of the parties in litigation by removing the defendant from the hot seat and instead putting the patentee in the dock. None of these motives, however, seems heavy enough to justify altering the rules of litigation in Europe. An additional reason for its popularity in the United States is related to litigation costs: although inequitable conduct does not automatically make a case exceptional to grant attorney fees,[482] it is very often considered to be so,[483] hence departing from the general principle in American litigation. In Europe, where courts tend to impose attorney fees to the losing party as a rule,[484] this does not seem to be a major concern, although it would probably be reasonable for courts to take into account the conduct of the patentee as a relevant—and even aggravating—factor when deciding on the legal costs.

In summary, it seems that it would not be advisable for European courts to implement an inequitable conduct doctrine or otherwise refuse to en-

481 Chiang (n 453) 1293.

482 *Lighting World Inc v Birchwood Lighting Inc* 382 F 3d 1354, 1367 (Fed Cir 2004).

483 See, eg, *BRASSELER, USA I, LP v Stryker Sales Corp* 267 F 3d 1370, 1386 (Fed Cir 2001). See also Wasserman (n 455) 11, fn 80.

484 Enforcement Directive, art 14.

force patent rights on the basis of what transpired before the patent office. Firstly, rather that high quality patents it would seem to warrant an increase in the costs of litigation and a distraction from important issues like infringement and validity. And more importantly, its contribution to the patent system would be either superfluous or indesirable. On the one hand, if a specific misconduct is tied to an invalid patent, the existence of an inequitable conduct would appear as clearly redundant and unnecessary, since challenging the validity of the patent is a much more straightforward defence which does not require delving into endless subjective matters. On the other hand, if the misconduct is tied to a patent that nevertheless meets all patentability requirements, it is not at all clear why a reproachable behaviour during prosecution should justify refusing the enforcement of a patent that protects a worthy invention and a valuable contribution to technical development.

PART II: THE IMPROPER ACQUISITION OF PATENTS AS A COMPETITION LAW PROBLEM

Over and above the way in which the respective patent laws may deal with situations involving devious conducts at the patent office, or the extent to which patent courts may take them into consideration during litigation, such conducts—and their immediate outcomes—can have, at least potentially, considerable implications for competition. By way of a plain, paradigmatic example, a deceptive conduct before the patent office could lead to the grant of an unwarranted patent, which could in turn hamper competitors' participation on an otherwise unrestricted market or even ban them from entering or remaining in it. In this context, laws protecting competition may have a role to play as a way of countering this kind of abuses and preventing them from unduly foreclosing the market. Part II of this work, thus, is precisely aimed at analysing the way and the extent to which competition rules can be applied within this quite peculiar context.

Part II is divided into three chapters. Chapter IV first briefly explains the rationale behind the protection of competition, develops some basic economic concepts and describes the essential features of EU competition and US antitrust laws,[485] particularly those referred to abusive unilateral conducts. Chapter V thence presents a synopsis of the general interplay between competition rules and intellectual property and analyses how American and European antitrust case law have dealt with abuses in patent prosecution until today. Finally, chapter VI critically appraises the approach assumed by courts and antitrust enforcers and, based on many of their underlying foundations, seeks to postulate a sound and systematic mechanism for the application of competition laws against this specific type of behaviour by presenting a workable, across-the-board theory of harm.

485 Whereas the term 'antitrust law' is commonly employed in US law, Europeans normally prefer the term 'competition law'. This work, however, uses both terms interchangeably, except where specifically noted.

Chapter IV: Competition and Competition Law Tools

1. *Goals of Competition Law*

As a general principle, an economy with free competition is widely recognised as the best possible mechanism for warranting allocative, productive and dynamic efficiency and hence achieving an optimal combination of products and services in the market in terms of price, quality, and consumer choice.[486] Instead, when an industry is monopolised, prices tend to rise above costs and output is reduced below the competitive level, which logically brings about considerable negative implications for consumers and for the market as a whole. Firstly, on an allocative efficiency dimension, those consumers who cannot afford the higher prices suffer an evident loss, which is usually referred to as deadweight loss since it is not offset by any gains by the monopolist. Moreover, those who can still afford the higher price are also harmed because they are compelled to pay prices above the competitive level, and their loss in this case is equal to the additional revenue that the monopolist obtains by charging a price above its costs. But monopolised markets might have an even more harmful impact on social welfare in terms of productive and dynamic efficiencies, since monopolists will often lack incentives to keep their production costs low or invest in innovation.[487]

Against this background, it is no surprise that the primary objective of competition law is to protect competition. The exact content of this proclamation, however, is far from clear and conceals a diversity of possible objectives.[488] If having firms with considerable market power leads to welfare

---

486 Frederic M Scherer and David Ross, *Industrial Market Structure and Economic Performance* (3rd edn, Houghton Mifflin 1990) 15; FTC, 'To Promote Innovation: The Proper Balance of Competition and Patent Law and Policy' (2003) ch 1, 3.

487 For a general overview of the social costs of monopolies see, among many others, Scherer and Ross (n 486) chs 2 and 18; Massimo Motta, *Competition Policy: Theory and Practice* (Cambridge Univ Press 2004) ch 2; Richard A Posner, 'The Social Costs of Monopoly and Regulation' (1975) 83 J Pol Econ 807.

488 Phillip E Areeda and Herbert Hovenkamp, *Antitrust Law: An Analysis of Antitrust Principles and Their Application* (3rd edn, Aspen 2011) para 100. For a more thorough debate on the objectives of competition, see Daniel Zimmer (ed), *The Goals of Competition Law* (Edward Elgar 2012).

losses, the first impulse would probably be to surmise that competition policy should predominantly aim at ensuring a permanent multiplicity of rival firms on the market and at limiting their individual market power to the greatest possible extent. Alas, basic economics attest that delineating a sound competition policy might be a little thornier than that. On the one hand, not every competitor might deserve to be protected, particularly not those who are less efficient and deliver less to consumers in terms of price, choice, quality and innovation.[489] On the other hand, there is no reason to condemn a dominant position as such when it is the result of superior performance in the market.[490] What is more, not every monopolised market will necessarily reduce social welfare. Firstly, from a productive efficiency dimension, it can enable the attainment of economies of scale.[491] And from a more Schumpeterian perspective, firms holding a dominant position can also be beneficial to social welfare in terms of dynamic efficiency, since they may be in a better position to invest in innovation than firms under fierce competition and with very tight profit margins.

What, then, do competition laws seek, if not to protect competitors and squash dominant firms? Antitrust enforcers in the EU and the US seem to agree today that, instead of specific competitors, competition policy should protect the competitive process.[492] Or more bluntly, that laws should not *mandate* competition, but rather intervene to condemn certain conducts that may obstruct it.[493] To determine how the competitive process should be protected, they seem to be slowly converging under the ban-

489 Communication from the Commission, Guidance on the Commission's enforcement priorities in applying Article 82 of the EC Treaty to abusive exclusionary conduct by dominant undertakings [2009] OJ C45/7, para 6 (EU Guidance Paper); Case C-209/10 *Post Danmark A/S v Konkurrencerådet* (CJEU, 27 March 2012), para 21.

490 Case 322/81 *Nederlandsche Banden-Industrie-Michelin* v *Commission* [1983] ECR 3461, para 57; Joined Cases C-395/96 P and C-396/96 P *Compagnie Maritime Belge Transports* v *Commission* [2000] ECR I-1365, para 37; *United States* v *Grinnell Corp* 384 US 563, 570-71 (1966); *Verizon Communications Inc v Law Offices of Curtis V Trinko, LLP* 540 US 398, 407 (2004). In this same line of thinking, Justice Learned Hand famously stated that 'The successful competitor, having been urged to compete, must not be turned upon when he wins.' *United States v Aluminium Company of America (Alcoa)*, 148 F 2d 416, 430 (2nd Cir 1945).

491 Scherer and Ross (n 486) 30.

492 Commission Notice, Guidelines on the application of Article 81(3) of the Treaty [2004] OJ C101/97, para 105 (Guidelines on Article 81(3)); EU Guidance Paper (n 489) para 6; FTC, 'To Promote Innovation' (n 486) ch 1, 3.

493 Eleanor M Fox, 'We Protect Competition, You Protect Competitors' (2003) 26 World Competition 149, 149.

ner of a more economic approach, aligning themselves behind a Post-Chicago School economic reasoning.[494] In this sense, the overarching rationale behind the protection of competition should be the enhancement of consumer welfare and the efficient allocation of resources,[495] and this language is observed more and more in decisions and opinions by antitrust enforcers and courts.

This growing consensus, however, by no means implies that US and EU competition policies entirely coincide; in fact, important differences can still be observed between the two jurisdictions.[496] Most significantly, conducts that can virtually eliminate competition, even if justified by economic efficiency, are normally judged with distrust by EU competition enforcers, and the goal of protecting effective competition somehow subdues other efficiency goals.[497] In this sense, European competition policy seems to lean towards a consumer surplus standard, which might not exactly match US' model of total consumer welfare.[498]

On the delineation of EU competition's objectives, the legal traditions of the EU Member States can also have a significant influence. Germany's

---

494 Josef Drexl, 'Is There a "More Economic Approach" to Intellectual Property and Competition Law?' in Josef Drexl (ed), *Research Handbook on Intellectual Property and Competition Law* (Edward Elgar 2008) 35.

495 FTC, 'To Promote Innovation' (n 486) ch 1, 3; Guidelines on Article 81(3) (n 492) para 33; EU Guidance Paper (n 489) para 19. See also, however, Robert H Lande, 'A Traditional and Textualist Analysis of the Goals of Antitrust: Efficiency, Preventing Theft from Consumers, and Consumer Choice' (2013) 81 Fordham L Rev 2349 (arguing that the overriding purpose of the antitrust statutes is actually to prevent firms from stealing from consumers by charging them supracompetitive prices and to warrant consumer choice, and that economic efficiency was only a secondary concern when the Sherman Act was drafted).

496 Fox, 'We Protect Competition' (n 493); Drexl, 'Is There a "More Economic" Approach?' (n 494) 35.

497 See, eg, the language of art 101(3)(b) of the TFEU (essentially banning per se any agreement that could permit firms to eliminate competition in respect of a substantial part of the market); Guidelines on Article 81(3) (n 492) para 105 ('Ultimately the protection of rivalry and the competitive process is given priority over potentially pro-competitive efficiency gains which could result from restrictive agreements.'). See also Joined Cases C-501/06 P, C-513/06 P, C-515/06 P and C-519/06 P *GlaxoSmithKline v Commission* [2009] ECR I-9291, para 63 (insinuating that consumer welfare is not the only goal of EU competition law and highlighting that it also aims to protect 'the structure of the market and, in so doing, competition as such.').

498 Josef Drexl, 'Real Knowledge is to Know the Extent of One's Own Ignorance: On the Consumer Harm Approach in Innovation-Related Competition Cases' (2010) 76 Antitrust L J 677, 678. See also Zimmer (n 488).

Kartellrecht, for instance, was in its origins very strongly inspired by the Freiburg school of ordoliberalism, which traditionally regarded economic freedom as one of its primary goals,[499] and it is widely believed that these principles have impinged upon the delineation of art 102.[500]

Lastly, non-economic principles often also play a role in defining competition policies. In this regard, the social and historical context in which European competition laws were passed and the place they occupy in the EU legal regime also leave an important imprint and instil law enforcers to conduct themselves with an eye on ancillary objectives.[501] In particular, competition law is viewed in the EU as a key mechanism for achieving market integration along the territory of the Union,[502] eg by severely judging conducts that could partition the internal market, even at the expense of economic efficiency.[503]

2. *Legal Framework in the EU and in the US*

In order to achieve their competition policy goals, both EU and US legal systems have in place their own sets of competition rules and guidelines, which in the case of the EU are built on the grounds of arts 101-106 TFEU and the Merger Regulation[504] and in the US on the basis of the Sherman

---

499 Pinar Akman, *The Concept of Abuse in EU Competition Law: Law and Economic Approaches* (Hart 2012) 103.

500 David J Gerber, *Law and Competition in Twentieth Century Europe: Protecting Prometheus* (OUP 2003) 261-65. Cf Pinar Akman, 'Searching for the Long-Lost Soul of Article 82 EC' (2009) 29 Oxford J Leg St 267 (2009) (suggesting that the ordoliberal influence might not be as strong as commonly thought).

501 Motta (n 487) 17.

502 ibid 23.

503 Giorgio Monti, *EC Competition Law* (Cambridge Univ Press 2007) 39-40. One of the areas where the contrast between free movement of goods and economic efficiency can be most clearly observed is that of vertical restraints. See, for instance, Joined Cases 56 and 58/64 *Établissements Consten SàRL and Grundig-Verkaufs-GmbH v Commission* [1966] ECR 299 (one of the first cases of the CJEU applying art 101 TFEU (then art 85 EEC Treaty), where a vertical territorial restraint based on trademark rights was judged anticompetitive). For a report of the facts of the case, see text at nn 853ff in ch 5.

504 Council Regulation (EC) 139/2004 of 20 January 2004 on the control of concentrations between undertakings [2004] OJ L24/1 (the EU Merger Regulation).

Act,[505] the Clayton Act[506] and the FTC Act.[507] Admittedly, rules and case law in both jurisdictions do not entirely coincide, but considering that they are based on a common analytical framework and that the historical underpinnings upon which they have been developed are to a large extent analogous, this chapter attempts to analyse their essential features side by side, particularly those referring to unilateral conducts, underlining their differences wherever appropriate.[508]

A. *Essential Pillars of the Competition Legal Framework*

In the realm of antitrust rules, a basic distinction can readily be made between unilateral conducts and contractual relations between two or more parties. Generally speaking, horizontal and vertical contracts—or any sort of concerted practices—are condemned when they have as a purpose or effect to restrict or distort competition,[509] or are concluded 'in restraint of trade or commerce'.[510] These may include, by way of example, price-fixing, market allocation, certain exclusivity arrangements, tying, etc. Moreover, when agreements have a more permanent nature and involve a change of control in one of them by way of a merger, purchase of shares, joint venture, etc., concerns grow and different, more stringent rules apply. In those cases, firms are normally required to inform the competition agencies before the change of control takes place, provided that certain conditions are met—most importantly in terms of turnover thresholds.[511]

But competition policy is not only concerned with the surveillance of bilateral or multilateral agreements, as unilateral conducts by individual firms might be equally capable of restraining competition—especially if

505 15 USC §§ 1-7.

506 15 USC §§ 12-27.

507 15 USC §§ 41-58.

508 In addition to the differences that may exist as to the core antitrust provisions of the EU and the US, significant differences also remain with regard to their remedial structure, ie how those rules are enforced and the sanctions that are associated thereto. Except for some specific questions, those dissimilarities exceed the scope of this work. The significance of these issues on competition policy, however, should not be underestimated. For a comparison of both jurisdictions, see Einer Elhauge and Damien Geradin, *Global Antitrust Law and Economics*, (2nd edn, Foundation Press 2011) 11-70.

509 TFEU, art 101.

510 § 1 Sherman Act.

511 EU Merger Regulation, art 4; § 7A Clayton Act.

the firms hold a high degree of market power. For this reason, antitrust rules also condemn certain forms of unilateral behaviours when at least some degree of market power is involved. In the US, § 2 Sherman Act is the central rule dealing with these conducts and condemns the act of monopolising or attempting to monopolise any part of the trade or commerce. EU law, on its turn, finds its key provision in art 102 TFEU, which bans the abuse of a dominant position. Considering that the scope of this work is concentrated on conducts by patent applicants taking place at the patent office, and that said conducts are not likely to be undertaken by more than one person, rules dealing with unilateral conducts become of utmost importance. Hence, a more thorough analysis of their content and scope seems obligatory before diving into the particularities of patent prosecution and its intersection with competition law.[512]

B. § 2 Sherman Act and Article 102 TFEU. Scope and Objectives

As it was mentioned above, the central provision in the US on the matter of unilateral conducts is § 2 of the Sherman Act, which reads as follows:

> Every person who shall monopolize, or attempt to monopolize, or combine or conspire with any other person or persons, to monopolize any part of the trade or commerce among the several States, or with foreign nations, shall be deemed guilty of a felony …

From the language of the statute, three separate offences can be clearly distinguished: monopolisation, attempt to monopolise and conspiracy to monopolise. As the latter logically does not regulate unilateral behaviour, emphasis will be placed on the first two variations.

With respect to the offence of monopolisation, courts have recognised that two elements are to be attested: '(1) the possession of monopoly power in the relevant market and (2) the willful acquisition or maintenance of that power as distinguished from growth or development as a consequence of a superior product, business acumen, or historic accident.'[513] In other

512 Rules referring to anticompetitive agreements, however, should not be entirely disregarded, particularly those norms concerning horizontal agreements, as a behaviour at the patent office could be the result of a conspiracy or concerted practice by more than one undertaking. In those cases, art 101 of the TFEU and § 1 of the Sherman Act might also become applicable, as well as the last part of § 2 of the Sherman Act, as it refers to conspiracy to monopolise.

513 *Grinnell* (n 490) 570-71.

words, the offense requires proof not only of monopoly power—which in itself cannot be condemned[514]—but also an exclusionary or anticompetitive conduct.[515]

On the other side, in the case of attempts to monopolise, the conditions are slightly different. To demonstrate this offence, courts require proof '(1) that the defendant has engaged in predatory or anticompetitive conduct with (2) a specific intent to monopolize and (3) a dangerous probability of achieving monopoly power.'[516] In attempt to monopolise cases, thus, the law softens the monopoly power requirement by replacing it by a dangerous probability that it will happen,[517] ie that such market power will be achieved, but adds as a counterbalance a specific intent element to the anticompetitive conduct. Such intent, courts conventionally acknowledge, goes beyond the mere intent to do the act and requires an aspiration to accomplish the anticompetitive objective.[518]

As far as EU competition law is concerned, the fundamental provision dealing with unilateral conducts is art 102 TFEU, which provides the following:

> Any abuse by one or more undertakings of a dominant position within the internal market or in a substantial part of it shall be prohibited as incompatible with the internal market in so far as it may affect trade between Member States.
> Such abuse may, in particular, consist in:
> (a) directly or indirectly imposing unfair purchase or selling prices or other unfair trading conditions;
> (b) limiting production, markets or technical development to the prejudice of consumers;
> (c) applying dissimilar conditions to equivalent transactions with other trading parties, thereby placing them at a competitive disadvantage;
> (d) making the conclusion of contracts subject to acceptance by the other parties of supplementary obligations which, by their nature or according to commercial usage, have no connection with the subject of such contracts.

---

514 *Trinko* (n 490) 407.
515 Phillip E Areeda and Herbert Hovenkamp, *Fundamentals of Antitrust Law* (4th edn, Wolters Kluwer 2011) para 6.03a.
516 *Spectrum Sports Inc v McQuillan* 506 US 447, 456 (1993).
517 *Swift & Co v United States* 196 US 375, 396 (1905).
518 *Aspen Skiing Co v Aspen Highlands Skiing Corp* 472 US 585, 602 (1985).

This provision hence contains one single offence, for which two separate points need to be shown: (1) a dominant position and (2) an abuse of that position. Like the Sherman Act in the US, EU law does not make it illegal to simply possess market power, but requires an additional anticompetitive behaviour. The language of art 102 TFEU, however, is clearly different from § 2 Sherman Act and may actually seem either narrower or broader, depending on the prism with which it is observed.[519] It appears narrower in the sense that its focus is placed not so much on the way in which market power is acquired, but rather on the way such power, once acquired, is employed. On the other hand, the scope of art 102 TFEU may seem broader than its US counterpart with regard to the type of behaviours it condemns, as it prohibits not only 'exclusionary' conducts but also 'exploitative' abuses that directly harm consumers—most significantly excessive pricing.[520] Moreover, the degree of market power required from the relevant undertaking has also been interpreted differently in both jurisdictions, the European standard probably standing someplace between the tough standard of monopolisation cases and the more lenient one of attempts to monopolise.[521]

Despite the ostensible dissimilarities in their wording and criteria, it seems that both art 102 TFEU and § 2 Sherman Act require proof—in one way or another—of two essential elements, ie market power and an anticompetitive conduct. The first element, which pertains to the definition of market power and the relevant market, stands beyond the scope of this work. Yet considering that many of the conducts studied in this work proceed from undertakings who might not—at least not yet—hold substantial market power, the issue can play a decisive role in the competition assessment. Therefore, a general overview of what constitutes market power is offered below, together with some of the most debated issues. Later, the second element (ie, the abusive or anticompetitive conduct) will be introduced and a general framework will be provided. This framework will then serve as a cornerstone for the succeeding chapters, where specific unilateral conducts are studied in detail.

519 Elhauge and Geradin (n 508) 271.

520 Alison Jones and Brenda Sufrin, *EU Competition Law* (5th edn, OUP 2014) 283.

521 Elhauge and Geradin (n 508) 272.

I. The First Element: Market Power

The concept of market power is essential to competition policy, and particularly in cases of unilateral behaviours.[522] In the US, monopolisation cases require (with a rather archaic vocabulary) 'the possession of monopoly power'[523] and attempt to monopolise situations demand a dangerous probability that it will be achieved.[524] In the EU, art 102 TFEU requires a dominant position within the internal market or a substantial part of it. Both jurisdictions thus penalise unilateral anticompetitive conducts only when they stem from a firm having (or threatening to have, in the case of attempts to monopolise) some degree of market power.

How is it possible, then, to determine whether a firm holds market power? Although in certain cases econometric techniques, evidence or indicia may allow to directly detect whether a firm holds such market power, the traditional approach is to evaluate it in an indirect way which comprises two separate steps. Firstly, the boundaries of the market in which the firms operate are analysed and the relevant market is defined. Secondly, and only once the relevant market has been defined, the degree of market power that the firm holds on that market is measured, with the aid of a range of methodological tools.[525]

a. Market Definition

In general terms, the task of defining the relevant market consists in identifying all those products which are interchangeable and can function as al-

522 Motta (n 487) 101. Along this work, the concepts of 'market power' and 'market dominance' are used interchangeably, though it is important to note that some difference between them exist. Most significantly, whereas the former is a purely economic term, the latter rather seems to be a legal one. Josef Drexl, 'The Relationship Between the Legal Exclusivity and Economic Market Power: Links and Limits' in Inge Govaere and Hans Ullrich (eds), *Intellectual Property, Market Power and the Public Interest* (Peter Lang 2008) 15.

523 *Grinnell* (n 490) 570-71. Monopoly power and market power are to be considered interchangeable concepts. Thomas G Krattenmaker, Robert H Lande and Steven C Salop, 'Monopoly Power and Market Power in Antitrust Law' (1987) 76 Geo L J 241.

524 *Swift* (n 517) 396.

525 Case 6/72 *Europemballage Corporation and Continental Can Company Inc v Commission* [1973] ECR 215, para 32; *Grinnell* (n 490) 570-71.

ternatives to one another in the eyes of the customers.[526] The definition of the relevant market in this field, however, might differ from definitions in other contexts, since its value here is purely instrumental to a later verification of whether a firm has market power or not.[527] In this regard, the CJEU has stated that

> ... an examination limited to the objective characteristics only of the relevant products cannot be sufficient: the competitive conditions and the structure of supply and demand on the market must also be taken into consideration.[528]

In a similar vein, the US Supreme Court has emphasised that, when determining the outer boundaries of a product market, physical or functional differences between products are not sufficient to prove separate markets,[529] and that the cross-elasticity of demand and supply constitute essential factors to be considered.[530]

The delimitation of the market, hence, does not depend so much on whether products or services are physically comparable, but rather on whether they can impose a competitive constraint on each other in an economic sense.[531]

i. Product and Geographical Markets. The Hypothetical Monopolist Test

In order to determine whether a product is subject to competitive constraints, different aspects of the market need to be analysed. In the first place, and since the constraints depend not only on the likeness of the alternative products but also on the geographical proximity of their supply, it is important to distinguish the product from the geographical dimension: both dimensions must be separately studied and later consolidated to establish the relevant market.[532]

---

526 *Continental Can* (n 525), para 32; *United States v EI du Pont de Nemours & Co* 351 US 377, 394 (1956).

527 Commission Notice on the definition of relevant market for the purposes of Community competition law [1997] OJ C372/5, paras 2-3 (EU Notice on Market Definition).

528 *Michelin* (n 490) para 37.

529 *du Pont* (n 526) 394.

530 *Brown Shoe Co v United States* 370 US 294, 325 (1962).

531 Motta (n 487) 102.

532 EU Notice on Market Definition (n 527) paras 1-4 and 9; *Brown Shoe* (n 530) 324.

As it was anticipated above, the relevant product market is comprised by products that have a sufficient degree of interchangeability, and such interchangeability is to be assessed from an economic standpoint so as to determine whether there can be 'effective competition between the products which form part of it'.[533] In order to make this assessment, the US Department of Justice introduced in 1982 a method commonly known as the SSNIP ('Small but Significant Non-transitory Increase in Prices') or Hypothetical Monopolist test,[534] which has become today the standard method for most competition agencies worldwide.[535]

Essentially, the purpose of the SSNIP test is to identify the smallest market within which a hypothetical monopolist would be able to profitably raise its prices in an appreciable and non-transitory way.[536] To this end, it is necessary to identify a group of products, assume that there is only one firm selling them (the 'hypothetical monopolist') and evaluate whether it would be profitable for that firm to impose a small but significant and non-transitory increase in price, or whether after such rise in price consumers would rather shift to readily available substitutes.[537] If the outcome reveals that such price rise would indeed prove profitable, it suggests that this group of products does not face significant competitive constraints, and hence that these products constitute the relevant product market. Conversely, if the result shows that the firm would not find such price increase profitable, additional products will need to be included into the group until an increase in their prices would become lucrative.[538]

It should be pointed out that, despite the SSNIP test's proven reliability when assessing merger cases,[539] its employment in situations involving unilateral conducts is not without difficulties, particularly when determining the benchmark price to which the hypothetical price increase should

533 Case 85/76 *Hoffmann-La Roche & Co AG v Commission* [1979] ECR 461, para 28. See also *Brown Shoe* (n 530) 325.

534 Gregory J Werden, 'The 1982 Merger Guidelines and the Ascent of the Hypothetical Monopolist Paradigm' (2003) 71 Antitrust L J 253, 254.

535 Elhauge and Geradin (n 508) 334.

536 DoJ and FTC, Horizontal Merger Guidelines (19 August 2010), para 9 (US Horizontal Merger Guidelines).

537 ibid para 4.1.1. US antitrust enforcers refer to a 5 percent increase. Ibid para 4.1.2. EU law refers to a range of five to ten percent. EU Notice on Market Definition (n 527) para 17.

538 EU Notice on Market Definition (n 527) para 17.

539 Simon Bishop and Mike Walker, *The Economics of Competition Law: Concepts, Application and Measurement* (3rd edn, Sweet & Maxwell 2010) para 10-002.

be exerted.[540] This problem is commonly known as the 'cellophane fallacy', due to an economic error in which the US Supreme Court incurred in the well-known *du Pont* case[541]—an error that has since been widely recognised.[542] The fallacy resides in the fact that, when assessing the conduct of firms which already possess a high degree of market power, their prices might already be at a monopoly level, ie high enough so as to make any further increase unprofitable. Thus, employing their current prices as yardsticks could lead to inaccurate market definitions, wrongly including products which do not truly constitute substitutes.[543]

Finally, in addition to the relevant product market, the geographical dimension should also be appraised. In essence, the geographical market refers to the relevant area in which the undertaking concerned is involved and where the conditions of competition are sufficiently homogeneous, taking particularly into account the characteristics of the products and the existence of entry barriers (most importantly transport costs) or consumer preferences.[544] As a rule, the demarcation of the relevant geographical market is also carried out with the aid of the SSNIP test.[545] The pertinent question is hence whether the consumers would be ready to switch to products located elsewhere should the hypothetical monopolist impose a small but appreciable price increase.[546]

ii. Demand and Supply Substitution

As it was explained above, the quest of defining the relevant product and geographical market consists of identifying substitutable products, and such substitutability can be approached from two different angles: demand

---

540 Jones and Sufrin (n 520) 71; Motta (n 487) 105.

541 *du Pont* (n 526).

542 See, eg, William M Landes and Richard A Posner, 'Market Power in Antitrust Cases' (1981) 94 Harv L Rev 937, 960-61. Although without expressly referring to this case, the EU Commission has recognised this difficulty in para 19 of the EU Notice on Market Definition (n 527).

543 Motta (n 487) 105. For a list of different solutions that have been suggested to this problem, see Robert O'Donoghue and A Jorge Padilla, *The Law and Economics of Article 102 TFEU* (2nd edn, Hart 2013) 113-16.

544 EU Merger Regulation, art 9(7); US Horizontal Merger Guidelines (n 536) para 4.2.

545 Monti (n 503) 139.

546 EU Notice on Market Definition (n 527) para 17; US Horizontal Merger Guidelines (n 536) paras 4.2.1 and 4.2.2.

substitution and supply substitution.[547] The former refers to the ability and willingness of customers to shift from one product to another—which they view as a substitute—in case of a change in the market such as the price increase posited within the SSNIP test.[548] This is naturally the most immediate and effective source of competitive constraints, and hence where competition enforcers normally focus most of their attention.[549]

But antitrust agencies, both in the EU and in the US, have recognised that supply substitution might also be an important factor to consider when defining the relevant market.[550] This principle refers to the ability of other suppliers, not currently active in the market, to switch their production to the relevant (or a substitute) product without substantial delay and without incurring in significant additional costs in case of a change in prices like the one hypothesised by the SSNIP test.[551] Thus, even if there are currently no alternative products in the market, competitive constraints might still exist from certain firms if switching production is for them easy, rapid and feasible.[552]

iii. Product and Technology Markets

When envisaging conventional scenarios that normally attract the attention of competition law enforcers, the types of markets that first come to mind are probably those consisting of physical goods or services. Markets where, eg, cars, apples, air tickets or telephone services are traded. Together, these markets are commonly referred to as product markets.[553] But when products incorporate technological developments protected by intel-

547 Jones and Sufrin (n 520) 66.

548 EU Notice on Market Definition (n 527) para 13; US Horizontal Merger Guidelines (n 536) para 4.

549 EU Notice on Market Definition (n 527) para 13.

550 ibid paras 20-23; US Horizontal Merger Guidelines (n 536) para 4. The US Supreme Court had long ago acknowledged this principle in *United States v Columbia Steel Co* 334 US 495 (1948) and so did the CJEU in *Continental Can* (n 525) para 33.

551 EU Notice on Market Definition (n 527) para 20; US Horizontal Merger Guidelines (n 536) para 5.1.

552 Motta (n 487) 104.

553 Communication from the Commission, Guidelines on the applicability of article 101 of the Treaty on the Functioning of the European Union to horizontal co-operation agreements [2011] OJ C 11/1, para 8 (EU Guidelines on Horizontal Cooperation Agreements).

lectual property rights and those rights are marketed independently from the products to which they relate, a separate technology market might also need to be acknowledged.[554] Indeed, technology can constitute an upstream market that plays the exact same role as any other input to the goods and services traded in the downstream product market—just like any other physical supply.[555] For instance, to manufacture and sell a certain gadget, a firm might not only need physical supplies like silicon, copper or plastic, but also licences for those intellectual property rights which protect the technology embedded in it, and each of them could thus constitute a separate market: the downstream product market for the gadget (and its possible substitutes), the upstream product markets for silicon, copper and plastic (and their possible substitutes) and the upstream technology market for the intellectual property licences (and their possible substitutes).

The existence of technology markets as a concept separate from product markets has been recognised both in the EU and in the US.[556] They are defined, in both jurisdictions, as the intellectual property rights that are licensed and their substitutes, ie technologies which are sufficiently close that customers could use them as substitutes,[557] or which are sufficiently close to constrain the exercise of market power.[558]

From a theoretical point of view, technology markets do not fundamentally differ from product markets.[559] As a matter of fact, they are treated like any other upstream supply market and the same methodology— ie,

554 ibid para 116.

555 Josef Drexl, 'Anticompetitive Stumbling Stones on the Way to a Cleaner World: Protecting Competition in Innovation Without a Market' (2012) 8 J Comp L & Econ 507, 514.

556 Commission Regulation (EC) 316/2014 of 21 March 2014 on the application of Article 101(3) of the Treaty on the Functioning of the European Union to categories of technology transfer agreements [2014] OJ L93/17, art 1 (TTBER); Commission Regulation (EU) 1217/2010 on the application of Article 101(3) of the Treaty on the Functioning of the European Union to certain categories of research and development agreements, [2010] OJ L335/36, art 1; DoJ and FTC, Antitrust Guidelines for the Licensing of Intellectual Property (12 January 2017) para 3.2.2 (US Antitrust Guidelines for the Licensing of IP).

557 EU Guidelines on Horizontal Cooperation Agreements (n 553) para 116; Communication from the Commission, Guidelines on the application of Article 101 of the Treaty on the Functioning of the European Union to technology transfer agreements [2014] OJ C89/3, para 22 (EU Guidelines on Technology Transfer Agreements).

558 US Antitrust Guidelines for the Licensing of IP (n 556) para 3.2.2.

559 Drexl, 'Anticompetitive Stumbling Stones' (n 555) 515.

the hypothetical monopolist or SSNIP test—is thus employed for defining their boundaries.[560] Therefore, in the case of technology markets, the conundrum is to identify the smallest group of technologies over which a hypothetical monopolist would be able to profitably impose a small but significant and non-transitory price increase.

Defining a technology market, however, might encounter some additional hurdles that do not emerge in traditional product markets.[561] Identifying the actual sources of competitive constraints for any given technology, for instance, can be particularly challenging. The main source of competitive constraints is undoubtedly incarnated by substitute technologies offered by competing licensors,[562] ie by the intellectual property rights owned by third parties to which customers could switch. But constraints to a technology to produce a certain good can also originate from technologies used to produce other goods that compete with the former in the downstream product market.[563] And what is more, competitive constraints might even stem from technologies that belong to the public domain—either because they are non-patented, non-patentable or the term already expired. Indeed, in those cases, a price increase by the licensor of the patented technology could lead customers to switch to alternative free technologies. Finally, competitive constraints can also derive from protected technologies which are only used in-house and hence not available for customers to license. In these cases, the competitive constraint of the alternative technology cannot be observed in the upstream market—because said technology is not open for licensing—but rather in the downstream product market, where the products implementing the alternative technologies actually compete. In light of the foregoing, and also bearing in mind the complications of employing the SSNIP test in upstream technology markets where information on royalty levels tends to be very scarce,[564] competition agencies often turn to look at the downstream product markets when defining the relevant technology market.[565]

560 EU Guidelines on Technology Transfer Agreements (n 557) para 22; US Antitrust Guidelines for the Licensing of IP (n 556) para 3.2.2.

561 See, eg, the discussions on defining the relevant market that preceded the adoption of the TTBER. Jones and Sufrin (n 520) 867-74.

562 EU Guidelines on Horizontal Cooperation Agreements (n 553) para 116; US Antitrust Guidelines for the Licensing of IP (n 556) para 3.2.2.

563 US Antitrust Guidelines for the Licensing of IP (n 556) para 3.2.2, fn 19.

564 Jones and Sufrin (n 520) 882.

565 EU Guidelines on Technology Transfer Agreements (n 557) para 25; US Antitrust Guidelines for the Licensing of IP (n 556) para 3.2.2.

An additional source of competitive constraint for technology markets—but one certainly not free from controversy—is the one stemming from potential competition. The EU Guidelines on Horizontal Cooperation Agreements, for instance, regard potential competition as a relevant factor for defining the relevant technology market, although they mainly seem to refer to supply substitution scenarios, ie firms which do not currently license their technology but might be willing to do so if the licensing prices increase.[566] But the concept of potential competition can be a bit of a quagmire, as it might also be interpreted to comprise less immediate sources of constraints.[567] Indeed, in the area of technology markets, potential competition could be interpreted as also embracing the hypothetical incentives that other firms might have for engaging in R&D activities to develop competing technologies. In view of the extended times ordinarily demanded by R&D activities, however, the likelihood of them configuring a competitive constraint seems rather strained and its inclusion in the definition of the relevant technology market may thus be far-fetched.

Finally, a question that might become particularly relevant for the object of this work is whether a technology market needs to be defined at all in those cases where the technology concerned is not open for licensing. A pharmaceutical firm, for instance, could be the owner of a patent and sell the pharmaceutical product implementing the technology without licensing the patent to any other party. In such cases, a product market certainly exists for the pharmaceutical product concerned and its substitutes, but is it necessary to define a separate technology market for the patented technology? A similar question arose in the context of the debate on refusal to license in the EU, where the CJEU stated that, in order for a refusal to license to violate competition laws, the existence of two separate markets (among other requirements) needed to be verified.[568] In that case, the CJEU also stated that, for identifying the upstream market, 'it is sufficient that a potential market or even hypothetical market can be identified'.[569]

566 EU Guidelines on Horizontal Cooperation Agreements (n 553) para 118. Such potential competition, however, is not considered in the TTBER when defining the relevant technology market. TTBER, art 1(n)(i).

567 The Commission Notice on the definition of the relevant market expressly states that potential competition should not be taken into account for defining relevant markets, although it might be taken into account at a later stage. EU Notice on Market Definition (n 527) paras 14 and 24.

568 Case C-418/01 *IMS Health GmbH & Co OHG v NDC Health GmbH & Co KG* [2004] ECR I-5039, para 38.

569 ibid para 44.

Such a definition, however, has been accused of artificial and criticised for the dangerous implications it entails,[570] and it might be possible to argue, in any case, that it was aimed to the specific circumstances of refusal to license cases. Such a definition in the context of this work could indeed lead to extremely narrow market definitions.

iv. Competition without markets. From Innovation Markets to Competition in Innovation

It is fairly clear today that firms do not only compete in terms of price over existing products, but also in terms of innovation by continually striving to generate new and better products.[571] From an economic perspective, this suggests that competition among companies can also be approached from a dynamic dimension and competition policy might hence have an important role to play in steering innovation. The idea is admittedly not new: rivers of ink have flowed seeking to recognise which market structure is more favourable for technological development and two major lines of thought are traditionally identified in this regard. Firstly, from a Schumpeterian perspective, the idea of temporary market power is considered an essential factor for motivating firms to engage in research and development activities, both as a stimulating reward and as a way to recover costs.[572] In apparent contradiction, Arrow argued that it is the existence of competitive constraints that predominantly encourages firms to innovate.[573] But these two fundamental insights are not necessarily irreconcilable, as they might both coalesce under the overarching principle of contestable markets.[574] In any case, that competition policy occupies a pivotal

570 Damien Geradin, 'Limiting the Scope of Article 82 EC: What can the EU Learn From the US Supreme Court's Judgment in *Trinko* in the Wake of *Microsoft*, *IMS*, and *Deutsche Telekom*?' (2004) 41 CML Rev 1519, 1530.

571 Drexl, 'Anticompetitive Stumbling Stones' (n 555) 513.

572 Joseph Schumpeter, *Capitalism, Socialism and Democracy* (Routledge 1992) 87-92.

573 Kenneth J Arrow, 'Economic Welfare and the Allocation of Resources for Invention' in National Bureau of Economic Research (ed), The Rate and Direction of Inventive Activity: Economic and Social Factors (Princeton Univ Press 1962) 620.

574 Carl Shapiro, 'Competition and Innovation: Did Arrow Hit the Bull's Eye?' in Josh Lerner and Scott Stern (eds), *The Rate and Direction of Inventive Activity Revisited* (Univ of Chicago Press 2012) 363-64.

position in spurring innovation can hardly be debated and both EU and US laws have long acknowledged this central role.[575]

When firms engage in innovation activities, they frequently do it in an 'incremental' or 'evolutionary' way, in the sense that they simply remodel or improve already existing products and processes. But innovation can also be—and occasionally is—'revolutionary' or 'drastic', as it can lead to the emergence of wholly new products and product markets.[576] Yet for this form of innovation, where firms compete for future, not-yet-existing technology and product markets, traditional competition laws might at times result ill-suited, seeing as their regulations and tools strongly rely on the notion of already existing markets.[577]

When competition agencies and scholars first took interest on this issue and began to realise that firms' incentives to innovate can be strongly affected by events taking place long before the emergence of the traditional product markets, the question immediately arose as to how could competition rules better adapt to this scenario. The initial reaction was to try to identify a further upstream market, and Gilbert and Sunshine suggested in this line that a separate 'innovation market' should be recognised.[578] The concept was first proposed for merger analysis, but the DoJ and the FTC quickly incorporated it in 1995 when issuing the Guidelines for the Licensing of Intellectual Property.[579] According to these guidelines, an innovation market 'consists of the research and development directed to particular new or improved goods or processes, and the close substitutes for that research and development.'[580] To define its boundaries, the guidelines

575 EU Guidelines on Technology Transfer Agreements (n 557) para 7; FTC, 'To Promote Innovation' (n 486) ch 2, 8-9.

576 See Drexl, 'Anticompetitive Stumbling Stones' (n 555) 513-14; Miguel Rato and Nicolas Petit, 'Abuse of Dominance in Technology-Enabled Markets: Established Standards Reconsidered?' (2013) 9 ECJ 1, 3.

577 Susan DeSanti and William Cohen, 'Competition to Innovate: Strategies for Proper Antitrust Assessments' in Rochelle C Dreyfuss, Diane L Zimmerman and Harry First (eds), *Expanding the Boundaries of Intellectual Property* (OUP 2001) 328; Drexl, 'Anticompetitive Stumbling Stones' (n 555) 508.

578 Richard J Gilbert and Steven C Sunshine, 'Incorporating Dynamic Efficiency Concerns in Merger Analysis: The Use of Innovation Markets' (1994) 63 Antitrust L J 569.

579 US Antitrust Guidelines for the Licensing of IP (n 556) para 3.2.3.

580 ibid.

even attempt to transplant the SSNIP test.[581] In a similar vein, the concept of innovation markets was also incorporated in the EU in the old Guidelines on Technology Transfer Agreements and in the old Guidelines on Horizontal Cooperation Agreements.[582]

Despite its laudable purposes, the notion of innovation markets rapidly became the object of intense criticism.[583] Among the many critiques yielded by such a proposal, perhaps the most important one lies on the fact that an 'innovation market' falls short of all the essential features that define a proper market, since there are absolutely no transactions taking place at that stage.[584] Speaking of an innovation market thus mistakenly leads to think that a relevant market can actually be defined and, most importantly, that the notion of market power can be transposed to this sphere.[585] In reality, however, innovation competition seems to work differently from traditional price competition; the economic theory behind the latter might not completely explain the structure of the former. From a Schumpeterian perspective, for instance, reducing the number of firms engaging in R&D does not necessarily have a negative impact on innovation.[586]

Considering these strong concerns, modern US and EU regulations seem to be shifting away from the concept of 'innovation markets'.[587] Without diminishing the importance of the dynamic dimension in the

---

581 ibid ('The close substitutes are research and development efforts, technologies, and goods that significantly constrain the exercise of market power with respect to the relevant research and development, for example by limiting the ability and incentive of a hypothetical monopolist to retard the pace of research and development.') (Citations omitted).

582 Communication from the Commission: Guidelines on the application of Article 81 of the EC Treaty to technology transfer agreements, O.J. C101/2 (27.04.2004) para 25 (repealed); Commission Notice, Guidelines on the applicability of Article 81 of the Treaty to horizontal cooperation agreements, [2001] OJ C3/2, para 60 (repealed).

583 See, eg, Richard T Rapp, 'The Misapplication of the Innovation Market Approach to Merger Analysis' (1995) 64 Antitrust L J 19; John Temple Lang, 'European Community Antitrust Law: Innovation Markets and High Technology Industries' (1997) 20 Fordham Int'l L J 717.

584 Rapp (n 583) 27.

585 Drexl, 'Anticompetitive Stumbling Stones' (n 555) 519.

586 Research joint ventures, for example, are a form of concentration that reduces competition between different R&D projects, and would hence be highly suspicious if viewed from a traditional competition standpoint. Rapp (n 583) 28-30 (1995). See also DeSanti and Cohen (n 577) 332.

587 Some, however, consider that the 'innovation market' analysis might still serve as a good starting point. See, eg, Benjamin R Kern, 'Innovation Markets, Future Markets, or Potential Competition: How Should Competition Authorities Ac-

overall competition assessment, they now refer to 'innovation competition'[588] or 'competition in innovation'[589] and avoid using the term 'market'. The TTBER Guidelines in the EU, for instance, explain that, in situations in which competition in innovation might be at stake, the Commission will normally confine to analyse existing product and technology markets or recognise innovation as a source of potential competition, and in exceptional cases it will proceed to analyse the effects on competition in innovation separately.[590] The new approach seems to provide more flexibility to the competition agencies in coping with these novel problems—though sometimes sacrificing legal certainty.[591]

Be that as it may, the discussion on innovation competition has mostly taken place within the framework of bilateral conducts, ie when two parties merge or enter into different types of agreements in such a way that mutual constraints to innovate are reduced. Much less debate seems to have arisen in the context of unilateral behaviours,[592] one of the most important reasons probably being that the relevant rules are deeply associated with the concept of market power and simply cannot be applied against conducts excessively remote from the emergence of a traditional market.[593] The state of affairs might be even more problematic under European law, for art 102 TFEU only condemns conducts carried out by firms already holding a dominant position—as opposed to § 2 Sherman Act in the US, which also censures behaviours taking place before that stage.

It is important to note that this riddle might become of utmost importance in circumstances like the ones targeted by this work, for conducts in the patent office sphere might take place long before a palpable market exists and hence only affect future product or technology markets.[594] Never-

---

count for Innovation Competition in Merger Reviews?' (2014) 37 World Competition 173.

588 US Horizontal Merger Guidelines (n 536) para 6.4.

589 EU Guidelines on Horizontal Cooperation Agreements (n 553) paras 119-22; EU Guidelines on Technology Transfer Agreements (n 557) para 26.

590 EU Guidelines on Technology Transfer Agreements (n 557) para 26.

591 Drexl, 'Anticompetitive Stumbling Stones' (n 555) 519.

592 An important exception in Europe is given by the investigation that the Commission carried in *Boehringer Ingelheim* (Case COMP/39.246). The conducts under analysis involved defensive patenting strategies in form of applications for blocking patents. The case was finally closed with a settlement agreement. See Commission Press Release IP/11/842, 'Antitrust: Commission Welcomes Improved Market Entry for Lung Disease Treatments' (6 July 2011).

593 Drexl, 'Anticompetitive Stumbling Stones' (n 555) 529.

594 See text at nn 1454ff in ch 6.

theless, many of these conducts might still not be captured by the concept of competition in innovation, since they may not truly entail constraints against other firms' incentives to innovate, but rather on traditional competition by imitation—though on a market which might not yet exist.[595]

b. Market Power

Once the relevant market is defined, the following step consists on determining whether a firm has market power on it. From an economic perspective, market power is traditionally defined as the ability of a firm or group of firms to profitably raise prices above marginal cost,[596] or above competitive levels.[597] Based on these definitions, most firms would actually hold at least some degree of market power, as it is only in hypothetical perfect competition models that prices equal marginal costs.[598] However, not any kind of market power in an economic sense constitutes relevant market power in the eyes of antitrust laws, but in those cases where such market power can be regarded as 'substantial' and durable.[599]

In any case, and despite a few concerns that might be posed from a theoretical dimension, these definitions are widely regarded as the cornerstone of any market power assessment[600] and its influence can clearly be perceived in the definitions that EU and US courts have offered for this concept. In the EU, the CJEU has defined a dominant position as

---

595 Josef Drexl, '*AstraZeneca* and the EU Sector Inquiry: When do Patent Filings Violate Competition Law?' in Josef Drexl and Nari Lee (eds), *Pharmaceutical Innovation, Competition and Patent Law: A Trilateral Perspective* (Edward Elgar 2013) 315-20. See also Marcus Glader, *Innovation Markets and Competition Analysis* (Edward Elgar 2006) 297-98 (arguing that, although there are good reasons to caution against the policy of innovation markets, it might provide an effective way of attacking unilateral anticompetitive behaviour affecting competition at an early stage, such as fraudulent procurement of patents).

596 Landes and Posner, 'Market Power in Antitrust Cases' (n 542) 939; Bishop and Walker (n 539) para 3-002.

597 Areeda and Hovenkamp, *Fundamentals* (n 515) para 5.02.

598 Motta (n 487) 115.

599 Jones and Sufrin (n 520) 59. For the complexities of determining what constitutes 'substantial' market power, see Einer Elhauge, 'Defining Better Monopolization Standards' (2003) 56 Stan L Rev 253, 259-60. It has also been argued that there is no reason to exclude short-lasting monopoly power from the scope of competition rules, provided that the anticompetitive harm can be proven. Luis Ortiz Blanco, *Market Power in EU Antitrust Law* (Hart 2012) 47-48.

600 Jones and Sufrin (n 520) 60.

> ...a position of economic strength enjoyed by an undertaking which enables it to prevent effective competition being maintained on the relevant market by giving it the power to behave to an appreciable extent independently of its competitors, customers and ultimately of its consumers.[601]

For its part, the Supreme Court in the US has defined market power (monopoly power) as 'the power to control prices or exclude competition'.[602]

Although both definitions seem to include two separate components—one referring to price discretion and the other one to the ability to exclude competition—it is widely understood that both elements represent simply one and the same thing,[603] as market power ultimately entails a certain level of discretion in price-setting.[604]

If market power, thus, is defined as the ability of a firm to independently set prices above marginal cost or competitive prices, a simple and direct method for proving market power in both jurisdictions would be to observe price levels in the market and compare them against their marginal costs or the prices that would be perceived as competitive.[605] In practice, however, that is rarely the case. Firstly, because estimating the marginal cost is in practice a quasi-impossible task.[606] The same can also be said about competitive prices, since unilateral behaviour cases are precisely based on the premise that the market is no longer competitive.[607] Furthermore, because even if it was possible to estimate the marginal cost, a firm might have inefficiently high costs (and hence price slightly above marginal cost) and still hold a dominant position,[608] or enjoy large profit margins in a market of effective competition.[609] It is for all these reasons

601 Case 27/76 *United Brands Co v Commission* [1978] ECR 207, para 65.

602 *du Pont* (n 526) 391.

603 Damien Geradin and others, 'The Concept of Dominance in EC Competition Law' (2005) GCLC Research Paper on the Modernization of Article 82 EC, 3 <http://ssrn.com/abstract=770144> accessed 14 February 2018.

604 EU Guidance Paper (n 489) paras 10-11; *du Pont* (n 526) 392.

605 The most cited method in this sense is the renowned 'Lerner index', which measures the difference between current prices and marginal cost. Abba P Lerner, 'The Concept of Monopoly and the Measurement of Monopoly Power' (1934) 1 Rev of Econ Stud 157.

606 Motta (n 487) 116.

607 Elhauge and Geradin (n 508) 279.

608 Motta (n 487) 116; Monti (n 503) 131.

609 *United Brands* (n 601) para 126. See also Landes and Posner, 'Market Power in Antitrust Cases' (n 542) 957 (1981).

that courts and competition agencies, both in the EU and the US, turn to alternative, indirect methods for determining market dominance, most commonly by observing market shares—which explains why the previous step of appropriately defining the relevant market is of utmost importance.[610]

i. Indirect Methods of Establishing Market Power. Market Shares, Entry Barriers and other Indicia

In actual practice, the most frequent way for determining market power is by inferring it from the market share that the concerned firm holds in the relevant market.[611] Although, as a rule, this factor cannot alone uphold a finding of dominance, it is often used as a valuable starting-point and regarded as the most important element in every market power assessment.[612]

Which precise levels of market share, then, do authorities normally regard as an indication of market power? In the case of the EU, the CJEU understands that, save in exceptional circumstances, a market share above 50% constitutes a presumption of market power[613] and it would hence be the concerned firm's burden to rebut it. On the other end of the spectrum, low levels of market share (below 25%) can establish a presumption of lack of market power.[614] In the US, market power thresholds seem to be somehow higher.[615] Courts normally regard more than 90% as certainly evidencing monopoly power, shares around 60% as doubtful scenarios and shares of 33% as clearly ruling it out.[616]

610 Jones and Sufrin (n 520) 61.

611 *Hoffmann-La Roche* (n 533) para 39; *Grinnell* (n 490) 571; *Jefferson Parish Hospital District No 2 v Hyde* 466 US 2, 17 (1984).

612 *Hoffmann-La Roche* (n 533) paras 39-40; Areeda and Hovenkamp, *Fundamentals* (n 515) para 5.03b. It has been argued, however, that in dynamic markets with short innovation cycles, even high market shares might not be indicative of market power. See, eg, Case T-79/12 *Cisco Systems Inc v Commission* (GC, 11 December 2013), para 69.

613 Case C-62/86 *AKZO Chemie BV v Commission* [1991] ECR I-3359, para 60.

614 Case 75/84 *Metro SB-Großmärkte GmbH & Co KG v Commission* [1986] ECR 3021, paras 85-86 (market shares of 10% and below practically preclude the existence of a dominant position); EU Merger Regulation, recital 32 (a market share below 25% is not likely to impede effective competition).

615 Monti (n 503) 143-44.

616 *Alcoa* (n 490) 424; *American Tobacco Co v United States* 328 US 781, 813-14 (1946).

Notwithstanding their somewhat diverse standards, both jurisdictions show that there is a wide range of situations where the market share is neither high nor low enough to constitute a decisive indicium.[617] Thus, anywhere between their upper and lower benchmarks, competition agencies will need to turn to additional factors.

One of the most important factors to be considered in this regard is the existence of entry barriers—a notion deeply intertwined with supply substitutability, potential competition and contestable markets.[618] Generally speaking, the concept of entry barriers refers to the level of difficulty for potential competitors to enter the relevant market and constrain the ability of the allegedly-dominant firm to raise prices.[619] In this sense, if an incumbent has a high market share but entry to the relevant market is extremely easy, it is likely that it has no significant market power.[620]

Entry barriers can result from a wide variety of factors, and in many cases hinge on the sunk costs involved.[621] Entry barriers can arise, firstly, from the very nature of the relevant market, eg due to the existence of economies of scale, natural monopolies, essential facilities, network effects, etc.[622] They can even arise from the restrictive behaviour of firms already in the market.[623] But most importantly for the purposes of this work, barriers to entry can be the result of governmental measures, including the grant of intellectual property rights.[624] Some patents, indeed, can significantly raise barriers to entry,[625] although others might play no role at all—the impact ultimately depending on its scope, the existence of alterna-

617 It has also been argued that the relevance of market share as a factor for finding market power should strongly depend or the reliability of the definition of the relevant market, although courts do not seem to pay much attention to this question. Areeda and Hovenkamp, *Fundamentals* (n 515) para 5.03a.

618 Motta (n 487) 120-21.

619 *Southern Pacific Communications Co v AT&T Co* 740 F 2d 980, 1002 (DC Cir 1984).

620 Monti (n 503) 144.

621 Commission Notice, Guidelines on Vertical Restraints [2010] OJ C130/1, para 117 (EU Guidelines on Vertical Restraints).

622 Ortiz Blanco (n 599) 60.

623 ibid 61.

624 EU Guidelines on Vertical Restraints (n 621) para 117. Other entry barriers emerging from governmental action include exclusive rights, state aid, import tariffs, special authorisation requirements, etc.

625 See, eg, *AstraZeneca* (Case COMP/A.37.507/F3) Commission Decision 2006/857/CE [2006] OJ L332/24, para 517.

tive technologies, etc.[626] The specifics of the relationship between patents and market power are more comprehensively analysed in the following chapter.[627]

In addition to entry barriers, other supplementary factors which are occasionally resorted to when assessing market power include the relative level of market share,[628] the structure of demand,[629] and the behaviour of the undertakings.[630] Lastly, specific industries might also merit particular factors to be taken into account. In the pharmaceutical sector, for instance, firms are often restrained in terms of price-setting, either directly through price controls or indirectly through reimbursement arrangements.[631]

ii. Is Market Definition Always Necessary? Direct Methods of Establishing Market Power

As previously explained, the rationale behind the traditional method of evaluating market power indirectly, and thereby first defining the relevant market, seems to be that any attempt to measure it in a direct way is doomed to fail—mostly due to the lack of reliable data.[632] Yet the task of defining the relevant market might sometimes present comparable hur-

---

626 Andreas Heinemann, 'The Contestability of IP-Protected Markets' in Josef Drexl (ed), *Research Handbook on Intellectual Property and Competition Law* (Edward Elgar 2008) 62-63; Sven Bostyn and Nicolas Petit, 'Patent=Monopoly: A Legal Fiction' (2013) 15 <http://ssrn.com/abstract=2373471> accessed 14 February 2018.

627 See text at nn 734ff in ch 5.

628 *Hoffmann-La Roche* (n 533) para 63 (a significant gap between the firm concerned and the next largest competitors is an additional factor for assessing market dominance); *Transource Int'l Inc v Trinity Industries Inc* 725 F 2d 274, 284 (5th Cir 1984).

629 Scherer and Ross (n 486) ch 14.

630 Ortiz Blanco (n 599) 57, 62-65. The CJEU has indeed acknowledged that the mere ability to engage in an anticompetitive behaviour can be indicative of market dominance. *Michelin* (n 490) para 60 (confirming the criteria used by the Commission).

631 Communication from the Commission, Pharmaceutical Sector Inquiry: Final Report (8 July 2009) paras 145-46 <http://ec.europa.eu/competition/sectors/pharmaceuticals/inquiry> accessed 14 February 2018. Yet it is also argued that, in the pharmaceutical industry, the market power held by firms is often larger due to the very limited elasticity of demand, and that price controls are just a means of curtailing to some extent such excessive market power. Commission Decision in *AstraZeneca* (n 625) paras 553-56.

632 Motta (n 487) 101.

dles, particularly when searching for a benchmark price for applying the SSNIP test in already monopolised markets.[633] Furthermore, market shares might not always constitute a reliable yardstick with which to determine market power.[634] It has even been argued that defining a market is impossible without first formulating an estimate of market power.[635] Thus, considering that econometric tools and evidence are sometimes available for assessing market power directly, competition agencies might as well, under certain circumstances, eschew the traditional structural analysis and dispense with the task of defining the relevant market.[636]

In the EU, indeed, recent cases in the Commission seem to evidence a subtle shift away from market definitions and towards directly testing market power.[637] Furthermore, the CJEU has admitted that, in certain cases, the behaviour of a firm in the market can itself demonstrate that it is able to impede effective competition and, hence, that it holds a dominant position.[638] A similar predisposition can be observed in US agencies and courts.[639]

II. The Second Element: the Abusive or Anticompetitive Behaviour

As it was mentioned earlier, neither EU nor US law condemn the holding of market power as such, but rather require on top some kind of anticom-

633 See text at nn 540ff.

634 Motta (n 487) 117.

635 Louis Kaplow, 'Why (Ever) Define Markets?' (2010) 124 Harv L Rev 437, 466-67.

636 James A Keyte and Neal R Stoll, 'Markets? We Don't Need no Stinking Markets! The FTC and Market Definition' (2004) 49 Antitrust Bull 593; Monti (n 503) 150-53.

637 Monti (n 503) 152. As a matter of fact, this was a central argument in the report of the Economic Advisory Group on Competition Policy (EAGCP) when advocating for an economic approach to competition law. European Commission, Econ Advisory Group on Competition Policy, Report on an Economic Approach to Article 82 (July 2005) 14 <http://ec.europa.eu/dgs/competition/economist/eagcp_july_21_05.pdf> accessed 14 February 2018. For a more thorough discussion, see Emanuela Arezzo, 'Is There a Role for Market Definition and Dominance in an Effects-Based Approach?' in Mark-Oliver Mackenrodt, Beatriz Conde Gallego and Stefan Enchelmaier (eds), *Abuse of Dominant Position: New Interpretation, New Enforcement Mechanisms?* (Springer 2008) 21.

638 *Michelin* (n 490) paras 60-61 (confirming a decision from the Commission in that sense).

639 *Tops Markets Inc v Quality Markets Inc* 142 F 3d 90, 98 (2nd Cir 1998); *Toys "R" Us v FTC* 221 F 3d 928, 937 (7th Cir 2000). See also Keyte and Stoll (n 636).

petitive behaviour on the part of the concerned firm: in the EU an *abuse* of that market power and in the US the *monopolising* conduct or the attempt to monopolise. Neither art 102 TFEU nor § 2 Sherman Act, however, offer a clear-cut definition of what such behaviours consist of. A list of specific conducts is admittedly offered in art 102 TFEU, but such list is merely illustrative and other behaviours not included therein can thus still fall within its scope.[640] Courts on both sides of the Atlantic have hence strived to provide some guidance on the issue, although an all-encompassing definition might be a well-nigh impossible task to achieve.[641]

On the US side, the Supreme Court long ago expressed that the monopolisation conduct consists of the 'willful acquisition or maintenance' of monopoly power 'as distinguished from growth or development as a consequence of a superior product, business acumen, or historic accident.'[642] The first problem with this definition probably arises with the fact that very often firms wilfully acquire or maintain market power *precisely* through superior products or business acumen.[643] These concepts, hence, are not mutually exclusive.[644] Moreover, the vagueness of terms like 'superior product' and 'business acumen' might bring unnecessary uncertainty to the legal standard, as it might often be difficult to distinguish, for instance, whether a certain business strategies represents a superior business acumen or an illicit, exclusionary conduct.[645] In an effort to clarify, modern case law seems to prefer the concept of 'competition on the merits' instead. In *Aspen Skiing*, for instance, the Supreme Court defined an anticompetitive behaviour as that which 'not only (1) tends to impair the opportunities of rivals, but also (2) either does not further competition on the merits or does so in an unnecessarily restrictive way.'[646]

In the case of the EU, the CJEU offered a seminal definition of abusive behaviour in *Hoffmann-La Roche*, where it stated that

---

640 *Continental Can* (n 525) para 26; Case C-95/04 P *British Airways v Commission* [2007] ECR I-2331, para 57; Case C-52/09 *Konkurrensverket v TeliaSonera Sverige AB* [2011] ECR I-527, para 26. See also O'Donoghue and Padilla (n 543) 257-58 (the list of examples of art 102 TFEU is not exhaustive, although it does set out an exhaustive list of *categories* of abuse).

641 Richard Whish, *Competition Law* (8th edn, OUP 2015) 208.

642 *Grinnell* (n 490) 570-71.

643 Elhauge, 'Defining Better Monopolization Standards' (n 599) 261.

644 ibid.

645 ibid 263.

646 *Aspen Skiing Co* (n 518) 605, fn 32. See also *Trinko* (n 490) 407 (stating that the possession of monopoly power is not unlawful 'unless it is accompanied by an element of anticompetitive *conduct*') (emphasis in original).

> [t]he concept of abuse is an objective concept relating to the behaviour of an undertaking in a dominant position which is such as to influence the structure of a market where, as a result of the very presence of the undertaking in question, the degree of competition is weakened and which, through recourse to methods different from those which condition normal competition in products or services on the basis of the transactions of commercial operators, has the effect of hindering the maintenance of the degree of competition still existing in the market or the growth of that competition.[647]

This is probably the most frequently cited definition of abuse in EU case law, although the question naturally remains as to what exactly constitutes 'normal competition'. In more recent cases, the CJEU seems to prefer a slightly different language by requiring dominant firms to 'compete on the merits',[648] in some way resembling the evolution of US Supreme Court's case law. The Commission, for its part, has also adopted this concept in its Guidance on the application of art 102 TFEU—and ventured to shed some light on it.[649] In the EU, the concept of abuse is also strongly influenced by the fact that courts have consistently recognised a 'special responsibility' upon dominant firms.[650] In this regard, the CJEU stated in *Michelin* that a firm holding a dominant position has 'a special responsibility not to allow its conduct to impair genuine undistorted competition on the common market.'[651] In later cases, the CJEU even suggested that said responsibility might increase along with the degree of market power.[652]

In any case, both jurisdictions seem to be slowly converging in delineating the scope of the reprehensible behaviour along the boundaries of the concept of 'competition on the merits'. The exact confines of this standard, however, are still strongly debated and there are in fact numerous exam-

---

647 *Hoffmann-La Roche* (n 533) para 91.

648 *AKZO* (n 613) para 70; *Post Danmark* (n 489) para 25.

649 EU Guidance Paper (n 489).

650 Jones and Sufrin (n 520) 374.

651 *Michelin* (n 490) para 57.

652 Case C-333/94 P *Tetra Pak International SA v Commission* [1996] ECR I-5951, para 24 (*Tetra Pak II*); *Compagnie Maritime Belge* (n 490) para 114. The idea of 'super dominance' and increased responsibilities has been often criticised for lack of economic basis and for adding significant legal uncertainty. O'Donoghue and Padilla (n 543) 206-08. *See also* Ekaterina Rousseva and Mel Marquis, 'Hell Freezes Over: A Climate Change for Assessing Exclusionary Conduct under Article 102 TFEU' (2013) 4 J Eur Comp L & Prac 32, 43 (suggesting that *Post Danmark* may indicate an attempt to read this concept from a more economic perspective).

ples of clashing interpretations, where conducts labelled as 'competition on the merits' in the United States were judged anticompetitive under EU law.[653] At the end of the day, the definition of what constitutes an anti-competitive behaviour seems to be strongly swayed by the ultimate interest that antitrust is believed to protect, although important differences also linger when observing the particulars of art 102 TFEU and § 2 Sherman Act and the conditions that each of these provisions demand. The following paragraphs analyse those that are most relevant for the purposes of this work.

a. Types of Anticompetitive Conducts: Exclusionary and Exploitative Behaviours

Under EU law, two types of abuse are commonly distinguished: exploitative and exclusionary.[654] The CJEU has recognised in *Continental Can* that both of them are captured within the scope of art 102 TFEU.[655] Simply put, exploitative abuses are those where firms take advantage of their market power in order to exploit their customers,[656] the classic example being the imposing of high prices. Exclusionary abuses, on the other hand, harm customers in a more indirect—but also more severe—way, by affecting the competitive process and hence preventing the development of competition.[657]

---

653 See, eg, Monti's case study on the British Airways/Virgin case on rebate schemes. Monti (n 503) 162-69.

654 Additional categories of abuses are occasionally mentioned, such as 'reprisal' abuses or 'single market' abuses. See, eg, John Temple Lang, 'Reprisals and Overreaction by Dominant Companies as an Anti-competitive Abuse under Article 82(b)' (2008) 29 Eur Comp L Rev 13. See also Jones and Sufrin (n 520) 371-72 (also highlighting that the line between exploitative and exclusionary abuses becomes blurred when approaching art 102 TFEU from a consumer welfare approach); Akman, The Concept of Abuse (n 499) ch 8 (suggesting that abusive behaviours under art 102 TFEU should be behaviours that are *both* exclusionary and exploitative).

655 *Continental Can* (n 525) para 26 ('…the provision is not only aimed at practices which may cause damage to consumers directly, but also at those which are detrimental to them through their impact on an effective competition structure…').

656 Jones and Sufrin (n 520) 367.

657 Whish (n 641) 212.

Exploitative abuses constitute the most obvious objection to a dominant firm, as they incarnate the core of competition policy's ultimate nemeses: monopolists reducing output and increasing prices.[658] There are, however, a number of compelling reasons that call for extreme caution in condemning this category of abuses and suggest that focusing on exclusionary conducts might be a more sensible policy. Firstly, exclusionary abuses are often much more harmful to consumers in the long-run. Indeed, if a dominant firm charges high prices in a market where the entry barriers are low, this conduct might in itself incite competition over time.[659] Furthermore, determining whether a price is excessive or not is a nearly impossible task, particularly taking into account that almost every firm prices, to a larger or smaller extent, above its marginal costs.[660] And even if a firm were found to charge too high a price, penalising this behaviours as a rule would virtually convert competition agencies into regulators[661] and could negatively affect investments and innovation.[662] In this regard, there does not seem to be any sound reason to penalise high prices as such, as the opportunity to charge high prices is what actually incentivises firms to engage in competition in the first place.[663]

It is precisely for these reasons that US antitrust law only focuses on exclusionary conducts and why exploitative behaviours are considered to be beyond the scope of § 2 Sherman Act.[664] The Supreme Court has indeed emphasised in this regard that the charging of high prices 'is not only not unlawful; it is an important element of the free-market system.'[665] The European stance, on its turn, does not seem to be as bold. For starters, because art 102(a) TFEU expressly mentions 'imposing unfair purchase or selling prices' as the first example of abusive behaviour. Admittedly, the

---

658 ibid.

659 ibid; Areeda and Hovenkamp, *Antitrust Law* (n 488) para 720b. See also *Trinko* (n 490) 407 ('The opportunity to charge monopoly prices –at least for a short period– is what attracts "business acumen" in the first place.').

660 Monti (n 503) 218.

661 Valentine Korah, *An Introductory Guide to EC Competition Law and Practice* (9th edn, Hart 2007) 135; *Trinko* (n 490) 414.

662 Lars-Hendrik Röller, 'Exploitative Abuses' in Claus-Dieter Ehlermann and Mel Marquis (eds), *European Competition Law Annual 2007: A Reformed Approach to Article 82 EC* (Hart 2008) 527.

663 Motta (n 487) 69-70.

664 Eleanor M Fox, 'Monopolization and Dominance in the United States and the European Community: Efficiency Opportunity and Fairness' (1986) 61 Notre Dame L Rev 981, 993.

665 *Trinko* (n 490) 407.

Commission and the courts have been rather cautious when dealing with exploitative abuses[666] and mostly concentrated their efforts against exclusionary abuses.[667] Under certain scenarios, however, the Commission has recognised the importance of attacking exploitative abuses and, for instance, has been relatively active in regulating prices in newly liberalised sectors.[668] And more importantly for the purpose of this work, it has been argued that the figure of exploitative abuses might also prove useful as an ancillary resource, eg for closing 'enforcement gaps' or for rectifying 'mistakes' by competition agencies.[669] A clear example of such use is explained in the following paragraph.

b. The Importance of Timing: Dominance as a Prerequisite under EU Law. Differences with US' Monopolisation and Attempt to Monopolise

The language of art 102 TFEU is clear in condemning the abuse *of a* dominant position. As it was anticipated above, this implies that the provision only captures abuses from firms which already hold a dominant position in the market, but not where the abusive behaviour leads to the *acquisition* of that dominant position.[670] In contrast, § 2 Sherman Act does capture conducts taking place before the acquisition of market power: on the one hand, the monopolisation offence comprises both the acquisition and maintenance of monopoly power; on the other hand, the concept of attempt to monopolise applies even if the behaviour does not result in the acquisition of such market power, provided that a dangerous probability of success can be verified.[671]

EU competition law's constrained focus on conducts taking place after the acquisition of market power and its failure to capture behaviours that lead to the attaining of that market power leave an important enforcement

666 Indeed, courts have very rarely attacked exploitative abuses under EU case law. Massimo Motta and Alexandre de Streel, 'Exploitative and Exclusionary Excessive Prices in EU Law' in Claus-Dieter Ehlermann and Isabela Atanasiu (eds), *European Competition Law Annual 2003: What is an Abuse of a Dominant Position?* (Hart 2006) 91.

667 Monti (n 503) 218; EU Guidance Paper (n 489) paras 5-7.

668 Monti (n 503) 220.

669 Röller (n 662) 528-29.

670 See, among others, Franklin M Fisher, 'Monopolization versus Abuse of Dominant Position: An Economist's View' in Barry Hawk (ed), *International Antitrust Law & Policy: Fordham Corporate Law 2003* (Juris Publishing 2004) 159.

671 ibid.

gap[672] and the consequences have become manifest in scenarios such as those involving patent ambush,[673] where an abusive conduct by a non-dominant firm can lead in a very short period of time to a position of significant market power. As a means to close this gap, it has been suggested that the concept of exploitative abuse could be employed.[674] In this sense, surveying the high prices charged by a monopolist could function as a gateway for indirectly tackling the exclusionary conduct that took place before the acquisition of market dominance. As a matter of fact, in the *Rambus* decision, which concerned a firm concealing information on its patents from the standard setting organisation and subsequently demanding high royalties, the Commission seemed to embrace such a theory.[675]

c. Causation: The Relationship between Market Power, Anticompetitive Conduct and Anticompetitive Effects

Associated with the above portrayed problem is the question as to the causal link that competition law requires between the anticompetitive conduct and the market power held by the concerned firm. Indeed, since art 102 TFEU speaks about the abuse *of a* dominant position, the syntax implies that there should be some kind of link between these two concepts.

672 Röller (n 662) 529; Elhauge, 'Defining Better Monopolization Standards' (n 599) 332.

673 Josef Drexl, 'Deceptive Conduct in the Patent World: A Case for US Antitrust and EU Competition Law?' in Wolrad Prinz zu Waldeck und Pyrmont and others (eds), *Patents and Technological Progress in a Globalized World: Liber Amicorum for Joseph Straus* (Springer 2009) 156; Inge Govaere, 'In Pursuit of an Innovation Policy Rationale: Stakes and Limits under Article 82 TEC' (2008) 31 World Competition 541, 550-51; Peter Picht, *Strategisches Verhalten bei der Nutzung von Patenten in Standardisierungsverfahren aus der Sicht des Europäischen Kartellrechts* (Springer 2013) 452.

674 Röller (n 662) 529.

675 *Rambus* (Case COMP/38.636) Commission Decision 2010/C 30/09 [2010] OJ C30/17, paras 27-39. See also Drexl, 'Anticompetitive Stumbling Stones' (n 555) 530-36 (generally endorsing the Commission's approach); Ian S Forrester, 'The Interplay Between Standardization, IPR and Competition Law' in Giandonato Caggiano, Gabriella Muscolo and Marina Tavassi (eds), *Competition Law and Intellectual Property: A European Perspective* (Wolters Kluwer 2012) 129 (highlighting that the indirect theory used by the Commission was necessary due to the limitations of art 102 TFEU). For a more detailed analysis of the case, see text at nn 1478-1486 in ch 6.

Vogelenzang[676] has distinguished, in this regard, three modalities in which abuse and dominance can be possibly connected:

(a)cases where the abuse itself can only be performed by a dominant firm (eg, predatory pricing);
(b)cases where the act can be performed by anyone, but where the anticompetitive effects would not occur if the firm were not dominant. Within this category, yet another distinction can be made between cases where the dominant position was the *condition sine qua non* of the anticompetitive effect (eg, refusal to deal) and cases where the anticompetitive effect is strengthened due to the dominant position of the firm (eg, rebate schemes); and
(c)cases where the act and the dominant position have no connection whatsoever.

In *Continental Can* and in *Hoffmann-La Roche*, the CJEU rejected a narrow interpretation whereby art 102 TFEU should only capture the first category of cases.[677] This interpretation necessarily implies that, as a minimum, the first set of cases from the second category should be comprised as well.[678] Yet the CJEU also stated in *Tetra Pak II* that art 102 TFEU 'presupposes a link between the dominant position and the alleged abusive conduct',[679] which seems to acknowledge that some kind of link is still necessary[680] and would hence leave the third category of cases outside the scope of the provision. The question, hence, is whether the required causation under art 102 TFEU embraces both cases in the second category or only the first one. The recent decision of the CJEU in *AstraZeneca* seems to incline towards the former alternative,[681] since anticompetitive effects could have existed

676 Pierre Vogelenzang, 'Abuse of a Dominant Position in Article 86: the Problem of Causality and Some Applications' (1976) 13 CML Rev 61, 66-67.

677 *Continental Can* (n 525) para 27; *Hoffmann-La Roche* (n 533) para 91 ('…the interpretation suggested by the applicant that an abuse implies that the use of the economic power bestowed by a dominant position is the means whereby the abuse has been brought about cannot be accepted.').

678 Vogelenzang (n 676) 70.

679 *Tetra Pak II* (n 652) para 27.

680 Thomas Eilmansberger, 'How to Distinguish Good From Bad Competition Under Article 82 EC: In Search of Clearer and More Coherent Standards for Anticompetitive Abuses' (2005) 42 CML Rev 129, 142; O'Donoghue and Padilla (n 543) 263. Cf Whish (n 641) 215 (arguing that in *Tetra Pak II* the Court was not really concerned with the problem of causation).

681 Case C-457/10 P *AstraZeneca v Commission* (CJEU, 6 December 2012, ECLI:EU:C:2012:770).

even if the conduct had been performed by non-dominant firms, yet the impact on competition was much larger because of the dominant position.[682] More specifically, the anticompetitive effect derived from the temporal extension of the dominant position by unduly acquiring SPC protection.

On the US side, the Supreme Court has suggested in *Kodak* that the monopolisation offence consists of the 'use of monopoly power to foreclose competition, to gain a competitive advantage, or to destroy a competitor',[683] which at first glance seems to imply that a certain causal link should also be proven under US antitrust law. Such a conclusion, however, does not stand up to scrutiny, as it lays in stark contrast to the traditional definition of monopolisation.[684] Indeed, because § 2 Sherman Act also captures behaviours leading to the initial acquisition of market power, debating whether causation in the European sense is required under US antitrust law seems unnecessary.

In any case, it is important to distinguish the above depicted question from the causation that competition laws require between the anticompetitive conduct and the anticompetitive effects. In this sense, US antitrust law does require a causal connection between those two elements, since § 2 Sherman Act requires the exclusionary conduct to be the cause of the acquisition (or maintenance) of market power.[685] The required causal link in monopolization offences would thus be 'conduct→market power'. Although it has been argued that this strongly differs from EU law,[686] the difference in practice does not seem to be significant.[687] While EU competition law undoubtedly postulates the dominant position as a prerequisite, it also requires a causal link between the conduct and the anticompetitive effects—especially with the increasing tendency towards an effect-based approach.[688] The causal sequence under art 102 TFEU would thus be 'dominance→ abuse→anticompetitive effect'.[689]

---

682 See Drexl, 'Deceptive Conduct in the Patent World' (n 673) 151-52.

683 *Eastman Kodak Co v Image Technical Services Inc* 504 US 451, 482-83 (1992).

684 Elhauge, 'Defining Better Monopolization Standards' (n 599) 333 (also emphasising that the Supreme Court's statement in *Kodak* was dicta).

685 *Grinnell* (n 490) 570-71.

686 Elhauge, 'Defining Better Monopolization Standards' (n 599) 331-33.

687 Thorsten Käseberg, *Intellectual Property, Antitrust and Cumulative Innovation in the EU and the US* (Hart 2012) 75.

688 Whish (n 641) 211.

689 Käseberg (n 687) 74.

d. The Role of Intent

It is commonly understood that, as a principle, unilateral conducts are to be assessed exclusively under objective parameters and do not depend on the concerned firm's subjective intent. In the EU, the CJEU has famously stated in *Hoffmann-La Roche* that '[t]he concept of abuse is an objective concept'.[690] In the US, intent did seem to play a significant role in the early cases,[691] but that role has been relegated with the wake of the Chicago and Post-Chicago school of antitrust analysis.[692] In *Aspen Skiing*,[693] for instance, the Supreme Court disparaged the weight of the intent factor and cited Judge Hand's renowned statement: 'no monopolist monopolizes unconscious of what he is doing.'[694] There are sound reasons for courts and competition agencies not looking at subjective elements as a rule, including the complications involved in proving it[695] and the fact that, in many cases, it is nearly impossible to distinguish an illegitimate intent to exclude rivals from a legitimate intent to maximise profits.[696]

In exceptional circumstances, however, courts and competition agencies have considered intent as a relevant factor in their assessments, mostly as a tool for understanding ambiguous behaviours or foreseeing their likely effects.[697] In predatory pricing cases, for instance, prices above average variable costs but below average total costs can be regarded abusive in the EU 'if they are determined as part of a plan for eliminating a competitor.'[698] In the US, predatory pricing cases require 'that the competitor had a reason-

690 *Hoffmann-La Roche* (n 533) para 91.

691 Herbert Hovenkamp, 'The Monopolization Offence' (2000) 61 Ohio St L J 1035, 1037-38. See also Denis Waelbroeck, 'Tough Competition: What is the Relevance of Intention in Article 82 cases?' (2006) 5(8) Comp Law Insight 5-7.

692 Marina Lao, 'Reclaiming a Role for Intent Evidence in Monopolization Analysis' (2004) 54 Am Univ L Rev 151, 164.

693 *Aspen Skiing Co* (n 518) 602-03.

694 *Alcoa* (n 490) 432.

695 Richard A Posner, *Antitrust Law* (2nd edn, Univ of Chicago Press 2001) 214-15.

696 Herbert Hovenkamp, 'The Monopolization Offence' (n 691) 1039-40. Cf Lao, 'Reclaiming a Role for Intent Evidence' (n 692) (generally vindicating intent evidence for monopolisation cases); Eilmansberger (n 680) 170-77 (arguing that, in market structure abuses, intent should be an essential factor).

697 Areeda and Hovenkamp, *Antitrust Law* (n 488) para 805c; O'Donoghue and Padilla (n 543) 280-82; EU Guidance Paper (n 489) para 20. See also Lao, 'Reclaiming a Role for Intent Evidence' (n 692) 181 (alleging that intent can be a powerful tool for understanding anticompetitive effects in innovation competition).

698 *AKZO* (n 613) para 72.

able prospect ... of recouping its investment in below-cost prices',[699] which in practice might involve diving into subjective considerations. There are, moreover, situations where the subjective element not only constitutes a relevant factor but steps forward as an essential requirement in competition assessment. In sham or vexatious litigation cases, for instance, both EU and US courts have found the intent of the concerned firm an indispensable requisite for any finding of anticompetitive behaviour.[700] Most notably, chapter 6 of the present work shows that intent may also constitute an extremely relevant factor in competition cases involving proceedings at the patent office.

C. *The Particular Case of § 5 FTC Act*

As a final remark, it should also be noted that, under US law, an additional provision governing unilateral behaviour exists in the FTC Act, namely § 5.[701] This norm essentially prohibits, with a very general and imprecise language, 'unfair methods of competition', and its meaning remains largely unsettled. Courts have interpreted that it somehow supplements other antitrust rules,[702] and can hence proscribe behaviours that lay beyond the scope of the Sherman Act.[703] Indeed, when enforcing this provision, the FTC has not only pursued conducts that violate the Sherman Act, but also so-called 'standalone' § 5 violations.[704] In cases of patent ambush, for example, the FTC initially attempted to address the problem as a 'standalone' § 5 violation in the *Dell Computer Corporation* case.[705] Later on, however, in

699 *Brooke Group Ltd v Brown & Williamson Tobacco Corp* 509 US 209, 224 (1993).

700 Case T-111/96 *ITT Promedia NV v Commission* [1998] ECR II 2937 (confirming the decision of the Commission without questioning the test suggested in it's decision); *Professional Real Estate Investors Inc v Columbia Pictures Industries Inc* 508 US 49, 60-61 (1993). See text at nn 1161ff in ch 6.

701 § 5 FTC Act ('Unfair methods of competition in or affecting commerce ... are hereby declared unlawful').

702 Areeda and Hovenkamp, *Fundamentals* (n 515) para 8.04f(1).

703 William E Kovacic and Marc Winerman, 'Competition Policy and the Application of Section 5 of the Federal Trade Commission Act' (2010) 76 Antitrust L J 929, 929.

704 Maureen K Ohlhausen, 'Section 5 of the FTC Act: Principles of Navigation' (2013) 1 J Antitrust Enforcement 1, 2.

705 *Dell Computer Corporation* (FTC Docket C-3658) 121 FTC 616 (1996).

the *Rambus* case,[706] the FTC seemingly changed its interpretation and assumed an integrative approach by applying § 5 FTC Act and § 2 Sherman Act.[707]

The vague wording of this rule, combined with the very scarce case law, remains the source of distressing legal uncertainty and has prompted many legal scholars, including Commissioners of the FTC, to advocate for clearer limiting principles.[708] In this sense, a policy statement has been put forward by a Commissioner of the FTC proposing that an unfair method of competition in the terms of § 5 should only be found when a conduct (1) harms or is likely to harm competition significantly and (2) lacks cognizable efficiencies.[709] Such an interpretation seems to reflect a more economic approach to the provision. In any case, it should be borne in mind that the role that this rule has played in the development of competition policy in the US is rather small when compared to § 2 Sherman Act.[710]

Finally, it should be borne in mind that similar unfair competition tools could also be envisaged in EU under the national laws of the Member States. In Germany, e.g., national unfair competition rules provide that deliberately hindering competitors shall be considered as unfair commercial practice and, as such, illegal.[711] Hence, in cases where art 102 TFEU becomes inapplicable due to lack of market dominance, the application of unfair competition provisions should not be ruled out.

706 *Rambus* (FTC Docket 9302) Opinion of the Commission of 2 August 2006 <www.ftc.gov/os/adjpro/d9302/060802commissionopinion.pdf> accessed 14 February 2018.

707 Drexl (n 673) 144.

708 Kovacic and Winerman (n 703) 944; Ohlhausen (n 704) 3; Joshua D Wright, 'Proposed Policy Statement Regarding Unfair Methods of Competition Under Section 5 of the FTC Act' (19 June 2013) 2 <www.ftc.gov/sites/default/files/documents/public_statements/statement-commissioner-joshua-d.wright/130619umcpolicystatement.pdf> accessed 14 February 2018.

709 Wright (n 708) 2-3. It might be interesting to point out that, among the examples of conducts that would fall within this novel scope, the proposal mentions the 'use by a firm of unfair methods of competition to acquire market power that does not yet rise to the level of monopoly power necessary for a violation of the Sherman Act.' Ibid 8.

710 Kovacic and Winerman (n 703) 934.

711 § 4 No. 4 UWG (*Gesetz gegen den unlauteren Wettbewerb* or German Act Against Unfair Competition).

Chapter V: Applying Competition Rules to Patent Proceedings: The Experience in the US and in the EU

1. *The Interaction between Intellectual Property Rights and Competition Law*

Having described the general functioning and essential features of the competition rules under EU and US law, a succinct analysis of the interplay between the latter and the intellectual property system represents an unavoidable step before immersing in the specifics of its role within the framework of patent procedures. The following paragraphs, hence, briefly explain the complex interaction between these two bodies of law, with a logical focus on patents over other intellectual property rights in view of the goals of this work.

A. *Tension and Complementarity*

In the eyes of the layperson, the goals of competition law and intellectual property law are likely to appear, at first glance, not only as conflicting but just plain contradictory. Indeed, while the former is designed to thwart monopolies, the latter seems to foster the exact opposite by creating monopoly rights over specific products or processes. However, a closer look reveals that neither of these statements is entirely accurate and that the collision between intellectual property and antitrust objectives is more ostensible than real.[712] On the one hand, intellectual property rights are not real monopolies and do not necessarily confer the kind of market power that is the concern of competition law.[713] On the other hand, competi-

712 Herbert Hovenkamp and others, *IP and Antitrust: An Analysis of Antitrust Principles Applied to Intellectual Property Law* (2nd edn Supp 2013, Wolters Kluwer) para 1.3; Luc Peeperkorn, 'IP Licences and Competition Rules: Striking the Right Balance' (2003) 26 World Competition 527, 527-28. For a seminal study on the complementarity between competition law and patent law see Ward S Bowman, *Patent and Antitrust Law: A Legal and Economic Appraisal* (Univ of Chicago Press 1973).

713 See text at nn 734ff.

tion law does not really seek to condemn monopolies as such, but rather specific undesired conducts connected to its attainment or to its improper exploitation.[714]

In fact, when studied in a broader context, both intellectual property rights and competition seem to have not opposing but rather reciprocal goals, as they both seek to promote innovation and enhance consumer welfare.[715] Although not completely evident in earlier times, this intelligence has since widely sprouted among most courts and competition agencies. The Commission in the EU, for instance, proclaims in its current Guidelines on Technology Transfer Agreements that:

> The fact that intellectual property laws grant exclusive rights of exploitation does not imply … that there is an inherent conflict between intellectual property rights and the Union competition rules. Indeed, both areas of law share the same basic objective of promoting consumer welfare and an efficient allocation of resources. Innovation constitutes an essential and dynamic component of an open and competitive market economy. Intellectual property rights promote dynamic competition by encouraging undertakings to invest in developing new or improved products and processes. So does competition by putting pressure on undertakings to innovate. Therefore, both intellectual property rights and competition are necessary to promote innovation and ensure a competitive exploitation thereof.[716]

In a similar vein, US courts and agencies have acknowledged that 'the patent and antitrust laws are complementary',[717] that they both promote

714 See text at nn 640ff in ch 4.

715 Josef Drexl, 'Intellectual Property and Antitrust Law - IMS Health and Trinko: Antitrust Placebo for Consumers Instead of Sound Economics in Refusal-to-Deal Cases' (2004) 35 IIC 788, 793; Bowman (n 712) 1 (antitrust and patent laws both pursue 'to maximize wealth by producing what consumers want at the lowest cost.'); Christopher R Leslie, 'Antitrust and Patent Law as Component Parts of Innovation Policy' (2009) 34 Iowa J Corp L 1259 (arguing that antitrust and patent law should both be conceived as interdependent parts of a general innovation policy).

716 Communication from the Commission, Guidelines on the application of Article 101 of the Treaty on the Functioning of the European Union to technology transfer agreements [2014] OJ C89/3, para 7 (EU Guidelines on Technology Transfer Agreements).

717 *Loctite Corp v Ultraseal Ltd* 781 F 2d 861, 877 (Fed Cir 1985).

consumer welfare over time[718] and that they 'both are aimed at encouraging innovation, industry and competition.'[719] The Supreme Court itself has also favoured this interpretation in its recent *Actavis* judgment.[720]

I. Social and Economic Functions of the Patent System

The understanding that patents and competition law share an ultimate common ambition is deeply intertwined with the patent system's raison d'être, and most significantly with its recognition as an essential tool for correcting market failure and incentivising innovation. In this regard, the development of new inventions commonly demands considerable efforts in terms of time and resources,[721] which translates into large fixed costs for the concerned inventors.[722] The fruit of these efforts, however, mainly consists of non-rivalrous goods in the form of intangible knowledge, which—as opposed to traditional physical property—lacks an inherent 'excludability' attribute.[723] For this precise reason, once it is achieved, an invention would be readily accessible for competitors, who would spare those fixed costs and hence run with a competitive advantage.[724] Against this backdrop, no businessperson would invest in innovation absent some

718 FTC, 'To Promote Innovation: The Proper Balance of Competition and Patent Law and Policy' (2003) ch 1, 7.

719 *Atari Games Corp v Nintendo of America Inc* 897 F 2d 1572, 1576 (Fed Cir 1990).

720 *FTC v Actavis Inc* 133 S Ct 2223 (2013). In this case, which essentially dealt with 'reverse payment' or 'pay-for-delay' settlement agreements, the majority rejected a sharp separation between the patent and the competition spheres. Ibid 2231. The dissent, in its turn, seemed to subscribe the more conventional view, according to which patent law and competition law remain two separate and essentially independent bodies of law, where the former 'carves out an exception to the applicability of antitrust laws.' Ibid 2238.

721 It should be borne in mind that the costs implicated might vary significantly between industries. It is widely recognised, for instance, that innovation within the life sciences industries often calls for particularly large investments. See, eg, Matthew Herper, 'The Cost of Creating a New Drug Now $5 Billion, Pushing Big Pharma to Change' *Forbes* (New York, 11 August 2013) <www.forbes.com/sites/matthewherper/2013/08/11/how-the-staggering-cost-of-inventing-new-drugs-is-shaping-the-future-of-medicine> accessed 14 February 2018 (estimating that the average total R&D cost per new drug is close to US$ 5 billion).

722 William M Landes and Richard A Posner, *The Economic Structure of Intellectual Property Law* (Harvard Univ Press 2003) 294.

723 Hovenkamp and others, *IP and Antitrust* (n 712) para 1.1.

724 Landes and Posner, *The Economic Structure of IP Law* (n 722) 294.

sort of incentive, hence leading to a suboptimal level of investment in socially desirable activities.[725] Patent protection, therefore, emerges as a crucial attempt to remedy this market failure by enabling firms to recoup those initial costs and incentivise them to engage in further innovation activities.[726]

The above described rationale is commonly referred to as the *incentive theory* and is the most widely recognised function of the patent system[727]—although certainly not the only one.[728] Further significant economic and social justifications for patent rights include the *exchange-for-secrets* theory,[729] the *prospect* theory,[730] the *commercialisation* theory[731] and the

---

725 Frederic M Scherer and David Ross, *Industrial Market Structure and Economic Performance* (3rd edn, Houghton Mifflin 1990) 624.

726 For a more detailed explanation of the economic rationale behind patents, see Scherer and Ross (n 725) 622-630; Landes and Posner, *The Economic Structure of IP Law* (n 722) 294-326; Gustavo Ghidini, *Innovation, Competition and Consumer Welfare in Intellectual Property Law* (Edward Elgar 2010) 33-97.

727 Hovenkamp and others, *IP and Antitrust* (n 712) para 1.1; William R Cornish, David Llewelyn and Tanya F Aplin, *Intellectual Property: Patents, Copyright, Trade Marks and Allied Rights* (8th edn, Sweet & Maxwell 2013) para 3-37. In this line of thought, Abraham Lincoln famously stated that the patent system 'added the fuel of *interest* to the *fire* of genius.' See B Zorina Khan and Kenneth L Sokoloff, 'History Lessons: The Early Development of Intellectual Property Institutions in the United States' (2001) 15 J Econ Perspectives 233, 244. The incentive theory, however, has not remained completely free from disputes. See, for instance, Rudolph J R Peritz, 'Competition within Intellectual Property Regimes: the Instance of Patent Rights' in Steven D Anderman and Ariel Ezrachi (eds), *Intellectual Property and Competition Law: New Frontiers* (OUP 2011) 27; Mark A Lemley, 'The Myth of the Sole Inventor' (2012) 110 Mich L Rev 709.

728 FTC, 'To Promote Innovation' (n 718) ch 1, 6.

729 The *exchange-for-secrets* theory relies on the assumption that patents result from a bargain between the inventor and society, whereby the former surrenders the secrecy of the invention in exchange for temporary legal exclusivity. Fritz Machlup, 'An Economic Review of the Patent System' (Study No 15 of the Subcommittee on Patents, Trademarks, and Copyright of the Committee on the Judiciary of the US Senate, 85th Congress, 2nd Session, Washington, 1958) 21. In the absence of patents, inventors would expend substantial resources on preserving secrecy, which would retard the spread of knowledge. Richard A Posner, 'The Social Costs of Monopoly and Regulation' (1975) 83 J Pol Econ 807, 825.

730 According to this theory first suggested by Edmund Kitch, patents are like prospects in mineral exploitation and incentivise firms to further develop technological possibilities. Edmund W Kitch, 'The Nature and Function of the Patent System' (1977) 20 J L & Econ 265.

731 Akin to the *prospect* theory, it is argued that patents can function as tools to bring new products to the market. Michael Abramowicz and John F Duffy, 'Intellectual Property for Market Experimentation' (2008) 83 NYU L Rev 337.

transaction costs theory.[732] In addition, intellectual property rights in general have been advocated on ethical grounds as well, ie as natural or personality rights or, from a more Lockean perspective, as a reward for the time and effort incurred by the inventor under the *labour* theory.[733]

II. Patents and Market Power

Patents confer upon the patentee the right to exclude others from manufacturing, selling, importing, etc the products or processes covered by the claims of the patent.[734] Because of this exclusive right that they ascribe, it is not unusual to find court decisions referring to patents as 'limited monopolies',[735] 'temporary monopolies',[736] or as rights conferring 'monopolistic, albeit lawful, market control'.[737] As a matter of fact, in cases involving tying arrangements, early Supreme Court cases in the US had even established a presumption that patents conferred monopoly power upon the patentees,[738] although such presumption was later repealed.[739]

The prevailing opinion in the antitrust spheres nowadays, however, clearly speaks out against equating patents with monopolies or market

732 Patents may also be justified based on the transaction costs savings that they offer in comparison to other alternatives for exploiting information assets. Paul J Heald, 'A Transaction Costs Theory of Patent Law' (2005) 66 Ohio St L J 473; Daniel F Spulber, 'How Patents Provide the Foundation of the Market for Inventions' (2014) Northwest L & Econ Research Paper 14/14, 12 <http://ssrn.com/abstract=2487564> accessed 14 February 2018.

733 Justin Hughes, 'The Philosophy of Intellectual Property' (1988) 77 Geo L J 287. See also Machlup (n 729) 21-23.

734 EPC, art 64; UK Patents Act, s 60; § 9PatG; § 154 US Patent Act.

735 *International Salt Co Inc v United States* 332 US 392, 395 (1947).

736 Joined Cases C-468/06 to C-478/06 *Sot Lélos kai Sia EE v GlaxoSmithKline* [2008] ECR I-7139, para 64.

737 *Times-Picayune Publishing Co v United States* 345 US 594, 608 (1953).

738 This presumption had first arisen as part of the patent misuse doctrine, outside the antitrust context. *Morton Salt Co v G S Suppiger Co* 314 US 488 (1942). Some years later, it migrated to the antitrust domain. *International Salt* (n 735) 396.

739 *Illinois Tool Works Inc v Independent Ink Inc* 547 US 28 (2006). For a critical analysis of this case, see Clifford A Jones, 'Patent Power and Market Power: Rethinking the Relationship Between Intellectual Property Rights and Market Power in Antitrust Analysis' in Josef Drexl (ed), *Research Handbook on Intellectual Property and Competition Law* (Edward Elgar 2008) 239.

power.[740] Quite on the contrary, it is widely acknowledged that the vast majority of patents do not confer the kind of market power that can be meaningful from a competition law perspective.[741] Firstly, it should be borne in mind that a patent only represent a negative right to exclude, but does not necessarily imply that there is a market for the products or processes protected by it.[742] Those products or processes might in fact never make it to the market, and studies indeed show that only a very small percentage of the universe of granted patents turns out to have some commercial significance.[743] Secondly, even if the patent protects a product that effectively sells on the market, it is likely that consumers are also able to find substitute products from other competitors, hence constraining the patentee's discretion over price.[744] Moreover, even if a patent can assure a large market share for a certain period of time, such position might still be threatened by *potential* substitutes, as competitors may come up with different—or even better—products falling outside the scope of the patent.[745]

---

740 Organisation for Economic Co-operation and Development (OECD), 'Competition, Patents and Innovation' (2008, DAF/COMP(2007)40) 9 <http://www.oecd.org/daf/competition/39888509.pdf> accessed 14 February 2018; Hovenkamp and others, *IP and Antitrust* (n 712) para 4.2a; Landes and Posner, *The Economic Structure of IP Law* (n 722) 374-75; Josef Drexl, 'The Relationship Between the Legal Exclusivity and Economic Market Power: Links and Limits' in Inge Govaere and Hans Ullrich (eds), *Intellectual Property, Market Power and the Public Interest* (Peter Lang 2008) 16; Andreas Heinemann, 'The Contestability of IP-Protected Markets' in Josef Drexl (ed), *Research Handbook on Intellectual Property and Competition Law* (Edward Elgar 2008) 62; Sven Bostyn and Nicolas Petit, 'Patent=Monopoly: A Legal Fiction' (2013) <http://ssrn.com/abstract=2373471> accessed 14 February 2018. For an alternative viewpoint, see Martin J Adelman, 'The Relevant Market Paradox: Attempted and Completed Patent Fraud Monopolization' (1977) 38 Ohio St L J 289 (arguing that proof of market power should not need to be proven in monopolisation cases); Ariel Katz, 'Making Sense of Nonsense: Intellectual Property, Antitrust, and Market Power' (2007) 49 Ariz L Rev 837 (criticising the conclusion of *Illinois Tool* and arguing that, in principle, patents do confer some market power).

741 Landes and Posner, *The Economic Structure of IP Law* (n 722) 374-75.

742 Bostyn and Petit (n 740) 5.

743 Mark A. Lemley and Carl Shapiro, 'Probabilistic Patents' (2005) 19 J Econ Perspectives 75.

744 Heinemann (n 740) 62.

745 Josef Drexl, 'Is There a "More Economic Approach" to Intellectual Property and Competition Law?' in Josef Drexl (ed), *Research Handbook on Intellectual Property and Competition Law* (Edward Elgar 2008) 46; Steven Anderman, 'The IP and Competition Interface: New Developments' in Steven D Anderman and Ariel Ezrachi (eds), *Intellectual Property and Competition Law: New Frontiers* (OUP 2011) 14.

Today, courts and agencies on both sides of the Atlantic seem to unanimously subscribe to this view. In the US, the Supreme Court acknowledged it in the above cited *Illinois Tool Works* decision.[746] In the same vein, the FTC's and DoJ's Antitrust Guidelines for the Licensing of Intellectual Property state the following:

> The Agencies will not presume that a patent, copyright, or trade secret necessarily confers market power upon its owner. Although the intellectual property right confers the power to exclude with respect to the specific product, process, or work in question, there will often be sufficient actual or potential close substitutes for such product, process, or work to prevent the exercise of market power.[747]

On the European side, the CJEU has also expressly recognised that the mere ownership of an intellectual property right does not necessarily confer a dominant position.[748]

The above does not mean, however, that patents do not have any role to play in establishing market power. It is undisputed that patents, just like physical property,[749] can occasionally raise barriers to entry into the market and constitute a relevant factor in the assessment of market power.[750] What is more, in some cases they can play a critical role in this assessment.[751] In any case, it should be reminded that, in the absence of an anticompetitive conduct, holding market power as such is not condemned by antitrust rules.[752]

---

746 *Illinois Tool Works* (n 739) 45-46. For non-tying cases, the Supreme Court had already recognised that ownership of intellectual property rights was insufficient to establish market power. Hovenkamp and others, *IP and Antitrust* (n 712) para 4.2e5.

747 DoJ and FTC, Antitrust Guidelines for the Licensing of Intellectual Property (12 January 2017) para 2.2 (US Antitrust Guidelines for the Licensing of IP).

748 Joined Cases C-241/91 P and C-242/91 P, *Radio Telefis Eireann (RTE) and Independent Television Publications Ltd (ITP) v Commission* [1995] ECR I-743, para 46 (*Magill*).

749 Hovenkamp and others, *IP and Antitrust* (n 712) para 4.2a.

750 EU Guidelines on Technology Transfer Agreements (n 716) para 166; Heinemann (n 740) 57; Robert O'Donoghue and A Jorge Padilla, *The Law and Economics of Article 102 TFEU* (2nd edn, Hart 2013) 156.

751 That was the case, for instance, of the AstraZeneca decision that is analysed in detail below. See *AstraZeneca* (Case COMP/A.37.507/F3) Commission Decision 2006/857/CE [2006] OJ L332/24, para 517 ('A factor of considerable importance in determining dominance in this case relates to AZ's technology in the form of intellectual property and other rights derived from pharmaceutical law.').

752 See text at nn 640ff in ch 4.

III. Reciprocal Goals but Conflicting Means

Even if agreed that patent law and competition law have a reciprocal relationship, that they strive towards ultimate common goals and that patents regularly do not confer significant market power in an economic sense, there is no denying that the methods employed by each of them are diametrically different and can occasionally generate tension.[753] In terms of traditional price competition, patents—as explained in the preceding paragraph—will often grant protection to only one of many products that effectively compete in the market, thus giving rise to few antitrust concerns.[754] But in those situations where they enfold larger portions of the market, or even prevent in effect all possible competition, patent and antitrust approaches will inevitably tend to clash.[755] On the other hand, from a dynamic competition perspective, even when patents and antitrust can both serve to spur innovation,[756] they both do it by undertaking different roles: the former temporarily limits competition by *imitation*, which incentivises rivals to compete by *substitution*.[757]

In view of this inescapable tension, it is important to recognise that, when both areas of law come into contact, each one of them may limit the reach of the other: whereas competition law has to tolerate some restrictions in the market, particularly in terms of competition by *imitation*, it may also impose constraints on what patentees can do with their patents.[758] In fact, identifying where exactly to draw the dividing line is probably one of the major challenges for competition agencies and courts. The next section describes the efforts undertaken by US and EU courts, legislators and scholars to that end.

753 Steven D Anderman and John Kallaugher, *Technology Transfer and the New EU Competition Rules: Intellectual Property Licensing after Modernisation* (OUP 2006) para 1.11.

754 *SCM Corp v Xerox Corp* 645 F 2d 1195, 1203 (2nd Cir 1981).

755 ibid.

756 Carl Shapiro, 'Competition and Innovation: Did Arrow Hit the Bull's Eye?' in Josh Lerner and Scott Stern (eds), *The Rate and Direction of Inventive Activity Revisited* (Univ of Chicago Press 2012) 363-64.

757 Drexl, 'Is There a "More Economic" Approach?' (n 745) 45.

758 Hovenkamp and others, *IP and Antitrust* (n 712) para 1.3b.

B. When is Competition Enforcement Warranted in the Intellectual Property Arena?

Despite their showing clear signs towards convergence, US' and EU's antitrust approaches vis-à-vis intellectual property rights have evolved someway differently, to a large extent due to their particular legal frameworks and jurisdictional and cultural backgrounds.[759] Because significant discrepancies still remain between both jurisdictions, it seems justified to break down the analysis and separately consider the path that each of them has followed in their efforts to strike a balance between the protection of intellectual property rights and the fostering of competition. The following paragraphs, hence, attempt to briefly depict the essential tools that courts and competition agencies have developed over time to unfold the entanglement.

I. The Scenario in the US

a. Evolution of the Interrelation between Antitrust and Intellectual Property

Since the enactment of the Sherman Act in 1890, the application of antitrust rules against intellectual property rights in the US has historically moved like a pendulum in search of the right balance.[760] In the early days, for instance, courts tended to solve the disputes strongly inspired by the 'freedom to contract' principle and granting an almost absolute deference to intellectual property holders,[761] yet the relation soon became much more hostile and, with the dawn of the Great Depression, a halo of suspicion hovered over most patent-related endeavours as their goals were increasingly perceived to be in tension with those of antitrust policy.[762] In

---

759 Mariateresa Maggiolino, *Intellectual Property and Antitrust: A Comparative Economic Analysis of US and EU Law* (Edward Elgar 2011) 207.

760 Hovenkamp and others, *IP and Antitrust* (n 712) para 1.3c.

761 Willard K Tom and Joshua A Newberg, 'Antitrust and Intellectual Property: From Separate Spheres to Unified Field' (1997) 66 Antitrust L J 167, 168-69. See, for instance, *Bement v National Harrow Co* 186 US 70 (1902) (where the Supreme Court ruled in favour of a price fixing agreement involving the licensing of patent rights).

762 FTC, 'To Promote Innovation' (n 718) ch 1, 15-16; Herbert Hovenkamp, 'IP and Antitrust Policy: A Brief Historical Overview' (2005) Univ Iowa Legal Studies

this context, the courts reacted by exploring new limits to the discretion of patent holders and expanding the reach of antitrust rules: it was during this period that they recognised that abuses in obtaining and in enforcing a patent could amount to an antitrust violation,[763] along with a vast number of different licensing practices.[764] Within the scope of the patent grant, it was argued, patent holders remained mainly unaffected, yet one step over the line and they became immediately subject to potential antitrust liability.[765] Therefore, in order to determine the circumstances under which antitrust laws should apply, courts mainly focused on identifying and condemning those conducts that could be considered to be beyond the scope of the patent[766]—a formalistic approach that seems to very much resemble the criteria that the CJEU developed a few decades later in the EU around the concept of 'specific subject-matter'.[767]

Around the mid-1970s, the perceived tension between patents and antitrust was gradually toned down. Firstly, a number of renowned scholars challenged the fundamental postulates of the approach in vogue and suggested that both bodies of law in fact share common, complementary goals.[768] The Supreme Court, on its turn, progressively modified its antitrust policy by limiting the use of *per se* rules in favour of a rule of reason and leaning towards a more economic analysis rather than the prior, more

---

Research Paper 05/31, 4 <http://ssrn.com/abstract=869417> accessed 14 February 2018.

763 *Walker Process Equipment Inc v Food Machinery & Chemical Corp* 382 US 172 (1965).

764 A paradigmatic example are the 'Nine No-No's' of intellectual property licensing: in 1970, the Deputy Assistant Attorney General of the DOJ's Antitrust Division gave a list of practices which were considered unlawful 'in virtually every context'. Bruce B Wilson, 'Patent and Know-How License Agreements: Field of Use, Territorial, Price and Quantity Restrictions' (Remarks Before the Fourth New England Antitrust Conference, 6 November 1970) 9.

765 Tom and Newberg (n 761) 172. See, in this regard, *Ethyl Gasoline Corp v United States* 309 US 436, 452 (1940); *United States v Line Material Co* 333 US 287, 308 (1948) ('[i]t is equally well settled that the possession of a valid patent or patents does not give the patentee any exemption from the provisions of the Sherman Act beyond the limits of the patent monopoly.').

766 See, eg, *United States v Univis Lens Co* 316 US 241, 251 (1942); *Line Material* (n 765) 310.

767 As a matter of fact, the Supreme Court even appears to have anticipated the existence-exercise dichotomy when, in a case involving cross-licensing arrangements, it stated that '[i]t is not the monopoly of the patent that is invalid. It is the use of that monopoly improperly.' *Line Material* (n 765) 310. For a description of the existence-exercise dichotomy in the EU, see text at nn 853ff.

768 Bowman (n 712) is a seminal work frequently cited in this regard.

formalistic approach.[769] Moreover, the creation of the Federal Circuit in 1982, with the aim of hearing all patent cases and delivering a more harmonised interpretation of the law, also offered a more reconciling view.[770] Similarly, the DoJ and the FTC relinquished the 'Nine No-No's'[771] and presented a renewed viewpoint with the release of the Guidelines for the Licensing of Intellectual Property in 1995, under the premises that intellectual property rights are essentially comparable to other forms of private property,[772] that they often do not accord market power[773] and that their licensing is 'generally procompetitive'.[774] Along similar lines, the Supreme Court more recently suggested in *Actavis* that IP and competition law should not be perceived as isolated bodies of law but should rather be applied as complementary instruments.[775]

Overall, the application of antitrust rules in the US is driven today by an updated economic framework,[776] which is often able to offer a more accurate—yet also more complex—answer to its interplay with intellectual property law. Against this backdrop, intellectual property rights are not seen as an 'exception' to the antitrust laws[777] and the existence of tort remedies under different areas of law is not pondered as necessarily precluding antitrust concern, 'for the public interest in competition is not necessarily vindicated by private tort remedies.'[778] At the same time, an-

---

769 See, eg, *Continental TV Inc v GTE Sylvania Inc* 433 US 36 (1977); *Broadcast Music Inc (BMI) v Columbia Broadcasting System (CBS)* 441 US 1 (1979).

770 See, eg, *Atari Games* (n 719) 1576 ('...the aims and objectives of patent and antitrust laws may seem, at first glance, wholly at odds. However, the two bodies of law are actually complementary, as both are aimed at encouraging innovation, industry and competition.').

771 Abbott B Lipsky Jr, 'Current Antitrust Division Views on Patent Licensing Practices' (1981) 50 Antitrust L J 515, 516-24 ('When one makes the analysis, one finds that the "Nine No-Nos,", as statements of rational economic policy, contain more error than accuracy.').

772 US Antitrust Guidelines for the Licensing of IP (n 747) para 2.1.

773 ibid para 2.2.

774 ibid para 2.0.

775 *Actavis* (n 720) 2231.

776 FTC, 'To Promote Innovation' (n 718) ch 1, 22.

777 *American Hoist & Derrick Co v Sowa & Sons Inc* 725 F 2d 1350, 1367 (Fed Cir 1984). See also *Re Independent Service Organizations Antitrust Litigation* 203 F 3d 1322, 1325 (Fed Cir 2000) ('Intellectual property rights do not confer a privilege to violate the antitrust laws.').

778 Phillip E Areeda and Herbert Hovenkamp, *Antitrust Law: An Analysis of Antitrust Principles and Their Application* (3rd edn, Aspen 2011) para 782a. In a similar

titrust is not normally perceived as a tool to correct all defects in intellectual property laws.[779]

b. Antitrust Immunity and the *Noerr* Doctrine

When examining the interface between antitrust and intellectual property under US law, some of the most important issues revolve around the *Noerr* immunity doctrine—especially when it comes to cases involving communications to different branches of the government. This doctrine, which emerged from that seminal Supreme Court judgment and which is also referred to as *Noerr-Pennington* or 'antitrust petitioning immunity', essentially refers to the set of principles that US courts have developed in order to protect private parties in their attempts to influence the passage or enforcement of laws, even if the law that they call for would produce restraints on trade.[780] Under the *Noerr* doctrine, thus, efforts to restrain trade by petitioning the government cannot constitute, as a rule, the basis for antitrust liability.[781]

In the famous *Noerr* case of 1961,[782] a group of railroad organisations had initiated a public campaign designed to encourage the adoption of laws against the trucking business and to disparage truckers among the general public, which prompted a group of truck operators to sue for conspiracy and monopolisation. The Supreme Court, however, considered that condemning such conducts could jeopardise the power of the government to take action and could raise important constitutional questions as

---

vein, see Rudolph J R Peritz, 'Competition Policy and its Implications for Intellectual Property Rights in the United States' in Steven D Anderman (ed), *The Interface Between Intellectual Property Rights and Competition Policy* (Cambridge Univ Press 2007) 193.

779 Herbert Hovenkamp, *The Antitrust Enterprise: Principle and Execution* (Harvard Univ Press 2005) 254. See also FTC, 'To Promote Innovation' (n 718) ch 1, 13 (stressing that mistaken antitrust enforcement may undermine the incentives that the patent system creates).

780 *Eastern Railroad Presidents Conference v Noerr Motor Freight Inc* 365 US 127, 135-36 (1961). For a systematic analysis of the doctrine, see FTC, 'Enforcement Perspectives on the Noerr-Pennington Doctrine: An FTC Staff Report' (2006) <www.ftc.gov/sites/default/files/documents/reports/ftc-staff-report-concerning-enforcement-perspectives-noerr-pennington-doctrine/p013518enfperspectnoerr-penningtondoctrine.pdf> accessed 14 February 2018.

781 *Allied Tube & Conduit Corp v Indian Head Inc* 486 US 492, 499 (1988).

782 *Noerr* (n 780).

well.[783] In this regard, it drew the attention to the *state action* doctrine[784] and highlighted that the right of petition is a freedom expressly recognised by the First Amendment.[785] In view of this, the court held that 'no violation of the Act can be predicated upon mere attempts to influence the passage or enforcement of laws'[786] and emphasised that it is irrelevant whether the sole purpose of the defendants is to destroy its competitors.[787] Shortly after *Noerr*, the Supreme Court extended the immunity beyond the legislative arena to the other branches of the government. First, in *Pennington*, it recognised that it also comprises lobbying the executive branch.[788] Later, in *California Motor Transport*, it held that the doctrine reached petitioning before courts and administrative agencies as well.[789]

Perhaps because these early cases were relatively straight-forward, the decisions did not seem to provide a clear doctrinal framework or offer any distinct guidelines for the lower courts.[790] In later cases, the Supreme

783 ibid 138.

784 ibid 136. In the landmark decision *Parker v Brown* which gave birth to the 'state action' doctrine, the Supreme Court had held that when restraints on trade are the result of a governmental action, as opposed to private action, antitrust laws are inapplicable. *Parker v Brown* 317 US 341, 350-51 (1943).

785 *Noerr* (n 780) 138. The First Amendment states that 'Congress shall make no law respecting an establishment of religion, or prohibiting the free exercise thereof; or abridging the freedom of speech, or of the press; or the right of the people peaceably to assemble, and to petition the government for a redress of grievances.'

786 ibid 135.

787 ibid 138-40.

788 *United Mine Workers of America v Pennington* 381 US 657 (1965). In this case, a miners' union and a group of large coal producers had lobbied the Secretary of Labor to establish a minimum wage that would impair smaller producers. The Supreme Court acknowledged that '[j]oint efforts to influence public officials do not violate the antitrust laws even though intended to eliminate competition.' Ibid 670.

789 *California Motor Transport Co v Trucking Unlimited* 404 US 508 (1972). In this case, the Supreme Court held that the right to petition extends to all departments of the Government, that '[t]he right of access to the courts is indeed but one aspect of the right of petition' and that the same rationale of *Noerr* and *Pennington* should govern the citizens's approaching to administrative agencies and courts. Ibid 510.

790 Marina Lao, 'Reforming the Noerr-Pennington Antitrust Immunity Doctrine' (2003) 55 Rutgers L Rev 965, 974.

Court admittedly attempted to shed some more light on the issue,[791] but a considerable number of questions still remain open.

In the first place, the doctrinal underpinnings on which the doctrine is grounded are not entirely clear hitherto. Whereas some argue that the immunity is rooted on the First Amendment,[792] others contend that it is exclusively a statutory construction, since petitioning is not the kind of conduct with which the antitrust laws are concerned.[793] The Supreme Court, for its part, has indiscriminately relied on one rationale or the other along its decisions,[794] which might suggest that the doctrine is actually based on both.[795] In any case, it should be noted that, although on the face of it this inquiry may seem purely theoretical, it can have significant effects in practice.[796] Indeed, while grounding the doctrine solely on constitutional principles probably implies that any conduct not covered by the right of petition can fall within the scope of antitrust scrutiny, a justification based on the Sherman Act is likely to lead to a more expansive reading of the immunity—thus excluding a larger number of conducts from the antitrust radar.[797]

Additional questions arise in connection with the scope and boundaries of the *Noerr* doctrine. At the outset, it is imperative to define what exactly

---

791 *Allied Tube* (n 781); *FTC v Superior Court Trial Lawyers Association (SCTLA)* 493 US 411 (1990); *City of Columbia v Omni Outdoor Advertising Inc* 499 US 365 (1991); *Professional Real Estate Investors Inc v Columbia Pictures Industries Inc* 508 US 49 (1993).

792 Daniel R Fischel, 'Antitrust Liability for Attempts to Influence Government Action: The Basis and Limits of the *Noerr-Pennington* Doctrine' (1977) 45 U Chi L Rev 80, 81; David McGowan and Mark A Lemley, 'Antitrust Immunity: State Action and Federalism, Petitioning and the First Amendment' (1994) 17 Harv J L & Pub Pol'y 293, 360-61.

793 Milton Handler and Richard A De Sevo, 'The *Noerr* Doctrine and Its Sham Exception' (1984) 6 Cardozo L Rev 1, 5.

794 *Noerr* (n 780) 136 (emphasising the 'essential dissimilarity' between lobbying and the type of conducts traditionally condemned by the Sherman Act); *California Motor Transport* (n 789) 510 (holding that the doctrine relies on the need to protect the governmental decision-making process and the right of petition); *SCTLA* (n 791) 424 (interpreting the Sherman Act in the light of the First Amendment's petition clause); *Omni* (n 791) 383 ('antitrust laws regulate business, not politics'); *PREI* (n 791) 56 ('the Sherman Act does not punish "political activity"').

795 Lao, 'Reforming the Noerr Doctrine' (n 790) 1002.

796 Stephen Calkins, 'Developments in Antitrust and the First Amendment: the Disaggregation of Noerr' (1988) 57 Antitrust L J 327, 330; McGowan and Lemley (n 792) 298.

797 Calkins (n 796) 330.

constitutes petitioning. The general rule is that 'no violation of the Act can be predicated upon mere attempts to influence the passage or enforcement of laws',[798] or upon conducts 'directed toward obtaining governmental action.'[799] Thus, it has been alleged that immunity is proffered to efforts to *convince* the government to do something, but not to those conducts that merely seek a ministerial response.[800] In those cases, it is argued, the results are in fact 'independent decisions' from private parties rather than a request for governmental action.[801]

Also connected to the boundaries of the antitrust petitioning immunity emerges the question as to the range of restraints that endure under the immunity umbrella: does it only comprise restraints produced by the governmental action sought after? Or does it also extend to restraints directly caused by private parties in their efforts to influence the government? Supreme Court case law appears to point at disparate directions. Under the *SCTLA* decision of 1990,[802] for instance, the court seemed to recognise that the principle was relatively straight-forward: antitrust immunity only protects restraints of trade which are a *consequence* of public action, but not when they are the *means* by which private parties seek to obtain favourable legislation.[803] Yet although it grounded its decision on *Noerr*, the fact is that immunity in that seminal case did extend to some of those *means*, provided that they could be considered an 'incidental effect' of the efforts to induce government action.[804] And the landscape becomes even cloudier when looking at *Allied Tube*,[805] where the Supreme Court gave *Noerr* a more nuanced reading and held that immunity does not really shield all

798 *Noerr* (n 780) 135.

799 ibid 140.

800 FTC, 'Enforcement Perspectives on the Noerr-Pennington Doctrine' (n 780) 18.

801 *Litton Systems Inc v American Telephone & Telegraph Co* 700 F 2d 785, 807 (2nd Cir 1983). For an analysis of this matter in the patent arena, see text at nn 1379ff in ch 6.

802 *SCTLA* (n 791). In this case, a group of lawyers had agreed to stop representing indigent defendants until their fees for doing so were increased.

803 ibid 424-25.

804 *Noerr* (n 780) 143. See also Einer Elhauge, 'Making Sense of Antitrust Petitioning Immunity' (1992) 80 Cal L Rev 1177, 1188 (arguing that the characterisation of *Noerr* in *SCTLA* was inaccurate, since *Noerr* did not involve only restraints caused by public action, but also restraints directly caused by private parties via the publicity campaign).

805 *Allied Tube* (n 781). In this case, a steel producer had packed the meeting of a private standard-setting association with new, bogus members in order to secure an electrical code that would exclude plastic manufacturers. Since such code was routinely adopted by a substantial number of state and local governments, the

means which are incidental, but only those which are 'incidental to a *valid* effort to influence governmental action.'[806] What exactly distinguishes a valid from an invalid effort, however, is nowhere to be found in this or other subsequent decisions and has elicited confusion among lower courts.[807]

Lastly, the most critical questions surrounding the antitrust petitioning immunity are probably those concerning its exceptions and limitations. The most widely recognised exception to this doctrine—and the only one explicitly acknowledged by the Supreme Court—is the 'sham exception', but a number of scholars, antitrust enforcers and case law suggest that it might not be the only one.

The 'sham exception' was established by the Supreme Court in *Noerr* itself and essentially refers to situations where private parties are not genuinely interested in the outcome of their petitioning. In that case, the court stated that petitioning might still justify the application of the Sherman Act when it is 'a mere sham to cover what is actually nothing more than an attempt to interfere directly with the business relationships of a competitor.'[808] In the years that followed, the concept of sham developed in the lower courts into a blanket concept to deny immunity to whatever forms of petitioning judges deemed improper,[809] but the Supreme Court has since warned against such an expansive reading and clarified that the sham exception is limited to 'situations in which persons use the governmental process itself—as opposed to the outcome of that process—as an anticompetitive weapon.'[810] This exception, thus, seems to be reserved to restraints imposed directly by the private parties in their (insincere) at-

---

steel producer invoked the *Noerr* immunity. The Supreme Court, however, held that *Noerr* was not absolute and that its scope, which depends on the source, context, and nature of the anticompetitive restraint, did not reach the conduct at issue.

806 ibid 499 (internal quotation and omitted) (emphasis added).

807 The Supreme Court had stated in that decision that the validity of those efforts 'varies with the context and nature of the activity.' Ibid 499. Then again, it is not clear which precise contexts and natures would be denied immunity. Calkins (n 796) 337. See also Elhauge, 'Making Sense of Antitrust Petitioning Immunity' (n 804) 1187.

808 *Noerr* (n 780) 144.

809 Calkins (n 796) 338-39; Elhauge, 'Making Sense of Antitrust Petitioning Immunity' (n 804) 1178; Lao, 'Reforming the Noerr Doctrine' (n 790) 967.

810 *Omni* (n 791) 380. See also *Allied Tube* (n 781) 507, fn 10 (the sham exception is limited to activities which are not 'genuinely intended to influence governmental action').

tempts to influence the government, but not to those imposed by the governmental action itself. Some years later, in *PREI*, the Supreme Court interpreted that proof of anticompetitive intent alone is not sufficient to find an antitrust violation and outlined a two-pronged test according to which, even before analysing the subjective intent, courts should first determine whether the petitioning activities were 'objectively baseless'.[811]

In addition to the 'sham exception', it has been argued that a separate exception to the *Noerr* immunity should be recognised for misrepresentations, ie situations where governmental action itself imposes restraints on trade but is triggered by from the deceitful conduct of a private party.[812] The Supreme Court had indeed suggested in earlier cases that misrepresentations could, under certain circumstances, result in an antitrust violation.[813] In *PREI*, however, where a 'sham exception' question was at issue, the Supreme Court specifically declined to provide an answer,[814] leaving the question open to this day.[815]

811 *PREI* (n 791) 60-61. For a more thorough analysis of the sham exception, see text at nn 1148ff in ch 6.

812 FTC, 'Enforcement Perspectives on the Noerr-Pennington Doctrine' (n 780) 22. A number of courts also deem misrepresentation as another exception to *Noerr*. See, eg, *St Joseph's Hospital Inc v Hospital Corp of America* 795 F 2d 948, 955 (11th Cir 1986); *Whelan v Abell* 48 F 3d 1247, 1255 (DC Cir 1995); *Nobelpharma AB v Implant Innovations Inc* 141 F 3d 1059, 1071 (Fed Cir 1998). Furthermore, a number of scholars also urge to recognise an exception for misrepresentations separate from sham. See, among others, Fischel (n 792) 106; C Douglas Floyd, 'Antitrust Liability for the Anticompetitive Effects of Governmental Action Induced by Fraud' (2001) 69 Antitrust L J 403, 410; Scott Filmore, 'Defining the Misrepresentation Exception to the Noerr-Pennington Doctrine' (2001) 49 Univ Kan L Rev 423, 443; Lao, 'Reforming the Noerr Doctrine' (n 790) 1022; James C Cooper and William E Kovacic, 'U.S. Convergence with International Competition Norms: Antitrust Law and Public Restraints on Competition' (2010) 90 Bost U L Rev 1555, 1605; Note, 'Deception as an Antitrust Violation' (2012) 125 Harv L Rev 1235. Against: *Armstrong Surgical Center Inc v Armstrong County Memorial Hospital* 185 F 3d 154, 160 (3rd Cir 1999); Handler and De Sevo (n 793) 47; James B Kobak Jr and Robert P Reznick, 'Antitrust Liability for Statements about Intellectual Property: Unocal, Unitherm and New Uncertainty' (2004) 19 Antitrust 87, 89-90.

813 *California Motor Transport* (n 789) 513; *Allied Tube* (n 781) 500.

814 *PREI* (n 791) 61, fn 6.

815 For a thorough analysis of the misrepresentation exception, see text at nn 1290ff in ch 6.

c. The Patent Misuse Doctrine

Another concept that has played a central role in shaping the boundaries of antitrust and patent law—although not so appreciably in the framework of deceptive behaviours at the patent office—is the patent misuse doctrine. This doctrine, which derives—as the inequitable conduct defence—from the equitable doctrine of unclean hands[816] and which does not seem to have a parallel in Europe,[817] has historically stood somewhere at the intersection between these two areas of law, originally stemming from the intellectual property system but incorporating numerous elements from traditional antitrust analysis along the way.[818]

In a nutshell, the patent misuse doctrine is an affirmative defence in patent litigation that proscribes patent holders from broadening 'the physical or temporal scope of the patent monopoly'.[819] The underlying rationale thus lies on the premise that 'the patentee may exploit his patent but may not use it to acquire a monopoly not embraced in the patent.'[820] If found, misuse renders the patent unenforceable until the misuse is purged[821]—in

---

816 *B Braun Medical Inc v Abbott Laboratories* 124 F 3d 1419, 1427 (Fed Cir 1997) ('… the patent misuse doctrine is an extension of the equitable doctrine of unclean hands, whereby a court of equity will not lend its support to enforcement of a patent that has been misused.'). See also *Morton Salt* (n 738) 492 ('It is a principle of general application that courts, and especially courts of equity, may appropriately withhold their aid where the plaintiff is using the right asserted contrary to the public interest.').

817 Dimitrios Riziotis, 'Patent Misuse als Schnittstelle zwischen Patentrecht und Kartellrecht: Eine Rechtsvergleichende Darstellung' [2004] GRUR Int 367. See also, however, Anne Flanagan, Federico Ghezzi and Maria Lillà Montagnani, 'The Search of EU Boundaries: IPR Exercise and Enforcement as "Misuse"' in Anne Flanagan and Maria Lillà Montagnani (eds), *Intellectual Property Law: Economic and Social Justice Perspectives* (Edward Elgar 2010) 126 (arguing that several potential sources are theoretically available to recognise a patent misuse doctrine in the EU).

818 Daryl Lim, *Patent Misuse and Antitrust Law: Empirical, Doctrinal and Policy Perspectives* (Edward Elgar 2013) 38.

819 *Blonder-Tongue Laboratories Inc v University of Illinois Foundation* 402 US 313, 343 (1971); *Windsurfing International Inc v AMF Inc* 782 F 2d 995, 1001 (Fed Cir 1986).

820 *Princo Corp v International Trade Commission* 616 F 3d 1318, 1327 (Fed Cir 2010) (en banc).

821 *Senza-Gel Corp v Seiffhart* 803 F 2d 661, 668 fn 10 (Fed Cir 1986).

that sense differing from inequitable conduct, which cannot be purged.[822] Under current patent litigation, misuse allegations are to be found mostly within the context of patent licensing,[823] eg in cases involving tying, bundling or demands for royalties beyond the patent term.

The origins of the patent misuse doctrine can be traced back to the Supreme Court's decision in the *Motion Picture Co* case of 1917,[824] in a period when antitrust laws still found themselves at an embryonic stage. In this case, the patentee held a patent on a mechanism for a movie projector and demanded licensees to bar the use of any film not manufactured by the patentee. The Court of Appeals found this restriction anticompetitive,[825] and the Supreme Court confirmed that it was invalid. Yet despite the obvious competitive concerns in its reasoning, the Supreme Court refused to rely on antitrust laws and instead based its decision on principles of patent policy,[826] stating that the conduct improperly expanded the scope of the patent.[827] In subsequent decisions, the Court continued developing this principle—particularly in *Morton Salt*, where it expressly held that patent misuse was an equitable principle entirely independent from antitrust law.[828] The scope of the doctrine was also broadened, most notably in *Mercoid*,[829] where the Court held that starting a contributory infringement suit could constitute patent misuse if the allegedly infringing product was not itself patented, even if it was a necessary element of a patented mechanism with no substantial non-infringing use.

Such expansive view on patent misuse raised concerns among scholars and in 1952 encouraged the Congress to limit its scope by identifying a number of circumstances that should not be considered misuse.[830] During the following years, the doctrine also gradually adopted elements of antitrust analysis and the trend was intensified during the 1970s, as a renewed economic approach gained attention and the focus shifted away from *per se* assessments and towards protecting competition rather than in-

---

822 The introduction of the Supplemental Examination procedure by the AIA, however, now seems to allow the purging of the inequitable conduct to a certain extent. See text at nn 279-281 in ch 3.

823 Marshall Leaffer, 'Patent Misuse and Innovation' (2010) 10 J High Tech L 142, 147; *Princo* (n 820) 1327.

824 *Motion Picture Patents Co v Universal Film Manufacturing Co* 243 US 502 (1917).

825 ibid 517.

826 Hovenkamp and others, *IP and Antitrust* (n 712) para 3.2a.

827 *Motion Picture Co* (n 824) 514.

828 *Morton Salt* (n 738) 490-92.

829 *Mercoid Corp v Mid-Continent Investment Co* 320 US 661 (1944).

830 Lim (n 818) 51-52.

dividual competitors.[831] In the following decades, the concepts of patent misuse and antitrust became yet more intertwined with the creation of the Federal Circuit in 1982[832] and a new amendment of the law in 1988, which required proof of market power in tying cases[833] and which the Federal Circuit took as an unequivocal message that misuse as a whole should be read under the light of antitrust principles.[834]

The Supreme Court's decision in *Kimble*,[835] however, did not seem to approve of this restrictive approach. In this case, the court was asked whether a patent holder was still barred from charging royalties for the use of an invention after its patent term has expired, as it had decided in *Brulotte*.[836] The claimant essentially argued that the referred holding should be overruled in favor of a case-by-case approach based on antitrust law's rule of reason.[837] However, the Supreme Court declined to do so adhering to the principle of *stare decisis*.[838] In doing so, the Supreme Court seems to have implicitly reinstated the approach based on patent policy, as laid down in *Morton Salt*, as the correct approach to patent misuse analysis.[839]

831 ibid 54-55.

832 *Windsurfing Int'l* (n 819) 1001 ('The doctrine of patent misuse is an affirmative defense to a suit for patent infringement ... and requires that the alleged infringer show that the patentee has impermissibly broadened the "physical or temporal scope" of the patent grant with anticompetitive effect.'). Chief Judge Markey himself, author of this decision, seemed to recoil soon after in *Senza-Gel* (n 821) 668 (evoking the Supreme Court stating that 'the patentee's act may constitute patent misuse without rising to the level of an antitrust violation.') but was not followed by later cases. Lim (n 818) 71.

833 § 271(d)(5) US Patent Act ('No patent owner otherwise entitled to relief for infringement or contributory infringement of a patent shall be denied relief or deemed guilty of misuse or illegal extension of the patent right by reason of his having ... conditioned the license of any rights to the patent or the sale of the patented product on the acquisition of a license to rights in another patent or purchase of a separate product, unless, in view of the circumstances, the patent owner has market power in the relevant market for the patent or patented product on which the license or sale is conditioned.').

834 Lim (n 818) 76; Mark D Janis, 'Transitions in IP and Antitrust' (2002) 47 Antitrust Bull 253. Indeed, in subsequent cases the Federal Circuit applied antitrust analysis in misuse cases not falling within § 271 of the US Patent Act. See, eg, *Mallinckrodt Inc v Medipart Inc* 976 F 2d 700 (Fed Cir 1992).

835 *Kimble v Marvel Entm't, LLC* 135 S Ct 2401 (2015).

836 *Brulotte v Thys Co* 379 US 29 (1964).

837 *Kimble* (n 835) 2408.

838 *Kimble* (n 835) 2406.

839 Daryl Lim, 'Revisiting the Patent Misuse Doctrine' in Josef Drexl (ed), *The Innovation Society and Intellectual Property* (Edward Elgar, forthcoming).

A number of commentators had long advocated for such a reading, highlighting the importance of retaining the patent misuse doctrine as a concept independent from antitrust law, at least for certain specific situations.[840] In this regard, these commentators essentially argue that misuse and antitrust do not necessarily have identical goals and that antitrust analysis might not be able to capture the entire range of policy concerns comprised in the misuse doctrine.[841] It has been suggested, for instance, that misuse comprises all practices that undermine patent policy by foreclosing innovation, competition or access to the public domain, even if they do not violate antitrust laws.[842] Furthermore, it is also argued that it might guarantee an optimal deterrence of antitrust violations, as it could even be used when conducts are anticompetitive in an economic sense 'but fall between the legislative cracks'.[843]

Other courts and commentators, however, have openly questioned the need for a patent misuse doctrine altogether.[844] On the one hand, for those cases where antitrust and misuse concerns in fact overlap, the question inevitably arises as to why holding a misuse doctrine at all. Its flexibility vis-à-vis antitrust does not appear to be sufficient reason, as invigorating antitrust scrutiny would probably constitute a more reasonable solution.[845] On the other hand, if misuse comprises behaviours which are not necessarily anticompetitive, it is not clear why those behaviours should be banned to any extent, let alone how uniform and coherent criteria can be defined beyond the reigning vagueness.[846] Such wide a scope might have been logical at a time when IP and antitrust were perceived as separate spheres,

840 Robert P Merges, 'Reflections on Current Legislation Affecting Patent Misuse' (1988) 70 J Pat & Trademark Off Soc'y 793; Note, 'Is the Patent Misuse Doctrine Obsolete?' (1997) 110 Harv L Rev 1922; Robin C Feldman, 'The Insufficiency of Antitrust Analysis for Patent Misuse' (2003) 55 Hastings L J 399; Leaffer (n 823) 147; Christina Bohannan, 'IP Misuse as Foreclosure' (2011) 96 Iowa L Rev 475; Lim (n 818) 418.

841 Feldman (n 840) 400.

842 Bohannan, 'IP Misuse as Foreclosure' (n 840) 526.

843 Hovenkamp, *The Antitrust Enterprise* (n 779) 273.

844 *USM Corp v SPS Technologies Inc* 694 F 2d 505, 511 (7th Cir 1982); Mark A Lemley, 'The Economic Irrationality of the Patent Misuse Doctrine' (1990) 78 Cal L Rev 1599; Thomas F Cotter, 'Four Questionable Rationales for the Patent Misuse Doctrine' (2011) 12 Minn J L Sci & Tech 457.

845 Cotter, 'Four Questionable Rationales for the Patent Misuse Doctrine' (n 844) 477.

846 Cotter, 'Four Questionable Rationales for the Patent Misuse Doctrine' (n 844) 470; *USM v SPS* (n 844) 510 (the misuse doctrine 'is too vague a formulation to be useful.').

when patents were presumed to grant market power and antitrust rules were applied in a much more formalistic fashion. Today, antitrust seems to be flexible enough to embrace the entirety of the policy concerns comprised in the misuse doctrine,[847] as it is acknowledged to have an active role not only in safeguarding competition, but also in fostering innovation. Against this backdrop, the existence of an auxiliary doctrine that suspects social costs without sound economic foundations seems much more questionable.

In any case, it should be noted that, although there have been attempts to invoke the patent misuse doctrine in cases involving fraud to the patent office, courts seem to be hesitant to admit it within this particular context.[848] Firstly, as the Federal Circuit specifically stated in an *en banc* decision in 2010, not any wrongful—or even anticompetitive—conduct necessarily configures a patent misuse.[849] But perhaps more importantly, the availability of a patent misuse defence in this context is unlikely to add much to the already broader inequitable conduct defence,[850] which configures a more attractive tool for defendants as it does not allow purging.

II. The European Approach

On the European side, the CJEU has strived to draw clear and workable lines with which to bring competition rules and intellectual property rights into harmony since its very early decisions, although it has not always found the task easy.[851] While sufficiently complex in itself, the analy-

---

847 *USM v SPS* (n 844) 511.

848 *CR Bard Inc v M3 Systems Inc* 157 F 3d 1340, 1373 (Fed Cir 1998) ('Although the law should not condone wrongful commercial activity, the body of misuse law and precedent need not be enlarged into an open-ended pitfall for patent-supported commerce.').

849 *Princo* (n 820) 1329 ('the defense of patent misuse is not available to a presumptive infringer simply because a patentee engages in some kind of wrongful commercial conduct, even conduct that may have anticompetitive effects. ... While proof of an antitrust violation shows that the patentee has committed wrongful conduct having anticompetitive effects, that does not establish misuse of the patent in suit unless the conduct in question restricts the use of that patent and does so in one of the specific ways that have been held to be outside the otherwise broad scope of the patent grant.').

850 Hovenkamp and others, *IP and Antitrust* (n 712) para 3.3i.

851 David T Keeling, *Intellectual Property Rights in EU Law Vol I: Free Movement and Competition Law* (OUP 2003) 51.

sis is rendered even thornier by the unique significance that market integration has had as an overriding goal for European competition law.[852] The following paragraphs analyse the most significant milestones in this regard.

a. Existence v Exercise Dichotomy

The CJEU's first attempt to reconcile intellectual property and competition consisted in distinguishing the existence of an intellectual property right from its exercise, a standard which was originally coined in the well-known *Consten and Grundig* decision of 1966.[853] In this case, Grundig, a German firm, had appointed Consten as its exclusive distributor in France and, to this end, had allowed it to register the trade mark GINT (Grundig International) in that country on its own name. As a result of this strategy, Consten was enabled to prevent in practice all parallel importation of Grundig's products into France. When the Commission ruled that the arrangement between Grundig and Consten constituted an infringement of art 101 TFEU, the parties appealed—among other grounds—on the basis of today's art 345 TFEU.[854] The French trade mark, they argued, had been legitimately granted under the French system of property ownership and could thus not be distorted by competition rules. The CJEU, however, confirmed the decision of the Commission and stated that the ruling 'does not affect the grant of those rights but only limits their exercise to the extent necessary to give effect to the prohibition under Article [101](1).'[855] Such remark shows the CJEU's caution in not trespassing the principle according to which, in the absence of harmonisation under EU law, the conditions governing the grant of intellectual property rights remain a matter exclusively for national laws.[856]

Shortly after this decision, the CJEU confirmed and further developed this standard in *Parke Davis*, where it stated that 'the existence of the rights

852 Richard Whish, *Competition Law* (8th edn, OUP 2015) 23-24; Valentine Korah, 'The Interface Between Intellectual Property and Antitrust: The European Experience' (2002) 69 Antitrust L J 801, 804.

853 Joined Cases 56 and 58/64 *Établissements Consten SàRL and Grundig-Verkaufs-GmbH v Commission* [1966] ECR 299.

854 Art 345 TFEU provides that '[t]he Treaties shall in no way prejudice the rules in Member States governing the system of property ownership.'

855 *Consten and Grundig* (n 853) 345.

856 Keeling (n 851) 57.

granted by a member state to the holder of a patent is not affected by the prohibitions contained in articles [101](1) and [102] of the treaty' and that 'the exercise of such rights cannot of itself fall … under article [102], in the absence of any abuse of a dominant position.'[857]

b. The Specific Subject-Matter Standard

The existence-exercise dichotomy drawn by the CJEU has been intensely criticised for constituting a vague, formal distinction without a sound underlying basis and mostly unhelpful in practice.[858] In this last regard, one of the main criticisms focused on the fact that the distinction left unanswered the crucial question as to in which specific circumstances the exercise of an intellectual property right could be considered abusive, hence signalling the need for supplementary criteria.[859] Against this backdrop, the CJEU attempted to shed some light by referring to the notion of the 'specific subject-matter' of the intellectual property right as a yardstick. In *Deutsche Gramophon v Metro*, a case concerning the freedom of movement of goods in the EU, the CJEU referred to the existence-exercise dichotomy and affirmed that derogations to that freedom are only admitted 'to the extent that they are justified for the purpose of safeguarding rights which constitute the specific subject-matter of such property.'[860] Some years later, in an effort to clarify the concept, the CJEU stated that the specific subject-matter of patents

> is the guarantee that the patentee, to reward the creative effort of the inventor, has the exclusive right to use an invention with a view to manufacturing industrial products and putting them into circulation for the first time, either directly or by the grant of licences to third parties, as well as the right to oppose infringements.[861]

---

857 Case 24/67 *Parke, Davis & Co v Probel* [1968] ECR 55, 72.

858 Keeling (n 851) 54; Valentine Korah, *Intellectual Property Rights and the EC Competition Rules* (Hart 2006) 3-4. Yet it has also been stated that most critics seem to ascribe the distinction ambitions that it never intended to have, as it did not mean to solve the entire universe of possible conflicts and should rather be taken as a starting point. Keeling (n 851) 61.

859 Keeling (n 851) 61.

860 Case 78/70 *Deutsche Grammophon GmbH v Metro-SB-Großmärkte GmbH* [1971] ECR 487, para 11.

861 Case 15/74 *Centrafarm BV v Sterling Drug Inc* [1974] ECR 1147, para 9.

The clarification, however, did not seem to advance the debate very far. On the one hand, the court left unclear whether the specific subject-matter referred to the policy reason for granting the patent or to its nature and scope.[862] Perhaps more significantly, critics emphasised that the test can be defined arbitrarily in every case in such a way that it determines *a priori* the result sougth.[863]

c. Current Stage of the Debate

Today, both standards have been virtually abandoned by the courts. The existence-exercise dichotomy had already been played down in several decisions following *Consten and Grundig*[864] and was clearly disregarded in *AstraZeneca*.[865] The specific subject-matter standard, on its turn, also fell in disgrace after the *Keurkoop v Nancy Kean Gifts* decision.[866] In a nutshell, this case referred to a firm who had copied and registered a design in Benelux without the authorisation of the original author and had later relied on it to stop the sale of similar products. It was, therefore, the perfect case to further develop specific subject-matter standard, its 'moment of truth',[867] although that would have probably forced the CJEU to recognise that an intellectual property right granted by a Member State was not worthy of protection.[868] Perhaps not ready to take such a courageous step, the CJEU did not even mention the standard in its decision and instead revert-

862 Valentine Korah, 'The Limitation of Copyright and Patents by the Rules for the Free Movement of Goods in the European Common Market' (1982) 14 Case W Res J Int'l L 7, 17.

863 ibid 19-20; Karen Banks and Giuliano Marenco, 'Intellectual Property and the Community Rules on Free Movement: Discrimination Unearthed' (1990) 15 E L Rev 224, 230.

864 Inge Govaere, *The Use and Abuse of Intellectual Property Rights in EC Law* (Sweet & Maxwell 1996) 168. An important decision in this regard is *Tetra Pak I*, where the Court of First Instance condemned the acquisition of an exclusive patent license by a dominant firm. Case T-51/89 *Tetra Pak Rausing SA v Commission* [1990] ECR II-309 (*Tetra Pak I*).

865 In this case, the Commission explicitly stated that the standard has 'gradually been abandoned in later case law'. Commission Decision in *AstraZeneca* (n 751) para 741. See also, in this connection, Katarzyna Czapracka, *Intellectual Property and the Limits of Antitrust: A Comparative Study of US and EU Approaches* (Edward Elgar 2010) 93-96.

866 Case 144/81 *Keurkoop BV v Nancy Kean Gifts BV* [1982] ECR 2853.

867 Banks and Marenco (n 863) 232.

868 Keeling (n 851) 70.

ed to the general principle according to which, in the absence of harmonisation, the conditions under which intellectual property protection is granted remain a matter for national law.[869] After this case, the specific subject-matter standard never fully recovered.[870]

Regrettably, subsequent decisions did not propose alternative criteria,[871] except perhaps for the vague distinction between 'legitimate' and 'improper' exercise of intellectual property rights[872] or the general yardstick of 'competition on the merits'.[873] In any case, what seems clear is that European competition law enforcers nowadays do not consider intellectual property rights to be immune from antitrust intervention.[874] The boundaries appear to be determined more by the constituent elements of the proscribed conduct than by the scope of the intellectual property rights.[875] Under the current practice of EU courts, not only the exercise of intellectual property rights can be challenged but also their very existence, and it is not necessary for the abusive behaviour to take place in the market.[876] For this reason, conducts like obtaining an exclusive license, acquiring a right or abusing administrative or judicial processes can amount to a breach of the EU competition law.[877] Even in situations where intellectual property laws themselves offer alternative remedies and try to strike a balance between public and private interests, antitrust intervention is usually still

869 *Keurkoop v Nancy Kean Gifts* (n 866) para 29. A similar approach was taken in *Thetford v Fiamma*, where the court refused to revise the UK patent system in force at that time, which allowed the grant of patents under the principle of relative novelty. Case 35/87 *Thetford Corp v Fiamma SpA* [1988] ECR 3585.

870 Banks and Marenco (n 863) 232; Keeling (n 851) 72. Yet it should be noted that cases like *AstraZeneca*, which is analysed below, seem to still find some inspiration from it. Commission Decision in *AstraZeneca* (n 751) para 742 ('AZ's conduct can hardly be described as belonging to the subject-matter of the rights in question. ... the making of misleading representations is not included in the bundle of rights forming part of the subject-matter of an SPC.').

871 Czapracka (n 865) 106.

872 Keeling (n 851) 73 (stressing the numerous concerns that it raised due to its ambiguity). Some scholars, however, seemed to consider it an adequate standard. See Friedrich-Karl Beier, 'Industrial Property and the Free Movement of Goods in the Internal European Market (1990) 21 IIC 131, 149-50.

873 Case C-62/86 *AKZO Chemie BV v Commission* [1991] ECR I-3359, para 70.

874 EU Guidelines on Technology Transfer Agreements (n 716) para 7.

875 Anderman, 'The IP and Competition Interface' (n 745) 24.

876 Commission Decision in *AstraZeneca* (n 751) para 328 and case law cited therein.

877 *Tetra Pak I* (n 864) para 23; Joined Cases C-395/96 P and C-396/96 P *Compagnie Maritime Belge Transports* v *Commission* [2000] ECR I-1365, paras 82-88; Case T-111/96 *ITT Promedia v Commission* [1998] ECR II-2937; Case C-457/10 P *AstraZeneca v Commission* (CJEU, 6 December 2012, ECLI:EU:C:2012:770).

considered justified, as the IP legislation might not be able to comprehensively take into account all the concerns in which the competition rules are inspired.[878]

Finally, it should be noted that EU courts and agencies at times conceive competition policy as a tool to correct imperfect intellectual property laws from the Member States.[879] Taking into account that most of those laws have not yet been fully harmonised, this might be viewed as advantageous from a community law perspective, yet caution is also required in order to avoid disrupting the internal coherence of the IP system.[880]

d. Is there a Petitioning Immunity Doctrine in Europe?

As a final point, it is important to consider whether EU law has developed any principles to protect private parties in their attempts to induce government action comparable to US' *Noerr* doctrine. On its face, no comparable immunity doctrine seems to exist in Europe and the case law on the matter is admittedly not as well established as in the US,[881] yet some analogous principles have been nevertheless developed. The Commission, for instance, has recognised that private parties' approaching public authorities in their own interest should not in itself amount to an infringement of competition law.[882] Furthermore, the Charter of Fundamental Rights of

878 Ghidini (n 726) 212 (despite of the synergic relationship, it is important to avoid attributing antitrust a *direct* role in promoting innovation and intellectual property rights a *direct* role in promoting competition); Keeling (n 851) 377-78 (since intellectual property law cannot examine whether effective competition in a particular market is being damaged as a result of the manner in which an exclusive right is being exercised, there seems to be a legitimate role for art 102 TFEU). Cf Govaere, *The Use and Abuse of IPRs in EC Law* (n 864) 305.

879 See, for instance, Case C-7/97 *Oscar Bronner v Mediaprint Zeitungs- und Zeitschriftenverlag* [1998] ECR I-7791, Opinion of AG Jacobs, para 63 ('[t]he ruling in Magill can in my view be explained by the special circumstances of that case ... the provision of copyright protection for programme listings was difficult to justify in terms of rewarding or providing an incentive for creative effort...').

880 Czapracka (n 865) 38; Lars Kjølbye, 'Article 82 EC as Remedy to Patent System Imperfections: Fighting Fire with Fire?' (2009) 32 World Competition 163.

881 Maggiolino (n 759) 190.

882 *French-West African Shipowners' Committees* (Case IV/32.450) Commission Decision 92/262/EEC [1992] OJ L134/1, para 68.

the EU expressly recognises the rights of petitioning and access to courts[883] and both the Commission and the General Court have acknowledged in the *ITT Promedia* case that 'it is only in wholly exceptional circumstances that the fact that legal proceedings are brought is capable of constituting an abuse of an dominant position.'[884] The CJEU subsequently came to a similar conclusion in *Huawei*, where it highlighted that the Charter of Fundamental Rights of the EU calls for a high level of protection for intellectual property rights and the right to effective judicial protection and that this 'means that, in principle, the proprietor may not be deprived of the right to have recourse to legal proceedings to ensure effective enforcement of his exclusive rights…'.[885] However, in that same case the CJEU also suggested that the fundamental right to legal redress must be balanced against the protection of competition, as certain circumstances may justify the imposition of limitations to those rights.[886]

Additionally, the CJEU clarified in *Compagnie Maritime Belge*[887] that conducts that merely seek a ministerial response from the government are entirely subject to competition law.[888] Likewise, the CJEU has also recognised that the submission of false or misleading information to public authorities can constitute a violation of competition rules.[889]

---

883 Charter of Fundamental Rights of the European Union [2012] OJ C 326/391, art 44 ('Any citizen of the Union and any natural or legal person residing or having its registered office in a Member State has the right to petition the European Parliament.'); art 47 ('Everyone whose rights and freedoms guaranteed by the law of the Union are violated has the right to an effective remedy before a tribunal…').

884 *ITT Promedia* (n 877) para 60. See also Case T-119/09 *Protégé International Ltd v Commission* [2012] OJ C319/6, para 48 ('l'accès au juge étant un droit fondamental et un principe général garantissant le respect du droit, ce n'est que dans des circonstances tout à fait exceptionnelles que le fait d'intenter une action en justice est susceptible de constituer un abus de position dominante au sens de l'article 82 CE.').

885 Case C-170/13 *Huawei Technologies Co. Ltd v ZTE Corp., ZTE Deutschland GmbH* (CJEU, 16 July 2015, ECLI:EU:C:2015:477) paras 57-58.

886 Ibid para 59.

887 *Compagnie Maritime Belge* (n 877) para 83 ('It is … unnecessary to consider whether, and in what circumstances, mere incitement of a government to take action may constitute abuse within the meaning of Article 86 of the Treaty').

888 ibid paras 81-83.

889 CJEU Decision in *AstraZeneca* (n 877) paras 93 and 99. In fact, in that case the CJEU also argued that even conducts that are deemed legal under a specific field of law may be considered anticompetitive. For a detailed analysis of this decision, see text at nn 977ff.

Finally, the Commission has attempted to define in *ITT Promedia* the circumstances under which sham or vexatious litigation can constitute an abusive behaviour and developed to that end a test which has also been employed by the General Court. According to this test, in order to determine in which cases the bringing of legal proceedings against a competitor can constitute an abuse, it is necessary to prove that the action

(i) cannot reasonably be considered as an attempt to establish the rights of the undertaking concerned and can therefore only serve to harass the opposite party, and
(ii) it is conceived in the framework of a plan whose goal is to eliminate competition.[890]

As can be observed, this two-step test very much resembles the sham litigation test developed by the US Supreme Court in *PREI*.[891]

2. *How can Deceptive Conducts before the Patent Office Affect Competition? The Experience and Challenges under US and EU law*

Having laid out the general framework on the interaction between intellectual property and antitrust, it is now possible to study how these two bodies of law interplay in the specific scenario that constitutes the essential object of this work: that which involves a deceptive behaviour before a patent office.

At the outset, it should be pointed out that this matter presents certain specific features that distinguish it from other discussions at the intersection of patent law and competition. Ordinarily, the focus is set on situations where both areas of law appear in tension, ie on ascertaining whether a specific behaviour that is legal under the eyes of patent law can nonetheless constitute a violation of the competition rules. Instead, in the cases at hand, the question is rather whether a conduct which might already be reprehensible from a patent law perspective[892] can also be condemned by

890 *ITT Promedia* (n 877) para 55; *Protégé* (n 884) para 49.
891 See text at n 811. For a more thorough analysis of the concept of sham, see text at nn 1148ff.
892 Indeed, as explained above, most patents obtained via deceptive demeanours are likely to be invalid, although it is also possible to conceive situations where, despite the existence of deceptive conduct, the invention still meets all patentability requirements. In those situations, the patent is likely to remain valid, al-

antitrust.[893] In principle, the fact that a conduct is condemned by patent laws should not present a major issue, since the existence of other tort remedies does not automatically exempt a specific conduct from antitrust scrutiny.[894] Remedies under different areas of law are likely to pursue different interests.[895] Moreover, hardly anyone could deny that deceptive conducts are socially undesirable and should be banned,[896] yet that alone is not sufficient to condemn every deceptive conduct as an antitrust violation.[897] Competition law is not about morality, but essentially about making sure that competition is not obstructed.[898] Thus, the essential question is whether deceptive conducts before the patent office cause the kind of anticompetitive harms that the competition rules are designed to go after.

Admittedly, the issue has been a long-standing concern under US antitrust law, with cases dating back to as early as 1965, whereas in Europe the question arose much more recently. What remains of this chapter is aimed at providing a synopsis of the most significant cases and reveal the at times converging, at times divergent approaches adopted on both sides of the Atlantic—thereby also laying the ground for Chapter VI to analyse in depth the questions that remain to be answered.

---

though it might be held unenforceable under US law based on the inequitable conduct doctrine. See text at nn 230ff in ch 3.

893 Christopher R Leslie, 'Antitrust, Inequitable Conduct, and the Intent to Deceive the Patent Office' (2011) 1 U C Irvine L Rev 323, 323.

894 Areeda and Hovenkamp, *Antitrust Law* (n 778) para 782a; Susan A Creighton and others, 'Cheap Exclusion' (2005) 72 Antitrust L J 975, 993; O'Donoghue and Padilla (n 750) 647.

895 O'Donoghue and Padilla (n 750) 647.

896 Josef Drexl, 'Deceptive Conduct in the Patent World: A Case for US Antitrust and EU Competition Law?' in Wolrad Prinz zu Waldeck und Pyrmont and others (eds), *Patents and Technological Progress in a Globalized World: Liber Amicorum for Joseph Straus* (Springer 2009) 139.

897 Harv L Rev note, 'Deception as an Antitrust Violation' (n 812) 1255. In this connection, the US Supreme Court has expressed the view that, in cases where a regulatory structure is already in place, the likelihood of major antitrust harm is diminished and the additional benefit to competition provided by antitrust enforcement is likely to be small. *Verizon Communications Inc v Law Offices of Curtis V Trinko, LLP* 540 US 398, 412 (2004).

898 See text at nn 492ff in ch 4.

A. *US Case Law. Fraud to the Patent Office and Misuse of Orange Book Listings*

In the US, deceptive conducts before the patent office were first addressed from an antitrust perspective in the Supreme Court's *Walker Process* decision of 1965. Since then, the decision has become a touchstone around which the doctrine has developed. Today, 'fraud to the patent office' constitutes one of the most popular antitrust defences in patent litigation together with the so-called *Handgards* or sham litigation claims[899]—although hardly ever are these antitrust defences successful.[900] The following paragraphs attempt to thoroughly explain how these antitrust doctrines have developed over time and conclude with an analysis of a series of more recent cases that have arisen in the context of Orange Book listings by patent applicants—and which provide the chance to put the underlying theories of harm under the microscope.

I. Walker Process and its Progeny

a. The *Walker Process* decision

The first case in which the US Supreme Court ruled on misleading behaviours before the patent office as possible antitrust violations was *Walker Process Equipment v Food Machinery & Chemical*.[901] In this case, Food Machinery had started a patent infringement action against Walker, who had in turn denied the infringement and counterclaimed that the patent was invalid. Since the patent had expired in the meantime, Food Machinery later made a motion to dismiss its complaint, but at that point Walker amended its counterclaim and accused the former of monopolisation, alleging that the patent had been fraudulently obtained and maintained. It argued that Food Machinery had sworn before the USPTO that it neither knew nor believed that the invention had been in public use for more than one year before the filing date when, in fact, it had been itself selling the invention before that date. It further argued that the existence of such

899 David R Steinman and Danielle S Fitzpatrick, 'Antitrust Counterclaims in Patent Infringement Cases: A Guide to Walker Process and Sham-Litigation Claims' (2001) 10 Tex Intell Prop L J 95, 95.

900 ibid 99; Joel Davidow, *Patent-Related Misconduct Issues in US Litigation* (OUP 2010) 118.

901 *Walker Process* (n 763).

patent had deprived Walker of business that it would have otherwise enjoyed and grounded its suit on the patent misuse doctrine: if using a valid patent to extend the protection on an unpatented product was considered illegitimate, then securing protection on an unpatentable product by a fraudulently obtained patent should also be.[902]

The district court, however, considered that Walker was attempting to use the issue of fraud to indirectly achieve what it could not do directly, since according to earlier case law only the US Government could 'annul or set aside' a patent based on fraud.[903] The district court thus rejected the antitrust counterclaim and the Court of Appeals later confirmed that decision, highlighting the lack of case law on the matter.[904] Against this context, the Supreme Court proposed a novel approach to the quandary and, without overruling the earlier case law, concluded that 'the enforcement of a patent procured by fraud on the Patent Office may violate of § 2 of the Sherman Act provided that the other elements necessary for a § 2 case are present.'[905]

To reach this conclusion, the Supreme Court first argued that Walker's claim was not barred by earlier case law, since it was based on antitrust laws rather than patent law and fraudulent procurement was only one of its elements.[906] It emphasised in this regard that defendants in patent infringement suits were already permitted to raise defences based on fraudulent procurement when invoking inequitable conduct and that allowing antitrust claims against said conducts could further promote the purposes of the inequitable conduct doctrine.[907]

When looking at the crux of the matter, the Supreme Court opened with the premise that patents are ordinarily exempted from antitrust laws and approached the issue in terms of whether such an exemption would be apposite in this particular case. To answer the question, the court held that proof that a patent has been obtained 'by knowingly and wilfully misrepresenting facts to the Patent Office' would be 'sufficient to strip [the paten-

---

902 *Food Machinery & Chemical Corp v Walker Process Equipment Inc* 335 F 2d 315, 316 (7th Cir 1964).

903 ibid 316. This rule had been allegedly acknowledged as a means to protect patentees from vexatious suits by defendants. B D Daniel, 'Walker Process Proof: The Proper Prescription' (2009) 41 Rutgers L J 105, 118.

904 *Walker Process* (Court of Appeals) (n 902) 316.

905 *Walker Process* (n 763) 174.

906 ibid 176.

907 ibid 176-77 (1965) (quoting reasoning given in *Precision Instrument*; see text at n 172 in ch 3).

tee] of its exemption from the antitrust laws.'[908] It further specified that, by the same token, patent assignees who maintain and enforce a patent 'with knowledge of the patent's infirmity' would also be stripped from their exemption.[909] On the other end of the spectrum, it stated that proof of good faith would provide a complete defence.[910]

The decision also included a much-cited concurring opinion by J Harlan. While entirely agreeing with the conclusions of the majority, J Harlan warned against an extensive interpretation that could affect patents 'that for one reason or another may turn out to be voidable under one or more of the numerous technicalities attending the issuance of a patent'.[911] As such a reading could have chilling effects on the disclosure of inventions, he continued, no antitrust case should be made out of a mere finding of invalidity, eg due to obviousness or 'technical fraud'. Even if the fraudulent behaviour is proven, the opinion concluded, no antitrust violation could exist if the assignee had no knowledge thereof.[912]

In any event, the Supreme Court majority reminded that stripping a patent of its exemption from antitrust laws only constitutes a first step in the antitrust analysis and refused to see the behaviour as a *per se* violation. The court observed that, to establish an antitrust violation, all other elements of § 2 Sherman Act should be present, including the exclusionary power of the concerned patent and the definition of the relevant market.[913]

At first glance, the conclusions of the decision seem to be relatively clear and precise, yet a closer look reveals a number of unsettled questions. In the first place, it is not entirely clear whether the patent misuse doctrine played any role in the case: the antitrust plaintiff had made it an essential part of the claim, but the Supreme Court does not seem to rely on it to reach its conclusion.[914] Most significantly, the decision does not explain how the *Noerr* petitioning immunity fits into the puzzle. While the decision in *Walker Process* was issued only four years after *Noerr*, the Supreme Court does not even mention it among its considerations—despite the fact

908 ibid 177.
909 ibid 177, fn 5.
910 ibid 177.
911 ibid 180.
912 ibid 179.
913 ibid 177-78.
914 While it is true that the decision cites a patent misuse decision, it appears to do so for merely illustrative purposes. Ibid 176.

that applying for a patent clearly constitutes an act of petitioning the government.[915]

Additional questions also arise in connection with the kind of deceptive conduct that needs to be shown to make an antitrust case. The majority speaks, in rather vague terms, of knowing and wilful misrepresentation of facts to the patent office, thus possibly suggesting that any misrepresentation could open the door for an antitrust analysis. The concurring opinion attempted to shed some light by listing a handful of circumstances that should not be considered relevant from an antitrust perspective, yet the boundaries of the reproachable conduct were still imprecise.[916]

Last, but certainly not least, the decision does not provide much of a guidance as to the underlying theory of harm that informed its reasoning. On the one hand, it seems to rely on a prevailing assumption at that time: patents are exempted from the antitrust laws as long as the patentees' behaviour remains within the patent scope, whereas any step beyond the line makes them automatically subject to antitrust liability.[917] On the other hand, it is not entirely clear whether the anticompetitive harm flows from the fraud at the patent office or from maintaining and enforcing the fraudulently obtained patent, and in the latter case whether the behaviour before the patent office is indeed meaningful. At parts, the decision focuses exclusively on the deceptive behaviour before the patent office,[918] but the conclusions suggest that it might rather be 'the enforcement of a patent procured by fraud' which triggers antitrust concerns.[919] What is more, the Supreme Court stated that assignees who maintain and enforce a patent 'with knowledge of the patent's infirmity' can also be anticompetitive, which might actually downplay the relevance of the fraud element altogether. In this regard, there does not seem to be much of a difference from an antitrust perspective between an assignee who enforces a patent with knowledge of a fraudulent procurement and a patentee or assignee who, despite an immaculate procurement, later finds out that the patent is invalid (eg, due to the emergence of an old piece of prior art) and nonethe-

915 Hovenkamp and others, *IP and Antitrust* (n 712) para 11.2b.

916 Raymond P Niro and J William Wigert Jr, 'Patents, Fraud and the Antitrust Laws' (1968) 37 Geo Wash L Rev 168, 176.

917 See text at n 765.

918 *Walker Process* (n 763) 177 (proof that a patentee 'obtained the patent by knowingly and willfully representing facts to the Patent Office … would be sufficient to strip [the patentee] of its exemption from the antitrust laws').

919 ibid 174.

less seeks to enforce it. In both cases, the parties would be maintaining and enforcing a right knowing that it is vitiated.[920]

b. The *Walker Process* Legacy

As stated earlier, *Walker Process* has become over the years one of the most often raised antitrust defences in US patent litigation. The Supreme Court, however, has not rendered any further decision on the issue ever since and the lower courts have sometimes struggled to cope with the questions that were left open.

In the first place, it is not yet clear how the *Noerr* immunity doctrine applies (or not) to these particular behaviours. The Supreme Court has had the chance to clarify it in subsequent decisions, but explicitly refused to do so.[921] Some lower courts have then ventured to suggest that misrepresentations in adjudicatory procedures—like patent applications—simply constitute a subset of the sham exception recognised in *Noerr*.[922] The Supreme Court case law, however, does not seem to allow such a view, since it has traditionally thought of sham as a narrow concept, limited to situations where the anticompetitive harm is caused by the governmental process it-

920 Ned L Conley, 'Considerations in Patent Litigation Brought About by Walker Process Equipment, Inc v Food Machinery & Chemical Corp' (1966) 9 S Tex L J 9, 13 ('the *Walker* decision might well be considered to be authority for finding an antitrust violation even in a case where there was no fraud on the Patent Office. For example, if, after the patent issues, the patentee learns that the patent is invalid, either for public use or for some other reason, and despite this he attempts to enforce the patent monopoly, the courts may well apply the reasoning in *Walker* and find this to be an attempt to enforce an illegal monopoly.'). See also Hovenkamp, *The Antitrust Enterprise* (n 779) 267 ('… the "intellectual property" content of Walker Process claims is easily exaggerated. The basis of the claim is that the antitrust defendant went to court or threatened to do so on a nonmeritorious claim. It in fact knew or should have known that the patent was invalid or unenforceable.').

921 *PREI* (n 791) 61, fn 6 ('In surveying the "forms of illegal and reprehensible practice which may corrupt the administrative or judicial processes and which may result in antitrust violations," we have noted that "unethical conduct in the setting of the adjudicatory process often results in sanctions" and that "[m]isrepresentations, condoned in the political arena, are not immunized when used in the adjudicatory process." We need not decide here whether and, if so, to what extent *Noerr* permits the imposition of antitrust liability for a litigant's fraud or other misrepresentations.') (citations omitted).

922 *Kottle v Northwest Kidney Centers* 146 F 3d 1056, 1060-61 (9th Cir 1998).

self rather than its outcome.[923] Others considered that *Walker Process* existed in a sort of 'patent-antitrust eddy' of its own, independent of the *Noerr* line of cases.[924] The Federal Circuit and the FTC have both provided a more sensible interpretation, stating that sham litigation and misrepresentations actually constitute two different alternatives on which a patentee may be stripped of its *Noerr* immunity.[925]

With respect to the kind of deceptive conducts before the patent office that can configure an antitrust violation, lower courts have consistently relied on the elements of common law fraud and adapted them to this particular scenario.[926] Accordingly, *Walker Process* claims are required to show the following elements:

> (1) a representation of a material fact, (2) the falsity of that representation, (3) the intent to deceive or, at least, a state of mind so reckless as to the consequences that it is held to be the equivalent of intent (scienter), (4) a justifiable reliance upon the misrepresentation by the party deceived which induces him to act thereon, and (5) injury to the party deceived as a result of his reliance on the misrepresentation.[927]

As for the materiality element, ie the patent office's reliance upon the misrepresentation, J Posner has elaborated on the topic and argued that only 'but-for' materiality would justify antitrust intervention and that no an-

---

923 *Omni* (n 791) 380.

924 James B Kobak Jr, 'Professional Real Estate Investors and the Future of Patent-Antitrust Litigation: *Walker Process* And *Handgards* Meet *Noerr-Pennington*' (1994) 63 Antitrust L J 185, 193.

925 *Nobelpharma* (n 812) 1071 ('Each provides its own basis for depriving a patent owner of immunity from the antitrust laws; either or both may be applicable to a particular party's conduct in obtaining and enforcing a patent. The Supreme Court saw no need to merge these separate lines of cases and neither do we.'); FTC, 'Enforcement Perspectives on the Noerr-Pennington Doctrine' (n 780) 22-23 ('There are instances in which parties may mislead government decision makers in an attempt to secure government action that harms competition. Such misrepresentations differ from traditional sham activities, such as the initiation of baseless litigation, in that the purpose of making the misrepresentations likely *is* to obtain government action.').

926 *Norton Co v Carborundum Co* 530 F 2d 435, 444-45 (1st Cir 1976); *Nobelpharma* (n 812) 1069. Cf Daniel (n 903) 156 (In *Walker Process*, the Supreme Court made no reference whatsoever either to "common law fraud" or to the elements of "common law fraud." … the Supreme Court's decision … affirmatively precludes any incorporation of elements from the common law cause of action.').

927 *Norton v Curtiss* 433 F 2d 779, 793 (CCPA 1970) (internal citations omitted).

titrust case should be made if the invention was nevertheless patentable.[928] Indeed, if the invention is patentable, it should not matter from an antitrust perspective how pristine or dishonest the patentee was in obtaining the patent.[929] The decision provides the example of a patent granted on a patentable invention to a person other than the real inventor, contending that the effect of that patent on the market 'is no greater than it otherwise would be just because the person exercising the rights is not the one entitled by law to do so.'[930] This reasoning has proved influential among other courts.[931]

Also related to the nature of the fraud necessary to support a *Walker Process* claim, the Federal Circuit had attempted to shed some light by distinguishing it from the conduct required in inequitable conduct cases and emphasising that '[t]o demonstrate *Walker Process* fraud, a claimant must make higher threshold showings of both materiality and intent than are required to show inequitable conduct.'[932] Furthermore, the Federal Circuit had highlighted that the 'sliding scale' employed in inequitable conduct cases[933] was not applicable in antitrust suits.[934] Subsequently, however, the Federal Circuit rendered an *en banc* decision in *Therasense* which has considerably heightened the inequitable conduct standards, asserting that 'but for' should be the governing materiality standard and ruling out the 'sliding scale'.[935] Therefore, although *Therasense* does not address *Walker Process*

928 *Brunswick Corp v Riegel Textile Corp* 752 F 2d 261, 265 (7th Cir 1984).

929 ibid.

930 ibid.

931 Kobak, 'PREI and the Future of Patent-Antitrust Litigation' (n 924) 198.

932 *Dippin' Dots Inc v Mosey* 476 F 3d 1337, 1346 (Fed Cir 2007). In a frequently cited passage, the Federal Circuit has claimed that '[i]nequitable conduct is … an equitable defense in a patent infringement action and serves as a shield, while a more serious finding of fraud potentially exposes a patentee to antitrust liability and thus serves as a sword.' *Nobelpharma* (n 812) 1069.

933 See text at nn 252-253 in ch 3.

934 *Dippin' Dots* (n 932) 1348 ('Weighing intent and materiality together is appropriate when assessing whether the patentee's prosecution conduct was inequitable. However, when *Walker Process* claimants wield that conduct as a "sword" to obtain antitrust damages rather than as a mere "shield" against enforcement of the patent, they must prove deceptive intent independently.') (internal citations omitted).

935 *Therasense Inc v Becton, Dickinson & Co* 649 F 3d 1276, 1290-91 (Fed Cir 2011) (en banc). See text at nn 243-248 and 252-253 in ch 3.

claims or antitrust, the differences in practice between these two standards might not be as sharp anymore.[936]

Finally, the most significant question mark that hovers over the courts as regards *Walker Process* claims is probably the one that refers to the underlying theory of harm. On one side of the spectrum, some have interpreted that *Walker Process* is actually a case of antitrust liability for inducing governmental action via misrepresentations.[937] In that event, the anticompetitive harm would flow from the decision of the government to mistakenly grant a patent due to the fraudulent conduct of the applicant and the impact that the granted patent has on the market. Yet one court has argued that, because the patent should have a 'colourable validity', its mere existence might not be sufficient to deter competitors and that some additional activity from the patentee might be required.[938] That same court also recognised, however, that a showing of enforcement is not indispensable because, after all, 'the concern of section 2 is with exclusion of competition, not with the particular means of exclusion.'[939]

On the other side of the spectrum, the prevailing reading of *Walker Process* today seems to consider that the antitrust offence consists not solely on the fraudulent behaviour before the patent office, but also on the enforcement of the fraudulently obtained patent. The Ninth Circuit, for instance, interpreted that, without some effort to enforce, the patent cannot serve as the foundation for a monopolisation case.[940] The Federal Circuit later embraced this reading[941] and in a subsequent decision confirmed that it is the *enforcement* of a patent procured by fraud, rather than the fraud itself, that

936 Herbert Hovenkamp, 'Patent Exclusions and Antitrust after *Therasense*' (2011) U Iowa Legal Studies Research Paper 11/39, 34 <http://ssrn.com/abstract=1916074> accessed 14 February 2018.

937 *Woods Exploration & Producing Co Inc v Aluminum Co of America* 438 F 2d 1286, 1295 (5th Cir, 1971) ('plaintiffs' basic claim is that the applicable production allowable formula which the state would have intended to utilize was subverted to the injury of plaintiffs by defendants' filing of false nomination forecasts. The situation is analogous to the filing of fraudulent statements with the Patent Office, which has been held to be evidence of an antitrust violation.'). Along the same lines, see L Barry Costilo, 'Antitrust's Newest Quagmire: The Noerr-Pennington Defense' (1967) 66 Mich L Rev 333, 348-50; Floyd (n 812) 422; Lao, 'Reforming the Noerr Doctrine' (n 790) 977.

938 *Brunswick* (n 928) 265-66.

939 ibid 266.

940 *California Eastern Laboratories Inc v Gould* 896 F 2d 400, 403 (9th Cir 1990).

941 *Cygnus Therapeutic Systems v Alza Corp* 92 F 3d 1153, 1161 (Fed Cir 1996).

can amount to an antitrust offence.[942] To that end, it stated that the standards developed for declaratory judgment actions 'also define the minimum level of "enforcement" necessary to expose the patentee to a *Walker Process* claim.'[943] More recent cases have clarified that said 'enforcement' does not necessarily require the patentee to initiate legal actions, but can also be configured, eg, by sending letters to competitors' customers notifying them of the existence of the patent.[944]

It is worth stressing at this point that, under the latter interpretation, the role played by the fraud element seems to be rather minor. As explained above, it is hard to see much of a difference from an antitrust perspective between (i) maintaining and enforcing a fraudulently procured patent, and (ii) maintaining and enforcing a patent known to be invalid, even if the prosecution was carried out in good faith, eg because the patentee only later became aware of the cause of invalidity. The focus here seems to be on maintaining and enforcing a patent knowing of its invalidity, and the fraud at the patent office would be just one of a ream of reasons why the patentees may be aware of it. In any case, it should also be acknowledged that, under this reading, the antitrust harm still seems to flow from the deterrent effect caused by the existence of the patent and its use by the patentee: if a patentee knowingly maintains and enforces an invalid patent while competitors are unaware—or unsure—of its invalidity, such circumstance itself can delay or dissuade the latter from entering or staying in a particular market.

c. The *Handgards* or 'Bad Faith Litigation' Antitrust Claim

Together with *Walker Process*, the other most common antitrust defence in US patent infringement cases is the *Handgards* or 'bad faith litigation' claim.[945] Both have similar origins and share some of their defining elements, yet the antitrust harm induced in each of them seems to be somewhat different.

---

942 *Unitherm Food Systems Inc v Swift-Eckrich Inc* 375 F 3d 1341, 1357-58 (Fed Cir 2004), revd on other grounds 546 US 394 (2006).

943 ibid 1358 ('In other words, if the patentee has done nothing but obtain a patent in a manner that the plaintiff believes is fraudulent, the courts lack jurisdiction to entertain either a Declaratory Judgment Action or a *Walker Process* claim.').

944 *Hydril Co LP v Grant Prideco LP* 474 F 3d 1344, 1350 (Fed Cir 2007).

945 Steinman and Fitzpatrick (n 899) 95.

The *Handgards* case,[946] which gives name to this antitrust defence, had started with an unsuccessful patent infringement suit, where the court had concluded that the patent was invalid due to the existence of a 'prior public use'. The alleged infringer thence filed an antitrust action initially invoking *Walker Process*, but the grounds of the complaint were revised when no proof of fraud at the patent office was found and a 'bad faith' theory was asserted instead. According to the antitrust plaintiff, the patentee had attempted to monopolise the relevant market by bringing a patent infringement action knowing that the patent was invalid, among other reasons, because the patentee had become aware that the defendants themselves had made a prior public use of the invention. The Court of Appeals confirmed that, by the time of the infringement suit, the patentee was aware that the patent was invalid and that this behaviour may constitute a violation of § 2 Sherman Act. In this regard, it stated that such a finding would configure a case of 'sham' that would exempt the patentees of the immunity that they would otherwise enjoy for petitioning the courts.[947]

It has been argued that a *Handgards* claim does not essentially differ from *Walker Process*, as both cases involve the enforcement of an invalid patent with an anticompetitive effect.[948] The *Walker Process* decision had indeed included a statement that very much resembles the offence in *Handgards*.[949] Yet in *Handgards*, the anticompetitive harm does not appear to be exactly the same, as it seems to flow not from the exclusionary effect of a patent whose invalidity is unknown by the general public, but rather from the harassing behaviour of the patentee. As a matter of fact, *Handgards* claims may be based not only on the enforcement of a patent known to be invalid, but also on the enforcement of a valid patent known not to be infringed,[950] thus evidencing that the focus is not set on the exclusionary effect of the patent but on the abusive use of the judicial system.

---

946 *Handgards Inc v Ethicon Inc* 601 F 2d 986 (9th Cir 1979) (*Handgards I*); *Handgards Inc v Ethicon Inc* 743 F 2d 1282 (9th Cir 1984) (*Handgards II*).

947 *Handgards II* (n 946) 1294-95.

948 Hovenkamp and others, *IP and Antitrust* (n 712) para 11.1 ('there is essentially no economic justification for treating *Walker Process* and *Handgards* claims differently.'); S W O'Donnell, 'Unified Theory of Antitrust Counterclaims in Patent Litigation' (2004) 9(8) Va J L & Tech 1, 45 ('It is difficult to see how the *Handgards* claim, based upon *Walker Process*, differs so radically from its progenitor that it implicates a completely different standard of analysis.').

949 The Supreme Court had stated that the conclusion reached in that decision 'applies with equal force to an assignee who maintains and enforces the patent with knowledge of the patent's infirmity.' *Walker Process* (n 763) 177, fn 5.

950 *Loctite* (n 717) 877.

In fact, the same anticompetitive harm is conceivable even in the absence of a patent, eg if the plaintiff attempts to enforce a trade secret[951] or, even outside the intellectual property sphere, if she initiates any kind of baseless court action.[952] The anticompetitive harm here does not flow from the exclusionary effects of an IP right, but rather consist on the plaintiff's harassing, deterring or delaying competitors through the petitioning activities—and not through the outcome of that petitioning, ie the governmental act. In other words, *Handgards* cases seem to be just the equivalent of sham litigation in patent infringement cases.[953]

II. Orange Book Cases

Within the highly regulated pharmaceutical industry, a series of cases have emerged which, although not directly taking place before the patent office, also concern deceptive conducts involving patent rights and raise very interesting questions in that regard. These cases refer to the complex system put in place by the Hatch-Haxman Act and, more particularly, to the inappropriate listing of patent rights in the so-called Orange Book run by the FDA.[954]

By way of background, under the Hatch-Waxman Act each company filing an NDA with the FDA in order to market a new drug in the US is also required to submit a list of the patents that it holds protecting the drug or methods of using such drug 'and with respect to which a claim of patent infringement could reasonably be asserted if a person not licensed by the owner engaged in the manufacture, use, or sale of the drug.'[955] Such list is then included by the FDA in what is commonly known as the Orange Book. If, subsequently, another company seeks approval of a generic version of that same drug, it must file an ANDA certifying that (i) no patent has been listed for that drug, (ii) the patent has expired, (iii) the patent will

951 *CVD Inc v Raytheon Co* 769 F 2d 842, 851 (1st Cir 1985) ('the assertion in bad faith of trade secret claims, that is, with the knowledge that no trade secrets exist, for the purpose of restraining competition does not further the policies of either the antitrust or the trade secrets laws.') (citations omitted).

952 See, eg, *Landmarks Holding Corp v Bermant* 664 F 2d 891, 896 (2nd Cir 1981) (where a firm initiated a series of court and administrative actions designed to delay the construction of a competitor's shopping mall).

953 O'Donnell (n 948) 22.

954 The publication is officially referred to as the list of 'Approved Drug Products with Therapeutic Equivalence Evaluations'.

955 21 USC § 355(b).

expire prior to the first sale; or (iv) the patent is invalid or will not be infringed.[956] In the latter case, which is commonly known as a 'Paragraph IV' certification, the NDA applicant must give notice to the patent owner,[957] who then has 45 days to bring an infringement action.[958] If said action is brought, the generic drug application at the FDA is automatically stayed for 30 months, unless the patent expires or is invalidated or declared not infringed before that period ends.[959]

Within this rather complex framework, a significant number of antitrust cases arose in the US—the most frequently cited ones referring to 'reverse payment' or 'pay-for-delay' settlement agreements.[960] Yet a different sort of antitrust cases, deeply connected to the theme of the present work, also developed when a number of generic companies complained that several NDA applicants had listed patents in the Orange Book knowing that those patents were invalid or would not be infringed. From the cases that emerged around this issue, the most frequently cited one is *In re Buspirone*,[961] where Bristol-Myers Squibb had listed a newly-obtained patent on the Orange Book in connection with buspirone only one day before the expiration of the patent originally listed and allegedly knowing that the new patent would not be infringed. When generic producers later attempted to obtain a market approval under a Paragraph IV certification, Bristol-Myers Squibb immediately brought infringement suits, thereby triggering the 30-month stay. The generic producers thus brought an antitrust complaint, which Bristol-Myers Squibb moved to dismiss essentially alleging that its activities constituted lawful petitioning immunised under the *Noerr* doctrine.

At the outset, the district court highlighted that, for the *Noerr* doctrine to apply, the conduct under analysis should first qualify as petitioning activity. To that end, it is important to distinguish between situations where the government acts only after an independent review of the merits of the decision and cases where the intervention of the government is merely ministerial or non-discretionary and directly relies on the private parties' representations. In the latter event, the court argued, the conduct of the private party does not really amount to petitioning and the *Noerr* doctrine

956 21 USC § 355(j)(2)(A)(vii).
957 21 USC § 355(j)(2)(B).
958 21 USC § 355(j)(5)(B)(iii).
959 21 USC § 355(j)(5)(B)(iii).
960 See, in this regard, the recent of the Supreme Court in *Actavis* (n 720) attempting to shed some light on the debate.
961 *Re Buspirone Patent Litigation* 185 F Supp. 2d 363 (SD New York 2002).

is thus not applicable.[962] On this basis, the court interpreted that the act of listing a patent in the Orange Book is not in fact an act of petitioning, since it merely seeks a ministerial response and the FDA has practically no margin for discretion.[963] And even assuming that *Noerr* was applicable, the court concluded that the listing and the subsequent litigation constituted clear cases of misrepresentation and sham that warranted an exception to immunity.[964]

Around the same time, a case also arose before the District Court of New Jersey which presented a relatively similar set of facts.[965] Not surprisingly, the court relied to a great extent on *In re Buspirone* and stated that listing a patent in the Orange Book does not amount to petitioning within the meaning of *Noerr*, since the FDA serves in that connection a purely ministerial function.[966] Interestingly, though, the analysis did not end at that point: even if the activities were not immunised against antitrust scrutiny, the court interpreted that the listings in this case did not violate any antitrust law because, at the time of listing the patent, the NDA applicant had a reasonable basis to believe that it could be infringed.[967] The court made it clear, thus, that, although requests merely seeking a ministerial response from the government are not immunised by *Noerr*, something more still needs to be shown in order to make an antitrust case.

Finally, an interesting decision dealing with Orange Book filings was also issued by another judge from the Southern District of New York in *Twin City Bakery Workers*.[968] The facts did not differ much from the above mentioned cases, yet in this one the judge held that the only possible exclusionary effect of an Orange Book listing was the 45-day delay in the FDA approval of the generic drug until the NDA applicant decides whether to sue or not. Since in this case the NDA applicant had made the contested patent listing at a time when the initial—and presumably valid—patent was still listed and not close to expiring, the court reasoned that the new listing did not lead to an extension of the exclusivity, as that

962 ibid 369-70. The court cites in this regard *Litton* (n 801), a leading case on this distinction, where the court had interpreted that tariff filings before the Federal Communications Commission do not constitute petitioning under *Noerr*. *Litton* (n 801) 807.

963 *Re Buspirone* (n 961) 371.

964 ibid 373-75.

965 *Organon Inc v Mylan Pharmaceuticals Inc* 293 F Supp 2d 453 (D NJ 2003).

966 ibid 458-59.

967 ibid 459-60.

968 *Twin City Bakery Workers v Astra Aktiebolag* 207 F Supp 2d 221 (SD NY 2002).

same delay would already have been triggered by the initial patent. According to the court, the 30-month stay is not the result of the Orange Book listing, but rather of the patentees' having commenced infringement lawsuits—activities which would be clearly protected under *Noerr*.[969]

This latter decision has been criticised by the FTC, who essentially contends that antitrust laws are in fact capable of condemning an action that causes an anticompetitive effect even if it is presented in conjunction with some other action that is beyond its reach.[970] As a matter of fact, when NDA applicants in other cases had argued that the Orange Book listings were an integral part of the (immunised) infringement suits, courts had pointed out that listings were distinct from the filing of the infringement suits, as the former do not *per se* affect the merits of the latter.[971] Moreover, it would also be possible to argue that the mere listing in the Orange Book might have an exclusionary effect on their own among competitors, aware as they are—even before any infringement suit is started—that the 30-month stay is available for the NDA applicant and will be automatically triggered with the sole filing of an infringement suit.

In any case, it should be reminded that placing these filings outside the scope of the antitrust immunity doctrine only constitutes the first step of the antitrust analysis. Evidently, not every filing seeking a ministerial response from the government should be banned by antitrust laws. The challenge is, thus, to determine in which specific cases those 'non-petitioning' activities can actually amount to an antitrust violation.[972]

B. EU Competition Law. Improper Acquisition of Intellectual Property Rights. Impact on Member States' Competition Practice

Although the history of European competition law had started with a strict differentiation between existence and exercise of intellectual property rights which virtually immunised the former from antitrust scrutiny, subsequent decisions gradually blurred the distinction and the bold approach was progressively relativized.[973] In *Tetra Pak I*, for instance, EU courts had decided that the acquisition of an exclusive patent licence by a dominant

969 ibid 225.

970 FTC, 'Enforcement Perspectives on the Noerr-Pennington Doctrine' (n 780) 21, fn 87.

971 *Re Buspirone* (n 961) 372; *Organon v Mylan* (n 965) 459.

972 For a more thorough analysis of this question, see text at nn 1379-1390.

973 See text at nn 864-880.

firm could amount to a competition law violation.[974] Moreover, in a dispute between Osram and Airam that concluded with a settlement between the parties, the Commission had expressed the opinion that registering a trade mark in bad faith, knowing that that mark is already used by a competitor, could infringe art 102 TFEU.[975] It was only in the *AstraZeneca* case, however, at the dawn of the new millennium, that EU courts for the first—and thus far only—time dealt with deceptive conducts before intellectual property offices as a source of competitive concern. Until then, EU case law on the interface of intellectual property and competition law had fundamentally concentrated on refusal to licence questions.[976] The following paragraphs hence describe the *AstraZeneca* case in detail, as well as the impact that it has had so far among national competition agencies.

I. The AstraZeneca Case

At the outset, it is interesting to point out that the facts and specific legal issues discussed in the *AstraZeneca* case were of a transitory nature and, hence, unlikely to arise again in the future.[977] Nevertheless, the case bears particular significance as it raises a number of crucial questions concerning the strategic use of patenting and other administrative procedures as po-

---

974 *Tetra Pak I* (n 864). Admittedly, that case did not deal with 'original' but with 'derivative' acquisition of rights, besides focusing on the acquisition itself rather than on the procedure for acquiring. Dirk Seidel, *Europäische Missbrauchsaufsicht nach AstraZeneca: Fallrelevante Problemkreise unter besonderer Berücksichtigung des Konfliktfeldes Immaterialgüter-/Wettbewerbsrecht* (Shaker 2008) 14.

975 Commission, Eleventh Report on Competition Policy 1981, para 97 (*Airam/ Osram*).

976 Case C-238/87 *AB Volvo v Erik Veng (UK) Ltd* [1988] ECR 6211; *Magill* (n 748); Case C-418/01 *IMS Health GmbH & Co OHG v NDC Health GmbH & Co KG* [2004] ECR I-5039; Case T-201/04 *Microsoft Corp v Commission* [2007] ECR II-3601. Interestingly, when the AstraZeneca case emerged, some scholars even wondered whether the criteria that had been developed in the context of refusal to license cases should also be applicable to the AstraZeneca case. Jacques-Philippe Gunther and Charlotte Breuvart, 'Misuse of Patent and Drug Regulatory Approval Systems in the Pharmaceutical Industry: An Analysis of US And EU Converging Approaches' (2005) 26 Eur Comp L Rev 669, 680.

977 Josef Drexl, '*AstraZeneca* and the EU Sector Inquiry: When do Patent Filings Violate Competition Law?' in Josef Drexl and Nari Lee (eds), *Pharmaceutical Innovation, Competition and Patent Law: A Trilateral Perspective* (Edward Elgar 2013) 291.

tential competition law violations and for the first time brings them forward to the EU courts.

In essence, the *AstraZeneca* decisions address two different types of conducts, both connected to Losec. Losec is an omeprazole-based pharmaceutical product launched by AstraZeneca in Europe at the end of the 1980s,[978] principally aimed at treating acid-related gastro-intestinal diseases and conditions. In 1999, two generic companies lodged a complaint contending that AstraZeneca had abused its dominant position by preventing them to bring generic versions of the product to a number of European markets.[979] In general terms, they argued that the company had (i) misled several national patent offices in order to obtain or unduly extend SPCs for the active ingredient omeprazole, and (ii) adopted an abusive strategy when switching from capsule to tablet formulations of Losec.

In 2005, after an extensive investigation, the Commission concluded that AstraZeneca had indeed infringed art 102 TFEU and imposed a 60 million euro fine.[980] The decision was subsequently appealed, but the General Court,[981] the Advocate General[982] and the CJEU[983] all essentially agreed with the Commission and confirmed both the infringement and the fine—although the latter was slenderly reduced because the effects on parallel imports had not been shown in certain markets.[984] The decisions of the Commission and the courts can all be divided into three essential parts: they begin by addressing the question of market definition and its dominance, followed by a separate analysis of each of the two abuses.

a. Market Definition and its Dominance

Although defining relevant markets and determining market dominance are issues that exceed the scope of this work, the AstraZeneca case raises interesting questions in this regard that should not go overlooked. Firstly, because it is the first time that European institutions address this matter in

978 As a matter of fact, the product was launched by Astra AB, which later merged with the Zeneca Group and formed AstraZeneca.

979 Commission Decision in *AstraZeneca* (n 751) paras 1-2.

980 ibid paras 913-24.

981 Case T-321/05 *AstraZeneca v Commission* [2010] ECR II-2805.

982 Case C-457/10 P *AstraZeneca v Commission* (CJEU, 6 December 2012, ECLI:EU:C:2012:293), Opinion of AG Mazák.

983 CJEU Decision in *AstraZeneca* (n 877).

984 GC Decision in *AstraZeneca* (n 981) paras 840-62.

the pharmaceutical sector within the framework of art 102 TFEU.[985] And perhaps most importantly, because a finding of market dominance constitutes a crucial issue under EU competition law in cases like the one at hand, as abuses can only be sanctioned when they stem from a firm who is already dominant on the market.[986]

As mentioned above, this case revolves around the active ingredient omeprazole, a so called proton pump inhibitor (PPI) for the treatment of acid-related gastro-intestinal diseases. Together with the H2 blockers, PPIs belong to the group of medicines which proactively inhibit the acid secretion into the parietal cells of the stomach, which is pumped by a specific enzyme normally known as the proton pump.[987] But whereas H2 blockers merely block some of the stimulants of the enzyme, PPIs act in a more direct way by inhibiting the enzyme itself. Omeprazole, which was launched at the end of the 1980s under the Losec brand, was the pioneer PPI and it was only during the 1990s that other PPIs entered the market—all containing molecules similar to omeprazole.[988] The first H2 blockers, on the other hand, had been launched considerably earlier, around the 1970s.[989]

Within this framework, the first step was to determine the relevant market in which Losec was immersed. To that end, it is important to take into consideration that competition in the pharmaceutical sector presents a number of special features that make it different it from other industries, particularly due to the high degree of market regulation and the fact that the consumers (patients) are neither the decision-makers nor the ones typically bearing the costs.[990] Against this background, EU competition enforcers tend to focus, in practice, on the function of the drugs to define the relevant market, thus ordinarily employing the third level of the WHO's Anatomical Therapeutic Chemical Classification System (ATC), which looks at their therapeutic indication.[991] In the present case, however, the Commission opted for the fourth level, which looks at the drug's mode of action, and therefore concluded that, in the period relevant for its assess-

---

985 Johanna Müller-Graff and Filipe Fischmann, 'Der Fall AstraZeneca: "Tool boxes" in Arzneimittelsektor – Wer hat die Bessere Werkzeuge und Welche sind Erlaubt? Zum Urteil des Gerichts der Europäischen Union vom 1. Juli 2010, Rs. T-321/05' [2010] GRUR Int 2010 792, 794.

986 See text at nn 670ff in ch 4.

987 Commission Decision in *AstraZeneca* (n 751) para 34.

988 ibid para 36.

989 Frances Murphy and Francesco Liberatore, 'Abuse of Regulatory Procedures: The AstraZeneca Case' (2009) 30 Eur Comp L Rev 223, 223.

990 Commission Decision in *AstraZeneca* (n 751) para 362.

991 ibid para 371.

ment (ie, between 1993 and 2000), the relevant product market was conformed exclusively by PPIs and that H2 blockers did not inflict significant competitive constraints.[992] In order to reach this conclusion, which both the General Court and the CJEU shared, the Commission highlighted the fundamental differences between PPIs and H2 blockers,[993] as well as the differences in price,[994] and interpreted that the shift in sales from H2 blockers towards PPIs during the relevant period had been slow largely due to inertia in prescribing practices.[995] According to the Commission and the courts, the gradual shift was not inconsistent with the finding of a separate market for PPIs,[996] but rather constituted a sign of the scant competitive constraints that H2 blockers were able to impose on them.[997] On a different note, the Commission also concluded that supply-side substitutability should not be taken into account.[998]

In view of the narrow market definition, which has been fiercely criticised by a number of scholars and practitioners,[999] it came as no surprise that AstraZeneca was found to enjoy a dominant position in the PPI mar-

992 ibid para 504.

993 ibid paras 380-86 (PPIs yield superior results and constitute the only effective remedy against a significant number of diseases); GC Decision in *AstraZeneca* (n 981) para 72.

994 Commission Decision in *AstraZeneca* (n 751) para 401; GC Decision in *AstraZeneca* (n 981) para 165.

995 Commission Decision in *AstraZeneca* (n 751) para 467.

996 ibid paras 388 and 467; GC Decision in *AstraZeneca* (n 981) para 96; CJEU Decision in *AstraZeneca* (n 877) para 48.

997 Commission Decision in *AstraZeneca* (n 751) paras 388-97. The General Court and the CJEU speak in this regard of 'asymmetrical substitution'. GC Decision in *AstraZeneca* (n 981) para 96; CJEU Decision in *AstraZeneca* (n 877) para 59.

998 Commission Decision in *AstraZeneca* (n 751) para 403 (essentially due to the long period required to develop new pharmaceutical products).

999 See, among others, David Hull, 'The Application of EU Competition Law in the Pharmaceutical Sector' (2011) 2 J Eur Comp L & Prac 480 (a narrow market definition represents a risk for new products); Jacob Westin, 'Defining Relevant Market in the Pharmaceutical Sector in the Light of the Losec-Case: Just How Different is the Pharmaceutical Market?' (2011) 32 Eur Comp L Rev 57, 60 (too narrow market definitions, especially concerning innovative products, not only risk being counterproductive but also stifle innovation); Ilaria Ottaviano, 'Industrial Property and Abuse of Dominant Position in the Pharmaceutical Market: Some Thoughts on the AstraZeneca Judgment of the EU General Court' in Giandonato Caggiano, Gabriella Muscolo and Marina Tavassi (eds), *Competition Law and Intellectual Property: A European Perspective* (Wolters Kluwer 2012) 197-98 (the temporary competitive advantage of an innovative drug compared to the methods of alternative treatment does not seem adequate to justify the con-

ket. This inference was already insinuated by AstraZeneca's market share, which during the relevant period had always remained over 50% and in most cases well above 70%,[1000] yet other factors were also taken into consideration. Based on the premise that the primary threat for Losec is the one stemming from generic omeprazole, it was interpreted that AstraZeneca enjoyed a particularly strong patent protection, which in practice implied a virtually unavoidable entry barrier.[1001] Even the alternative source of threat, derived from the other PPIs that subsequently entered the market, had played in practice a minor role, also thanks to AstraZeneca's robust patent portfolio.[1002] Also mentioned as influential factors were the first mover advantages[1003] and the inertia in doctor's prescribing behaviour that hindered alternative PPIs' market penetration.[1004] AstraZeneca had argued that, in any case, the particular features of the pharmaceutical industry left firms very little room for manoeuvre, which diminished the relevance of market dominance, but the Commission was of a different opinion.[1005] As a matter of fact, AstraZeneca had been able to maintain high prices during a large period of time[1006] and was, in practice, the sole undertaking in a position to implement an exclusionary strategy.[1007]

sideration of that drug as an autonomous market); Adrian Spillmann, 'Transparency Obligation for Holders of EU IP Assets in the Pharmaceutical Industry' (2014) 9 J Intell Prop L & Prac 125, 127 (it would have been fairer to acknowledge a common product market for H2 blockers and PPIs in the beginning of the relevant period, and only accept a separate product market once the superiority of the PPIs was clearly established).

1000 Commission Decision in *AstraZeneca* (n 751) para 567; GC Decision in *AstraZeneca* (n 981) para 253.

1001 Commission Decision in *AstraZeneca* (n 751) para 526; GC Decision in *AstraZeneca* (n 981) para 271.

1002 Commission Decision in *AstraZeneca* (n 751) paras 521-25.

1003 ibid para 541; GC Decision in *AstraZeneca* (n 981) para 278.

1004 Commission Decision in *AstraZeneca* (n 751) para 542; GC Decision in *AstraZeneca* (n 981) para 278.

1005 Commission Decision in *AstraZeneca* (n 751) paras 553-61.

1006 ibid paras 544-48; GC Decision in *AstraZeneca* (n 981) para 261.

1007 Commission Decision in *AstraZeneca* (n 751) para 528.

b. The First Abuse

AstraZeneca's first abuse referred to a deceptive handling of SPC applications before the national patent offices of Germany, Belgium, Denmark, Norway, the Netherlands and the United Kingdom.

The SPC regime had been introduced in the EU in 1992 as a means for compensating pharmaceutical firms for the delays that regularly occur between the filing of a patent application and the date the medicinal product is finally authorised to enter the market.[1008] In a nutshell, an SPC is a sui generis right[1009] that extends the duration of a patent and confers essentially the same rights, yet its scope is limited to the product covered by the market authorisation that suffered the delays.[1010] As to its duration, it compensates delays between the patent's filing date and the date of the first market authorisation exceeding five years, although the total duration of an SPC itself cannot go beyond five years.[1011]

Importantly for the case at hand, when the SPC Regulation entered into force, it was aimed to be applied not only to future products but also to a large range of products which were already on the market[1012]—a decision which may be seen as rather arbitrary.[1013] According to the transitional provisions, those products which were already on the market were still eligible for SPC protection provided that they had obtained their 'first authorization to place it on the market as a medicinal product in the Community' after 1 January 1985.[1014] Some countries, however, had managed to negotiate tailored transitional provisions on the grounds of internal public

---

1008 Council Regulation (EEC) 1768/92 of 18 June 1992 concerning the creation of a supplementary protection certificate for medicinal products [1992] OJ L182/1 (Old SPC Regulation, subsequently amended by Regulation (EC) 469/2009). Such delays, the regulation specifies, make the period of effective patent protection 'insufficient to cover the investment' and in practice penalise pharmaceutical research. See text at nn 125-132 in ch 2.

1009 Katarzyna Zbierska, *Application and Importance of Supplementary Protection Certificates for Medicinal Products in the European Union* (Shaker 2012) 40.

1010 Regulation (EC) 469/2009 of 6 May 2009 concerning the supplementary protection certificate for medicinal products [2009] OJ L152/1, arts 4-5 (SPC Regulation).

1011 SPC Regulation, arts 13(1) and (2).

1012 Zbierska (n 1009) 250-51 (certain countries had advocated for a regime to only reward future products, but ultimately the view of the Commission prevailed).

1013 See Drexl, 'Deceptive Conduct in the Patent World' (n 896) 155 (arguing that the retroactive effect of this provision does not seem to incentivise innovation).

1014 Old SPC Regulation 1768/92, art 19.

health issues.[1015] In this sense, SPCs could only be obtained in Denmark and Germany if the first market authorisation had been obtained after 1 January 1988, whereas Italy and Belgium went in the opposite direction and admitted SPCs for products that had obtained their first market authorisation already in 1982.[1016] The SPC Regulation was later incorporated into the EEA Agreement, where Finland and Norway joined the '1988 countries' and Austria became a '1982 country'.[1017]

Having been launched on the European market by the end of the 1980s, Losec was one of the products to which the transitional provisions applied when the SPC regime entered into force. The patents protecting omeprazole had been filed before the EPO and different national patent offices in 1979 and were due to expire in the course of 1999.[1018] Its first technical market authorisation, however, had been issued in France in 1987, which suggested that AstraZeneca might not be entitled to obtain SPCs in the '1988 countries'. In this context, and taking into consideration that, in many countries, product registrations are not considered complete—and products cannot be launched—until the price negotiations are concluded,[1019] the company decided to try out a novel interpretation of the SPC regime and instructed its patent agents to submit the SPC applications declaring March 1988 as the first relevant authorisation in the EU.[1020] March 1988 was, in this regard, the date of publication of a list of authorised products in Luxembourg, which AstraZeneca believed to be the first 'effective' marketing date in the Community.[1021] For the sake of consistency,[1022] the strategy was implemented not only in the '1988 countries', but also in the '1982' and '1985 countries'. It should be kept in mind that, until then, courts had not defined the concept of 'first authorisation'; it was only in 2003 that the CJEU clarified that the term refers solely to the technical market authorisation and not to other authorisations such as those referring to pricing or reimbursement.[1023]

1015 Zbierska (n 1009) 251.
1016 Old SPC Regulation 1768/92, art 19.
1017 Decision of the EEA Joint Committee 7/94 of 21 March 1994 amending Protocol 47 and certain Annexes to the EEA Agreement [1994] OJ L160/1, Annex 15.
1018 Commission Decision in *AstraZeneca* (n 751) paras 20-21.
1019 ibid para 166-68. In France itself, for instance, the product had only been introduced to the market in 1989. Ibid para 171.
1020 ibid para 173.
1021 ibid.
1022 ibid para 180.
1023 Case C-127/00 *Hässle AB v Ratiopharm GmbH* [2003] ECR I-14781, para 79.

The general practice of national patent offices when receiving SPC applications was to rely, without verification, on the information submitted by the applicants with regard to the first market authorisation.[1024] Therefore, when in 1993 and 1994 AstraZeneca set in motion its strategy, many patent offices proceeded to grant AstraZeneca's SPC, although the course of events was not in any way smooth.[1025] In some countries, for instance, the patent agents did not follow AstraZeneca's instructions and refused to use Luxembourg's price list: while some of them relied on France's first technical market authorisation,[1026] others, unaware of the latter date, relied instead on Luxembourg's first technical authorisation—even though it was clearly not the first one in the EU.[1027] In other countries, the patent office itself questioned AstraZeneca's attempt or revoked the SPC following complaints lodged by competitors.[1028] And even in those countries where the SPC had been granted, competitors later started court actions that eventually resulted on the respective SPCs being revoked.[1029] It is also important to point out that, at some point during the implementation of its strategy, AstraZeneca had become aware that Luxembourg's price list was in fact a private publication,[1030] irrelevant for the commercialisation of Losec,[1031] yet it did not reveal this information to all patent offices concerned.[1032]

Against this background, the Commission interpreted that AstraZeneca had developed a 'pattern of misleading misrepresentations' in order to acquire SPCs to which it was not entitled, or to which it was only entitled for a shorter period, and concluded that said behaviour constituted a violation of art 102 TFEU.[1033] Both the General Court[1034] and the CJEU later confirmed such findings.[1035] In essence, the abuse was divided into two

1024 Commission Decision in *AstraZeneca* (n 751) para 154.
1025 ibid paras 185-245.
1026 ibid paras 194 and 208.
1027 The General Court further highlights that AstraZeneca did not subsequently intervene at those patent offices to rectify the SPCs. GC Decision in *AstraZeneca* (n 981) para 594.
1028 Commission Decision in *AstraZeneca* (n 751) paras 209-15 (United Kingdom), 218 (Ireland), 219 (Denmark).
1029 ibid paras 227 (Germany), 234 (Norway).
1030 GC Decision in *AstraZeneca* (n 981) para 497.
1031 CJEU Decision in *AstraZeneca* (n 877) para 92.
1032 ibid paras 88-92.
1033 Commission Decision in *AstraZeneca* (n 751) para 626.
1034 GC Decision in *AstraZeneca* (n 981) para 609.
1035 CJEU Decision in *AstraZeneca* (n 877) paras 100 and 113.

tute a *carte blanche* to use any means imaginable to obtain the right it believed it was entitled to.[1046]

A particularly relevant factor in that respect was the margin of manoeuvre enjoyed by the authorities concerned. In the view of the CJEU, every case should be analysed *in concreto*,[1047] because misleading representations before public authorities to obtain an exclusive right can only constitute an abuse if, in view of the specific circumstances of the case, those representations are actually liable to lead them to grant the right applied for.[1048] In this case, the margin of manoeuvre enjoyed by the different patent offices was particularly limited,[1049] as they relied in practice on the information provided by the applicants without further verification.[1050] AstraZeneca's conduct, thus, was indeed liable to lead them to grant the exclusive rights. The CJEU, however, tried to make clear that this conclusion does not imply that dominant firms need to be infallible in their dealings with all public authorities.[1051] The CJEU hence seemed to suggest that the broader the margin of manoeuvre of the public authorities, the narrower the burden on the petitioner.

As to the market impact of AstraZeneca's, the Commission highlighted that an extra SPC protection in practice prevents market entry by all potential competitors,[1052] which in the end also affects national health systems and consumers.[1053] Those exclusionary effects are caused by the mere existence of the SPC, particularly considering that IPRs are presumed valid,[1054] even if in practice some generic firms ignored the SPCs.[1055] For this very reason, the General Court stated that the enforcement of the improperly obtained IPR is not a necessary requirement to attain anticompetitive effects on the market[1056]—which somehow seems to call into question the prevailing view of US courts. The General Court further pointed out that

1046 ibid para 98.
1047 ibid para 99.
1048 ibid para 106.
1049 ibid para 105.
1050 Commission Decision in *AstraZeneca* (n 751) para 680.
1051 ibid para 99.
1052 ibid para 762.
1053 ibid paras 771-72.
1054 ibid paras 762 and 765.
1055 ibid para 767.
1056 GC Decision in *AstraZeneca* (n 981) para 362. In that connection, the General Court argued that the *ITT Promedia* decision, which deals with vexatious litigation, in fact addresses a different problem and its conclusions are not applicable to the present case.

the fact that alternative remedies under different areas of law could—and in fact did—limit the effects of the exclusionary strategy did not exclude the existence of an abuse.[1057]

The CJEU, seemingly agreeing with the conclusions of the Commission and the General Court as to the anticompetitive effects, paid particular attention to the question as to their materialisation. As it was mentioned above, the pattern of deceptive conducts fundamentally took place between 1993 and 1994, whereas the SPCs applied for were expected to enter into force only in 1999, upon the expiry of the basic patents. In the interim, most SPCs were either rejected by the patent offices, revoked by the patent offices or struck down by the courts, which effectively meant that, by the time the basic patents expired, most SPCs had already been eliminated. On this particular issue, the CJEU held that 'the existence of an abuse is not affected by the fact that the strategy did not succeed in some countries.'[1058] On the one hand, in those countries where the SPCs had been rejected from the start, it was deemed sufficient to demonstrate that the misleading representations 'were very likely to result' in their issuance.[1059] On the other hand, in those countries where the SPCs had been initially granted and only revoked at a later stage, it was highlighted that also the effects taking place before the expiry of the basic patents should be considered, as those imminent SPCs were liable to alter the structure of the market by affecting potential competition[1060] and generating uncertainty.[1061] On the whole, the CJEU concluded that, even though the finding of an abuse necessarily requires proof of anticompetitive effects on the market, it is not necessary for them to be concrete: potential anticompetitive effects suffice.[1062]

Finally, another noteworthy point as to AstraZeneca's conduct was its timing. As it was mentioned above, the abuse was deemed to have taken place at different stages, which led the Commission and the General Court to interpret that, as a whole, such pattern of conduct configured a 'single and continuous' infringement.[1063] On the other hand, the CJEU stated that the anticompetitive nature of those acts is to be evaluated at the time when

---

1057 ibid para 366.
1058 CJEU Decision in *AstraZeneca* (n 877) para 111.
1059 ibid.
1060 ibid para 108.
1061 Commission Decision in *AstraZeneca* (n 751) para 760.
1062 CJEU Decision in *AstraZeneca* (n 877) para 112.
1063 Commission Decision in *AstraZeneca* (n 751) para 628, 774; GC Decision in *AstraZeneca* (n 981) para 895.

they were committed.[1064] Hence, the fact that AstraZeneca may no longer have been dominant by the time those acts were able to produce their effects was deemed irrelevant.[1065]

c. The Second Abuse

The second abuse does not really consist of a deceptive conduct before a patent office, but of a sequence of strategic registrations and withdrawals of marketing authorisations of medicinal products before national health authorities. Some of the questions addressed, however, may have a strong impact on how competition rules generally apply to cases involving petitioning public authorities.

In order to be able to market a medicinal product in the EU, firms need to obtain an authorisation from the competent authority in the relevant Member State. To that end, Directive 65/65/EEC, the legislation in force at the time of the abuse, required firms to submit a series of data and documents including the results of chemical, pharmaceutical and toxicological tests and clinical trials.[1066] Yet Directive 65/65 also provided for a number of simplified procedures, the most important being the abridged procedure used by generic producers by relying on products already existing on the market.[1067] The abridged procedure essentially enables them to bring cheaper products to the market and avoids the need to repeat tests on humans or animals.[1068] Through this procedure, firms basically rely on the data that has been submitted for the already authorised reference product, provided that they show that the generic version is 'essentially similar'.[1069] However, in order to ensure that innovative firms are not placed at a disadvantage, abridged procedures are only made available after the innovative company has enjoyed a period of exclusivity.[1070] Importantly for the case at hand, the legislation also required that the reference product 'is marketed'

1064 CJEU Decision in *AstraZeneca* (n 877) para 110.

1065 GC Decision in *AstraZeneca* (n 981) para 379.

1066 Council Directive 65/65/EEC of 26 January 1965 on the approximation of provisions laid down by Law, Regulation or Administrative Action relating to proprietary medicinal products [1965] OJ Spec Ed 24, art 4.

1067 Directive 65/65/EEC (as amended by Council Directive 87/21/EEC of 22 December 1986 [1987] OJ L15/36) art 4(8)(a)(iii).

1068 Directive 87/21/EEC, recital 4.

1069 Directive 65/65/EEC, art 4(8)(a)(iii).

1070 Directive 87/21/EEC, recital 2.

in the Member State concerned.[1071] The exact meaning of this last requirement was only clarified in 2003, when the CJEU ruled that, in order to obtain a generic market authorisation, it is 'necessary and sufficient' that the reference market authorisation is in force on the date the application is filed.[1072]

Against this background, AstraZeneca was accused of developing a strategy to prevent or delay competition by generics and parallel importers in Denmark, Norway and Sweden through technical and legal hurdles,[1073] which essentially consisted of registering and launching a new form of omeprazole (Losec MUPS tablets) and simultaneously withdrawing the registration of the product that had been commercialised until then (Losec capsules).[1074] Losec MUPS tablets had a magnesium salt of omeprazole as their active substance,[1075] yet it was recognised that the difference between capsules and tablets was clinically irrelevant.[1076] Due to the uncertainty that reigned until 2003 as to the need of having the reference product on the market for generic applications, AstraZeneca's capsule/tablet switch was accused of preventing competing firms from obtaining marketing authorisations for generic capsules in those countries where the reference authorisation had been withdrawn.[1077]

In the first place, the courts recognised that, as a rule, strategies for minimising erosion of sales are not necessarily anticompetitive, as long as they do not depart from practices 'coming within the scope of competition on the merits'.[1078] In the case at hand, however, AstraZeneca's strategy was deemed not to come within that scope,[1079] even though Directive 65/65 clearly allowed the firm to withdraw its market authorisations and register

---

1071 Directive 65/65/EEC, art 4(8)(a)(iii).

1072 Case C-223/01 *AstraZeneca* [2003] ECR I-11809, para 58. Yet the CJEU also recognised that, in order to grant market authorisations, 'what matters is that all the particulars and documents relating to the reference medicinal product remain available to the competent authority for the Member State where the application for the marketing authorisation is made and not that the reference medicinal product has in fact been placed on the market.' Ibid para 27.

1073 Commission Decision in *AstraZeneca* (n 751) para 788.

1074 The Commission also judged this second abuse as one of a single and continuous nature. Ibid para 861. The conclusion was not revised by the courts. GC Decision in *AstraZeneca* (n 981) para 896.

1075 Commission Decision in *AstraZeneca* (n 751) para 17.

1076 Commission Decision in *AstraZeneca* (n 751) para 30.

1077 GC Decision in *AstraZeneca* (n 981) para 670.

1078 CJEU Decision in *AstraZeneca* (n 877) para 129.

1079 ibid para 130.

different ones.[1080] In this regard, attention was drawn to the fact that in the majority of the cases anticompetitive abuses consist of behaviours which are otherwise lawful under other branches of law.[1081]

Contrary to AstraZeneca's contentions, the abuse did not consist of a misuse of property rights, but of government procedures.[1082] In this regard, the central element constituted the deregistration of market authorisations, which was liable to produce alone the anticompetitive effects.[1083] Those market authorisations are not designed to protect any legitimate investment after the expiry of the period of exclusivity,[1084] nor do they constitute property rights.[1085] Hence, a finding of abuse could not be considered an 'effective expropriation' of AstraZeneca's market authorisations[1086] and AstraZeneca's behaviour did not configure an 'essential facilities' case[1087] nor was it comparable to the situations which gave rise to 'refusal to license' cases such as *IMS Health*.[1088] Rather, the CJEU suggested a different test and, highlighting the special responsibility that rests with dominant firms when making use of governmental procedures, stressed that

> an undertaking which holds a dominant position ... cannot ... use regulatory procedures in such a way as to prevent or make more difficult the entry of competitors on the market, in the absence of grounds relating to the defence of the legitimate interests of an undertaking engaged in competition on the merits or in the absence of objective justification.[1089]

The CJEU recognised that, in cases like the one at hand, onerous pharmacovigilance obligations could have constituted a valid justification for deregistering the marketing authorisations.[1090] AstraZeneca, however, only raised this argument for the first time when appealing the case to the General Court, plus its internal documents did not make any reference to

---

1080 ibid para 132.
1081 ibid.
1082 ibid para 149; GC Decision in *AstraZeneca* (n 981) para 682; Commission Decision in *AstraZeneca* (n 751) para 817.
1083 CJEU Decision in *AstraZeneca* (n 877) para 140.
1084 ibid para 131.
1085 ibid para 149.
1086 ibid.
1087 GC Decision in *AstraZeneca* (n 981) para 684.
1088 CJEU Decision in *AstraZeneca* (n 877) para 148.
1089 ibid para 134.
1090 ibid para 135.

those justifications.[1091] Furthermore, the fact that Losec capsules had remained registered in other European countries suggested that the additional burden of maintaining the registration in Denmark, Sweden and Norway would not have required additional efforts.[1092]

Incidentally, the Commission also highlighted that requests for deregistration are automatic procedures where authorities have no discretion,[1093] and further stressed that a finding of an abuse cannot be ruled out merely because the legislation was not perfect and could have amended any incorrect balancing of interests,[1094] eg by admitting generic market authorisations despite of the reference authorisation having been withdrawn.

As to the anticompetitive effects of this abuse, the verdict was relatively straight-forward, despite a few passages of the General Court's decision which seem to mix up the anticompetitive effects of deregistration with other legitimate conducts such as patent enforcement.[1095] AstraZeneca's strategy, and particularly the deregistration of its market authorisations, had the effect of making the abridged procedure unavailable for competitors and, thus, of delaying the grant of marketing authorisations in Denmark, Norway and Sweden.[1096] The fact that the regulatory framework offered alternative abbreviated procedures, such as the reference to published scientific literature,[1097] did not prevent the conduct from being abusive, particularly because said alternative means were longer and more expensive.[1098] Equally irrelevant to those effects was the fact that some competitors had been able to use the abridged procedure before the withdrawal of the reference product, since AstraZeneca's strategy still made the abridged procedure unavailable to other potential competitors.[1099] Furthermore, even if AstraZeneca was able to stop generics from entering the market based on other legitimate grounds, such as its formulation patents, deregistration still constituted one additional and illegitimate entry barrier.[1100]

1091 ibid para 136.
1092 ibid para 137.
1093 Commission Decision in *AstraZeneca* (n 751) para 819.
1094 ibid para 836.
1095 See GC Decision in *AstraZeneca* (n 981) paras 791-801.
1096 ibid para 828; Commission Decision in *AstraZeneca* (n 751) para 849.
1097 Directive 65/65/EEC, art 4(8)(a)(ii) (the applicant should provide detailed references to published scientific literature showing that the medicinal product has 'a well established medicinal use, with recognised efficacy and an acceptable level of safety').
1098 CJEU Decision in *AstraZeneca* (n 877) para 154.
1099 GC Decision in *AstraZeneca* (n 981) para 837.
1100 ibid para 836.

It is interesting to point out that, in its decision, the Commission found that AstraZeneca's strategy had not only had anticompetitive effects on generic competition, but also on the parallel trade of Losec capsules in Denmark, Norway and Sweden.[1101] The General Court, however, understood that the Commission had not demonstrated that parallel trade licenses had been revoked in Denmark and Norway due to the deregistration of the reference product.[1102] Hence, if there had been any decrease in parallel importation in those countries, it could not be blamed on AstraZeneca's deregistration.[1103] As for Sweden, the Commission had indeed demonstrated that the parallel import licenses had been withdrawn and, therefore, that AstraZeneca had effectively impeded parallel imports.[1104] The CJEU later confirmed these conclusions.[1105]

II. AstraZeneca's Aftermath: Cases in EU Member States

There seems to be a high level of uncertainty surrounding the actual effects of *AstraZeneca* on intellectual property practice and on the general application of competition law. While some seem to take a rather positive stance on its outcome,[1106] others fear that it might have a negative impact on in-

1101 Commission Decision in *AstraZeneca* (n 751) paras 857-58.

1102 GC Decision in *AstraZeneca* (n 981) paras 843 and 857.

1103 ibid paras 852 and 861.

1104 ibid para 862.

1105 CJEU Decision in *AstraZeneca* (n 877) para 155.

1106 See, eg, Emmanuel Dieny, 'The Pharmaceutical Industry and Competition Law between the Present and the Future' (2007) 28 Eur Comp L Rev 223; Matteo Negrinotti, 'Abuse of Regulatory Procedures in the Intellectual Property Context: The AstraZeneca Case' in Inge Govaere and Hans Ullrich (eds), *Intellectual Property, Market Power and the Public Interest* (Peter Lang 2008); Müller-Graff and Fischmann (n 985) 794; John Kallaugher and Andreas Weitbrecht, 'Developments under Articles 101 and 102 TFEU in 2010' (2011) 32 Eur Comp L Rev 333; Mariateresa Maggiolino and Maria Lillà Montagnani, 'Astrazeneca's Abuse of IPR-Related Procedures: A Hypothesis of Anti-Trust Offence, Abuse of Rights and IPR Misuse' (2011) 34 World Competition 245; Jonathan Galloway, 'Driving Innovation: A Case for Targeted Competition Policy in Dynamic Markets' (2011) 34 World Competition 73; Drexl, 'When do Patent Filings Violate Competition Law?' (n 977) 290; Matthew Cole, 'Pharmaceuticals and Competition: First Strike to the Commission?' (2013) 34 Eur Comp L Rev 227.

different stages, the first one consisting of the first round of SPC applications[1036] and the second one comprising the second round of SPC applications in the context of the EEA Agreement, together with the misleading responses to patent offices who had raised objections and the misleading representations before the courts.[1037]

At the outset, the Commission clarified that the old dichotomy between existence and exercise of IPRs had been abandoned by EU competition law practice and that the acquisition of a right can indeed amount to a violation of art 102 TFEU, even if the accused conduct does not take place in the market.[1038] Rather, what defines a conduct's legality is whether it qualifies as 'normal competition'[1039] or, in the words of the General Court and the CJEU, as 'competition on the merits'.[1040] As for the question of causation, the General Court emphasised that an abuse of a dominant position does not necessarily require the use of the economic power conferred by such position.[1041]

Moving on to AstraZeneca's intent and based on the objective nature of the concept of abuse, it was highlighted that proof of bad faith or of a deliberate conduct were not inexorably required, although they can at times constitute relevant factors.[1042] In the case at hand, the courts considered that AstraZeneca's behaviour was characterised by highly misleading representations and a manifest lack of transparency,[1043] which indicated that it indeed had had the intention to mislead the patent offices.[1044] In this regard, the CJEU stressed that the 'special responsibility' that rests upon dominant firms would have required AstraZeneca to disclose all the relevant information to the different patent offices so as to allow them to decide.[1045] Even if AstraZeneca's interpretation of the SPC regime was legally defensible, the CJEU further explained that that fact itself did not consti-

1036 The Commission had interpreted that the first stage of the abuse had started with AstraZeneca's instructions to its patent agents, but the General Court understood that it could only begin with the actual filing of the SPC applications. GC Decision in *AstraZeneca* (n 981) para 370.

1037 CJEU Decision in *AstraZeneca* (n 877) paras 77 and 85.

1038 Commission Decision in *AstraZeneca* (n 751) paras 741-43.

1039 ibid para 677.

1040 CJEU Decision in *AstraZeneca* (n 877) paras 75 and 93; GC Decision in *AstraZeneca* (n 981) paras 355 and 608.

1041 GC Decision in *AstraZeneca* (n 981) para 354.

1042 ibid paras 356 and 359.

1043 CJEU Decision in *AstraZeneca* (n 877) para 92.

1044 ibid para 84.

1045 ibid para 95.

novation and disrupt general IP practice,[1107] yet most of them tend to converge in highlighting the need for clearer guidelines. Be that as it may, the decision seems to have made an impression on some national competition authorities. In the UK, for instance, the OFT imposed a fine upon Reckitt Benckiser for delisting a product from the NHS in order to hinder the development of generic competition.[1108] But a case which had enormous repercussions in this regard and which is worth describing in further detail is the one prosecuted by the Italian competition authorities against Pfizer.[1109]

The *Pfizer* saga began in 2012, when the AGCM (the Italian Competition Authority) fined the international pharmaceutical firm for delaying generic competition in the market for glaucoma eye drops in Italy by 'artificially prolonging' its patent protection.[1110] In a nutshell, Pharmacia (later merged into Pfizer) had filed a patent application in 1989 before the EPO which claimed the active ingredient latanoprost. The patent was granted in 1994 and validated in a number of Member States, including Italy. In 1996, the firm launched on the EU market the product Xalatan, based on the active ingredient latanoprost, and subsequently filed the corresponding

1107 See, eg, Sophie Lawrance and Pat Treacy, 'The Commission's AstraZeneca Decision: Delaying Generic Entry is an Abuse of Dominant Position' (2005) 1 J Intell Prop L & Prac 7; Maria Isabel Manley and Anna Wray, 'New Pitfall for the Pharmaceutical Industry' (2006) 1 J Intell Prop L & Prac 266; Kjølbye (n 880); David Hull, 'The AstraZeneca Judgment: Implications for IP and Regulatory Strategies' (2010) 1 J Eur Comp L & Prac 500; Joseph Straus, 'Patent Application: Obstacle for Innovation and Abuse of Dominant Position under Article 102 TFEU?' (2010) 1 J Eur Comp L & Prac 189; Christian Miege, Anette Gärtner and Marc Besen, 'Missbrauch einer marktbeherrschenden Stellung durch Irreführende Angaben bei Patentanmeldungen: Anmerkung zu EuG, Urt v 01.07.2010 – EUG 01.07.2010 – T-321/05' (2010) 11 PharmR 586; Christopher Stothers and Marco Ramondino, 'Aftermath of AstraZeneca and the Pharmaceutical Sector Inquiry: the Big Chill?' (2011) 32 Eur Comp L Rev 591; Ottaviano (n 999) 191; Pieter-Augustijn Van Malleghem and Wouter Devroe, 'AstraZeneca: Court of Justice Upholds First Decision Fiding Abuse of Dominant Position in Pharmaceutical Sector' (2013) 4 J Eur Comp L & Prac 228; Claudia Seitz, 'Klare Grenzlinie und Minenfeld: Die Marktmissbrauchskontrolle im Arzneimittelsektor nach dem AstraZeneca-Urteil des EuGH' [2013] EuZW 377; Spillmann (n 999).

1108 Case CE/8931/08 *Reckitt Benckiser Healthcare (UK) Ltd* (OFT Decision of 12 April 2011 CA98/02/2011).

1109 Decision of the Consiglio di Stato (Italy) 693/2014 of 12 February 2014 *Pfizer Italia srl*.

1110 Decision of the Autorità Garante della Concorrenza e del Mercato (AGCM) 23194 of 11 January 2012 - *A431: Ratiopharm/Pfizer* (Bollettino 2/2012).

SPC applications in a number of Member States, although it missed the deadline in Italy and hence could not obtain the SPC in that Member State.[1111] As a result, the patent in Italy would expire in September 2009, whereas the SPCs in the other Member States would expire in July 2011. In the meantime, however, the firm had applied for a divisional patent application based on that main patent, which was granted after a long procedure in January 2009. This patent, which originally claimed a group of molecules comprising latanoprost,[1112] was only validated in Italy and, based on it, Pfizer requested and obtained an SPC.

Against this context, the AGCM interpreted that Pfizer's behaviour constituted an abuse of a dominant position contrary to art 102 TFEU. First of all, to define the relevant market, the AGCM relied on *AstraZeneca* by employing the fourth level of the ATC and found Pfizer to enjoy a dominant position in it.[1113] On that basis, it judged that the firm had made an 'instrumental' use of the patent system[1114] so as to 'artificially extend' its patent protection,[1115] thus coming outside the scope of 'competition on the merits'.[1116] The AGCM alleged that divisional patent applications normally lead to the placing of new products on the market, yet in this case its scope was 'identical' to that of the parent patent[1117] and the intention of the firm was simply to 'correct' the patent situation in Italy[1118] and exclude generic competition from the market.[1119]

In reaching its conclusion, the AGCM seems to have relied ambiguously on a number of different theories of harm. In the first place, it cited the EU Pharmaceutical Sector Inquiry and argued that Pfizer's behaviour constituted a 'defensive patenting strategy' aimed at blocking the development

1111 SPC applications are to be filed within six months of the first authorisation to place the product on the market or, if the patent is granted after that date, within six months of the grant of the patent. Art 7(1) and (2), Regulation (EC) No 469/2009 of 6 May 2009.
1112 *Ratiopharm/Pfizer* (n 1110) para 79.
1113 ibid paras 151-52, 172
1114 ibid para 203.
1115 ibid para 139.
1116 ibid para 175.
1117 ibid para 193. See, however, Amedeo Arena, Bettina Bergmann and Jay L Himes, 'Two Bodies of Law Separated by a Common Mission: Unilateral Conduct by Dominant Firms at the IP/Antitrust Intersection in the EU and the US' (2013) 9 Eur Comp J 623, 634 (explaining that, because of their very nature, divisional patents cannot extend the content of the original application nor the protection period).
1118 *Ratiopharm/Pfizer* (n 1110) para 200.
1119 ibid para 198.

of new competing drugs,[1120] even though the competitors in this case did not seem to be interested in developing new drugs but on introducing generic versions on the market. Secondly, the AGCM contended that Pfizer's conduct resembles *AstraZeneca*'s first abuse, as it also provided 'evasive' information that led to the grant of an IPR to which it was not entitled.[1121] It should be noted that, at the time of AGCM's decision, Pfizer's divisional patent had been revoked by the EPO, although later on the validity of the patent was confirmed by the EPO Boards of Appeal. Thirdly, the AGCM argued that Pfizer's behaviour created a state of legal uncertainty among competitors, thus delaying the entry of generic products on the market and raising the production costs.[1122] In this last regard, it should be noted that the Pfizer's abuse was in fact deemed to be of a 'single and continuous' nature and encompassing a number of additional conducts,[1123] including the application for an extension of the Italian SPC based on paediatric trials,[1124] the delivery of warning letters and the involvement in civil and administrative litigation.[1125] According to the AGCM, Pfizer was asserting its rights aware of the poor chances of success and, if the criteria devised in *ITT Promedia* for vexatious litigation were to be applicable, both requirements would hence be met.[1126] Altogether, Pfizer's patenting and litigation strategy was deemed to have delayed market entry by generics and, therefore, caused significant damages to the national healthcare system.[1127]

It is interesting to point out that, although the decision of the AGCM was revoked by the court of first instance (Regional Administrative Court of Lazio),[1128] the higher tribunal in administrative matters (Council of State) ultimately annulled the latter judgment and confirmed AGCM's

1120 ibid para 178.
1121 ibid para 179.
1122 ibid para 177.
1123 ibid para 176.
1124 ibid para 212. According to the AGCM, the paediatric trials had only been carried out to obtain a further extension of the SPC. Ibid para 214. As finally granted, the patent claimed the use of a specific dose of latanoprost together with another compound for the preparation of an ophthalmological composition.
1125 ibid paras 204-05.
1126 ibid paras 208 and 211.
1127 ibid paras 233 and 245.
1128 Decision of the Tribunale Amministrativo Regionale per il Lazio 7467/2012 of 3 Septeeember 2012 *Pfizer Italia srl*.

finding of abuse.[1129] In essence, the Council of State highlighted that Pfizer's divisional patent had not been followed by the introduction of a new product on the market[1130] and reminded that conducts which are legitimate under patent law can still amount to an anticompetitive abuse, as antitrust and patent laws have different goals.[1131] In the present case, it stated that Pfizer had used the patent procedures for a purpose different from that intended by the legislator, as the firm's sole purpose had been to exclude competitors from the market.[1132]

As a final remark, it is worth mentioning that a very similar case arose against Pfizer in Spain, with a very similar fact pattern, yet the Spanish Competition Authority ultimately decided to conclude the procedure based on the lack of evidence of abuse.[1133]

3. *Closing Remarks and Open Questions*

There can be little doubt that the case law developed around the *Walker Process* decision in the US, as well as around the *AstraZeneca* case on the EU side, raise genuine concerns from a competition law perspective. As most of the cases described above show, a deceptive conduct before the patent office has the potential to cause severe restraints on competition. Against this context, it is crucial to have a clearly defined set of criteria and to identify the correct theory of harm underlying those conducts.

In this last regard, the *Pfizer* decision in Italy may be a paradigmatic example of the importance of having clear guidelines. In that case, the Italian authorities seem to have misinterpreted not only the underlying legal principles informing *AstraZeneca*, but also a number of basic principles on the functioning and rationale of the patent system. The AGCM, for instance, referred to a defensive patent strategy and a misleading behaviour before the patent office similar to *AstraZeneca*'s first abuse, although neither of them seem to have taken place in this case.[1134] The Council of State possi-

---

1129 *Pfizer* (n 1109).
1130 ibid para V(A).
1131 ibid para V(C).
1132 ibid.
1133 Decision of the Comisión Nacional de los Mercados y la Competencia (Spain) of 13 February 2014 Case S/0441/12: *Pfizer Health AB*.
1134 Stothers and Ramondino (n 1107) 594; Daniela Ampollini, 'Looking for Sense in the Italian Antitrust Authority Decision in the *Pfizer Xalatan* Case' [2012] Antitrust Chronicle vol 7(2); Damien Geradin, 'When Competition Law Analy-

bly offered a more sensible interpretation by emphasising the idea of an abuse of administrative and judicial procedures, thereby also bringing the case closer to *AstraZeneca*'s second abuse—yet the circumstances appear to be slightly different. In *AstraZeneca*, the firm had employed administrative procedures for a purpose different from that intended by the legislator, whereas Pfizer's conduct appears to conform precisely to the legislator's purpose.[1135] In this sense, the Italian authorities mistakenly state that divisional patents ordinarily lead to new products on the market[1136] and assert that, in this case, parent and divisional patents have 'identical' scope, although that is not legally possible.[1137] Therefore, considering that the scope of an SPC is defined by the scope of the underlying patent,[1138] an SPC based on a parent patent necessarily has a different scope from an SPC based on a divisional patent. The Council of State seems to have overlooked the fact that the SPC regime itself acknowledges that there might be more than one patent covering different aspects of a product, and for that reason permits only one SPC per product[1139] and allows the applicant to use as a basis the patent it deems appropriate.[1140] On a different note, the AGCM also questioned Pfizer's 'utilitarian' purposes in applying for a

---

sis Goes Wrong – The Italian Pfizer/Pharmacia Case' (2014) 14 <http://ssrn.com/abstract=2393383> accessed 14 February 2018.

1135 David Hull, 'The Application of EU Competition Law in the Pharmaceutical Sector' (2012) 3 J Eur Comp L & Prac 473, 478.

1136 Gianni De Stefano, 'Tough Enforcement of Unilateral Conduct at the National Level: Italian Antitrust Authority Sanctions Bayer and Pfizer for Abuse of Dominant Position (aka AstraZeneca Ruling and Essential Facility Doctrine in Italian Sauce)' (2012) 3 J Eur Comp L & Prac 396, 400.

1137 According to the EPO's Examination Guidelines, '[t]he parent and divisional applications may not claim the same subject-matter. This means not only that they must not contain claims of substantially identical scope, but also that one application must not claim the subject-matter claimed in the other, even in different words. The difference between the claimed subject-matter of the two applications must be clearly distinguishable.' EPO, Guidelines for Examination in the European Patent Office (EPO November 2014) pt C(IX) para 1(6). The Italian authorities also mistakenly assume that divisional patents normally lead to the launching of new products, when the limitations of this kind of patents in fact make that very difficult. See EPC, art 76 ('A European divisional application … may be filed only in respect of subject-matter which does not extend beyond the content of the earlier application as filed …').

1138 SPC Regulation, art 5 ('…the certificate shall confer the same rights as conferred by the basic patent and shall be subject to the same limitations and the same obligations.').

1139 ibid, art 3(c).

1140 Zbierska (n 1009) 160.

paediatric extension of the SPC, although that seems to be precisely the legislator's rationale behind those extensions: because the market itself does not provide sufficient incentives to stimulate research into paediatric products, additional protection is offered.[1141] Finally, the decisions seem to overly rely on malleable and subjective terms, eg by alleging that the patent situation had been 'crystallised' after the firm failed to apply for an SPC on the parent patent, or that the patent protection was 'artificially' extended,[1142] thereby raising additional problems in terms of legal certainty.

In any case, the *Pfizer* saga serves to highlight the importance of having clear standards and evidences that the guidelines offered by the EU courts in *AstraZeneca* might need to be further developed. As indicated above, the landscape in the US does not seem to be very different, as a number of significant questions still remain open, particularly as to identifying the correct theory of harm. It is not completely clear in that jurisdiction whether the emphasis should be placed on the act of obtaining the patent or on maintaining and enforcing it. In the latter case, it is worth asking what distinguishes a fraudulently obtained patent from any other invalid patent and, on a more general level, whether it would just constitute a particular form of sham litigation. The next chapter attempts to provide an answer to these questions by critically appraising the existing case law described in this chapter, distinguishing the possible theories of harm and offering workable, across the board criteria for the cases to come.

1141 Regulation (EC) 1901/2006 of 12 December 2006 on medicinal products for paediatric use [2006] OJ L378/1, recitals 2-4.

1142 Geradin, 'When Competition Law Analysis Goes Wrong' (n 1134) 15.

Chapter VI: Searching for a Workable Theory of Harm

1. *Introduction*

Having analysed the most prominent case law in the US and in the EU on the question of deceptive behaviour before the patent office, it is now possible to turn to the underlying theory of harm in a more methodical fashion and from a more academic perspective. Most of the cases described along the previous chapter certainly provide valuable insights, yet—for different reasons—the theoretical criteria underpinning the decisions are at times ambiguous or imprecise and have left a number of questions open.

At the outset, it is noteworthy that antitrust cases involving a deceptive conduct before the patent office frequently arise amidst accusations of sham and abuses of administrative and judicial procedures. As a matter of fact, deceptive behaviour and sham are often invoked concurrently and, in the view of a considerable number of courts and scholars, there are in fact no significant differences among them, since the former would simply be a specific variant of the broader sham doctrine—or at least should be analysed under equivalent principles.[1143]

1143 As for US law, see, eg, *Kottle v Northwest Kidney Centers* 146 F 3d 1056, 1060-61 (9th Cir 1998) (treating misrepresentations as a variant of sham); *Cheminor Drugs Ltd v Ethyl Corp* 168 F 3d 119, 123 (3rd Cir 1999) (applying the sham criteria to a case involving misrepresentations); Robert H Bork, *The Antitrust Paradox: A Policy at War with Itself* (Basic 1978) 353 (arguing that, in a case involving the enforcement of a fraudulently obtained patent, the fraud is simply a way to show bad faith in litigation); Herbert Hovenkamp, *The Antitrust Enterprise: Principle and Execution* (Harvard Univ Press 2005) 267 (arguing that *Walker Process* is not really different from any other abusive litigation technique); S W O'Donnell, 'Unified Theory of Antitrust Counterclaims in Patent Litigation' (2004) 9(8) Va J L & Tech 1, 61 (interpreting that the sham litigation criteria is also applicable to cases like *Walker Process*); Christopher C Klein, 'The Economics of Sham Litigation: Theory, Cases, and Policy' (Bureau of Economics Staff Report to the FTC, April 1989) 9 <www.ftc.gov/sites/default/files/documents/reports/economics-sham-litigation-theory-cases-and-policy/232158_0.pdf> accessed 14 February 2018 (reasoning that sham litigation strategies either involve fraudulent use of the courts or they are special cases of nonprice predation); Rudolph J R Peritz, 'Competition Policy and its Implications for Intellectual Property Rights in the United States' in Steven D Anderman (ed), *The Interface Between Intellectual Property Rights and Competition Policy* (Cambridge

Against this background, it seems appropriate to first examine the sham doctrine in greater depth, scrutinise its underlying economic principles and verify whether deceptive conducts before the patent office can indeed qualify as a mere variant of a sham strategy. The first part of the present chapter, therefore, is devoted to this enterprise.

Parenthetically, it is important to recall that the US and the EU do not have the exact same starting points when approaching questions that involve petitioning public authorities. The US, on the one hand, starts from the premise that petitioning activities are, as a principle, immune from antitrust laws.[1144] Doctrines like sham, hence, are merely exceptions that strip the private party from that immunity and only mean that the act can be subject to antitrust scrutiny.[1145] In the EU, on its turn, no comparable immunity doctrine has been developed and authorities hence set off from a seemingly more open starting line. This, however, does not mean that EU competition rules know no boundaries, as limits to their reach can also be found on basic rights and constitutional principles. As a matter of fact, in the few cases in which the problem has been addressed, EU authorities have found in US case law an important source of inspiration.[1146] Therefore, the fact that the starting point may be different does not necessarily mean that the final outcome should also differ: ultimately, the common question in both jurisdictions seems to be whether a specific conduct has a negative effect on competition and, if yes, whether there are any overriding reasons that vindicate it.

Univ Press 2007) 193 (referring to the *Walker Process* doctrine as a type of sham litigation). As for EU law, see, eg, Mariateresa Maggiolino, *Intellectual Property and Antitrust: A Comparative Economic Analysis of US and EU Law* (Edward Elgar 2011) 103-05 (suggesting that *AstraZeneca*'s first abuse constitutes an abusive enforcement of a patent, similar to any other vexatious litigation situation); Valéria Guimarães de Lima e Silva, 'Sham Litigation in the Pharmaceutical Sector' (2011) 7 Eur Comp J 455, 496 (proposing to interpret vexatious litigation in a broader way, so as to include other abuses of governmental procedures 'that cause even more harmful effects than groundless litigation itself').

1144 *Professional Real Estate Investors Inc v Columbia Pictures Industries Inc* 508 US 49, 56 (1993).

1145 ibid 61.

1146 Katarzyna Czapracka, *Intellectual Property and the Limits of Antitrust: A Comparative Study of US and EU Approaches* (Edward Elgar 2010) 28.

2. *The Sham or Vexatious Litigation Doctrine*

The question of sham[1147] was briefly introduced in the previous chapter, when analysing the exceptions to the *Noerr* immunity in the US and its EU counterpart. The following paragraphs succinctly recount the most relevant decisions in both jurisdictions[1148] and later tease out their most important elements, study their underlying theory of harm and juxtapose it against different scenarios involving deceptive conducts before the patent office.

A. *The Development of Sham as an Antitrust Doctrine in the US and in the EU*

I. *Sanctions under Other Areas of Law*

Before addressing the question of sham as a competition law concern, it is worth pointing out that this sort of behaviour—ie, the use of court or governmental procedures with the intent of harassing rivals rather than obtaining a favourable outcome—is not the exclusive domain of competition law. Quite the contrary, these conducts have long raised concerns among other areas of law, predominantly in the context of procedural or civil law abuses. Admittedly, the fact that a certain behaviour is illegal under other areas of law does not exempt it from competition law scrutiny, as the sanctions imposed in those other areas are likely to pursue different objectives. Yet looking at these fields might nonetheless prove relevant for a couple of

---

1147 By way of clarification, it should be noted that the terms 'sham' and 'vexatious' litigation essentially refer to one and the same legal concept, ie the specious use of court and governmental procedures with the purpose of harassing competitors and indifferent of their outcome. See Case T-111/96 *ITT Promedia v Commission* [1998] ECR II-2937, para 30; *City of Columbia v Omni Outdoor Advertising Inc* 499 US 365, 380 (1991). While the former is often used in the context of US litigation, the latter is a more customary expression among European courts and scholars. Throughout this work, both terms are used interchangeably.

1148 It may be interesting to note that cases of sham litigation have arisen in other jurisdictions as well, although their analysis exceeds the scope of this work. See, eg, Decision of the Conselho Administrativo de Defesa Económica (Brasil) of 20 August 2014 Case 08012.011508/2007-91 *Eli Lilly do Brasil Ltda* (recommending to condemn the firm for sham litigation); *Monsanto Co s/ Apel Resol Comisión Nacional de Defensa de la Competencia* (decision of the Argentine Federal Court of Appeals of 30 Semptember 2008, case 13676/07) (revoking de decision of the NCA that had condemned the firm for sham litigation).

reasons. In the first place, it evidences that competition law is not the only tool available to address these concerns and that, under certain circumstances, other areas of law might be better suited to tackle them. Secondly, and perhaps more importantly, it may also help to shape competition law's constitutional boundaries. It has been argued in this regard that if a particular behaviour can be sanctioned under procedural laws without raising any constitutional concerns, it would be incongruous to argue that that same conduct cannot be sanctioned by competition law for the same reasons.[1149]

In the US, abuses of the judicial proceedings may be countered through different channels. Firstly, the Federal Rules of Civil Procedure establish that, when parties make presentations before the courts, they implicitly certify that they are not being made for any improper purpose and courts can impose sanctions in case of violation.[1150] Furthermore, under common law, two basic torts exist: malicious prosecution and abuse of process. Malicious prosecution refers to legal actions characterised in that they are undertaken without probable cause and for an improper purpose,[1151] whereas

1149 *Grip-Pak Inc v Illinois Tool Works Inc* 694 F 2d 466, 470-71 (7th Cir 1982) (arguing that, if a legal action with improper motivations can be sanctioned by procedural law even if brought with probably cause, that same conduct cannot be considered immunised for competition law purposes). See also Daniel R Fischel, 'Antitrust Liability for Attempts to Influence Government Action: The Basis and Limits of the *Noerr-Pennington* Doctrine' (1977) 45 U Chi L Rev 80, 101-06; C Douglas Floyd, 'Antitrust Liability for the Anticompetitive Effects of Governmental Action Induced by Fraud' (2001) 69 Antitrust L J 403, 434-35; Marina Lao, 'Reforming the Noerr-Pennington Antitrust Immunity Doctrine' (2003) 55 Rutgers L Rev 965, 1011. Cf Milton Handler and Richard A De Sevo, 'The *Noerr* Doctrine and Its Sham Exception' (1984) 6 Cardozo L Rev 1, 36-37 (1984) (challenging such a view on the basis that immunity does not stem from constitutional principles but on an interpretation of the antitrust rules).

1150 US Federal Rules of Civil Procedure, r 11(b) and (c) ('By presenting to the court a pleading, written motion, or other paper ... an attorney or unrepresented party certifies that to the best of the person's knowledge, information, and belief, formed after an inquiry reasonable under the circumstances ... it is not being presented for any improper purpose, such as to harass, cause unnecessary delay, or needlessly increase the cost of litigation ...').

1151 *Restatement (2d) of Torts* (1977) para 674 ('One who takes an active part in the initiation, continuation or procurement of civil proceedings against another is subject to liability to the other for wrongful civil proceedings if (a) he acts without probable cause, and primarily for a purpose other than that of securing the proper adjudication of the claim in which the proceedings are based, and (b) except when they are ex parte, the proceedings have terminated in favor of the person against whom they are brought.').

the tort of abuse of process only requires the action to have an improper purpose, even if the claim is asserted with probable cause.[1152]

On the European side, the regulation of court proceedings remains essentially a matter of national law. In the UK, courts also recognise the common law torts of malicious prosecution and abuse of process and their parameters are very similar to their US equivalents.[1153] Indeed, the tort of malicious prosecution requires to establish both a purpose not within the scope of the action and a lack of reasonable cause, whereas the tort of abuse of process does not include this last requirement.[1154] Moreover, in the specific field of patent litigation, the UK Patents Act even provides for sanctions for groundless threats.[1155] In Germany, on the other hand, ungrounded infringement accusations (*Unberechtigte Schutzrechtsverwarnungen*) also entitle the wrongly accused parties to claim damages on the basis of § 823 of the BGB and §§ 3, 4 and 9 of the UWG (*Gesetz gegen den unlauteren Wettbewerb* or German Act Against Unfair Competition).[1156] Moreover, courts may dismiss actions on the basis of the ZPO (*Zivilprozessordnung* or German Civil Procedural Rules)[1157] and the BGB[1158] if they believe that they lack of a legitimate interest for legal protection.[1159] It is also interesting to note that, for the Unitary Patent system which is yet to enter into force, the proposed Rules of Procedure seem to recognise to the courts

1152 *Restatement (2d) of Torts* (1977) para 682 ('One who uses a legal process, whether criminal or civil, against another primarily to accomplish a purpose for which it is not designed, is subject to liability to the other for harm caused by the abuse of process.').

1153 Neil Andrews, 'Abuse of Process in English Civil Litigation' in Michele Taruffo (ed), *Abuse of Procedural Rights: Comparative Standards of Procedural Fairness* (Kluwer 1999) 75-79.

1154 *Crawford Adjusters v Sagicor General Insurance (Cayman) Ltd* [2013] UKPC 17, [2014] 1 AC 366 [62].

1155 UK Patents Act, s 70.

1156 Ansgar Ohly and others, *Gesetz gegen den unlauteren Wettbewerb* (6th edn, Beck 2014) para 10/41. See also Hans-Peter Brack, 'Patent Infringement Warnings in a Common Law versus a Civil Law Jurisdiction - An Actionable Threat?' (2006) 37 IIC 1, 15-22.

1157 § 138 ZPO (duty to tell the truth).

1158 §§ 226 and 242 BGB (prohibition of chicanery and general good faith obligation).

1159 Burkhard Hess, 'Abuse of Procedure in Germany and Austria' in Michele Taruffo (ed), *Abuse of Procedural Rights: Comparative Standards of Procedural Fairness* (Kluwer 1999) 157.

the same power to dismiss claims when they are manifestly inadmissible or unfounded.[1160]

II. Sham as an Antitrust Injury in US Case Law

The concept of sham as an antitrust concern was originally introduced in the US in *Noerr*. Indeed, in the same decision in which the Supreme Court first recognised an antitrust immunity for petitioning the government, it also acknowledged that said immunity could be stripped away if the petition 'is a mere sham to cover what is actually nothing more than an attempt to interfere directly with the business relationships of a competitor.'[1161] However, since the Supreme Court considered that *Noerr* was not a case of sham, it failed to explain in detail which elements would actually establish one.

A few years later, in the *California Motor Transport* decision, the Supreme Court shed some light on the question. In this case, a group of highway carriers had been accused of systematically instituting proceedings and legal actions against competitors in order to stop them from acquiring or registering operating rights.[1162] The court immediately acknowledged its resemblance to *Noerr*, but pointed out that this time the behaviour of the group of highway carriers could justify the applicability of the sham exception. It stated in this regard that, in the case at hand, the transporters had instituted proceedings and legal actions 'with or without probable cause, and regardless of the merits of the cases'[1163] and that they had used their power, strategy and resources 'to harass and deter respondents in their use of administrative and judicial proceedings.'[1164] This kind of behaviour, reckoned the court, could indeed come within the sham exception to *Noerr* immunity.[1165] It should be noted that, although the decision seemed to recognise the relevant anticompetitive harm solely in restricting competitors' access to agencies and courts,[1166] the court later clari-

---

1160 17th draft of the Rules of Procedure of the Unified Patent Court, rr 361-63.

1161 *Eastern Railroad Presidents Conference v Noerr Motor Freight Inc* 365 US 127, 144 (1961).

1162 *California Motor Transport Co v Trucking Unlimited* 404 US 508, 509 (1972).

1163 ibid 512.

1164 ibid 511-12.

1165 ibid 516.

1166 See, in this regard, Thomas A Balmer, 'Sham Litigation and the Antitrust Laws' (1980) 209 Buffalo L Rev 39, 42-43.

fied that any other kind of anticompetitive effect (eg, by raising rivals' costs) could equally qualify as sham.[1167]

In the decades that followed, the Supreme Court had the opportunity to decide on a number of additional cases involving the *Noerr* immunity. Although most of those cases were not directly concerned with sham, they did provide some additional guidance as to its characterisation. In *Allied Tube*,[1168] for instance, the issue arose whether the manipulation of a private standard setting organisation to exclude competitors could be subject to competition law, considering that the results of those standards were widely used by local governments. The Supreme Court decided that the conduct was not immunised, although it refused to qualify it as sham because the standard had actually been approved by many local statutes and ordinances.[1169] According to the court, the concept of sham should be restricted to actions which are not genuinely aimed at procuring favourable government action.[1170] The court also warned against a broad reading that would encompass actions which genuinely seek to achieve a governmental result, even if through improper means.[1171] Later, in *Omni*,[1172] the Supreme Court continued along those lines by reaffirming that sham refers only to 'situations in which persons use the governmental process—as opposed to the outcome of that process—as an anticompetitive weapon.'[1173] Since the case concerned a conspiracy between a private firm and city officials to restrict potential competition through the enactment of local ordinances, the court understood that the restriction to competition would stem from the ultimate *product* of lobbying and hence did not constitute a case of sham.[1174] In the view of the court, the purpose of harassing competitors can only constitute sham if it is sought by the lobbying process itself, and not by the governmental action that the lobbying seeks.[1175]

In 1993, the Supreme Court was finally faced again with a pure sham question in *PREI*,[1176] which probably constitutes the most important deci-

1167 *Otter Tail Power Co v United States* 410 US 366, 380 (1973).
1168 *Allied Tube & Conduit Corp v Indian Head Inc* 486 US 492 (1988).
1169 ibid 502.
1170 ibid 500, fn 4.
1171 ibid 507, fn 10.
1172 *Omni* (n 1147).
1173 ibid 380.
1174 ibid 381.
1175 ibid.
1176 *PREI* (n 1144).

sion in the US on this issue to date. In this case, a hotel operator had installed videodiscs players on the rooms and rented videodiscs to its guests for in-room viewing. Columbia Pictures, who held copyrights on many of those movies, sued the hotel operator for copyright infringement. The hotel operator, on its turn, counterclaimed accusing Columbia of sham litigation, essentially arguing that the suit had been brought with anticompetitive purposes. Against this background, the main question presented to the Supreme Court was whether litigation may be considered sham merely because a subjective expectation of success does not motivate the petitioner.[1177] The court answered in the negative and interpreted that the sham doctrine contains not only a subjective element but also an 'indispensable objective component',[1178] whereby the baseless nature of the claim should also be shown. For the sake of clarity, the court outlined a two-pronged test:

> First, the lawsuit must be objectively baseless in the sense that no reasonable litigant could realistically expect success on the merits. If an objective litigant could conclude that the suit is reasonably calculated to elicit a favorable outcome, the suit is immunized under *Noerr*, and an antitrust claim premised on the sham exception must fail. Only if challenged litigation is objectively meritless may a court examine the litigant's subjective motivation. Under this second part of our definition of sham, the court should focus on whether the baseless lawsuit conceals "an attempt to interfere *directly* with the business relationships of a competitor," through the "use [of] the governmental *process* —as opposed to the *outcome* of that process—as an anticompetitive weapon." This two-tiered process requires the plaintiff to disprove the challenged lawsuit's *legal* viability before the court will entertain evidence of the suit's *economic* viability.[1179]

In other words, according to the Supreme Court's sham test, anticompetitive litigation contains both an objective component—a baseless suit—and a subjective component—the anticompetitive motivation. The objective baselessness should be the first element to consider; only if proven can the courts proceed to determine the anticompetitive purposes.

As it may be recalled, US courts in the patent litigation forum have developed an antitrust defence normally referred to as *Handgards* which, al-

1177 ibid 57.
1178 ibid 58.
1179 ibid 61-62 (internal citations omitted) (emphasis in original).

though initially viewed as an aftermath of *Walker Process*, ultimately developed into the equivalent of sham litigation in the patent sphere.[1180] Although the Supreme Court in *PREI* did not explicitly refer to it in its decision, there is little doubt that it had a profound impact on it and that *Handgards* claims should now be judged under the *PREI* standards.[1181]

III. Vexatious Litigation in the EU

Considering that no comparable immunity doctrine has been developed under European law,[1182] the starting point in this jurisdiction seems to be somehow easier. Indeed, as a general principle, any act can be subject to EU competition rules, even if it does not take place on the market, provided that it at least has some effects on it.[1183] The sham use of administrative and judicial procedures, hence, would be undoubtedly comprehended by that definition. As a matter of fact, this behaviour would even have been deemed within the scope of EU competition law under the old existence-exercise dichotomy,[1184] since it would clearly not affect the existence of any intellectual property right.

In spite of this, when shaping the boundaries of the competition rules, EU authorities have taken into consideration essentially the same concerns as their US counterparts in terms of fundamental rights and freedoms, habitually highlighting the importance of the right to access to courts—a right protected by art 47 of the Charter of Fundamental Rights of the

---

1180 See text at nn 945ff in ch 5.

1181 James B Kobak Jr, 'Professional Real Estate Investors and the Future of Patent-Antitrust Litigation: *Walker Process* And *Handgards* Meet *Noerr-Pennington*' (1994) 63 Antitrust L J 185, 201 (both the objective and the subjective test developed in *PREI* must also be satisfied in *Handgards* claims); S W O'Donnell (n 1143) 44 ('it is conventional wisdom that *Handgards* bad faith prosecution is the patent apposite of sham litigation. ... As a result, courts and scholars now formulate *Handgards* bad faith prosecution within the *Professional Real Estate* rubric.').

1182 See text at nn 881-891 in ch 5.

1183 *AstraZeneca* (Case COMP/A.37.507/F3) Commission Decision 2006/857/CE [2006] OJ L332/24, para 328. It has been argued, however, that the fact that the conduct occurs outside the market may indicate that competition law might not be the optimal remedy. Mario Siragusa, 'The EU Pharmaceutical Sector Inquiry: New Forms of Abuse and Article 102 TFEU' in Giandonato Caggiano, Gabriella Muscolo and Marina Tavassi (eds), *Competition Law and Intellectual Property: A European Perspective* (Wolters Kluwer 2012) 186.

1184 See text at nn 853-857 in ch 5.

European Union.[1185] In this sense, the CJEU has recognised that the right to assert one's claims in court reflects a general law principle that underlies the constitutional traditions of all EU Member States[1186] and that 'in principle, the proprietor may not be deprived of the right to have recourse to legal proceedings to ensure effective enforcement of his exclusive rights'.[1187] Similarly, the EU Commission has recognised that, as a principle, enforcing patents in court is a legitimate and fundamental right.[1188] In this light, it is no surprise that the cases adjudicated in the EU on the issue of sham or vexatious litigation bear many similarities to those decided in the US.[1189]

That being said, case law addressing sham as a competition law concern in Europe is scarce and relatively new.[1190] The first opportunity in which EU authorities seem to have acknowledged the issue is in the *BBI/Boosey & Hawkes* decision.[1191] In this case, a manufacturer of musical instruments had been accused of restraining competition mainly by refusing to supply products to potential competitors, although the complaint also included accusations of pursuing unjustified litigation for copyright infringement 'which had the effect of imposing a heavy financial burden on the appli-

1185 Charter of Fundamental Rights of the European Union [2012] OJ C 326/391.

1186 Case C-222/84 *Johnston v Chief Constable of the Royal Ulster Constabulary* [1986] ECR I-1651, para 18. See also Case T-5/97 *Industrie des Poudres Sphériques (IPS) SA v Commission* [2000] ECR II-3755, para 213 ('recourse to a remedy in law and, in particular, participation by an undertaking in an investigation conducted by the Community institutions, cannot be deemed, of itself, to be contrary to Article 86 of the Treaty.').

1187 Case C-170/13 *Huawei Technologies Co. Ltd v ZTE Corp., ZTE Deutschland GmbH* (CJEU, 16 July 2015, ECLI:EU:C:2015:477).

1188 See, eg, *Motorola - Enforcement of GPRS standard essential patents* (Case AT.39985) Commission Decision C(2014) 2892 [2014] OJ C344/6, paras 504-505; *Samsung - Enforcement of UMTS standard essential patents* (Case AT.39939) Commission Decision C(2014) 2891 [2014] OJ C350/8, paras 55 and 71-73.

1189 Abbe E L Brown, *Intellectual Property, Human Rights and Competition* (Edward Elgar 2012) 101.

1190 One of the reasons of the reduced number of cases might be the fact that, in order to find an abuse of dominance under art 102 TFEU, the firm already needs to be dominant at the time of the abuse. Eva Luterkort, 'Vexatious (Patent) Litigation & Art. 82 EC Following *AstraZeneca*: EC and US Converging Approaches?' (Master thesis, University of Lund 2007) 85 <http://lup.lub.lu.se/luur/download?func=downloadFile&recordOId=1559936&fileOId=1565148> accessed 14 February 2018.

1191 *BBI/Boosey & Hawkes: Interim Measures* (Case IV/32.279) Commission Decision 87/500/EEC [1987] OJ L286/36.

cants and of delaying the launching' of new products.[1192] Since the decision solely concerned the imposition of interim measures compelling the dominant company to resume the supply of its products, the Commission did not rule on the issue of sham, yet it did recognise that such behaviour could eventually fall foul of competition laws.[1193]

Soon after, in *Decca Navigator System*,[1194] the Commission rendered a decision on a case that presented clear elements of vexatious litigation, although regrettably it was decided on different grounds. The case concerned a navigation system originally created by Racal Decca and mostly used for maritime navigation, whereby land-based stations transmit signals which are received by devices placed on board. When a number of firms attempted to enter the market of receivers after Racal Decca's basic patents expired, the latter attempted to maintain its dominant position by implementing a mixed strategy essentially consisting in (i) varying the transmission signals of the land-based stations to obstruct the operation of competing receivers, and (ii) initiating numerous legal proceedings for unfair competition. These lawsuits were primarily grounded on the fact that Racal Decca was allegedly put in a competitive disadvantage by having to bear alone with the costs of signal transmission, yet complainants claimed that they were rather aimed to 'fatigue' and 'exhaust' competitors.[1195] In any case, Racal Decca and the different defendants ultimately settled these legal actions by entering into coordinated license agreements that fragmented the market, which on its turn led to several antitrust complaints from third parties. After analysing the market and the conducts in detail, the Commission interpreted that both the agreements and the changes in the signals were anticompetitive: the former because they amounted in practice to illegal market partitioning and the latter because it caused the malfunctioning of competitors' devices and discouraged competition.[1196] It refused to analyse, however, whether the ungrounded litigation could constitute an anticompetitive conduct on its own.

The issue of vexatious litigation was finally addressed in depth in the EU in the well-known *ITT Promedia* case.[1197] Promedia had been the exclusive publisher of telephone directories in Belgium for many years, but when its

1192 ibid para 9.
1193 ibid para 19.
1194 *Decca Navigator System* (Case IV/30.979 and 31.394) Commission Decision 89/113/EEC [1989] OJ L43/27.
1195 ibid, para 50.
1196 ibid paras 102 and 108.
1197 *ITT Promedia* (n 1147).

exclusive license was close to expire in 1993, a series of conflicts arose with Belgium's telecommunications operator, Belgacom. Claims and counter-claims were filed by both parties on different issues such as spreading false information, demands for supplying information on FRAND terms and demands for performance of agreement, with Promedia emerging victorious from all of them. Against this backdrop, Promedia submitted a complaint to the EU Commission asserting that Belgacom had abused its dominant position by, among other reasons, 'initiating vexatious litigation'.[1198]

The Commission stated at the outset that 'in principle the bringing of an action, which is the expression of the fundamental right of access to a judge, cannot be characterised as an abuse'.[1199] In order to qualify as an anticompetitive abuse, continued the Commission, it would be necessary to show the following cumulative conditions:

i. that the action 'cannot reasonably be considered as an attempt to establish [the dominant undertaking's] rights and can therefore only serve to harass the opposite party'; and
ii. that the action 'is conceived in the framework of a plan whose goal is to eliminate competition.'[1200]

Although not expressly referred to in the decision, the influence of the US Supreme Court's *PREI* judgment, which had been rendered only a few years before, is undeniable.[1201] In fact, the first part of the *ITT Promedia* test seems to embrace the whole of the *PREI* test, as it makes reference to both objective and subjective elements.[1202] In any case, the Commission concluded that, in the light of the proposed standard, Belgacom's conduct could not be considered anticompetitive, since its actions could reasonably be regarded 'as having been brought with a view to asserting its rights'.[1203]

1198 ibid para 23.
1199 ibid para 30.
1200 ibid para 30.
1201 Adrian J Vossestein, 'Corporate Efforts to Influence Public Authorities, and the EC Rules on Competition' (2000) 37 CML Rev 1383, 1395; Simonetta Vezzoso, 'Towards an EU Doctrine of Anticompetitive IP-Related Litigation' (2012) 3 J Eur Comp L & Prac 521, 530.
1202 It may well be that the raison d'être of *ITT Promedia*'s second part of the test responds to the different starting points already mentioned above: whereas US courts see sham as an exception to antitrust immunity, and hence solely as a first step, EU law conceives it as a definite test to find an abuse. See Vezzoso (n 1201) 533.
1203 *ITT Promedia* (n 1147) para 41.

Interestingly, when the decision was appealed before the General Court (then called Court of First Instance), the appellant did not challenge the two cumulative criteria, but simply its application by the Commission.[1204] The court hence reckoned that it was not necessary to rule on its correctness,[1205] although it did acknowledge the importance of respecting the fundamental right of access to the court and agreed with the Commission in the sense that 'it is only in wholly exceptional circumstances that the fact that legal proceedings are brought is capable of constituting an abuse of a dominant position'.[1206] Moreover, when scrutinising the way in which the Commission had applied the two cumulative criteria, the General Court offered some further guidance. Firstly, it explained that the test laid down by the Commission contains one objective and one subjective element: on the one hand, the action should be 'manifestly unfounded',[1207] which should be proven by analysing whether the action 'was intended to assert what the undertaking could, at that moment, reasonably consider to be its rights';[1208] on the other hand, the aim of the action must be 'to eliminate competition.'[1209] The court ultimately interpreted that the first part of the test had not been met and confirmed the Commission's decision.[1210]

Over the following years, the issue attracted little attention from courts and competition authorities and *ITT Promedia* became the leading precedent on vexatious litigation under EU competition law.[1211] It has been argued, however, that the CJEU's decision in *AstraZeneca* might have modified the landscape, particularly when examining AstraZeneca's second abuse.[1212] As it may be recalled, AstraZeneca's second abuse had essentially consisted in deregistering marketing authorisations for Losec with the sole purpose of obstructing and delaying generic competition.[1213] The anticompetitive harm, hence, seems to be somehow similar to that which constitut-

1204 ibid para 57.
1205 ibid para 58.
1206 ibid para 60.
1207 ibid para 56.
1208 ibid para 73.
1209 ibid para 56.
1210 ibid para 116.
1211 Robert O'Donoghue and A Jorge Padilla, *The Law and Economics of Article 102 TFEU* (2nd edn, Hart 2013) 652.
1212 Matteo Negrinotti, 'Abuse of Regulatory Procedures in the Intellectual Property Context: The AstraZeneca Case' in Inge Govaere and Hans Ullrich (eds), *Intellectual Property, Market Power and the Public Interest* (Peter Lang 2008) 143.
1213 See text at nn 1066ff in ch 5.

ed the main concern in *ITT Promedia*,[1214] ie a competition restraint imposed by the collateral effects of a bogus use of governmental procedures. In *AstraZeneca*, however, neither the General Court nor the CJEU used the two-pronged criteria nor paid any attention to the objective element—ie, whether AstraZeneca could have reasonably believed to be exercising its rights—but rather focused on the subjective aspect and the absolute lack of any economic rationalisation for its conduct other than stymieing competitors.[1215] Perhaps the courts implicitly understood that, in cases where the role of the administration is limited to rubber-stamping, the objective element of a sham test becomes less relevant. Be that as it may, the relation between *ITT Promedia* and *AstraZeneca* remains unclear, as the CJEU did not make any reference to the former case and the previous instances only referred to it in connection to the first abuse—and merely to underline its irrelevance on that specific issue.[1216]

Finally, the situation might have become yet thornier after the General Court's decision in *Protégé International*.[1217] This decision was rendered shortly after *AstraZeneca* and referred to a complaint for abusive use of opposition procedures in different countries during the registration of a number of trademarks. The General Court, however, did not allude to *AstraZeneca* at all and simply reiterated and confirmed the two-pronged criteria formulated in *ITT Promedia*.[1218] This might suggest that, in its view, *ITT Promedia* remains the governing test for sham cases, at least where they involve the assertion of an undertaking's right during an adjudicatory procedure, whereas *AstraZeneca*'s conclusions on the second abuse might come

---

1214 Negrinotti (n 1212) 163; Dirk Seidel, *Europäische Missbrauchsaufsicht nach AstraZeneca: Fallrelevante Problemkreise unter besonderer Berücksichtigung des Konfliktfeldes Immaterialgüter-/Wettbewerbsrecht* (Shaker 2008) 68.

1215 Case C-457/10 P *AstraZeneca v Commission* (CJEU, 6 December 2012, ECLI:EU:C:2012:770) para 132.

1216 Case T-321/05 *AstraZeneca v Commission* [2010] ECR II-2805, para 363; Case C-457/10 P *AstraZeneca v Commission* (CJEU, 6 December 2012, ECLI:EU:C:2012:293), Opinion of AG Mazák, para 52.

1217 Case T-119/09 *Protégé International Ltd v Commission* [2012] OJ C319/6.

1218 ibid para 49 ('Afin de conclure qu'une action en justice peut constituer, en réalité, un abus de position dominante, deux conditions cumulatives doivent être réunies. En premier lieu, il faut que l'action ne puisse être raisonnablement considérée comme visant à faire valoir les droits de l'entreprise en cause et ne puisse dès lors servir qu'à harceler la partie adverse. En deuxième lieu, l'action doit être conçue dans le cadre d'un plan ayant pour but d'éliminer la concurrence ... Ces deux conditions doivent être interprétées et appliquées restrictivement, de manière à ne pas tenir en échec l'application du principe général d'accès au juge.') (internal citations omitted).

into play in situations where the role of the governmental agency is merely ministerial.

Regardless of the above, it may be worth asking whether the subsequent decision rendered by the CJEU in *Huawei* may represent an overruling of *ITT Promedia* taking into consideration that it calls for a balance of the fundamental right to legal redress and the application of competition rules.[1219]

B. The Theory of Harm Underlying the Sham Doctrine

The cases examined in the preceding paragraphs altogether denote that, despite their somehow different points of departure, when competition authorities and courts in the US and the EU address the issues of sham or vexatious litigation, they essentially refer to the same conduct, ie the use of court and governmental proceedings irrespective of its outcome and with the main purpose of harassing, deterring or hindering competitors, and the standards developed seem to be very much alike.[1220] The following paragraphs will hence attempt to analyse the economic rationale underlying this exclusionary behaviour in order to more accurately understand how it affects competition and, ultimately, determine whether a deceptive behaviour before the patent office may have the same economic effects and be analysed under the same patterns.

I. Antitrust Injury

That a sham use of court and governmental procedures may represent a real and serious threat to competition does not appear to be in dispute. Not only courts on both sides of the Atlantic but even scholars with a more sceptical view on antitrust laws have acknowledged the considerable threats it entails.[1221] An undertaking well-established on a certain market may, for instance, decide to start legal actions on dubious grounds against

1219 *Huawei* (n 1187) para 59.

1220 Institute for Applied Economic Research (IPEA Brasilia), 'Study on the Anti-Competitive Enforcement of Intellectual Property (IP) Rights: Sham Litigation' (Report for the WIPO Committee on Development and Intellectual Property CDIP/9/INF/6 REV, 2012) 14 <www.wipo.int/edocs/mdocs/mdocs/en/cdip_9/cdip_9_inf_6_rev.pdf> accessed 14 February 2018.

1221 See, eg, Bork (n 1143) 347.

a myriad of new entrants, which would not only force the latter to incur in legal costs to defend themselves but could also delay their entry to the market, obstruct their access to financial funding and even deter other parties from even entering the market altogether. It is true that, in most cases, those effects must be tolerated as inevitable by-products of the judicial system, since private parties have an undeniable right to access the courts and assert their rights. Yet those rights are clearly not absolute and, if they are abused, competition law intervention may be justified.[1222]

At this point it should be clarified that this kind of exclusionary behaviour is not the exclusive domain of intellectual property rights, as the same kind of anticompetitive harm is conceivable with the assertion of any other non-meritorious claim.[1223] Indeed, a plaintiff can harass competitors not only by baselessly suing for the infringement of an IP right, but also by starting legal actions, eg, for an alleged breach of contract or a non-existing tort: the harmful effect does not depend so much on the right asserted but on the collateral damage inflicted because of the process. Moreover, even though courts and scholars often speak of sham or vexatious 'litigation', the anticompetitive conduct does not necessarily need to occur in court. As observed in some of the cases described above, it can also take place in administrative or regulatory settings, eg by filing ungrounded oppositions or complaints. As a matter of fact, when the concept of sham was first coined in the US, it did not refer to judicial procedures.[1224]

From an economic perspective, sham can be classified as a variant of the more general strategy of raising rivals' costs.[1225] As Salop and Scheffman explained, a company can incur in predatory practices not only by temporarily lowering their own revenues to deter competitors, but also by non-price predatory practices that aim at raising competitors' costs.[1226] Broadly speaking, these non-price predatory strategies can be of two different types. On the one hand, they can refer to the attempt to raise the pro-

---

1222 ibid 358-59.

1223 Hovenkamp, *The Antitrust Enterprise* (n 1143) 267.

1224 *Noerr* (n 1161) 144.

1225 Christopher C Klein, 'Strategic Sham Litigation: Economic Incentives in the Context of the Case Law' (1986) 6 Int'l Rev L & Econ 241, 244.

1226 Steven C Salop and David T Scheffman, 'Raising Rivals' Costs' (1983) 73 Am Econ Rev 267. As a matter of fact, non-price predatory practices like strategic litigation may constitute a much more attractive and profitable tool to restrain competition, as it is much easier and cheaper for the predator than, eg, predatory pricing. Susan A Creighton and others, 'Cheap Exclusion' (2005) 72 Antitrust L J 975, 977; Einer Elhauge, 'Making Sense of Antitrust Petitioning Immunity' (1992) 80 Cal L Rev 1177, 1230.

duction costs of some or all of the participants on the market.[1227] On the other hand, a predator may attempt to impose costs on rivals without affecting post-entry production costs.[1228] Cases of sham or vexatious litigation would clearly fall under the second category, as they impose costs on competitors which are not production-related.[1229]

In practice, determining in which cases the act of petitioning a governmental agency or court should be considered anticompetitive can be extremely difficult. One interesting proposal, based on a deeply economic understanding of sham, suggests that the decisive question should be whether the predator's expenditures on litigation can be expected to pay off absent any effect on competition[1230] or, in other words, whether the benefits that the plaintiff would obtain from a favourable outcome alone surpass its litigation costs. For that, it would be necessary to firstly determine the expected gains from succeeding on the merits, properly discounted, and secondly the expected costs of litigation. If the expected costs outweigh the expected benefits that would be obtained directly by the judgment, the plaintiff would necessarily be suing to provoke collateral effects, as otherwise the decision would not make economic sense.[1231] In simple economic equations proposed by Klein,[1232] an *honest* plaintiff would sue only if

$$B > L$$

where B are the expected benefits from a successful suit and L the expected litigation costs. *Dishonest* or sham litigants, on their turn, would sue if

$$X > L$$

where X are the expected collateral benefits to be obtained that do not depend on the outcome of the lawsuit. In reality, a plaintiff could even start a sham legal suit if

$$X < L$$

1227 Christopher C Klein, 'Predation in the Courts: Legal Versus Economic Analysis in Sham Litigation Cases' (1990) 10 Int'l Rev L & Econ 29, 32 (also stressing that the conduct might even raise the predators' production costs themselves, provided that the costs fall disproportionately on their rivals).

1228 ibid.

1229 ibid 33.

1230 Klein, 'Strategic Sham Litigation' (n 1225) 243.

1231 Klein, 'The Economics of Sham Litigation' (n 1143) 16.

1232 For a more thorough explanation of the economics of litigation and sham, see ibid 16-20.

provided that

$$(B + X) > L$$

This strictly economic reading of sham litigation has been supported by different scholars[1233] and J Posner arrived to a very similar conclusion in the *Grip-Pak* decision.[1234] In his view, the relevant question should be whether the 'purpose is not to win a favorable judgment against a competitor but to harass him, and deter others, by the process itself—regardless of outcome—of litigating' and should not depend on whether the plaintiff has a probable cause.[1235] Many claims which are not wholly baseless, he emphasised, may still constitute sham.[1236] What is more, sanctioning this kind of behaviour under antitrust laws should not present any constitutional impediment,[1237] as US procedural laws already include a tort against bad faith litigation even when it is not entirely groundless—and the same

---

1233 Gary Myers, 'Antitrust and First Amendment Implications of Professional Real Estate Investors' (1994) 51 Wash & Lee L Rev 1199, 1227; Scott D Helsel, 'Preventing Predatory Abuses in Litigation between Business Competitors: Focusing on a Litigant's Reasons for Initiating the Litigation to Ensure a Balance between the Constitutional Right to Petition and the Sherman Acts Guarantee of Fair Competition in Business' (1995) 36 Wm & Mary L Rev 1135, 1164; Christopher C Klein, 'Anticompetitive Litigation and Antitrust Liability' (2007) Middle Tennessee State University, Department of Economics and Finance Working Paper 2007/13, 2 <http://capone.mtsu.edu/berc/working/SHAM07WP.pdf> accessed 14 February 2018.

1234 *Grip-Pak* (n 1149).

1235 ibid 472.

1236 ibid ('Suppose a monopolist brought a tort action against its single, tiny competitor; the action had a colorable basis in law; but in fact the monopolist would never have brought the suit — its chances of winning, or the damages it could hope to get if it did win, were too small compared to what it would have to spend on the litigation — except that it wanted to use pretrial discovery to discover its competitor's trade secrets; or hoped that the competitor would be required to make public disclosure of its potential liability in the suit and that this disclosure would increase the interest rate that the competitor had to pay for bank financing; or just wanted to impose heavy legal costs on the competitor in the hope of deterring entry by other firms. In these examples the plaintiff wants to hurt a competitor not by getting a judgment against him, which would be a proper objective, but just by the maintenance of the suit, regardless of its outcome.').

1237 *Grip-Pak* (n 1149) 471 ('If all nonmalicious litigation were immunized from government regulation by the First Amendment, the tort of abuse of process would be unconstitutional -something that, so far as we know, no one believes.').

could probably be argued in the EU at least with regard to UK law, where a very similar tort exists.[1238]

In any case, some of the promoters of this interpretation have themselves recognised that, even if the approach is economically sensible, it would make it easier for defendants to claim sham litigation and could incentivise them to target legitimate suits—thereby leading to 'sham-sham' suits.[1239] The most severe drawback, however, probably resides in the fact that this proposal instinctively assumes that all benefits not directly deriving from the outcome of the procedure are illegitimate and anticompetitive when, in fact, the inference is at least arguable. A trade mark owner, for instance, could decide to sue a small-scale counterfeiter aware that the litigation costs will not be recovered, but also knowing that it would dissuade other potential counterfeiters. Provided that the trade mark is valid and infringed, it would be difficult to argue that the deterrent effect sought by the owner is illegitimate. For the same reason, a patent owner could take legal actions against an infringer without even demanding damages, with the purpose of having a swift procedure and send a signal to the market. In this case, too, it would be hard to conclude that the purpose is anticompetitive if the patent is both valid and infringed, despite the fact that the litigation costs would clearly surpass the direct benefits stemming from the favourable judgment.

The question hence arises as to which of the collateral effects should be considered legitimate and which anticompetitive. Against this background, the two-pronged test advocated by the US Supreme Court in *PREI*—and largely mirrored by the EU's General Court in *ITT Promedia* and *Protégé*—might emerge, after all, as a reasonable first footstep to solve the conundrum.[1240] Under such view, legal actions with some probable cause would be automatically shielded and the 'economic' test suggested above could still enter into play, but only if the action is manifestly baseless.

1238 See text at nn 1153-1154.

1239 Klein, 'Strategic Sham Litigation' (n 1225) 249. Nevertheless, the same author argues that this upshot can be mitigated if courts award attorney fees. Klein, 'Anticompetitive Litigation and Antitrust Liability' (n 1233) 18.

1240 Against, arguing that this test may unduly shelter predatory conducts, see Myers (n 1233) 1221; David McGowan and Mark A Lemley, 'Antitrust Immunity: State Action and Federalism, Petitioning and the First Amendment' (1994) 17 Harv J L & Pub Pol'y 293, 397; Helsel (n 1233) 1138; Lao, 'Reforming the Noerr Doctrine' (n 1149) 986.

II. The Two-Pronged Test in the US and in the EU

As mentioned above, the tests advocated by US and EU courts, at least for adjudicatory procedures, are very much alike and, in general terms, include one objective and one subjective step. Therefore, the following paragraphs separately describe each of those steps and attempt to determine whether a scenario involving a deceptive behaviour before the patent office can be subsumed under their defined parameters. As will be seen, in most cases an antitrust enforcer would not face major difficulties when applying the objective part of the test against that setting, as a patent application that comprises deceiving representations is very likely to be without merit too. When moving on to the second portion of the test, however, problems would probably arise, since the patent applicant might not be interested in harassing or raising rivals' costs—as is the case in regular sham cases—but plainly in obtaining an exclusive right and, in that way, having the government directly bar those rivals from even entering the market.

a. Objective Baselessness or 'Legal Inviability'

According to the test proposed by the US Supreme Court in *PREI*, an action can only be classified as sham if it is, in the first place, 'objectively baseless', ie when 'no reasonable litigant could realistically expect success on the merits.'[1241] In other points of the decision, however, the court defines the objective test in slightly different terms, by speaking of lack of 'probable cause'[1242] and of 'some chance of winning',[1243] which render the standard somewhat imprecise.[1244] On the European side, the objective part of the test is quite similar, as it refers to actions 'which cannot reasonably be considered as an attempt to establish' the undertaking's rights.[1245] Ac-

1241 *PREI* (n 1144) 61.

1242 ibid 62.

1243 ibid 65.

1244 Kobak, 'PREI and the Future of Patent-Antitrust Litigation' (n 1181) 205; Mark A Lemley, 'Antitrust Counterclaims in Patent and Copyright Infringement Cases' (1994) 3 Tex Intell Prop L J 1, 3-4; Lao, 'Reforming the Noerr Doctrine' (n 1149) 985. See also the concurring opinion of J Stevens and J O'Connor in *PREI* (n 1144) (arguing that the definition of objective baselessness offered by the majority is imprecise and broad and suggesting that actions which might have an insignificant chance of success may still be *unreasonable* and, hence, objectively baseless).

1245 *ITT Promedia* (n 1147) para 30.

cording to the General Court, this means that the action should be 'manifestly unfounded'[1246] and that the plaintiff could not 'reasonably consider' to be asserting her rights.[1247]

Whichever definition of the objective test is ultimately employed, the first conclusion that may be drawn is that, if a plaintiff succeeds on the merits, the action must be considered as a reasonable petition to the courts and, hence, not a sham.[1248] That does not mean, however, that all actions which are ultimately dismissed automatically indicate that they were sham,[1249] as citizens have, as a principle, an undeniable right to petition the authorities. Courts on both jurisdictions thence agree that, in those cases, what matters in broad terms is whether the plaintiffs could have reasonably believed that they had some chance of winning.

In this context, the question that follows for the purposes of the present work is whether a patent applicant incurring in misrepresentations before the patent office could be considered to be making a petition which is 'objectively baseless' or 'manifestly unfounded'. The patent applicant would probably allege she is not, since—in the words of the US Supreme Court—there was indeed 'some chance of winning', ie some chance of obtaining the patent—particularly because of the dishonest manners. Provided that the misrepresentations referred to material elements relevant to the grant of the patent, however, a court would probably be more likely to find that the patent application is indeed baseless, since the applicant was aware that the patent would not be granted if the examiner became aware of all the pertinent facts.[1250]

1246 ibid para 56.

1247 ibid para 73.

1248 *PREI* (n 1144) 60, fn 5. As explained above, this conclusion would not be shared by J Posner, Klein and other scholars who advocate for an exclusively 'economic' or subjective test and would hence rule out the objective prong altogether. See text at nn 1230-1238.

1249 ibid 60; *ITT Promedia* (n 1147) paras 60-61 (also emphasising that bringing legal proceedings may only constitute an anticompetitive conduct in exceptional circumstances and that the criterion should be construed strictly, in a manner which does not defeat the fundamental right of access to courts).

1250 *Hydranautics v FilmTec Corp* 70 F 3d 533, 538 (9th Cir 1995) (highlighting that the question had been left open by the courts and interpreting that the enforcement of a patent obtained by 'intentional fraud' cannot be considered to have probable cause); James B Kobak Jr, 'The Doctrine that Will Not Die: Nobelpharma, Walker Process, and the Patent-Antitrust Counterclaim' (1998) 13 Antitrust 47, 47.

An additional question would also emerge as to whether a patent infringement action based on a fraudulently-obtained patent could be considered as manifestly unfounded as well. The plaintiff could again allege that there were some chances of winning—as long as the fraud and the cause of invalidity remained unnoticed—yet a court would most probably conclude that the action is indeed unfounded, as the plaintiff could not reasonably consider to be asserting her rights.[1251]

Consequently, both a deceptive behaviour before the patent office and the enforcement of a patent obtained through that behaviour would most likely meet the first prong of a sham test both in the US and in the EU.

b. Intent or 'Economic Inviability'

Proof that an action is objectively baseless, however, only constitutes the first step of the test. In order to establish an anticompetitive conduct, courts in the US and in the EU understand that a subjective component should also be established. In the case of the US, the Supreme Court stated that the baseless action should conceal 'an attempt to interfere *directly* with the business relationships of a competitor through the use of the governmental process—as opposed to the outcome of that process.'[1252] In the EU, the action would be inadmissible when it 'can ... only serve to harass the opposite party.'[1253] Additionally, the EU courts specifically require that the action 'is conceived in the framework of a plan whose goal is to eliminate competition.'[1254]

As already noted, this part of the test seems to very much resemble the more 'economic' test for sham advocated by Judge Posner and Klein,[1255] as it draws the attention to the collateral benefits that the plaintiff could expect to obtain besides the outcome of the procedure itself. As a matter of fact, the US Supreme Court itself acknowledges that this part of the test refers to the 'economic viability' of the contested lawsuit—as opposed to the 'legal viability' embodied in the objective prong portrayed above.[1256] Even so, this second prong has not been able to escape criticism. Firstly, it has been argued that it might be redundant, at least within a two-step test,

1251 O'Donnell (n 1143) 25; *Hydranautics* (n 1250) 538.
1252 *PREI* (n 1144) 60-61 (emphasis in original) (internal citations omitted).
1253 *ITT Promedia* (n 1147) para 30.
1254 ibid.
1255 See text at nn 1230-1238.
1256 *PREI* (n 1144) 61.

because an action that fails the objective part of the test would necessarily fail the subjective one too.[1257] In other words, if a plaintiff starts a legal action aware that it is manifestly baseless, it would be extremely difficult to argue that it was not started with improper purposes.[1258] In fact, the language of the test proposed in *ITT Promedia* seems to insinuate itself that the intent to harass competitors would be a natural consequence of the action being baseless.[1259] Secondly, it has also been pointed out that a literal application of this test might unduly shield baseless suits, considering that it requires that the plaintiff's *sole* purpose should be to harass competitors.[1260] In practice, it might be difficult to conceive a situation where the only intent of litigation is to harass rivals, since a plaintiff may always have at least some minimal hope of success.[1261] And if the plaintiff did seek to win the lawsuit despite of it being manifestly unfounded, a literal construction of the test would not permit the court to deem it sham—particularly under the language of the US Supreme Court in *PREI*. Finally, and on a more general level, it has been argued that intent often constitutes an unreliable guide to assess competition cases.[1262] This might be particularly so in the case of intellectual property rights, as the improper exclusionary intent might be difficult to distinguish from the intent to exclude competitors that is present in every IP infringement claim.[1263]

Be that as it may, the sham tests sketched by US and EU courts both clearly require to look into the subjective stance or 'economic viability' of the plaintiff. At this point, hence, a question necessarily arises within the context of this work: would it be possible to apply that subjective test vis-à-vis a mischievous handling of a patent application at the patent office? Hypothetically, a firm could apply for a patent for an assumed invention which is clearly ineligible for protection (eg, because it had been publicly

1257 Myers (n 1233) 1226; Lao, 'Reforming the Noerr Doctrine' (n 1149) 986.

1258 Myers (n 1233) 1226; Kobak, 'PREI and the Future of Patent-Antitrust Litigation' (n 1181) 208.

1259 *ITT Promedia* (n 1147) para 30 (emphasising that an action would be anticompetitive when it cannot reasonably be considered as an attempt to establish the firm's rights 'and can *therefore* only serve to harass the opposite party.') (emphasis added).

1260 Lao, 'Reforming the Noerr Doctrine' (n 1149) 986-87.

1261 Elhauge, 'Making Sense of Antitrust Petitioning Immunity' (n 1226) 1231; Jonathan Galloway, 'Driving Innovation: A Case for Targeted Competition Policy in Dynamic Markets' (2011) 34 World Competition 73, 88.

1262 Denis Waelbroeck, 'Tough Competition: What is the Relevance of Intention in Article 82 cases?' (2006) 5(8) Comp Law Insight 5, 6.

1263 Lao, 'Reforming the Noerr Doctrine' (n 1149) 987.

used and sold by the applicant for several years before the filing date), yet the patent may be nonetheless granted because the cause of invalidity could not be detected during the examination at the patent office.[1264] Assuming that the patent applicant was well aware of the invalidity, it would be hard to argue that the decision to nonetheless pursue the application by deceptive demeanours was made with the purpose to 'harass' competitors or to 'interfere' with them through the use of the patent procedure. Admittedly, it is possible to conceive a firm making sham patent applications with the sole purpose of harassing competitors, eg by inducing them to incur in legal costs by lodging observations and oppositions, by generating legal uncertainty or even by hindering competitors' innovation efforts.[1265] Yet if patent applicants deliberately conceal relevant information or make misrepresentations to the patent office, it seems more likely that their ultimate purpose is to obtain the unwarranted patent rather than to cause collateral harm through the process. Put another way, their focus would not be so much on raising their rivals' costs but on obtaining a governmental adjudication that directly forbids third parties from manufacturing or selling a specific product. Under these circumstances, the application of the subjective test of *PREI* and *ITT Promedia* against scenarios involving a deceptive behaviour before the patent office would probably leave the latter without antitrust sanction.

At this point, it seems fair to enquire why the *PREI* and *ITT Promedia* criteria do not adequately apply to cases involving deceptive conducts. Is it because a deceptive conduct does not actually raise any antitrust concerns? Because the tests are not correctly formulated? Or is it simply that the antitrust concerns that they raise are somehow different from those posed by sham or vexatious litigation strategies? As previously mentioned, when the US Supreme Court drafted the two-pronged test in *PREI*, it explicitly refused to decide whether—and, if so, how—that test could apply to cases of

---

1264 See *Les Laboratoires Servier v Apotex Inc* [2008] EWCA Civ 445 [9].

1265 See, eg, *Boehringer Ingelheim* (Case COMP/39.246), Commission Press Release IP/11/842 'Antitrust: Commission welcomes improved market entry for lung disease treatments (6 July 2011) (where Boehringer was accused by the Commission of having filed for patent applications for combinations of substances with a new active substance that had been discovered by Almirall a potential competitor and could block or considerably delay its market entry; the case was concluded with a settlement agreement between the parties).

fraud or misrepresentations,[1266] thereby leaving the question open.[1267] EU courts, on their turn, adopted a less ambiguous approach. When discussing *AstraZeneca*'s first abuse—which concerned a deceptive conduct before the patent office—the General Court indeed refused to apply the *ITT Promedia* criteria, emphasising that these two cases involved different antitrust concerns. The harm to competition in *AstraZeneca*'s first abuse, explained the General Court, did not stem from the legal procedures but from the mere possession of the intellectual property right, which may alone lead to keeping competitors away.[1268] The harm that a deceptive conduct may impose on competition, hence, might simply be of a different nature and incapable of being analysed as a sham case.

Finally, and despite of the above, the question might arise as to whether the subsequent enforcement of a patent obtained through deceptive means could anyway fulfil the subjective part of the sham test. In that scenario, the patent holder could indeed decide to start legal proceedings aware that the suit will be ultimately dismissed because of the invalidity of the enforced right, with the sole purpose of harassing competitors and forcing them to incur in expensive legal costs, deterring third parties from entering or remaining in the market, or even hampering innovation.[1269] In that case, the situation would not essentially differ from a typical sham litigation case: it would restrain competition in a very similar way and the subjective element of the sham test would be easily applicable. In fact, under that scenario the relevance of the deceptive behaviour seems to be rather secondary. The analysis would be essentially the same if the patentee, instead of having deceived the patent office, only later became aware of the invalidity of the patent and nonetheless decided to proceed with the infringement suit.[1270]

1266 *PREI* (n 1144) 61, fn 6.

1267 The Supreme Court did clarify, however, that misrepresentations outside the political arena would not be entitled to antitrust immunity. *Allied Tube* (n 1168) 504.

1268 GC Decision in *AstraZeneca* (n 1216) paras 362-63. See also Opinion of AG Mazák in *AstraZeneca* (n 1216) para 52 (essentially agreeing with the understanding of the General Court).

1269 Christina Bohannan and Herbert Hovenkamp, *Creation without Restraint: Promoting Liberty and Rivalry in Innovation* (OUP 2012) 247.

1270 It is important to remember at this point that not any enforcement of an invalid patent justifies antitrust intervention as long as the patentee had a reasonable ground for bringing the suit. As mentioned above, patentees have an undeniable right to enforce their patents, which should include those patents that are declared invalid but which the patentee could have reasonably believed to

It is also conceivable, however, that a plaintiff enforces a fraudulently-obtained patent with the undisputed purpose of obtaining a favourable judgment, trusting that the cause of invalidity will remain undetected. In this case, applying the *PREI* and *ITT Promedia* criteria would again become problematic,[1271] as the competitive harm suffered by rivals would not stem from the procedures themselves but from their outcome and the continued existence of the underlying intellectual property right: the lawsuit would just be a continuation of the exclusionary effect that the patent right already had. As the General Court explained in *AstraZeneca*, the anticompetitive harm can be inflicted without even attempting to enforce the patent, as the mere grant and subsequent possession of a patent can already have an impact on competition.[1272]

Notwithstanding the correctness or not of the sham criteria—a question which is beyond the scope of the present work—what seems clear from the above is that, even when a deceptive conduct before the patent office may, under certain circumstances, pave the way for a sham case, the anticompetitive concerns that it raises are of a different nature and merit a distinct analysis.[1273]

III. *Individual vs Patterns of Anticompetitive Litigation*

An interesting discussion that emerged in the US after the *PREI* decision refers to the question whether the test therein developed should also be applied—particularly as to its objective part—to situations where an undertaking institutes not one but multiple administrative or judicial proceed-

---

be valid, or at least to discuss it in court. Otherwise, the right of petitioning and access to courts would be severely curtailed. *BE&K Construction Co v National Labor Relations Board* 536 US 516, 532-33 (2002).

1271 See, however, O'Donnell (n 1143) 29 (arguing that the *PREI* criteria should be interpreted more broadly as encompassing any unlawful purpose, which would hence include the enforcement of improperly obtained patents).

1272 GC Decision in *AstraZeneca* (n 1216) paras 362-63. See also, in the same vein, Christopher R Leslie, 'The Anticompetitive Effects of Unenforced Invalid Patents' (2006) 91 Minn L Rev 101, 113.

1273 Scott Filmore, 'Defining the Misrepresentation Exception to the Noerr-Pennington Doctrine' (2001) 49 Univ Kan L Rev 423, 446; Floyd (n 1149) 407; James C Cooper and William E Kovacic, 'U.S. Convergence with International Competition Norms: Antitrust Law and Public Restraints on Competition' (2010) 90 Bost U L Rev 1555, 1606; Lemley, 'Antitrust Counterclaims in Patent and Copyright Infringement Cases' (n 1244) 6.

ings.[1274] The debate essentially emerged because, before *PREI*, the US Supreme Court had ruled in *California Motor Transport* that a pattern of repetitive petitioning and litigation can amount to an antitrust violation even despite the fact that more than half of the claims conforming the pattern had been ultimately successful.[1275] Given that PREI—which concerned one single sham suit—had cited *California Motor Transport* approvingly, the FTC and a number of scholars have interpreted that the latter decision has not been overruled and that cases involving multiple suits should be governed by it rather than by the *PREI* criteria.[1276] According to this view, if a plaintiff starts numerous legal actions, the fact that some of them may be meritorious should not affect the overall antitrust assessment as long as it can be proved that the plaintiff sought to impose collateral harm on defendants and was indifferent to the outcome.[1277] At least two appellate courts in the US have followed this interpretation.[1278] Others scholars, however, consider that *PREI* may have actually overruled *California Motor Transport* on that particular aspect, since nothing in the former decision suggests that the number of lawsuits makes a substantial difference.[1279] In this sense, it has been argued that the *PREI* criteria should simply be applied to each of the different actions initiated, and the ones which are found to be baseless can make for an antitrust case. Moreover, the find-

1274 Lemley, 'Antitrust Counterclaims in Patent and Copyright Infringement Cases' (n 1244) 5.

1275 Kobak, 'PREI and the Future of Patent-Antitrust Litigation' (n 1181) 203.

1276 FTC, 'Enforcement Perspectives on the Noerr-Pennington Doctrine: An FTC Staff Report' (2006) 29 <www.ftc.gov/sites/default/files/documents/reports/ftc-staff-report-concerning-enforcement-perspectives-noerr-pennington-doctrine/p013518enfperspectnoerr-penningtondoctrine.pdf> accessed 14 February 2018; Eugene Crew, 'The Use of Patent Litigation to Violate the Antitrust Laws' (2006) 11 Intell Prop L Bull 69, 74; Cooper and Kovacic (n 1273) 1603.

1277 FTC, 'Enforcement Perspectives' (n 1276) 31.

1278 *USS-Posco Industries v Contra Costa County Building & Construction Trades Council* 31 F 3d 800, 811 (9th Cir 1994) ('[w]hen dealing with a series of lawsuits, the question is not whether any one of them has merit –some may turn out to, just as a matter of chance– but whether they are brought pursuant to a policy of starting legal proceedings without regard to the merits and for the purpose of injuring a market rival.'); *Primetime 24 Joint Venture v National Broadcasting Co Inc* 219 F 3d 92, 101 (2nd Cir 2000) (interpreting that the two-step inquiry proposed by *PREI* is only applicable in case of a single legal action).

1279 Russell Wofford, 'Considering the "Pattern Litigation" Exception to the *Noerr-Pennington* Antitrust Defense' (2003) 49 Wayne L Rev 95, 99.

ing of numerous baseless actions could even be used as evidence of subjective motivation.[1280]

On the European side, it has been argued that the slightly different language used in *ITT Promedia*'s test vis-à-vis *PREI* may respond to the fact that, in that case, the suits initiated against ITT Promedia had been in fact multiple.[1281] The test in *ITT Promedia*, therefore, would be equally applicable to scenarios involving both single and patterns of suits, although its language may allow courts to apply it in a way that, even if some of the numerous suits are not objectively baseless, the baselessness of the litigation pattern as a whole may be considered.[1282]

In any case, even if both jurisdictions admitted that the objective part of the sham test must be applied in a less rigid fashion in cases involving patterns of litigation, the difficulties to categorise a deceptive conduct as sham would probably remain. As explained above, it is the subjective part of the sham test—as well as the differences in the ultimate effects that they may have on competition—that proves more problematic for cases involving misrepresentations.

IV. Litigation as part of a Broader Pattern of Conduct

Finally, it has been argued that antitrust rules may also apply differently in cases where litigation is only a part of a broader anticompetitive scheme.[1283] This interpretation dates back to *Kobe*, a US decision of 1952 where a Court of Appeals had held that a pattern of conduct involving the acquisition of every relevant patent in a particular market, the forming of a 'closed' patent pool and the subsequent enforcement of those rights could amount to an antitrust violation.[1284] In the view of the court, even when the infringement suits themselves could have been lawful and would not suffice to sustain an antitrust case when considered in isolation, they could still form a broader, unlawful 'monopolistic scheme'.[1285] The decision was rendered even before *Noerr* and some have argued that it might not be

1280 Herbert Hovenkamp and others, *IP and Antitrust: An Analysis of Antitrust Principles Applied to Intellectual Property Law* (2nd edn Supp 2013, Wolters Kluwer) para 11.3b3.

1281 Vezzoso (n 1201) 533.

1282 ibid.

1283 See, eg, Crew (n 1276) 74.

1284 *Kobe Inc v Dempsey Pump Co* 198 F 2d 416 (10th Cir 1952).

1285 ibid 425.

good law any more,[1286] yet competition law enforcers both in the US and Europe have occasionally shown signs in favour of analyses which focus on overall strategies or conduct patterns that may cumulatively restrain competition—even when, individually considered, those conducts may not amount to an abuse.[1287]

In this light, if a deceptive conduct before the patent office is perceived simply as one additional element of a broader anticompetitive strategy, it would not be necessary to analyse it in isolation but under a more general standard to determine whether the whole strategy could be deemed to remain within the scope of 'competition on the merits'. Such an approach may, however, raise concerns in terms of legal certainty and could be used as a subterfuge to avoid the ordinary antitrust standards.[1288]

C. *Wrapping-up: A Simple Genus-Species Relationship?*

On the basis of the foregoing, it can be observed that courts and competition authorities in the US and in the EU both recognise the question of sham or vexatious litigation as a genuine competition law concern which, in general terms, refers to situations where a firm is able to raise rivals' costs by a harassing use of court or governmental procedures without a sincere interest on their outcome. At the same time, the same courts and authorities do not hesitate to recognise that citizens have an undeniable right to petition the government which may, in practice, limit competition law's

---

1286 Fischel (n 1149) 113.

1287 See, eg, *Intel Corporation* (FTC Docket 9341) Statement of Chairman Leibowitz and Commissioner Rosch of 16 December 2009 <www.ftc.gov/system/files/documents/public_statements/568601/091216intelchairstatement.pdf> accessed 14 February 2018 (finding that the antitrust concern is raised by a 'course of conduct' that includes deception and coertion to stall competitors); *Intel* (Case COMP/C-3/37.990) Commission Decision of 13 May 2009 [2009] OJ C227/13, para 1747 (holding that Intel's conducts should not be viewed in isolation but as a 'long-term comprehensive strategy' to foreclose competition); Decision of the Autorità Garante della Concorrenza e del Mercato (AGCM) 23194 of 11 January 2012 - *A431: Ratiopharm/Pfizer* (Bollettino 2/2012) paras 233 and 245 (finding that the anticompetitive violation arose from a general strategy conformed by patenting and litigation activities).

1288 Herbert Hovenkamp and others, *IP and Antitrust* (n 1280) para 11.4f; Nicolas Petit, 'Microsoft v Google – Karate Competition Law?' (*Chillin' Competition*, 7 April 2011) <http://chillingcompetition.com/2011/04/07/microsoft-v-google-karate-competition-law> accessed 14 February 2018.

range of application. In an attempt to find a proper balance, each has developed a set of criteria along similar lines. In order to amount to an antitrust violation, they both agree, an act of petitioning the government should be objectively baseless and aimed at harassing competitors by means of the procedure itself.

As noted above, these tests do not seem to be particularly well suited against scenarios involving a deceptive conduct before the patent office—or before any other governmental office for that matter. Admittedly, there are situations where a mischievous behaviour may precede a sham enforcement, yet deceptive behaviours seem to be capable of harming competition in their own way and may not always be reachable by the sham or vexatious litigation tests. This, however, does not necessarily prove that those tests are in themselves inadequate, but rather that the antitrust concerns raised by the deceptive conduct itself may be of a somehow different nature. The sham doctrine, indeed, is probably more akin to doctrines against predatory strategies, in this case aimed at preventing undertakings from artificially raising rivals' costs by resorting to public procedures in which they are not really interested. A misleading conduct before the patent office, in turn, may lead to a different injury to competition, in which a governmental act—triggered by the deceptive petitioning—impedes third parties from even competing in the market. In that case, the anticompetitive injury (ie, the reduction of price competition) flows directly from the governmental act rather than as a collateral effect of the act of petitioning. For this very reason, a set of standards that can equally fit both scenarios seems difficult to conceive.[1289]

Against this backdrop, it is necessary to analyse scenarios involving deceptive representations before public authorities under a different light. The next section of this chapter constitutes an effort in this direction.

3. *Deceptive Conduct before the Patent Office as a Case of Inducing Government Action through Improper Means*

From a theoretical point of view, statutes, regulations, court rulings, and any other type of governmental action—including patent grants—are all equally capable of restraining competition. They can create legal monopolies, fix prices, create barriers to entry, grant exclusive rights or privileges to a particular undertaking, etc. As a matter of fact, governments restrain

1289 Cooper and Kovacic (n 1273) 1606.

competition in different ways all the time, yet in many cases they have legitimate reasons to do so and are, as a principle, excluded from competition law scrutiny in the US[1290] and, to a lesser extent, also in the EU.[1291] But when a governmental act imposes a restraint on competition triggered by a private party who, eg, submits misleading information to the decision-maker, the question inevitably arises as to whether, from an antitrust perspective, said party may be held responsible for those restraints. In other words, whether the act of providing false or misleading information to obtain a certain ruling from a public authority can amount to a violation of the competition laws. As explained above, these situations appear to bring forward a problem different from sham and may entail even greater

1290 See text at nn 780-815. In the US, immunity is recognised as a principle under the *state action* doctrine, which was coined by the Supreme Court in *Parker v Brown* 317 US 341 (1943). Later, the Supreme Court explained that, in order to recognise antitrust immunity, the restraint must be "one clearly articulated and affirmatively expressed as state policy" and said policy must be actively supervised by the state itself. *California Retail Liquor Dealers Assn v Midcal Aluminum Inc* 445 US 97, 105 (1980). See also Hovenkamp, *The Antitrust Enterprise* (n 1143) 236 ('antitrust is concerned about the private, discretionary exercise of market power, *not* with government decision making.') (emphasis in original); McGowan and Lemley (n 1240) 320-21 (the state action doctrine in the US 'protects both governments and the private enterprises that lobby them from liability for anticompetitive government conduct, without regard to the consequences for competition or the legitimate concerns of the antitrust laws.').

1291 See text at nn 881-891. See also Case 13/77 *SA GB-INNO-BM v Association des Détaillants en Tabac (ATAB)* [1977] ECR 2115, para 31 ('while it is true that article 86 is directed at undertakings, nonetheless it is also true that the Treaty imposes a duty on Member States not to adopt or maintain in force any measure which could deprive that provision of its effectiveness'); Case 267/86 *Pascal Van Eycke v ASPA NV* [1988] ECR 4769, para 16 (explaining that such would be the case 'if a Member State were to require or favour the adoption of agreements, decisions or concerted practices contrary to Article 85 or to reinforce their effects, or to deprive its own legislation of its official character by delegating to private traders responsibility for taking decisions affecting the economic sphere'); Case C-185/91 *Bundesanstalt für den Güterfernverkehr v Gebrüder Reiff GmbH & Co KG* [1993] ECR I-5801, para 24 (further clarifying that Member States are not precluded from establishing restraints when imposed on the basis of considerations of public interest and under the supervision of public authorities). For a general view, see Fernando Castillo de la Torre, 'State Action Defence in EC Competition Law' (2005) 28 World Competition 407. For a comparative analysis, see Eleanor M Fox and Deborah Healey, 'When the State Harms Competition: the Role for Competition Law' (2014) 79 Antitrust L J 769; Daniel A Crane, 'Judicial Review of Anticompetitive State Action: Two Models in Comparative Perspective (2013) 1 J Antitrust Enforcement 418.

threats to competition.[1292] As the FTC explains, misrepresentations can 'subvert governmental processes, resulting in well-intentioned but ill-informed rules or regulations that grant firms monopoly power or otherwise harm consumers.'[1293]

Provided that this kind of behaviour indeed falls within the scope of competition laws,[1294] a myriad of new questions emerge. On the one hand, it may not always be easy to recognise the causal link between the private party's behaviour and the governmental act, ie whether the latter was the direct result of the former or whether the former had only a marginal or insignificant impact on the judgment of the decision-maker. On the other hand, even assuming that a deceptive conduct directly leads to the passing of a governmental act, its potential and actual effects on competition should be evaluated as well—particularly bearing in mind that not every public act has the same effects on the market and that tools under other areas of law may be capable of diluting their actual impact.

In the light of the above, this section is first devoted to briefly analyse how US and EU competition agencies and courts have dealt with the general issue of antitrust liability due to improper inducement of governmental action and then moves to understand how a deceptive conduct before the patent office may be deemed as a specific variety within that category of misconducts. Subsequently, the section attempts to articulate the suitable theory of harm in the context of patent grants and examines in detail the different elements that should be taken into account in order to turn a deceptive conduct before the patent office into a competition law case, particularly with regard to the materiality of the offensive conduct, the level of discretion of the decision-maker and the concrete effects of the conduct on competition. Finally, and in view that an invalid patent which remains in force may have a continued effect on the market, the chapter concludes by raising the question whether the subsequent ownership or enforcement of an illicitly-obtained patent may also warrant competition law interven-

1292 Phillip E Areeda and Herbert Hovenkamp, *Antitrust Law: An Analysis of Antitrust Principles and Their Application* (3rd edn, Aspen 2011) para 204a; Richard A Posner, *Antitrust Law* (2nd edn, Univ of Chicago Press 2001) 260 ('Some acontractual methods of monopolizing, such as fraud on the Patent Office, are among the most serious exclusionary practices.').

1293 FTC, 'Enforcement Perspectives on the Noerr-Pennington Doctrine' (n 1276) 16.

1294 Christopher R Leslie, 'Patents of Damocles' (2008) 83 Ind L J 133, 139 ('When a patent applicant commits fraud against the Patent Office and subsequently achieves monopoly power because of the fraudulently issued patent, antitrust laws are implicated.').

tion—a question that may become of utmost importance in the EU, considering the limitations of art 102 TFEU when dealing with situations that involve an illegal acquisition of monopoly power by non-dominant undertakings.

Before proceeding, a brief clarification deserves to be made. Because this issue mainly refers to the unlawful acquisition of patents, it may be appealing to draw a parallel with abuses in derivative acquisition—or exclusive licensing—of patents from third parties, which have occasionally been the object of concern of both EU and US competition agencies and courts.[1295] Despite the apparent similarity, though, the scenarios do not seem to be entirely comparable. In cases of derivative acquisition of intellectual property rights, the focus is put on seemingly legitimate legal acts which result in an undertaking relinquishing part of its influence on the market—its exclusive right—in favour of another market participant, therefore somehow resembling the concerns of traditional merger control. The same way competition law tends to pay more attention to firms who increase their market power by acquiring or merging with competitors rather than to those who improve their market share on their own merits, the acquisition of intellectual property rights from third parties raises more competitive concerns than the development of an IP portfolio through internal R&D efforts. In cases of deceptive conduct before the patent office, however, the focus is not set on the accumulation of valid intellectual property rights but on the illegitimate procurement of an exclusive right which should not have been granted at all.

A. *Deceptively Inducing Government Action as a Competition Law Concern*

I. *The General Question under US Law*

As previously mentioned, US courts have consistently acknowledged that the act of petitioning a public authority is, as a principle, immune from the antitrust rules.[1296] To date, the only exception expressly admitted by

1295 Case T-51/89 *Tetra Pak Rausing SA v Commission* [1990] ECR II-309 (*Tetra Pak I*) (finding that the acquisition by a dominant firm of an exclusive patent license may constitute an abuse of a dominant position); *SCM Corp v Xerox Corp* 645 F 2d 1195 (2nd Cir 1981) (recognising that the acquisition by a dominant competitor in a market of a patent covering a substantial share of the same market can configure a monopolisation case).

1296 See text at nn 780ff in ch 5.

the Supreme Court is the sham defence described in the previous section. Less clear is the question whether a separate exception endures for cases where the private party furnishes the governmental body with false information in an attempt to secure a governmental act that harms competition.

As it may be recalled, the US Supreme Court had decided in *Omni* that a conspiracy between a private party and a governmental agency does not justify an exception to the general petitioning immunity.[1297] This conclusion has been interpreted by the Court of Appeals for the Third Circuit as implying that sham should remain the only exception to the *Noerr* immunity and that no antitrust liability can be predicated when the anticompetitive injuries are inflicted directly by the state—even if a deceitful conduct affects the decision-making process.[1298] The Supreme Court, however, had hinted in *California Motor Transport* and in *Allied Tube*—though in both cases in *dicta*—that deceptive practices are not always immunised, particularly when the petitioning takes place in adjudicatory processes and other non-political arenas.[1299] Even so, when the Supreme Court later had the opportunity to shed some more light on the question, it expressly declined to decide whether such an exception really exists.[1300]

It has been suggested that recognising an exception to *Noerr* for misrepresentations is in fact a natural consequence of *Walker Process*,[1301] despite the fact that *Noerr* was not even mentioned in that case. As explained above, the Supreme Court held in that decision that the enforcement of a patent procured by fraud on the patent office can amount to a violation of the Sherman Act.[1302] On this basis, Lao interprets that *Walker Process* is more than a case about the intersection of patent and antitrust law and

---

1297 *Omni* (n 1147) 383.

1298 *Armstrong Surgical Center Inc v Armstrong County Memorial Hospital* 185 F 3d 154, 162 (3rd Cir 1999). See also *Premier Electrical Construction Co v National Electrical Contractors Assn Inc* 814 F 2d 358, 376 (7th Cir 1987) (arriving to the same conclusion before *Omni* was decided). In a similar vein, see Handler and De Sevo (n 1149) 10-14.

1299 *California Motor Transport* (n 1162) 513 ('Misrepresentations, condoned in the political arena, are not immunized when used in the adjudicatory process'); *Allied Tube* (n 1168) 500 ('in less political arenas, unethical and deceptive practices can constitute abuses of administrative or judicial processes that may result in antitrust violations').

1300 *PREI* (n 1144) 61, fn 6.

1301 Floyd (n 1149) 422; Lao, 'Reforming the Noerr Doctrine' (n 1149) 977.

1302 *Walker Process Equipment Inc v Food Machinery & Chemical Corp* 382 US 172, 174 (1965).

supports the general principle that fraud in any petitioning process deprives the petitioner from antitrust immunity.[1303] Others, however, understand that the fraud element in *Walker Process* is overestimated and that it does not differ much from any other sham case.[1304] If interpreted under this light, *Walker Process* would not truly support a separate and more general exception for misrepresentations.[1305]

Be that as it may, the FTC has carried out a comprehensive study on the existing case law on the issue and concluded that—whether on the basis of *Walker Process* or not, deemed as a separate exception or treated under the sham rubric—the vast majority of lower courts understand that misrepresentations in non-political arenas are not worthy of antitrust immunity.[1306] Yet considering that the rigid definition of sham advanced by the Supreme Court in *PREI* has made it difficult to squeeze misrepresentations into those standards,[1307] a number of scholars and the FTC itself advocate for a separate exception.[1308]

1303 Lao, 'Reforming the Noerr Doctrine' (n 1149) 977-78.

1304 Hovenkamp, *The Antitrust Enterprise* (n 1143) 267. This, however, does not seem to be the view of the Federal Circuit, who has refused to consider *Walker Process* as a sham case and recognises that they both represent two alternative grounds of defence in patent litigation. *Nobelpharma AB v Implant Innovations Inc* 141 F 3d 1059, 1071 (Fed Cir 1998) ('*PRE* and *Walker Process* provide alternative legal grounds on which a patentee may be stripped of its immunity from the antitrust laws …').

1305 James B Kobak Jr and Robert P Reznick, 'Antitrust Liability for Statements about Intellectual Property: Unocal, Unitherm and New Uncertainty' (2004) 19 Antitrust 87, 90. See also Filmore (n 1273) 444 (arguing that a general misrepresentation exception should be recognised but stating that *Walker Process* does not provide sufficient basis).

1306 *Union Oil Company of California (Unocal)* (FTC Docket 9305) Opinion of the Commission of 7 July 2004, 16-17 <http://www.ftc.gov/sites/default/files/documents/cases/2004/07/040706commissionopinion.pdf> accessed 14 February 2018.

1307 Cooper and Kovacic (n 1273) 1606.

1308 Filmore (n 1273) 443; Floyd (n 1149) 455; Lao, 'Reforming the Noerr Doctrine' (n 1149) 1022; FTC, 'Enforcement Perspectives on the Noerr-Pennington Doctrine' (n 1276) 23; Cooper and Kovacic (n 1273) 1606; Note, 'Deception as an Antitrust Violation' (2012) 125 Harv L Rev 1235, 1255. See also Elhauge, 'Making Sense of Antitrust Petitioning Immunity' (n 1226) 1247-48 (arguing that, in misrepresentation cases, *Noerr* immunity can be denied on two doctrinal grounds: (i) because petitioning is only immunised when the restraint is the result of a 'valid' governmental action, and that would not be the case if the action is procured by fraud; or (ii) because the restraint does not truly result from the governmental action when that action is tainted by fraud).

II. The General Question under EU Law

On the European side, the question has drawn fairly limited attention.[1309] In general terms, EU courts also recognise that approaching the government on itself does not ordinarily clash with the competition rules. This principle can already be spotted in *Hilti*, where the Court of First Instance (today General Court) tacitly suggested that petitioning the government does not raise competitive concerns, even if the result of the petitioning would in fact lead to restraints on competition.[1310] Soon afterwards, in *French-West African Shipowners' Committees*, the Commission acknowledged in a more explicit way that approaching a public authority is not in itself an infringement of competition law.[1311]

An exception to this principle was first found by the Commission and the Court of First Instance in the *ITT Promedia* case described above, in the context of petitioning the courts.[1312] While highlighting that it is 'only in wholly exceptional circumstances' that the bringing of legal proceedings can constitute an abuse of a dominant position, it was recognised that vexatious litigation may constitute one of those exceptional cases.[1313] The question whether misrepresentations to public authorities justify a separate exception, however, remained unanswered.

That the question remained unanswered was explicitly acknowledged by the CJEU in *Compagnie Maritime Belge*, yet the court also considered that it was not necessary to solve the controversy at that point either.[1314] In that case, a shipping conference (Cewal) had entered into an agreement

1309 Richard Wainwright and André Bouquet, 'State Intervention and Action in EC Competition Law' in Barry Hawk (ed), *International Antitrust Law & Policy: Fordham Corporate Law 2003* (Juris Publishing 2004) 560. For a thorough review of the case law, see Vossestein (n 1201).

1310 Case T-30/89 *Hilti AG v Commission* [1991] ECR II-1439, para 117 (stating that, if instead of incurring in commercial practices designed to exclude competitors Hilti had approached the government to request a ruling that restrained competition based on safety reasons, such conduct would not have raised concerns under competition law).

1311 *French-West African Shipowners' Committees* (Case IV/32.450) Commission Decision 92/262/EEC [1992] OJ L134/1, para 68 (also suggesting that there might be situations were approaching the government may not be exempted, eg when the undertakings' sole purpose is for public authorities to shield their restrictive practices).

1312 See text at nn 1197ff.

1313 *ITT Promedia* (n 1147) paras 58-61.

1314 Joined Cases C-395/96 P and C-396/96 P *Compagnie Maritime Belge Transports* v *Commission* [2000] ECR I-1365, para 83 ('It is therefore unnecessary to consider

with the Zairean government which provided for exclusivity for the members of the conference, although it also allowed derogations to said exclusivity subject to the agreement of the two parties. When the Zairean government later unilaterally authorised an independent shipping operation, Cewal approached the authorities of that country demanding strict observance of the agreement and of its exclusive right. In its defence, Cewal argued that its demands constituted legitimate petitioning to the government, yet the CJEU interpreted that requesting a public authority to comply with a contractual obligation cannot be compared with a mere incitement of the authority to take action.[1315] In the view of the court, these cases cannot be treated in the same way because in the former scenario the public authority has no discretion and is bound to observe the legal rights enforced.[1316] In that case, hence, the exclusionary effect would not flow from a governmental decision nor from the agreement itself—which allowed derogations to the exclusive right—but from the private party's discretionary vetoing.[1317] A somehow similar conclusion was reached by the CJEU in *CIF*, where it stated that competition law may be applied against an undertaking's exclusionary conduct even if that conduct is facilitated or encouraged by national legislation—yet not when it is legally *required*.[1318]

Around the same time that the CJEU declined to decide on the issue in *Compagnie Maritime Belge*, the Court of First Instance seemed to insinuate in *IPS* that the submission of misleading information to a public authority cannot amount to a competition law infringement when the authority has the necessary powers to verify the information submitted and when the aggrieved party actively intervenes in the proceedings.[1319] That case, however, was ultimately decided on different grounds and it was only in *AstraZeneca*, several years later, that the courts were finally presented with a case that involved misleading representations before a governmental agency as a core question. Although the case involved a very singular set of facts, the General Court—whose decision was later confirmed by the CJEU—attempted to draw a more general conclusion by stating that

whether, and in what circumstances, mere incitement of a government to take action may constitute abuse within the meaning of Article 86 of the Treaty.').

1315 ibid para 82.

1316 ibid.

1317 Vossestein (n 1201) 1398.

1318 Case C-198/01 *Consorzio Industrie Fiammiferi (CIF) v AGCM* [2003] ECR I-8055, para 58.

1319 *IPS* (n 1186) paras 200-03.

> the submission to the public authorities of misleading information liable to lead them into error and therefore to make possible the grant of an exclusive right to which an undertaking is not entitled, or to which it is entitled for a shorter period, constitutes a practice falling outside the scope of competition on the merits which may be particularly restrictive of competition.[1320]

As the Commission explained, the special responsibility that endures on dominant firms not to impair genuine undistorted competition[1321] also covers the use of public procedures or regulations.[1322] The courts further stressed that the assessment of whether representations are misleading or not may vary according to the circumstances of each case[1323] and that the level of discretion of the public authorities and the extent to which they are compelled to verify the accuracy of the information provided may constitute decisive factors.[1324] In that case, for instance, the national patent offices were deemed to have exercised a rather limited degree of discretion and this factor spoke in favour of a broader antitrust accountability.[1325]

III. Can a Deceptive Conduct before the Patent Office be analysed as an Illegitimate Inducement of Government Action?

From a constitutional or administrative law angle, a patent office does not essentially differ from any other governmental agency, nor does the grant of a patent from any other governmental action. In the same vein, an undertaking's application for a patent is just one of the many ways of seeking governmental action—in this case to award a patent right. Therefore, provided that both US and EU law admit that, at least under certain circumstances, the submission of false information to a public authority in order to secure a specific ruling may amount to an antitrust infringement, so should in principle a deceptive conduct during the course of a patent application.

In the US, because an application for a patent is an act of petitioning the government and petitioning is in principle immune from antitrust scruti-

1320 GC Decision in *AstraZeneca* (n 1216) para 355.
1321 See text at nn 650-652 in ch 4.
1322 Commission Decision in *AstraZeneca* (n 1183) para 747.
1323 CJEU Decision in *AstraZeneca* (n 1215) para 99.
1324 ibid para 105.
1325 Commission Decision in *AstraZeneca* (n 1183) para 626.

ny, antitrust liability can only arise if a separate exception to *Noerr* is recognised for misrepresentations.[1326] As explained above, such an exception has not been explicitly acknowledged by the Supreme Court but was hinted by various circuits of the US Court of Appeals and has been advocated by the FTC and a number of scholars.

As for EU law, the leading case on competition law liability for deceptively inducing governmental action dealt precisely with conducts before the patent office, yet its value for assessing cases involving regular patent applications may be limited.[1327] In that specific case, the level of discretion of the patent offices vis-à-vis SPCs was restricted and the firm was under an obligation to inform them about the relevant dates, whereas regular patent applicants' disclosure duties are usually more limited and patent offices have a more stringent responsibility to examine whether each patent application fulfils all the patentability requirements.[1328] Then again, the courts in *AstraZeneca* held that the abuse also comprised misleading statements before the courts, who do have the duty to critically assess the parties' statements. Hence, if a deceptive conduct before the courts can be considered an abuse, the same conclusion may also be valid for statements during patent prosecution.[1329]

At all events, it may also be worth considering, from a more general perspective of innovation and competition policy, to what extent it is desirable for competition law to encroach on the sphere of patent applications, particularly taking into account the essential role that both patents and competition play on innovation and the very careful balance that should be kept between them. There is no doubt that deceptive conducts are socially unacceptable and lack any redeeming virtues, yet that alone does not justify antitrust intervention.[1330] Hovenkamp, for instance, argues that the conduct of patent applicants before the issuance of a patent is sufficiently regulated and supervised by the patent office and should not be subject to

1326 Lao, 'Reforming the Noerr Doctrine' (n 1149) 977.

1327 Josef Drexl, '*AstraZeneca* and the EU Sector Inquiry: When do Patent Filings Violate Competition Law?' in Josef Drexl and Nari Lee (eds), *Pharmaceutical Innovation, Competition and Patent Law: A Trilateral Perspective* (Edward Elgar 2013) 319.

1328 See text at nn 322ff in ch 3.

1329 Werner Berg and Sean-Paul Brankin,'Das AstraZeneca-Urteil des Gerichts der Europäischen Union' [2011] EuZW 91, 94.

1330 Harv L Rev note, 'Deception as an Antitrust Violation' (n 1308) 1255.

additional antitrust scrutiny.[1331] Similarly, on the European side, Käseberg understands that competition agencies should be reluctant to interfere against unilateral conducts that only harm price competition when IP laws already provide a solution to reduce such harm.[1332]

On the other hand, it is common ground that patent law and competition law, though complementary, do not share the exact same concerns.[1333] Even if the patent system provides for remedies aimed at reducing competitive harms, eg by providing for exceptions and limitations to patent rights, those remedies are probably incapable of addressing all the concerns that imprint the competition laws.[1334] Indeed, while patent law plays an essential role in encouraging innovation and competition by substitution, it does not seem to be apt to affirmatively punish abuses that are harmful to competition by innovation.[1335] In case of deceptive behaviour, all patent law can do is take the invalid patent away, and perhaps impose disciplinary sanctions in the most blatant cases, but that merely places the patent holders in the position they would have been in had they never engaged in deceptive practices.[1336] After all, when a conduct reaches the stage of offending the competition rules, antitrust intervention may be justified no matter what kind of remedies other areas of law may offer.[1337]

1331 Herbert Hovenkamp, 'Antitrust and the Patent System: A Reexamination' (2014) U Iowa Legal Studies Research Paper 14/27, 11-12 and 40 <http://ssrn.com/abstract=2486633> accessed 14 February 2018 (arguing that antitrust scrutiny should be limited to post-issuance conducts, like enforcement).

1332 Thorsten Käseberg, *Intellectual property, Antitrust and Cumulative Innovation in the EU and the US* (Hart 2012) 67. In a similar vein, see Lars Kjølbye, 'Article 82 EC as Remedy to Patent System Imperfections: Fighting Fire with Fire?' (2009) 32 World Competition 163 (arguing that competition law should, in principle, avoid intervening in abusive patent strategies, although admitting that it might be justified if there is a 'plus factor'); Joseph Straus, 'Patent Application: Obstacle for Innovation and Abuse of Dominant Position under Article 102 TFEU?' (2010) 1 J Eur Comp L & Prac 189, 201 (maintaining that art 102 TFEU should come into operation against the exercise of intellectual property rights rather than against the filing of an application).

1333 See text at nn 753-758 in ch 5.

1334 David T Keeling, *Intellectual Property Rights in EU Law Vol I: Free Movement and Competition Law* (OUP 2003) 377; Floyd (n 1149) 445.

1335 Christopher R Leslie, 'Antitrust and Patent Law as Component Parts of Innovation Policy' (2009) 34 Iowa J Corp L 1259, 1269.

1336 Leslie, 'Patents of Damocles' (n 1294) 168.

1337 Steven Anderman, 'The IP and Competition Interface: New Developments' in Steven D Anderman and Ariel Ezrachi (eds), *Intellectual Property and Competition Law: New Frontiers* (OUP 2011) 24.

Notwithstanding the foregoing, it would seem advisable to take a cautious approach in the sense that antitrust intervention should not lead to imposing additional obligations upon patent applicants or have a deterrent effect on legitimate patent activities. Patent laws are probably much better equipped to regulate the whole patent application procedure and to decide on technical questions, and competition agencies should thus be careful of not becoming 'supreme patent offices' or 'patent courts' in the name of protecting competition.[1338] Under this light, it could be argued that, notwithstanding how meritorious or absurd the alleged invention may be or how audaciously or ambitiously an applicant may behave, patent applications should largely remain a patent law concern.[1339] Yet when an applicant behaves with a clear, deliberate intent to deceive, grounds against antitrust intervention seem to vanish, as punishing intentional and calculated fraud is not likely to chill legitimate patenting activity or disrupt the smooth functioning of the patent system as long as the reprehensible conduct is precisely defined and does not trespass on legitimate practices.[1340] The following section analyses a myriad of different elements that may be taken into account in order to adequately identify anticompetitive conducts while at the same time maintaining a proper balance and avoiding undesired interferences on the patent sphere.

1338 See, in particular, Josef Drexl, '"Pay-for-Delay" and Blocking Patents: Targeting Pharmaceutical Companies under European Competition Law' (2009) 40 IIC 751, 753.

1339 See, eg, Simon Priddis and Simon Constantine, 'The Pharmaceutical Sector, Intellectual Property Rights, and Competition Law in Europe' in Steven D Anderman and Ariel Ezrachi (eds), *Intellectual Property and Competition Law: New Frontiers* (OUP 2011) 266 (arguing that, outside cases such as intentional deceitful behaviour, the application of art 102 TFEU against the acquisition of patents should be carefully circumscribed).

1340 See, eg, GC Decision in *AstraZeneca* (n 1216) para 367 (interpreting that a finding of abuse in these cases should not freeze patent applications but that, on the contrary, it is such misuse of the patent system that can lead to a reduction in the incentives to engage in innovation); Leslie, 'Antitrust and Patent Law' (n 1335) 1281 (arguing that, if proof of intent to deceive is required, the risk of creating a disincentive to engage in research and other patentable activity is largely mitigated).

B. Elements for Competition Assessment

Agreeing that private parties may be held liable from a competition law perspective for the anticompetitive effects of a patent obtained by fraud is only the first step of the antitrust enterprise, which in fact gives rise to a number of striking practical issues.[1341] This section analyses some of the most important challenges that competition enforcers might face when addressing this problem and attempts to provide some guiding input for that quest.

I. Materiality and Causal Connection

It is generally understood that, in order to hold a private party responsible for the anticompetitive effects of a governmental act, the private party's conduct must have been material and central to the outcome of the proceeding.[1342] One of the main problems that may arise in this regard refers to the difficulty of identifying the causal link,[1343] as it is often complex to deconstruct a governmental procedure and the mental process of the decision-maker.[1344] There may be some extreme cases (eg, when a public authority explicitly bases its entire decision on false information submitted by the applicant, or when that information is openly disregarded by the decision-maker) that do not pose major difficulties, but unfortunately the answer is not always so straight-forward.[1345]

In the US, some courts and scholars draw a line separating political lobbying from adjudicatory proceedings and argue that no antitrust liability should attach in the former case.[1346] But while it is true that establishing causation in political decisions is a nearly impossible task, there does not seem to be any compelling reason to provide wider protection to false speech in the political arena.[1347] Therefore, the fundamental question

---

1341 Floyd (n 1149) 425.

1342 FTC, 'Enforcement Perspectives on the Noerr-Pennington Doctrine' (n 1276) 25; Filmore (n 1273) 452; Czapracka (n 1146) 105.

1343 Areeda and Hovenkamp, *Antitrust Law* (n 1292) para 203a.

1344 Floyd (n 1149) 435.

1345 Areeda and Hovenkamp, *Antitrust Law* (n 1292) para 203f3.

1346 McGowan and Lemley (n 1240) 382; Filmore (n 1273) 449. See also *California Motor Transport* (n 1162) 513.

1347 Lao, 'Reforming the Noerr Doctrine' (n 1149) 1023-24; Cooper and Kovacic (n 1273) 1607.

should simply be whether it is possible to establish that a particular governmental action has been directly caused by a private misrepresentation, whatever the forum.[1348] In any case, patent procedures before the patent office are probably closer to adjudication processes than to political discussions.[1349]

In this context, the question arises as to how to determine whether a patent that restrains competition was granted *because* of the alleged deceptive conduct. To answer it, Lao suggests that there should be a 'substantial likelihood that a reasonable decision-maker would consider it important in her decision.'[1350] Others seem to prefer a slightly stricter standard, interpreting that a misrepresentation would only be material if, absent that misrepresentation, the patent would not have been granted, or at least not with the same scope.[1351] J Posner seems to be of the latter opinion, arguing that, if an invention is patentable, it is irrelevant from an antitrust standpoint what kind of shameful conduct the applicant may have embraced in order to obtain it.[1352] Since the question very much resembles the 'materiality' element of inequitable conduct cases discussed above,[1353] many of the opinions expressed by the courts in those cases may also be transposed to the antitrust sphere. On the European side, the question of materiality does not seem to have been discussed in detail in *AstraZeneca*—probably because it was quite clear that the patent offices in that case had exclusively relied on the information provided by the SPC applicants.[1354] In any case, the fact that a patent has survived in other jurisdictions, or that it is not unanimously invalidated, may be indicative factors in this regard.

Interestingly, Floyd has suggested that, in order to make sure that the misrepresentation was indeed material and to avoid constitutional objections, the vacatur of the governmental act by the competent authorities should be an indispensable prior requirement before imposing competition law sanctions.[1355] In the case of patent grants this would imply that,

1348 Floyd (n 1149) 463.

1349 Areeda and Hovenkamp, *Antitrust Law* (n 1292) para 203e.

1350 Lao, 'Reforming the Noerr Doctrine' (n 1149) 1023 (also suggesting that it should not be indispensable to prove that, but for the misrepresentation, the government outcome would have been different).

1351 Arun Chandra, 'Antitrust Liability for Attempting to Enforce a Fraudulent Patent' (1999) 81 J Pat & Trademark Off Soc'y 201, 214. See also Filmore (n 1273) 452.

1352 *Brunswick Corp v Riegel Textile Corp* 752 F 2d 261, 265 (7th Cir 1984).

1353 See text at nn 230ff in ch 3.

1354 CJEU Decision in *AstraZeneca* (n 1215) para 87.

1355 Floyd (n 1149) 446.

before assessing the conduct from a competition law perspective, either the patent office itself or the competent courts should first invalidate the patent. This could certainly constitute a sensible solution to avoid undesired interference upon the patent sphere and to make sure that the patent should not have been granted, even though cases like the ones involving 'pay-for-delay' settlement agreements evidence that there may be situations where, even when the patent may seem unwarranted, competitors may nonetheless be discouraged to challenge its validity in court.[1356] In any case, even if a patent is invalidated, that sole fact does not in itself indicate that the conduct of the patent applicant was inappropriate, which leads to a second and perhaps even more problematic question: what exactly constitutes a deceptive conduct relevant from a competition law viewpoint?

II. Conceptualisation of the Misconduct

At first glance, it may be appealing to think that every patent granted by the patent office which is later invalidated by the courts necessarily involved a misleading handling from the patent applicant. It could be argued on these lines that, if the applicant declared that she had an invention but later turned out not to have one, one cannot but conclude that such declaration was untruthful. A closer look, however, reveals that this is a far cry from reality. Despite the predominantly technical nature of the issues with which it ordinarily deals, patent law is in itself no exact science. Courts, patent offices and even examiners forming part of the same Examining Division disagree every day about what may be patented and what may not and the discussions often involve extremely complex technologies. Also, patent attorneys cannot be blamed for drafting their patent applications in wide terms,[1357] particularly bearing in mind that the scope of patent applications, once filed, can be subsequently narrowed down but never broadened.[1358] Patent offices, on their turn, do not always perform

1356 *FTC v Actavis Inc* 133 S Ct 2223, 2231-2233 (2013).

1357 Robin Jacob, 'Patent Thickets: A Paper for the European Patent Office Economic and Scientific Advisory Board Meeting' (2013) 8 J Intell Prop L & Prac 203, 204 ('It must be understood that any well-drafted patent application will have claims wider than those which will eventually be granted. No competent patent attorney would claim narrowly in the first instance. He goes wide to see what prior art is found and shapes his eventual widest claim around that. It would be negligent for him not to do so.').

1358 See text at n 85 in ch 2.

flawless examinations, yet that seems to a large extent inevitable.[1359] The occasional invalidation of patents, hence, seems to be inherent to the patent system without that meaning that their holders behaved inadequately when they first obtained it.

Against this backdrop, the opinions of the Commission, the General Court and the Advocate General in *AstraZeneca* had raised some concerns among practitioners in the EU.[1360] Those opinions indeed seemed to advocate a low threshold to define misleading conducts, highlighting that it was not necessary to show that the applicant intended to mislead the patent office but should rather be analysed under objective criteria.[1361] The CJEU, however, seems to have toned down that conclusion by imposing a higher standard.[1362] The CJEU indeed stressed that, in that particular case, the firm's representations had been highly misleading and intentional[1363] and explained that sanctioning those conducts does not imply that appli-

1359 Robin Jacob, 'Patent Thickets' (n 1357) 204. See also Mark A Lemley, 'Rational Ignorance at the Patent Office' (2001) 95 Northwest U L Rev 1495 (arguing that, even if patent offices do not do a perfect job in examining patents, better examinations may be too costly and not socially desirable because of the few patents asserted in practice vis-à-vis the number of patent applications annually filed).

1360 See, eg, Sven B Völcker, 'Developments in EC Competition Law in 2005: An Overview' (2006) 43 CML Rev 1409, 1432; David Hull, 'The AstraZeneca Judgment: Implications for IP and Regulatory Strategies' (2010) 1 J Eur Comp L & Prac 500, 502; Berg and Brankin (n 1329) 94; Gavin Bushell, 'AstraZeneca v Commission: Advocate-General Mazak's Opinion of 15 May 2012' (*Kluwer Competition Blog*, 11 June 2012) <http://kluwercompetitionlawblog.com/2012/06/11/astrazeneca-v-commission-advocate-general-mazaks-opinion-of-15-may-2012> accessed 14 February 2018.

1361 See, eg, GC Decision in *AstraZeneca* (n 1216) para 356 ('It follows from the objective nature of the concept of abuse that the misleading nature of representations made to public authorities must be assessed on the basis of objective factors and that proof of the deliberate nature of the conduct and of the bad faith of the undertaking in a dominant position is not required for the purposes of identifying an abuse of a dominant position.') (citations omitted).

1362 Bill Batchelor and Melissa Healy, 'CJEU AstraZeneca Judgment: Groping Towards a Test for Patent Office Dealings; (2013) 34 Eur Comp L Rev 171, 171-72; Van Malleghem and Devroe (n 1107). Cf Adrian Spillmann, 'Transparency Obligation for Holders of EU IP Assets in the Pharmaceutical Industry' (2014) 9 J Intell Prop L & Prac 125, 129 (arguing that the CJEU's threshold is still too low, as it is not sufficiently clear in requiring intent).

1363 CJEU Decision in *AstraZeneca* (n 1215) para 98.

cants need to be infallible when dealing with the patent offices.[1364] Ultimately, the assessment of whether representations are misleading or not must be made *in concreto* and may vary according to the specific circumstances of each case.[1365]

On the US side, the Supreme Court defined the reprehensible conduct by employing the concept of 'intentional fraud'.[1366] In this light, the Federal Circuit has interpreted that, to qualify as fraud, the conduct should include all the elements of common law fraud, including the falsity of the representation and the intent to deceive or, at least, 'a state of mind so reckless as to the consequences that it is held to be the equivalent of intent'.[1367] Similarly, the FTC understands that a misrepresentation relevant from an antitrust perspective must be both deliberate and factually verifiable.[1368]

Both jurisdictions, hence, seem to pay particular attention to the undertakings' specific intent. As it may be recalled, competition agencies both in the US and the EU ordinarily attempt to approach unilateral conducts under objective parameters, avoiding as much as possible the assessment of the undertakings' subjective intent.[1369] The case of misrepresentations before public authorities, thus, may embody one of those exceptional circumstances where intent can be not only a useful factor but also a quite decisive one. Despite of that, considering that in practice it may be difficult

---

1364 ibid para 99 (concluding that it 'cannot be inferred from that judgment that any patent application made by such an undertaking which is rejected on the ground that it does not satisfy the patentability criteria automatically gives rise to liability under Article 82 EC.').

1365 ibid.

1366 *Walker Process* (n 1302) 176. See also Concurring Opinion by Justice Harlan. Ibid 179 (explaining that fraud cannot be found by merely showing the invalidity of the patent arising, eg, from obviousness or other factors ordinarily referred to as 'technical fraud').

1367 *Nobelpharma* (n 1304) 1069-70. The Federal Circuit had also emphasised that the intent element in antitrust cases might be different from that of inequitable conduct cases. *Dippin' Dots Inc v Mosey* 476 F 3d 1337, 1347 (Fed Cir 2007). However, after *Therasense* heightened the inequitable conduct standards, that conclusion was very likely overruled. Herbert J Hovenkamp, 'Patent Exclusions and Antitrust after *Therasense*' (2011) U Iowa Legal Studies Research Paper 11/39, 34 <http://ssrn.com/abstract=1916074> accessed 14 February 2018.

1368 FTC, 'Enforcement Perspectives on the Noerr-Pennington Doctrine' (n 1276) 25. See also Filmore (n 1273) 453 (stating that the misrepresentation should be substantially false and the person must have known that the representation was false).

1369 See text at nn 690-700 in ch 4.

to prove subjective knowledge, courts could eventually draw upon objective tools, eg establishing that a representation is false when a reasonable person in the applicant's position would have known of its falsity.[1370]

The final question that arises at this point refers to the categories of conducts that can be classified, in practice, as deceptive. As a general principle, there is little doubt that an undertaking can engage in misleading behaviour via positive misrepresentations, but the Federal Circuit has clarified that a fraudulent conduct before the patent office can also be premised on an intentional omission.[1371] In the EU, the CJEU also highlighted in *AstraZeneca* that omissions could be relevant, particularly when the undertaking has a duty to disclose information.[1372] In spite of this, and considering that ordinary patent applicants in Europe do not have the same duties as those in the US,[1373] it seems difficult for an omission to make for a misconduct under EU competition law. A case could however arise, for instance, if an undertaking files a patent application while fully aware that it is not new,[1374] eg because it has itself been selling the invention for many years. In any case, as the CJEU explained in *AstraZeneca*, what is misleading and what is not is a question that very much depends on the specific circumstances of each case.[1375]

All things considered, it seems advisable to underscore that, when assessing what transpires before the patent office, antitrust should be wary of undermining the integrity of the patenting procedure and the decision-making functions of the patent offices.[1376] This would involve, in the first place, that competition agencies should not concentrate on patents which are merely weak, or whose claims are broad, or on patent applicants who apply for patents even when they are not fully convinced of their strength.[1377] Also, they should avoid imposing additional requirements through the back door,[1378] eg by imposing new disclosure requirements or modifying their drafting practices. Patent laws and patent offices are probably much better equipped to regulate on these technical questions.

1370 Areeda and Hovenkamp, *Antitrust Law* (n 1292) para 705h1.
1371 *Nobelpharma* (n 1304) 1070.
1372 CJEU Decision in *AstraZeneca* (n 1215) para 95.
1373 See text at nn 322ff in ch 3.
1374 Drexl, 'When do Patent Filings Violate Competition Law?' (n 1327) 320.
1375 CJEU Decision in *AstraZeneca* (n 1215) para 99.
1376 *Unocal* FTC Opinion (n 1306) 48.
1377 Drexl, 'When do Patent Filings Violate Competition Law?' (n 1327) 319.
1378 David Hull, 'The Application of EU Competition Law in the Pharmaceutical Sector' (2012) 3 J Eur Comp Law & Prac 473, 477.

III. Ministerial Acts and Discretion of the Patent Office

When assessing issues of antitrust liability for the anticompetitive effects of public actions, both EU and US courts have paid particular attention to the margin of discretion enjoyed by the issuing government authority and regarded it as an essential factor. This issue might become extremely important in cases where the patent office performs only limited or formal examinations, as is the case in Germany with utility models or in several other national patent offices with patents.[1379]

In the US, one of the leading cases on this question is *Litton*,[1380] which referred to tariff filings made by AT&T before the Federal Communications Commission. Because the public authority in that case had very limited discretion and the decision on the tariff had been in fact made by AT&T on its own, the court considered that its filing could not be compared to an act of petitioning and hence did not merit *Noerr* immunity.[1381] Similarly, in the Orange Book cases described above, the courts interpreted that the listings of patents before the FDA in the framework of the Hatch-Waxman Act could not be considered an act of petitioning because they only sough a ministerial response and the FDA had practically no margin of discretion.[1382] On this basis, it has been argued that, when an undertaking makes a submission to the government which does not call for a discretionary act, *Noerr* immunity is not even part of the equation and antitrust laws can be readily applied.[1383]

By the same token, courts in the EU have also drawn the attention to the public authority's room for manoeuvre and regarded it as a decisive element in their decisions. Firstly, in *Compagnie Maritime Belge*, the CJEU stated that situations in which the public authority has no discretion and is bound to observe what the private party requests cannot be treated in the same way as regular incitements to take action.[1384] Later, in *AstraZeneca*, it confirmed that 'the limited discretion of public authorities or the absence

---

1379 Berg and Brankin (n 1329) 94.

1380 *Litton Systems Inc v American Telephone & Telegraph Co* 700 F 2d 785 (2nd Cir 1983).

1381 ibid 807.

1382 See text at n 963 in ch 5.

1383 FTC, 'Enforcement Perspectives on the Noerr-Pennington Doctrine' (n 1276) 22; Lao, 'Reforming the Noerr Doctrine' (n 1149) 1005.

1384 *Compagnie Maritime Belge* (n 1314) paras 82-83. See text at n 1315.

of any obligation on their part to verify the accuracy or veracity of the information provided' can constitute relevant factors.[1385]

These conclusions can be explained by the fact that, when the patent office—or any other public authority—has ample discretion vis-à-vis an undertakings' request, the latter can only obtain the anticompetitive effects after convincing the former.[1386] Conversely, when the government has no discretion, the resulting public act is less likely to embrace public policy concerns and its potential anticompetitive effects flow directly from the undertakings' own judgment.[1387]

Nevertheless, it should be noted that the mere fact that government discretion is limited does not automatically render a private approach anticompetitive. Patent holders in the US, for instance, are evidently entitled to list on the Orange Book the patents that could be infringed by generic applicants;[1388] patent holders in the EU are equally entitled to request SPCs in case of delays in the administrative procedures. The crucial question is, hence, where to draw the line of acceptable conducts. In the Orange Book cases, for example, the Hatch-Waxman Act does provide some guidance by stating that patents can be listed as long as 'a claim of patent infringement could reasonably be asserted'.[1389] Other cases are much less clear. In *AstraZeneca*, for instance, the CJEU stated that, because of the limited duties of the patent offices to verify the accuracy of the submissions, even if an undertaking sincerely believes that she has a legitimate claim, she must clearly communicate her novel interpretation to the patent office when it goes out of the ordinary.[1390] Ultimately, it seems clear that, as a general rule, the undertakings' duty of transparency becomes stricter in inverse proportion to the government office's margin of discretion and will vary depending on the factual circumstances of each case.

To conclude, it should also be borne in mind that, even though their exposure to antitrust scrutiny may be larger, public acts that result from non-discretional procedures may nonetheless have a lesser impact on competition than those emanating from a discretionary governmental decision. German utility models, for instance, clearly do not have the same deterring effect as patents, which are granted after a fully-fledged examination proce-

1385 CJEU Decision in *AstraZeneca* (n 1215) para 105.

1386 FTC, 'Enforcement Perspectives on the Noerr-Pennington Doctrine' (n 1276) 22.

1387 Vossestein (n 1201) 1397-98.

1388 See, in this regard, text at n 967 in ch 5.

1389 21 USC § 355(j)(2)(A)(vii).

1390 CJEU Decision in *AstraZeneca* (n 1215) para 95.

dure, and are not perceived in the same way by the market or by the courts themselves. The following paragraphs analyse the public acts' effects on competition in further detail.

IV. *Effects on Competition*

Even if proven that a patent applicant indeed deceived the patent office and that such behaviour directly led to the issuance of an exclusive right, these facts alone do not necessarily render the behaviour anticompetitive: evidence that the public act—in this case the patent—has an exclusionary effect in the market is also required.[1391]

a. Exclusionary Effects of Improperly Granted Patents

From an economic perspective, there is little doubt that patents are capable of imposing restraints on competition.[1392] But whereas these restraints are entirely justified and desirable for the grant of valid patents, those which are obtained through misleading means and do not truly protect inventive ideas do not have any redeeming virtues and do not seem worthy of the same deference.[1393] How exactly those patents may impact the market, however, has been interpreted somehow differently by US and EU courts.

As it may be recalled, the US Supreme Court's first decision on the issue had concluded that 'the enforcement of a patent procured by fraud on the Patent Office may be violative of § 2 of the Sherman Act provided the other elements necessary to a § 2 case are present.'[1394] The emphasis on enforcement may be partly explained by historical reasons: since the patent invalidity action was at that time barred for the antitrust plaintiff, the

1391 *Walker Process* (n 1302) 174; CJEU Decision in *AstraZeneca* (n 1215) para 106. Cf Martin J Adelman, 'The Relevant Market Paradox: Attempted and Completed Patent Fraud Monopolization' (1977) 38 Ohio St L J 289 (arguing that fraud to the patent office should be considered a *per se* violation of antitrust law).

1392 Drexl, 'When do Patent Filings Violate Competition Law?' (n 1327) 296.

1393 William M Landes and Richard A Posner, *The Economic Structure of Intellectual Property Law* (Harvard Univ Press 2003) 20-24; Leslie, 'Antitrust and Patent Law' (n 1335) 1269. See also Drexl, 'When do Patent Filings Violate Competition Law?' (n 1327) 319.

1394 *Walker Process* (n 1302) 174.

court attempted to disconnect the validity claim from the antitrust action to the maximum possible extent.[1395] In spite of that, lower courts held that, in order to prevail in an antitrust claim, the claimant must show that the patentee attempted to *enforce* the fraudulently-obtained patent,[1396] as the sole grant of the patent would not be sufficient to trigger antitrust liability.[1397] The Federal Circuit reasoned in this regard that the minimum level of enforcement should be the same as that which determines jurisdiction in a declaratory judgment action for patent invalidity.[1398] Along the same lines, Areeda and Hovenkamp have stressed that merely obtaining a patent by fraud rarely has anticompetitive effects,[1399] although they added that antitrust liability may be prompted not only by the patentee's bringing of infringement actions or threats, but also by refusing to license or by licensing a patent while knowing that it is invalid.[1400]

EU courts seem to have chosen a different route,[1401] as they acknowledged in *AstraZeneca* that the grant of exclusive rights by the patent office

---

1395 See Ned L Conley, 'Considerations in Patent Litigation Brought About by Walker Process Equipment, Inc v Food Machinery & Chemical Corp' (1966) 9 S Tex L J 9, 10.

1396 *Struthers Scientific and Int'l Corp v General Foods Corp* 334 F Supp 1329, 1331 (D Del 1971); *Unitherm Food Systems Inc v Swift-Eckrich Inc* 375 F 3d 1341, 1355 (Fed Cir 2004), revd on other grounds 546 US 394 (2006).

1397 *Struthers* (n 1396) 1332 ('It is not the mere obtaining of a fraudulent patent which brings antitrust liability to its owner; it is the assertion or enforcement of the issued patent acquired by fraud which creates antitrust liability.'); *California Eastern Laboratories Inc v Gould* 896 F 2d 400, 403 (9th Cir 1990) ('Without some effort at enforcement, the patent cannot serve as the foundation of a monopolization case.').

1398 *Unitherm* (n 1396) 1357. See also, however, *Ritz Camera & Image LLC v SanDisk Corp* 700 F 3d 503, 508 (Fed Cir 2012) (clarifying that direct purchasers may have standing to sue in *Walker Process* claims even if they do not have standing to sue for patent invalidity).

1399 Areeda and Hovenkamp, *Antitrust Law* (n 1292) para 705a. See also Herbert Hovenkamp, 'The Walker Process Doctrine: Infringement Lawsuits as Antitrust Violations' (2008) U Iowa Legal Studies Research Paper 08/36, 10 <http://ssrn.com/abstract=1259877> accessed 14 February 2018 ('simply obtaining a patent fraudulently with no subsequent enforcement activity does not violate the Sherman Act, although it may violate the FTC Act.').

1400 Areeda and Hovenkamp, *Antitrust Law* (n 1292) para 705a. As already mentioned above, Hovenkamp has also stated that, because the deciding element is the enforcement, the fraud element in *Walker Process* is overestimated and the latter decision does not differ much from any other sham case. Hovenkamp, *The Antitrust Enterprise* (n 1143) 267.

1401 See, however, Maggiolino (n 1143) 104 (arguing that the courts in *AstraZeneca* arrived to a conclusion similar to *Walker Process*, because applying for an SPC

may itself have exclusionary effects[1402] and expressly rejected the idea that a finding of abuse of a dominant position requires the enforcement of the patent.[1403] In the same vein, a number of scholars have disputed the interpretation that US lower courts have made of *Walker Process* and argued against the enforcement requirement.[1404] Particularly noteworthy in this regard is the work of Leslie, who has dedicated a couple of extensive articles to this particular enterprise and comprehensively described the different kinds of anticompetitive effects that may stem from the sole procurement of a patent through improper means.[1405]

The most evident anticompetitive effect induced by the sole grant of fraudulently-obtained patents is connected to the general duty that rests upon every citizen to abide by patents. It should be borne in mind that, once a patent is granted, patent laws provide as a rule that nobody can make use of it without the authorisation of the patent holder.[1406] In fact, patents can be assimilated to a governmental order that bars competitors from performing a particular activity. For this reason, a patent grant sends a clear signal to the market that is likely to deter actual or potential competitors from marketing or using that particular product or process, aware as they are that they are bound by law to respect the exclusive right.[1407] In connection with the latter, EU courts have highlighted in *AstraZeneca* that intellectual property rights, when granted by a public authority, are 'normally assumed to be valid.'[1408] UK courts, in their turn, understand that, in patent infringement actions, claimants benefit from a presumption that

---

would be comparable to an abusive enforcement). Cf Sven Gallasch, 'AstraZeneca v the Walker Process – A Real EU-US Divergence or Just an Attempt to Compare Apples to Oranges?' (2011) 7 Eur Comp J 505 (arguing that *AstraZeneca* and *Walker Process* are not comparable).

1402 CJEU Decision in *AstraZeneca* (n 1215) para 108.

1403 GC Decision in *AstraZeneca* (n 1216) para 362.

1404 See, eg, Neil A Smith, 'Fraud upon the Patent Office as a Violation of the Sherman Antitrust Law' (1970) 14 Pat Trademark & Copyright J Res & Educ 507, 546; Floyd (n 1149) 424; Leslie, 'The Anticompetitive Effects of Unenforced Invalid Patents' (n 1272). See also Leslie, 'Patents of Damocles' (n 1294) 133 ('weapons need not actually be fired in order to have a deterrent effect on one's enemies.'). See also *Brunswick* (n 1352) 265 (enforcement actions are not a *sine qua non* of monopolizing by patent fraud.').

1405 Leslie, 'The Anticompetitive Effects of Unenforced Invalid Patents' (n 1272); Leslie, 'Patents of Damocles' (n 1294).

1406 § 271 US Patent Act; § 9 PatG; UK Patents Act, s 60.

1407 GC Decision in *AstraZeneca* (n 1216) para 362, confirmed by CJEU Decision in *AstraZeneca* (n 1215) para 108.

1408 ibid.

their patent is valid.[1409] In Germany, because of the bifurcation system that separates infringement from invalidity proceedings, patentees also get a running start when pursuing infringement actions.[1410] In the case of the US, the presumption of validity is explicitly recognised by the patent act.[1411] The Supreme Court has interpreted this provision to entail that, if a patent is challenged, the petitioner must prove its invalidity by 'clear-and-convincing' evidence and that a mere preponderance standard does not suffice.[1412]

Additionally, the existence in the market of invalid patents obtained through deceptive means may lead to increased costs of market entry[1413] or intimidate third parties who would otherwise be interested in doing business with competitors.[1414] The existence of a fraudulently-obtained patent could, eg, leave competitors at a serious disadvantage in public and private tenders or deter their customers, partners or investors. In certain scenarios, such as Orange Book patent listings before the FDA, a misrepresentation can prompt even more immediate consequences, as the petitioning can automatically block competitors from obtaining market authorisations during a period of 30 months.[1415]

Along with the restraints upon static competition described above, invalid patents obtained by misleading representations may be capable, in some instances, of hampering dynamic competition as well. Competitors could indeed refuse to engage in R&D activities in technical areas tainted by invalid patents, particularly if they are unaware of the invalidity, which

---

1409 *Hormel Foods Corp v Antilles Landscape Investments NV* [2005] EWHC 13 (Ch), [2005] RPC 28 [73]. See also Richard Miller and others, *Terrell on the Law of Patents* (17th edn, Sweet & Maxwell 2011) para 18.194.

1410 See Katrin Cremers and others, 'Invalid But Infringed? An Analysis of Germany's Bifurcated Patent Litigation System' (2014) Max Planck Institute for Innovation & Competition Research Paper 14/14, 2 <http://ssrn.com/abstract=2504507> accessed 14 February 2018.

1411 § 282(a) US Patent Act.

1412 *Microsoft Corp v i4i Ltd Partnership* 131 S Ct 2238, 2252 (2011).

1413 Leslie, 'The Anticompetitive Effects of Unenforced Invalid Patents' (n 1272) 119-22 (citing as examples the necessary investigations on patent scope and validity and the hypothetical entering into a license agreement with the patent holder).

1414 ibid 125-27 (explaining that invalid patents scare away competitors' customers or venture capital).

1415 See text at n 959 in ch 5.

would result in an overall slowing-down of technological development.[1416] The situation could be even more serious in the US, where the experimental use exception has been interpreted in narrow terms.[1417] In any case, both US and EU competition agencies have acknowledged the risks that improperly obtained patents may represent on innovation. The FTC, on the one hand, has stated that a questionable patent 'may lead its competitor to forgo R&D in the areas that the patent improperly covers.'[1418] On the other hand, Neelie Kroes, the EU Competition Commissioner at the time *AstraZeneca* was decided, also highlighted that misleading the patent office can act as a disincentive to innovate.[1419]

As a final point, a question regarding competitors' awareness should be considered. J Posner has argued in this respect that, in order for a fraudulently obtained patent to constitute an antitrust violation, an additional requirement should be met, namely that the patent should also have 'some colorable validity'.[1420] Although it is true that such feature would be required in order to discourage actual or potential competitors from making the patented product, the myriad of anticompetitive effects described above evidence that invalid patents may still have a negative impact on competition even if competitors are aware of such invalidity.[1421] On the one hand, the invalid patent may still act as a deterrent element for third parties dealing with competitors. On the other hand, the competitor herself could nonetheless be dissuaded from entering the market in view of the general presumption of validity of the patent and the high costs that the invalidity proceedings could entail.

1416 Leslie, 'The Anticompetitive Effects of Unenforced Invalid Patents' (n 1272) 127-28 (arguing that 'competitors fearful of infringement litigation may decline to invest in research and development (R&D) in areas tainted by invalid (but unexposed) patents.').

1417 *Madey v Duke University* 307 F 3d 1351, 1362 (Fed Cir 2002) (concluding that the experimental use defence is 'very narrow and limited to actions performed for amusement, to satisfy idle curiosity, or for strictly philosophical inquiry.') (citations omitted). For a general overview of the experimental use exception in the US, see Katherine J Strandburg, 'What Does the Public Get: Experimental Use and the Patent Bargain' [2004] Wis L Rev 81.

1418 FTC, 'To Promote Innovation: The Proper Balance of Competition and Patent Law and Policy' (2003) Executive Summary, 5.

1419 Commission Press Release IP/05/737, 'Competition: Commission fines AstraZeneca €60 million for misusing patent system to delay market entry of competing generic drugs' (15 June 2005).

1420 *Brunswick* (n 1352) 265.

1421 Leslie, 'The Anticompetitive Effects of Unenforced Invalid Patents' (n 1272) 132.

b. Scope of and Entitlement to the Patent

When assessing the effects that a patent may have on competition, particular attention should also be paid to the scope of its claims. The deceptively obtained patent could, for instance, refer to an exceptionally popular product or incorporate far-reaching claims. But the patent could also refer to trivial products or processes, contain narrow claims or refer to only one of many equally valuable alternatives available in the relevant market. In the former case, the impact of the patent on competition is likely to be more meaningful, as the patent would act as a significant entry barrier. Conversely, the exclusionary effects in the latter case may be less considerable if competitors' activities are not substantially affected or if they have at their disposal further alternatives that do not infringe the patent and whose use does not entail additional costs. When analysing the anticompetitive effects of a patent obtained by fraud, hence, it is advisable to first define the relevant market and then weigh it against the scope of the patent claims.[1422]

A final relevant factor to consider refers to the materiality of the deceptive behaviour vis-à-vis the justification of the issuance of the patent as such. J Posner has suggested in this regard that deceptive conducts leading the patent office to grant a non-patentable invention should be clearly distinguished from those conducts that concern patents that would have been granted anyhow, though to a different person.[1423] In the latter case, argues Posner, the effects that the patent has on competition are exactly the same as the effects that would have been observed had the patent been granted to the legitimate inventor.[1424] Hence, even when the applicant's conduct was material in the sense that it directly led to the grant of the patent on her name, it would not be material with regard to the existence of the patent as such and would hence render it irrelevant from an antitrust standpoint. By the same token, it could be argued that, when an applicant applies for a patent that meets all patentability requirements but nonetheless submits false information to the patent office, eg to meet a deadline or to amend an accidental mistake, such behaviour should not be considered anticompetitive either—even if, formally speaking, it was material for the

1422 *Delano Farms Co v The California Table Grape Commission* 655 F 3d 1337, 1351 (Fed Cir 2011).

1423 *Brunswick* (n 1352) 265.

1424 ibid. Cf Kobak, 'PREI and the Future of Patent-Antitrust Litigation' (n 1181) 198 (contending that the identity of the party holding the patent could have competitive and antitrust significance).

procurement of the patent. Indeed, although the conduct is certainly worthy of sanctions under other areas of law, this type of misrepresentations do not seem to affect in any way the patents-competition equation, as the latter is not opposed to the grant of patents on valuable inventions. Competition law is probably too cumbersome an instrument to be used to monitor unscrupulous applicants who, despite of that, make beneficial contributions to innovation.

c. Consumer Harm and Objective Justifications

As it may be recalled, the CJEU held in *AstraZeneca* that the fact that misleading representations do not ultimately lead to the grant of an exclusive right—or that, if granted, the exclusive right is subsequently revoked—does not necessarily exempt the undertaking from antitrust liability. In the view of the court, those conducts can still constitute a violation of competition law if they 'were very likely to result' in the issuance of the exclusive right.[1425] In a similar vein, the court also highlighted that the anticompetitive effects of the conduct do not need to be concrete to find an abuse, as it would be sufficient to show that those effects are at least potential.[1426]

If US courts were confronted with a similar question, their answer would probably be quite different, as no antitrust case can even be made in that jurisdiction unless the undertaking both obtains the patent and attempts to enforce it.[1427] As already noted, this enforcement requirement has been a subject of debate among several scholars on the grounds that the mere existence of patents is already capable of affecting the market. In fact, by waiting until the patentee enforces the patent, US courts appear to show more concern for the protection of specific competitors—those against whom the patent is enforced—than the competitive process as a whole.[1428]

Be that as it may, the alternative position adopted by EU courts in *AstraZeneca*, though on its face more appealing, has been target for criticism

1425 CJEU Decision in *AstraZeneca* (n 1215) para 111.
1426 ibid para 112.
1427 See text at nn 1396-1400.
1428 For the distinction between protecting competitors and protecting competition, see text at nn 492ff in ch 4.

as well.[1429] Most significantly, it has been pointed out that the CJEU's malleable stance towards the necessary evidence on anticompetitive effects shows that the court continues to perceive modern economic theory and the more economic approach to competition with excessive scepticism.[1430] Even granting that, under common European competition practice, consumer harm is not considered a conditio sine qua non in order to find anticompetitive effects and that evidence of market foreclosure may be sufficient to that end,[1431] the scarce references in *AstraZeneca* to the specific effects of the behaviour on competition seem to make for an unsound economic basis.[1432] Admittedly, the General Court and the CJEU did allude to alterations in the market structure, effects on potential competition and even the possible deterring effects on innovation, yet the high level of abstraction in their language makes these conducts appear almost like *per se* abuses.

Equally arguable seems to be the absolute disdain that the courts in *AstraZeneca* have demonstrated towards remedies offered by other areas of law and their ability to forestall competitive harm.[1433] If interpreted broadly, the conclusions of the courts could lead to a situation of daunting legal uncertainty among patent applicants, as even refused patent applications with no perceivable effects on the market could fall under the competition law radar as long as those effects are 'potential' and the behaviour 'likely' to lead to the grant of a patent—two criteria tainted with a high level of ambiguity. Also in this regard, the CJEU's return to the vague standard of 'competition on the merits' does not make the task of patent applicants any easier,[1434] in particular taking into account that patents are, in their very essence, meant to impose some limitations on competition.

This being said, it could also be argued that the conclusions of the courts in *AstraZeneca* are not automatically transplantable to scenarios involving regular patents. Indeed, while the courts in that case interpreted

---

1429 Czapracka (n 1146) 105; Rupprecht Podszun, 'Can Competition Law Repair Patent Law and Administrative Procedures? *AstraZeneca* ' (2014) 51 CML Rev 281, 292-94.

1430 Claudia Seitz, 'Klare Grenzlinie und Minenfeld: Die Marktmissbrauchskontrolle im Arzneimittelsektor nach dem AstraZeneca-Urteil des EuGH' [2013] EuZW 377, 380; Podszun (n 1429) 292.

1431 Josef Drexl, 'Real Knowledge is to Know the Extent of One's Own Ignorance: On the Consumer Harm Approach in Innovation-Related Competition Cases' (2010) 76 Antitrust L J 677, 683-88.

1432 Podszun (n 1429) 293.

1433 Czapracka (n 1146) 105.

1434 Podszun (n 1429) 293.

that SPCs can produce anticompetitive effects even before coming into effect, it should be borne in mind that, under that specific regime, there is a large time span between the grant of the exclusive right and its entering into force. AstraZeneca's SPCs, eg, had been majorly granted around 1993-1994, yet they were expected to enter into force only in 1999.[1435] Conversely, regular patents enter into force immediately after being granted. Before that, patent applications are still under examination and the fact whether they will be granted or not remains uncertain, hence yielding a different impact on the market.

Also worth mentioning is the efficiency defence or objective justification that patent applicants may have and which could exonerate their behaviour from antitrust liability. In the US, courts have acknowledged that, even if a certain conduct is proven to have anticompetitive effects, the concerned undertaking may be vindicated if 'valid business reasons' or a 'pro-competitive justification' are shown.[1436] Similarly, the CJEU has also accepted an efficiency defence for art 102 TFEU cases provided that the exclusionary effects are 'counterbalanced, or outweighed, by advantages in terms of efficiency which also benefit the consumer.'[1437] That notwithstanding, neither US nor EU courts have paid particular attention to this question when gauging misrepresentations before public authorities.

In particular, the Commission and the EU courts in *AstraZeneca* did not ponder the pro-competitive elements that the grant of the SPC could have had, eg in terms of dynamic competition.[1438] To that end, they could have analysed whether the grant of the SPC would have created additional incentives to innovate or aided the concerned undertaking to recoup prior expenditures on R&D, and could have subsequently balanced those pro-competitive effects against the restrictions that the SPC would impose on

---

1435 See text at n 1058 in ch 5.

1436 *Eastman Kodak Co v Image Technical Services Inc* 504 US 451, 483 (1992); *United States v Microsoft Corp* 253 F 3d 34, 59 (DC Cir 2001).

1437 Case C-95/04 P *British Airways v Commission* [2007] ECR I-2331, para 86. This defence, however, differs from the US standard in that it requires that the efficiencies should also benefit consumers. Josef Drexl, 'Deceptive Conduct in the Patent World: A Case for US Antitrust and EU Competition Law?' in Wolrad Prinz zu Waldeck und Pyrmont and others (eds), *Patents and Technological Progress in a Globalized World: Liber Amicorum for Joseph Straus* (Springer 2009) 150.

1438 Drexl, 'Deceptive Conduct in the Patent World' (n 1437) 152; Podszun (n 1429) 293.

competition.[1439] In this last regard, the EU courts do not seem to have considered the rather arbitrary transitional provisions of the SPC Regulation, which not only offered protection for new pharmaceutical products but also retroactively extended it in favour of already launched products, although with outwardly capricious date limitations.[1440] The regulation justified the retroactive effect on the European companies' need to 'catch up with its main competitors'.[1441] On this basis, AstraZeneca could have argued that it was as much entitled to catch up with its main competitors as other companies who had launched their products only a couple of months after Losec. Furthermore, it could have argued that the SPC would have acted as an incentive to invest more in R&D in the future.[1442] Be that as it may, it would seem advisable for competition enforcers, as a rule, to avoid questioning a specific regulation's assessment on its effects on innovation and accept the legislator's judgment.[1443]

On the US side, courts and antitrust enforcers do not seem to have addressed the question of efficiency defences in the context of *Walker Process* claims, though they did acknowledge that it may be a valid justification in cases involving other kinds of deceptive conducts.[1444] In any case, it should be noted that acknowledging that efficiency defences may constitute a

---

1439 Drexl, 'Deceptive Conduct in the Patent World' (n 1437) 151. See also Podszun (n 1429) 293.

1440 Drexl, 'Deceptive Conduct in the Patent World' (n 1437) 155.

1441 Council Regulation (EEC) 1768/92 of 18 June 1992 concerning the creation of a supplementary protection certificate for medicinal products [1992] OJ L182/1, recital 10 (Old SPC Regulation, subsequently amended by Regulation (EC) 469/2009).

1442 Drexl, 'Deceptive Conduct in the Patent World' (n 1437) 155. An analogous question arose in a case concerning restrictions on parallel trade. Advocate General Jacobs understood that certain limitations on parallel trade by a pharmaceutical company could have pro-competitive effects and incentivise the company to invest in further R&D. Case C-53/03 *Synetairismos Farmakopoion Aitolias & Akarnanias (Syfait) v GlaxoSmithKline plc* [2005] ECR I-4609, Opinion of AG Jacobs, paras 91-95. That conclusion, however, was disputed by AG Ruiz-Jarabo Colomer, who contended that there is no causal link between the companies' losses due to parallel trade and a hypothetical decrease in R&D. Joined Cases C-468/06 to C-478/06 *Sot Lélos kai Sia EE v GlaxoSmithKline* [2008] ECR I-7139, Opinion of AG Ruiz-Jarabo Colomer, para 109. The CJEU ultimately refused to provide a final answer on this question. Joined Cases C-468/06 to C-478/06 *Sot Lélos kai Sia EE v GlaxoSmithKline* [2008] ECR I-7139, para 70.

1443 Drexl, 'Deceptive Conduct in the Patent World' (n 1437) 155.

1444 *US v Microsoft* (n 1436) 77 (involving deceptive representations to software developers); *Rambus* (FTC Docket 9302) Opinion of the Commission of 2 August

valid justification for deceptive strategies by no means implies a full-fledged absolution for the concerned undertaking, who may still have to face liability under other areas of law.

V. *Market Power*

As explained in the opening of the second part of this work, proof of an anticompetitive conduct alone is not sufficient for a finding of antirust liability neither under § 2 Sherman Act nor under art 102 TFEU: in both cases, an element of market power must also be shown.[1445] Although questions concerning the definition of the relevant market and the assessment of market power are beyond the scope of this work, it is important to bear in mind that this element may acquire a special significance in the cases at hand. Undertakings may, in this regard, hold negligible market power by the time they make a deceptive representation before the patent office, yet they may achieve a strong position in the market precisely due to the wrongful behaviour, once the patent is granted.

Considering that the treatment of this issue by US courts somehow differs from EU law, the following paragraphs separately review in a succinct manner the main questions and problems that arise in each of these jurisdictions.

a. The Case under § 2 Sherman Act. Monopolisation and Attempt to Monopolise

As mentioned earlier, situations involving a deceptive behaviour before the patent office may pose significant hurdles in this respect. Admittedly, a patent applicant could already hold some market power at the time of the patent procurement, eg when the application refers to further developments of products or processes already established on the market. But the application could also refer to technologies which are still under develop-

---

2006, para 68-69 <www.ftc.gov/os/adjpro/d9302/060802commissionopinion.pdf> accesed 14 February 2018 (involving a deceptive strategy before a standard-setting organisation, although the FTC also highlighted in this case that deceptive conducts are 'extraordinarily difficult to justify.').

1445 See text at nn 522ff in ch 4.

ment and which do not even exist on the market at that point, in which case the applicant would not have any market power at all.

Under US antitrust law, this factor does not necessarily raise enforcement problems, as § 2 Sherman Act, with the figures of monopolisation and attempt to monopolise, enables antitrust enforcers to capture abusive conducts even if the firm does not enjoy monopoly power at that point—and even if it does not subsequently acquire it.

In order to qualify as an attempt to monopolise, however, additional elements should also be shown.[1446] On the one hand, there should be a dangerous probability that the monopoly power will be achieved, which would require 'inquiry into the relevant product and geographic market and the defendant's economic power in that market.'[1447] Although determining whether such probability exists or not appears to be a challenging enterprise, it is at least conceivable that it could occur in the cases under review. Indeed, the grant of a patent could render the patent holder the exclusive supplier of the product, particularly if the fraud and the cause of invalidity remain unknown to other market participants and to potential competitors.

On the other hand, attempt to monopolise cases require evidence of a specific intent,[1448] which goes beyond the mere intent to perform the act[1449] and has been interpreted as a purport 'to destroy competition or build monopoly'.[1450] In some cases, this intent may be readily inferred from the evidence of the patent applicant's deliberate deceit. As a matter of fact, because of the very nature of patents, every patent applicant can be presumed to have the purpose of imposing at least some restraints on competition. The latter, however, may not necessarily denote an intent to build a monopoly or destroy competition, though the distinction may be at times quite subtle.[1451]

In any event, at least from a theoretical perspective, US antitrust laws seem to be capable of reaching deceptive behaviours before the patent office under § 2 Sherman Act even if the patent applicant does not hold substantial market power at that specific point in time or is ultimately not able to attain it. Paradoxically, however, US courts in practice do not con-

---

1446 *Spectrum Sports Inc v McQuillan* 506 US 447, 456 (1993). See text at n 516 in ch 4.

1447 ibid 459.

1448 ibid 456.

1449 *Aspen Skiing Co v Aspen Highlands Skiing Corp* 472 US 585, 602 (1985).

1450 *Times-Picayune Publishing Co v United States* 345 US 594, 626 (1953).

1451 See Smith (n 1404) 543-44.

demn these conducts on their own as antitrust violations and interpret that antitrust law only becomes applicable when the patentee obtains the patent and makes at least some effort to enforce it.

As a final point, one could ask whether the deceptive behaviour before the patent office may also be assessed under § 5 FTC Act. In fact, there is at least one case where a Court of Appeals interpreted that deliberate fraud before the patent office can constitute an unfair method of competition under the FTC Act.[1452] However, as the current interpretation of § 5 FTC Act advocated by the FTC itself tends to subsume the boundaries of this provision within the general economic principles of antitrust law, the considerations made in this work with regard to § 2 Sherman Act became equally applicable to § 5 FTC Act and render a separate analysis of the latter superfluous.[1453]

b. The Case under art 102 TFEU. Market Dominance as a Pre-requisite

The panorama looks quite different under European competition law, where the focus of art 102 TFEU is set not so much on anticompetitive conducts that lead to a dominant position but rather on what undertakings do once that position has been attained.[1454] In fact, as a result of the language of this provision, anticompetitive abuses can only be sanctioned if the undertaking already holds a dominant position by the time of the abuse. Because the provision does not include an offence equivalent to US' attempt to monopolise, market dominance constitutes an inescapable precondition for the application of competition law against any kind of unilateral conducts. In this light, EU competition law seems perfectly suited to counter those abusive behaviours which are designed to *extend* market dominance, eg by filing patent applications associated with technologies already established on the market, yet it seems to become toothless against patent applicants who are not yet dominant—even if, after obtaining the patent, they do acquire a strong position on the market.

1452 *American Cyanamid Company v FTC* 363 F 2d 757, 771 (6th Cir 1966).

1453 See text at nn 701-710 in ch 4.

1454 Case 322/81 *Nederlandsche Banden-Industrie-Michelin* v *Commission* [1983] ECR 3461, para 57. See also Franklin M Fisher, 'Monopolization versus Abuse of Dominant Position: An Economist's View' in Barry Hawk (ed), *International Antitrust Law & Policy: Fordham Corporate Law 2003* (Juris Publishing 2004) 159.

Against this background, it has been suggested that, at least in some cases, a narrow definition of the relevant market may help to enable the applicability of art 102 TFEU, as it would evidently make it easier to ascertain dominance.[1455] In fact, narrow market definitions may be particularly appealing when dealing with innovative products and the Commission and the EU courts in *AstraZeneca* seem to have opted for a rather narrow market definition themselves when assessing the relevant market for Losec.[1456] That notwithstanding, caution is strongly advised in this regard, as too narrow market definitions may lead to unreasonable assessments that could bring every single new product within the scope of art 102 TFEU and, in so doing, backfire as a disincentive for innovation.[1457]

In addition, even if narrow market definitions were to be favoured, there may nevertheless be circumstances in which, by the time the applicant applies for a patent at the patent office, a market does not yet even exist for the products involved in the application. In those cases, regardless of how narrowly markets are defined, it would still seem quite challenging to capture the conduct under art 102 TFEU. One alternative to that conundrum could be provided by the adoption of the concept of 'innovation markets', although—as earlier explained—the concept is highly controversial today and increasingly neglected by competition enforcers.[1458]

Alternatively, it could be argued that, based on European case law, it is not necessary for a firm to be dominant in the market where the anticompetitive effects take place, provided that the firm is dominant in a neighbouring market.[1459] The CJEU, however, clarified that such finding should be reserved for very particular circumstances.[1460] In any case, that construction seems to be better suited for predatory strategies, such as predatory

1455 See, eg, Steven Anderman, 'The Strategic Use of Patent Enforcement and Acquisition Methods and Competition Law' in Inge Govaere and Hans Ullrich (eds), *Intellectual Property, Market Power and the Public Interest* (Peter Lang 2008) 181.

1456 Drexl, 'Deceptive Conduct in the Patent World' (n 1437) 147; Steven Anderman, 'New Developments' (n 1337) 10-11.

1457 Jacob Westin, 'Defining Relevant Market in the Pharmaceutical Sector in the Light of the Losec-Case: Just How Different is the Pharmaceutical Market?' (2011) 32 Eur Comp L Rev 57, 60; Spillmann (n 1362) 128.

1458 Drexl, 'When do Patent Filings Violate Competition Law?' (n 1327) 317. For a concise description of the concept of 'innovation markets' and the challenges it poses, see text at nn 571-595 in ch 4.

1459 See, eg, Case C-333/94 P *Tetra Pak International SA v Commission* [1996] ECR I-5951, para 27 (*Tetra Pak II*).

1460 ibid.

pricing or sham litigation, where the market power—even if on a different, connected market—does play an important role in the overall assessment. In cases like the ones at hand, it could put large firms at a disadvantage, as in practice the gravity of the anticompetitive harm derived from a deceptive behaviour does not seem to be affected in any way by the size and power of the applicant on other markets.[1461]

Ultimately, the case of deceptive conducts before the patent office appears to constitute just another example of the limitations of art 102 TFEU for capturing abuses that relate to the acquisition of market power—limitations which have already been vigorously highlighted by the scholarship, particularly in scenarios involving collective standard settings and patent ambush.[1462] Indeed, because the provision is essentially aimed at preventing dominant undertakings from abusing the strong position they already enjoy on the market, the question on *how* such position is attained seems to linger as a neglected spot in the overall operation of art 102 TFEU and may justify an amendment in the language of the provision.[1463]

In spite of that, and considering that an improperly obtained patent which remains in force may have a continued impact on the market and that the patent holder may engage in subsequent behaviours that help endure or strengthen the anticompetitive effects of the patent on competition, it is worth considering whether the ownership or enforcement of a patent so obtained may also warrant competition law intervention. The final section of this work is devoted to this endeavour by introducing the essential challenges that are likely to emerge and laying the groundwork for further exploration.

1461 Under the different modalities of causation identified by Vogelenzang, this would seem to belong to the third one, where the act and the dominant position have no connection whatsoever. See text at nn 676-689 in ch 4.

1462 Inge Govaere, 'In Pursuit of an Innovation Policy Rationale: Stakes and Limits under Article 82 TEC' (2008) 31 World Competition 541, 549; Drexl, 'Deceptive Conduct in the Patent World' (n 1437) 146; Peter Picht, *Strategisches Verhalten bei der Nutzung von Patenten in Standardisierungsverfahren aus der Sicht des Europäischen Kartellrechts* (Springer 2013) 164. See also Josef Drexl, 'Anticompetitive Stumbling Stones on the Way to a Cleaner World: Protecting Competition in Innovation Without a Market' (2012) 8 J Comp L & Econ 507, 540 (highlighting the limitations of art 102 TFEU vis-à-vis defensive patent strategies).

1463 See, eg, Govaere, 'In Pursuit of an Innovation Policy Rationale' (n 1462) 554; Drexl, 'Anticompetitive Stumbling Stones' (n 1462) 542.

C. Ownership or Enforcement of an Improperly Obtained Patent as an Antitrust Concern

Regardless of how competition laws apply to deceptive conducts during patent prosecution, once the patent is granted the question inevitably arises as to whether the continuing existence of the patent and its exploitation or enforcement by the patent holder may also constitute relevant conducts under an antitrust law standpoint. The existing differences between US and EU law, both in terms of the language of the applicable provisions and the paths taken by the existing case law, again call for an individual analysis for each jurisdiction.

I. The Case under US Law and Walker Process' Enforcement Requirement

Taking into account the existing case law, there is little doubt that, under US antitrust law, the enforcement of a patent obtained by deceptive means can configure a case of monopolisation or attempt to monopolise. In fact, although the language of § 2 Sherman Act seems to be sufficiently flexible to also capture what transpires during patent prosecution, US courts have consistently interpreted that it is only the enforcement of those patents that merits antitrust intervention, as the obtaining of a patent by fraud alone would not generate sufficient competitive concerns.[1464] What is more, courts have defined the concept of enforcement in considerably narrow terms. As referred above, the Federal Circuit understands that, as a rule, the minimum degree of enforcement necessary to trigger antitrust liability should be defined on the basis of the standards for admitting locus standi in declaratory judgment actions for patent invalidity.[1465] The concept therefore encompasses the patent holder's bringing of infringement suits as well as the explicit threats to sue, either against competitors or their customers,[1466] but probably not much more.[1467] Any conduct by the

1464 See text at nn 1396-1400.

1465 *Unitherm* (n 1396) 1357. More recently, it stressed that parties not having standing to start a declaratory judgment action may still have standing to start an antitrust claim, yet this conclusion does not seem to modify the fact that a minimum enforcement of the patent will have to be shown in order to succeed. See *Ritz Camera* (n 1398) 508.

1466 *Hydril Co LP v Grant Prideco LP* 474 F 3d 1344, 1350 (Fed Cir 2007).

1467 See Leslie, 'Patents of Damocles' (n 1294) 141-42.

patent holder falling short of enforcement would seem to take the deceptively obtained patent away from the radar of the Sherman Act.

In addition to showing that the patent has been enforced, *Walker Process* claims logically also require evidence that the patent was obtained by fraud.[1468] To this end, it is sufficient to reproduce here the considerations set out above when analysing whether the deceptive conduct alone could be regarded as anticompetitive.[1469] Accordingly, in order to regard a patent as fraudulently obtained, the representations of the patent applicant before the patent office should have been unmistakably false, material for the grant of the patent and made with a deliberate intent to deceive, and particular attention should be paid to the scope of the patent vis-à-vis the relevant market. Furthermore, *Walker Process* also requires all other elements necessary to a § 2 Sherman Act case to be present.[1470] By and large, all the conclusions exposed above are equally applicable to the cases at hand, with the fundamental difference that the deceptive behaviour here will need to be accompanied by a subsequent enforcement.

It is precisely the addition of that enforcement element, however, that may bring about a number of particularities that are worth considering. In the first place, it insinuates that, for a *Walker Process* claim to succeed, two separate conducts need to be proven: the enforcement and the fraud. For this reason, it is certainly possible to envisage cases where those conducts are performed by different undertakings, eg when a firm obtains a patent by fraud and assigns it to a third party who later decides to enforce it. In such cases, Justice Harlan's concurring opinion in *Walker Process* clarified that it would be sufficient to show that the patent holder enforced the patent 'with knowledge of the fraudulent manner in which it was obtained'.[1471]

On the other hand, the anticompetitive effects are not particularly easy to identify. By looking into the patent applicant's fraudulent conduct before the patent office, courts certainly seem to ponder all the concerns associated with such conducts which were described earlier in this chapter. Yet by making the enforcement of the patent an indispensable part of the *Walker Process* claim, they seem to ignore the anticompetitive effects that may already derive from the grant and sole existence of that patent. In any case, the enforcement may admittedly contribute to its anticompetitive ef-

1468 *Walker Process* (n 1302) 179.

1469 See text at nn 1341ff.

1470 *Walker Process* (n 1302) 174.

1471 ibid 179. In the same vein, see *Tyco Healthcare Group LP v Mutual Pharmaceutical Co Inc* 762 F 3d 1338, 1349 (Fed Cir 2014).

fects, as it would amount to a corroboration of the exclusionary nature of this right and could further deter competitors or their customers.

If viewed under this perspective, it may not be erroneous to state that the relevance of the fraud element in *Walker Process* claims is overstated.[1472] Indeed, if the essential element of the misconduct is the enforcement, fraud seems to be just one of the many ways to prove that the patent holder is aware of the invalidity of the patent. Exactly the same anticompetitive restraints may be envisaged if an undertaking, even after an impeccable conduct before the patent office, later finds out that the patent is unequivocally invalid and nonetheless decides to enforce it.

In addition, the anticompetitive effects stemming from the fraudulently obtained patent at an enforcement stage seem to be harder to tell apart from the anticompetitive harm that derives from sham litigation. When a plaintiff enforces a patent which she knows has been obtained by fraud, she may do so in order to obtain a favourable judgment from the court, hoping that the cause of invalidity remains unnoticed, but she may also aim at raising rivals' costs and deterring potential competitors regardless of the final judgment. In fact, as stated above, those two purposes may very well overlap and the *Handgards* case described in the previous chapter is a perfect example in this regard.[1473] Although this case was originally conceived as a natural consequence of *Walker Process*, in *Handgards* it was irrelevant whether the patent had been obtained by fraud, or even whether the patent was valid or not: what mattered was whether an undertaking had pursued legal actions with absolute indifference towards their outcome, with the purpose of raising rivals costs and deterring other competitors. Hence, even if the patent was valid, the enforcement could still configure an anticompetitive sham strategy if the plaintiff was aware that there was no infringement.

On a different note, as a final and perhaps more complex point, it may be interesting to consider whether the antitrust laws may be applied against the sole ownership, ie in situations where the patentee has not yet enforced the patent she knows is invalid. As explained above, US courts do not endorse such a view, yet those invalid and unenforced patents can certainly have an anticompetitive impact. For this reason, Leslie argues that firms having monopoly power should have a duty to disavow patents 'that they know to be invalid and that are used to maintain their monopoly

1472 Hovenkamp, *The Antitrust Enterprise* (n 1143) 267.

1473 See text at nn 945-953.

power.'[1474] In his opinion, *Walker Process*' enforcement requirement should be eliminated and the relevant conduct should become the 'knowing maintenance of invalid patents'.[1475] The proposal certainly deserves serious consideration, although the idea of a unilateral conduct consisting of not doing anything (except, perhaps, for the annual payment of patent renewal fees) does seem to make for a rather vague and daunting duty, particularly in the case of patents which were not obtained through deceptive means, as the relevant conduct would merely be an alteration in the state of mind of the owner. In the case of patents obtained by fraud, on the other hand, the anticompetitive effects seem hard to tell apart from those stemming from its grant, which US antitrust rules are already enabled to tackle. In any case, if such an approach were accepted, it would be imperative to have the standard carefully demarcated, as imposing this sort of duties upon patent holders bears the serious risk of deterring many patent applications and valuable inventive activity.[1476] As patents involve extremely complex technologies and patentability requirements are a question of eternal debate, the fact that a patent is weak or that the patent holder is not entirely certain about its validity should not be sufficient to deem its ownership anticompetitive—a strict 'bad faith' standard would probably be advisable.

II. The Case under EU Law

As stated earlier, art 102 TFEU is more concerned with how firms behave when they hold a dominant position in the market than with the way in which such position is attained. Hence, the question whether the ownership or enforcement of a patent obtained through deceptive means may configure an abusive behaviour seems to be particularly pertinent in this jurisdiction.

In the leading case on deceptive conducts before the patent office, however, the courts unfortunately did not deal with this specific issue. Because in that case AstraZeneca happened to already enjoy a dominant position by the time it applied for the SPCs, courts were able to tackle the acquisition of the IPR on itself and did not need to consider subsequent events.

1474 Leslie, 'The Anticompetitive Effects of Unenforced Invalid Patents' (n 1272) 161.

1475 ibid 155.

1476 See Robert P Merges, 'As Many as Six Impossible Patents before Breakfast: Property Rights for Business Concepts and Patent System Reform' (1999) 14 Berkeley Tech L J 577, 599.

Despite of that, in practice there may certainly be cases where the undertaking attains market power only after having deceived the patent office, precisely as a result of the improperly obtained patent. In such a case, it is worth asking whether art 102 TFEU may enter into play against any of the subsequent conducts that the patent holder may perform.

a. A case for Article 102(a) TFEU or duty to license?

In the first place, it would be interesting to analyse whether solutions presented in other areas under analogous circumstances may be borrowed and transplanted to the cases at hand. In fact, the interpretation insinuated by the Commission in the framework of 'patent ambushing' or 'patent hold-up' cases may be of particular interest in this regard.

Patent ambush is a concept that arose in the context of private standard-setting organisations (SSOs) and essentially refers to a complex strategy that comprises two basic steps. In the first place, the holder of a patent (or patent application) takes part in a standard-setting procedure without disclosing the existence of her IPRs, often actively participating in the discussions and striving to have the SSO embrace a standard that would infringe those IPRs. Subsequently, and provided that this standard is ultimately adopted by the SSO and implemented by the industry, the undertaking puts those IPRs to use by suing those firms who implement the standard or by demanding from them royalty fees that probably would not have been able to ask for had those IPRs been disclosed earlier—either because the SSO would have chosen a different standard or because the undertaking would have had to commit to license those IPRs on FRAND terms.[1477] As it may be noticed, this scenario bears some resemblance to the cases that constitute the target of this work, as they both involve deceptive conducts stemming from a firm which may not hold a dominant position at that exact point in time but which may later attain it for the very reason of the deceitful behaviour. In other words, they both deal with problems in the *acquisition* of market power rather than on its subsequent use or abuse.

The most significant case with which the Commission has dealt on the particular question of patent ambush is *Rambus*.[1478] In this case, an SSO

1477 See Andreas Fuchs, 'Patent Ambush Strategies and Article 102 TFEU' in Josef Drexl and others (eds), *More Common Ground for International Competition Law* (Edward Elgar 2011) 177-180.

1478 *Rambus* (Case COMP/38.636) Commission Decision 2010/C 30/09 [2010] OJ C30/17.

had adopted a particular standard on 'Dynamic Random Access Memory' (DRAM) chips that embodied, among others, a technology covered by Rambus' patents. During the discussions at the SSO that led to the adoption of the standard, Rambus had deliberately concealed the existence of those patents (by then patent applications), despite the fact that the SSO patent policy urged their disclosure and that Rambus had actively taken part in those discussions.[1479] In fact, Rambus was even accused of tailoring its pending patent applications on the basis of the SSO discussions so as to ensure that the claims would comprise the adopted standard.[1480]

While Rambus' behaviour indubitably raised the Commission's concern, the case presented a particular obstacle under the light of art 102 TFEU, namely that the undertaking did not hold a dominant position by the time it concealed its patent portfolio. By the time it started asserting its patents, however, Rambus had already acquired a substantial level of market power, which led the Commission to implement a quite creative approach by grounding its accusation on excessive pricing. In the view of the Commission, Rambus seemed to have abused its dominant position 'by claiming royalties ... at a level which, absent its allegedly intentional deceptive conduct, it would not have been able to charge.'[1481] In other words, the Commission analysed the case, on its face, as an exploitative abuse, yet it seemed to employ it purely as a back door to bring to the spotlight the conduct in which it was really interested: the concealment of the patent portfolio at the standard-setting procedure—which, on its own, could not have been reached by the language of art 102 TFEU.[1482] Ultimately, the case did not end with the finding of an antitrust violation be-

---

1479 ibid 42.

1480 ibid 40.

1481 ibid 28.

1482 Interestingly, the exact same case was also considered by US courts and they concluded that Rambus' conduct did not violate § 2 Sherman Act. Even though this provision allows antitrust enforcers to directly tackle the deceptive behaviour before the SSO, the Court of Appeals for the District of Columbia reversed the decision of the FTC and considered that there was not sufficient evidence that the SSO would have adopted a different standard and that the mere possibility to charge higher prices does not harm competition. *Rambus Inc v FTC* 522 F.3d 456, 463-64 (DC Cir 2008). For a critical analysis of this decision, see Drexl, 'Deceptive Conduct in the Patent World' (n 1437) 139ff; Joel M Wallace, 'Rambus v FTC in the Context of Standard-Setting Organizations, Antitrust, and the Patent Hold-Up Problem' (2009) 24 Berkeley Tech L J 661, 683 ff.

cause the Commission accepted the commitments offered by Rambus.[1483] The approach implied by the Commission, nevertheless, does offer some insight into the alternatives that EU competition enforcers may have at their disposal for coping with the practical limitations imposed by the language of art 102 TFEU.

In the light of the particular approach adopted in *Rambus*, the Commission could argue that the same logic would be equally applicable to scenarios involving a deceptive behaviour before the patent office, where that conduct leads to the attainment of market power. Indeed, if a firm is granted an unwarranted patent as a result of it employing dishonest means and later is able to secure a dominant position on the market, the Commission could contend that the prices charged by the patent holder become excessive 'in light of the specific circumstances of the case'. Those excessive prices could be either in the form of licencing royalties or those paid by end consumers for the final products; the special circumstances, on the other hand, would be given by the way in which the patent has been obtained. In this way, the Commission would be enabled in practice to analyse the specific behaviour of the patent holder at the patent office, even if it took place at a time when she was not yet dominant on the market.

As explained above, EU competition authorities ordinarily avoid prosecuting exploitative abuses and there are a number of reasons why this is a sensible policy.[1484] In fact, exploitative abuses like the ones observed in these cases appear to be a symptom of something that went wrong at a prior instance—and may thus suggest that competition law should ideally tackle that original source of competitive concerns rather than its effects. Yet considering the constraints of art 102 TFEU to face those concerns, it has been argued that the figure of exploitative abuses constitutes a legitimate alternative for EU competition enforcers in order to close 'enforcement gaps'.[1485] And in the specific case of patent ambush, it can be employed as a tool for bringing to the table not only questions on price competition but also on competition in innovation, as antitrust intervention would also be able to protect the pro-competitive and pro-innovation features of standard-setting processes.[1486]

1483 ibid 76.

1484 See text at nn 654-669 in ch 4.

1485 Lars-Hendrik Röller, 'Exploitative Abuses' in Claus-Dieter Ehlermann and Mel Marquis (eds), *European Competition Law Annual 2007: A Reformed Approach to Article 82 EC* (Hart 2008) 528-29.

1486 Drexl, 'Anticompetitive Stumbling Stones' (n 1462) 533-34.

Be that as it may, the fact must not be overlooked that the application of art 102(a) TFEU as an oblique scheme for tackling prior exclusionary conducts may also pose a number of challenges. For starters, because determining when a price is excessively high is often complex[1487] and may be particularly burdensome for competition agencies, which cannot be expected to possess pricing expertise on every singular market. Furthermore, if the prices imposed by the patent holder are ultimately found not to be excessive (or 'unfair', in the terms of art 102(a) TFEU), the prior deceptive behaviour would remain unpunished.[1488] Perhaps more importantly, additional hurdles may arise if it becomes necessary to scrutinise the price of a final product instead of licensing royalties, as there may be innumerable factors (including or not the fraudulently obtained patent) that allow a firm to charge the prices that it charges.

Additionally, as explained above in the context of *Walker Process*,[1489] having competition law focus not on one but on two different conducts (in this case the deceptive conduct and the excessive pricing) can also become problematic, as it is perfectly conceivable that those conducts are performed by two different undertakings. If that were the case, it would probably be necessary to look into the current patent holder's awareness about how that patent was obtained.

Finally, if antitrust intervention against exploitative abuses were to be justified only in those situations where competition in innovation is at stake,[1490] intervention against deceptive conducts before a patent office would make for a more debatable case, as this conduct essentially represents a restraint against price competition rather than on dynamic competition.[1491]

Regardless of the above, it should be noted that in *Rambus* and other patent ambush scenarios the patent holders are not ordinarily interested in excluding competitors but instead are ready to license their patent rights to third parties—only that they want to license them at high royalty rates. In the case of improperly obtained patents, however, it is very likely that the

1487 Urška Petrovčič, 'Patent Hold-Up and the Limits of Competition Law: A Trans-Atlantic Perspective' (2013) 50 CML Rev 1363, 1371-1373.

1488 See Picht (n 1462) 573-74. See however, Fuchs (n 1477) 194 (arguing that, if a patent holder did not act bona fide during the standardisation procedure, there should be a presumption that the subsequent royalties are excessive).

1489 See text at n 1471.

1490 See Drexl, 'Anticompetitive Stumbling Stones' (n 1462) 535.

1491 See text at nn 1406-1421.

patent holders have no intention of licensing their rights but only of reserving the market for their own and refuse to grant any license.

In view of this significant difference, it may be worth considering whether the EU 'refusal to license' case law[1492] could offer an alternative course of action by providing a duty to license.[1493] This could be particularly relevant in view of the criteria of the CJEU in *Huawei* which somehow showed a more flexible approach towards the 'exceptional circumstances' that may warrant the application of competition rules.[1494]

Although an objective justification would hardly be recognized in a case where a patent holder refuses to license an improperly obtained right, other factors and requirements ordinarily contemplated in 'refusal to license' cases, such as the indispensable nature of the right or exclusion of any effective competition, may pose significant challenges for the application of competition law. Perhaps more importantly, the grant of a compulsory license would appear as a rather abnormal remedy when considering that the question of competition law will likely arise, as a rule, after the patent has been declared invalid. The prior invalidation of tha patent would render any subsequent licensing uncalled for.

b. 'Single and Continuous' Abuses

Alternatively, it could be argued that the subsequent ownership and hypothetical enforcement of the patent actually constitute, together with the deceiving representations at the patent office, a 'single and continuous' abuse. In *AstraZeneca*, for instance, the Commission interpreted that the whole ensemble of misrepresentations before the different patent offices and courts constituted an abuse of a single and continuous nature.[1495] In

1492 For a detailed review of the EU case law on refusal to license see Beatriz Conde Gallego, 'Unilateral Refusal to License Indispensable Intellectual Property Rights – US and EU Approaches' in Josef Drexl (ed), *Research Handbook on Intellectual Property and Competition Law* (Edward Elgar 2008) 215-38.

1493 In fact, when the *AstraZeneca* case emerged, some scholars wondered whether the criteria that had been developed in the context of refusal to license cases should also be applicable to that case. Jacques-Philippe Gunther and Charlotte Breuvart, 'Misuse of Patent and Drug Regulatory Approval Systems in the Pharmaceutical Industry: An Analysis of US And EU Converging Approaches' (2005) 26 Eur Comp L Rev 669, 680.

1494 *Huawei* (n 1187) para 59.

1495 Commission Decision in *AstraZeneca* (n 1183) paras 774-76.

Rambus, the opinion of the Commission was not as explicit, but it is one of its possible readings.[1496]

The theory of 'single and continuous' anticompetitive behaviour is certainly not new under EU law. Courts have consistently admitted, when analysing cases under art 101 TFEU, that anticompetitive agreements or concerted practices may result not only from an isolated act but also from a series of associated acts,[1497] and the doctrine was developed in order to capture the whole dynamic of an agreement over its lifetime.[1498] Whether the same doctrine may be transplanted to art 102 TFEU cases, however, is still highly debatable.[1499] On the one hand, it may imply in practice imposing a 'special responsibility' upon firms who were not dominant when the conduct begun.[1500] On the other hand, it may be used as a mere pretext to stretch the scope of art 102 TFEU to reach conducts that the provision is not really designed to reach. If the relevant conduct took place before the patent office, it appears somehow arbitrary to claim that the same conduct lingers over time without clear boundaries and may become a source of legal uncertainty.

c. Ownership or Enforcement as Separate Exclusionary Abuses?

In the light of the foregoing, it would be important to analyse whether, under EU law, the ownership or enforcement of patents obtained by deceptive means may be considered as separate, individual exclusionary abuses. As already hinted when analysing the situation under US law, conducts

---

1496 See Drexl, 'Anticompetitive Stumbling Stones' (n 1462) 532 (eventually tipping against said interpretation).

1497 See, eg, Joined Cases C-204/00 P, C-205/00 P, C-211/00 P, C-213/00 P, C-217/00 P and C-219/00 P *Aalborg Portland A/S v Commission* [2004] ECR I-123, para 258 ('An infringement of Article 85(1) of the Treaty may result not only from an isolated act but also from a series of acts or from continuous conduct.').

1498 Julian Joshua, 'Single Continuous Infringement of Article 81 EC: Has the Commission Stretched the Concept beyond the Limit of its Logic?' (2009) 5 Eur Comp J 451, 452.

1499 See Fuchs (n 1477) 191; Drexl, 'Anticompetitive Stumbling Stones' (n 1462) 532.

1500 Fuchs (n 1477) 191-92. Although this may not particularly come out as undesirable in the case of deceptive behaviours before the patent office, it may generate legal uncertainty under different scenarios where conducts are perfectly admissible for non-dominant firms and only banned for those undertakings holding a dominant position in the market. See text at nn 650-652 in ch 4.

taking place once a patent has been granted such as its public disclosure, licensing or hypothetical enforcement—and maybe even its mere holding over time—may help to reinforce its exclusionary effects, as they would either alert or remind actual or potential competitors of the existence of the exclusive right. As opposed to the situation under US case law, however, EU competition enforcers have not particularly analysed whether those conducts can raise competitive concerns. In fact, the question has been incidentally raised,[1501] but it does not seem to have attracted much attention from scholars or antitrust enforcers yet.

As referred above, the application of competition laws against the mere ownership of a right is a question certainly worth asking, though special attention should be devoted to the potential negative effects that such a duty might entail for patenting activity. In practice, such a burden would imply for patent holders a positive obligation to renounce to patents provided that they are connected to markets in which they hold a dominant position.[1502] The considerations made when analysing this hypothesis under US antitrust law seem to be equally applicable here.

On the whole, the question whether the holding or assessment of knowingly invalid patents merits competition law intervention exceeds the question of deceptive behaviour (and hence the scope of this work), as it encompasses all invalid patents, no matter how they have been obtained. The question is certainly worth considering and deserves further research, though for the very reason of its wide reach, no additional duties should be imposed upon patent holders without meticulous consideration of their potential implications.

1501 See, eg, Robin Jacob, 'Patents and Pharmaceuticals: A Paper given on 29th November at the Presentation of the Directorate-General of Competition's Preliminary Report of the Pharma-Sector Inquiry' in Hugh C Hansen (ed), *Intellectual Property Law and Policy: Volume 12* (Hart 2013) 655.

1502 Leslie, 'The Anticompetitive Effects of Unenforced Invalid Patents' (n 1272) 161.

PART III: CONCLUSIONS

Part I of this work described the patenting procedure both in the US and in Europe, analysed the behavioural duties of patent applicants in both jurisdictions and concluded by examining the advantages and drawbacks of both systems.

Part II, on the other hand, dealt with the behaviour of patent applicants from a competition law perspective. To that end, this part of the work briefly described the fundamental aims and components of competition law, explained the general interaction between intellectual property rights and competition, analysed the relevant case law in the EU and in the US on the specific concerns raised by fraudulently obtained patents and concluded by exploring the appropriate theory of harm.

By way of conclusion, this Part III intends to provide a succinct summary of the complete analysis performed in this work, as well as to briefly explain the results and recommendations that may be drawn and on which further study and practice could continue.

Chapter VII: Summary and Conclusions

At the very beginning of this work, when referring to the *Servier* case heard by the UK courts, a decision from J Jacob was cited raising a handful of appealing remarks surrounding the examination procedure before the patent office, namely the concerns that can emerge from a dishonest conduct by a patent applicant and the legal remedies that are or should be available to offset them. Although the dishonest conduct in that case is far from certain and was in fact called into question at a later stage by the General Court,[1503] those general remarks essentially pertained to two basic challenges, the first one connected to the available remedies under patent law itself and the other one to the role that competition law should play in that particular scenario.

The topic has not traditionally attracted much attention within European courts and scholars, although it seems to have gained some ground ever since—particularly with respect to the application of competition law. In the US, the picture looks quite different. On the one hand, patent applicants have a strict duty of candour which includes, inter alia, the disclosure of relevant information for patentability and US courts are repeatedly asked to delve into these questions within the context of the inequitable conduct defences. On the other hand, the US Supreme Court has expressly acknowledged several decades ago that fraud to the patent office can be a source of serious antitrust concern and lower courts and scholars have long strived to develop appropriate legal standards thereto.

Against this backdrop, LJ Jacob's judgment offers a unique opportunity to study these two matters in greater depth. This has been, in point of fact, the main aim of the present work, which has analysed deceptive conducts before the patent office from those two markedly different angles. On one side, it has explored the question as to the alternatives that exist under patent law, either *de lege lata* or *de lege ferenda*, to cope with deceitful conducts before the patent office and has, to that end, critically compared the models in place in the US and in Europe. On the other side, it has explored how competition laws have tackled this kind of behaviour thus far and attempted to identify the appropriate theory of harm in order to develop coherent standards for assessment.

1503 See text in n 2 in ch 1.

1. *The Role of Patent Applicants in the US and in Europe. Duties and Remedies under Patent Law*

It is well known that European and American patent laws have completely different approaches when it comes to the duties imposed upon patent applicants. In fact, US represents a rather isolated case as to the degree of responsibilities imposed upon patent applicants and the severe consequences that a failure to comply with them can have. In times when patent laws around the world become increasingly homogeneous, the question emerges as to why US law remains so different on this particular aspect and whether Europe (or any other jurisdiction with a comparable patent law framework) should learn any lessons from that experience.

A. *The Scenario under US Law. A Strict Duty of Candour and the Inequitable Conduct Doctrine*

The duty of candour that rests upon patent applicants in the US today springs from two main institutions, namely the inequitable conduct doctrine developed by the courts and the specific regulations enacted by the USPTO, the latter overall following the parameters traced by former—but not necessarily congruent with it *in toto*. The origins of the doctrine are rooted in the equity principle of unclean hands, although scholars prevailingly perceive it as a tool for optimising the quantity and quality of information available to patent examiners.

Under US law, patent applicants are required to conduct their proceedings in a frank manner and in good faith, which is interpreted to also include the disclosure of all relevant information they are aware of that could be material to patentability. This burden comprises not only own disclosures, such as prior uses or exhibitions, but also publications or patents emanating from third parties, and a failure to comply with this duty can have drastic consequences on patentees. Indeed, if courts find that patentees have knowingly withheld relevant information during patent prosecution, or that they have submitted false or misleading data, even in connection with one single claim, the whole patent can be rendered unenforceable under the inequitable conduct doctrine, without even analysing whether the patent is valid or has been infringed—and even if the patent covers a genuine invention and would have otherwise been declared valid.

In order to be reputed inequitable, the conduct of the patentees must meet two central requirements: intent and materiality. In other words, the patent applicant must have had the specific intention to mislead the patent office and such conduct must have had a significant effect on the decision of the examiner. The exact characterisation of these elements, however, has been fiercely debated and different courts often use different standards, hence leading to a high level of legal uncertainty over the specific scope of patent applicants' duties.

Over time, due to the ambiguity surrounding it and the enormous reward for defendants in case of success, inequitable conduct allegations have become almost a standard plead in US patent litigation, regardless of the merits of the defence. In many lawsuits, the focus actually shifted from core issues, like infringement or validity, to questions more concerned with the morality of the patent applicants and with the minutiae of the patent's procedural history, which also increases the costs for the parties. Be that as it may, few courts or scholars dare to advocate for the complete eradication of the inequitable conduct doctrine, most of them rather suggesting amendments to reduce the number of frivolous suits or a revamp into an economic tool. In recent years, eg, the US Patent Act has incorporated a Supplemental Examination procedure allowing patentees to purge their patents before going to court so as to later avoid inequitable conduct accusations. The Federal Circuit, for its part, rendered an *en banc* decision in *Therasense*[1504] in a clear attempt to increase legal certainty and narrow down the circumstances under which inequitable conduct can be found.

B. *The Scenario under EU Law*

When it comes to the manner in which patent applicants are required to conduct their proceedings before the patent office, two central differences between Europe and the United States are to be noted: the extent of the duties upon the applicants and the legal consequences that a failure to meet them could later have on the patent and on its owner.

Firstly, although European patent applicants are undeniably expected to behave with candour and good faith in their affairs at the patent office, neither the EPC nor the major national patent offices in Europe provide for a stringent duty to disclose relevant prior art such as scientific publications, prior patents, etc. Admittedly, the EPC requires patent applicants to reveal proximate prior art in the specification, when describing the invention, but such a duty has been interpreted rather laxly by the Boards of Appeal of the EPO. The requirement appears to be aimed at ensuring that

---

1504 *Therasense Inc v Becton, Dickinson & Co* 649 F 3d 1276 (Fed Cir 2011) (en banc).

patent specifications disclose sufficient information to the public rather than at imposing a duty to collaborate with the examiners in the search for prior art. The Preparatory Works of the EPC, although not directly approaching the issue, seem to be on the same wavelength. It should be borne in mind, nevertheless, that there are specific circumstances under which applicants are expected to provide the examiners with specific information, particularly in the case of rule 141 EPC with regard to reports produced by foreign patent offices, but the duty remains rather negligible.

Secondly, in addition to the precise scope of the duties that lie upon the patent applicants, stark differences also exist between Europe and the US as to the legal effects that the behaviour at the patent office can later have over the enforceability of the patent as such. In the first place, under the EPC, a patent cannot be declared invalid for the mere fact that the applicant conducted the procedure in a dishonest or deceitful manner, so long as it is not also shown that the patent does not meet one of the patentability criteria. Similarly, those circumstances do not seem to play any role vis-à-vis the enforceability of the patent, as courts in the Member States tend to give short shrift to allegations concerning the circumstances under which patents were granted.

C. *Would it be Desirable for Europe to Implement an Increased Duty of Candour or an Inequitable Conduct Doctrine?*

At this point, it is worth asking whether the approach taken by US legislators and courts presents any benefits that would make it advisable from a European standpoint—or for any other jurisdiction having a legal framework akin to European laws. As mentioned, there are two essential issues in this regard which, although deeply intertwined, may be set apart and demand to be treated separately. The first one is connected to the extent of duties that are laid upon patent applicants and particularly the question whether they should be required to bring to the examination proceedings information relevant to patentability. The second one refers to the legal consequences that an inadequate prosecution of a patent application may have on the later enforcement of the patent if it were to be granted.

I. Extent of Patent Applicant's Duties

It seems undisputable that high quality patents can deliver benefits to all users of the patent system and to general welfare and that in order to issue high quality patents patent offices need to have at their disposal as much information as possible. Hence, at first glance, the idea of extending the patent applicants' duties and compelling them to bring forward background information on the invention appears as a rather logical and appealing approach—particularly considering that they are often knowledgeable on the field of the invention and that the proceedings up to the grant of the patent are, apart from a few exceptions, essentially ex parte. A closer look, however, reveals that this apparently straightforward solution may bring forward a number of serious problems.

First, it seems tremendously challenging to define the scope of patent applicants' disclosure duties in clear terms. Should the duty be restricted to relevant information they are aware of? Or should they be compelled to disclose the entirety of the existing prior art relevant to the invention? US practice is inclined towards the former, although both solutions seem to face severe drawbacks. The US approach makes the duty extremely difficult to supervise, as authorities need to investigate in every case whether the applicant was indeed aware of any specific piece of prior art and hence delve into subjective factors. Moreover, it may induce applicants to remain deliberately oblivious to reduce risks. But expecting applicants to disclose all existing prior art wouldn't make things much easier, as it would require them to become absolute experts on their fields and would hence raise their patenting costs significantly. In either case, applicants might be encouraged to err on the side of over-disclosure, which may end up burying important pieces of prior art inside long lists of less relevant information. Besides, the duty of advocacy that lies upon patent attorneys may constitute an additional hurdle in shaping the boundaries of these duties, as they may be required to put on the table arguments that they are later expected to rebut.

Moreover, even if a practical way of implementing such a duty were to be found, the information submitted by the applicants does not necessarily warrant the issuance of higher quality patents. As a matter of fact, in practice US examiners tend to pay very little attention to the background art brought forward by the patent applicants. The reasons are varied and may be related to the examiners' limited allocated time, today's vast sources of information at hand, self-confidence, distrust, etc. Moreover, in the case of the EPO, relevant information overlooked or hidden from the examiners may be promptly revealed by third parties not only via observations but also later, by filing an opposition. Hence, the practical value of such a duty may be much less significant than first expected.

Finally, it should be borne in mind that, in many cases, patent applicants themselves may be personally interested in having their inventions examined against the closest prior art, since emerging victorious of an accurate examination with relevant prior art is likely to put them in a better position during licensing negotiations or litigation.

In view of the above, any amendment to the current laws in the EPC in connection to the role of the patent applicants during the examination procedure seems ill-advised. At any rate, should proposals be made in this direction, additional empirical research would be required and revisions should only be implemented after very careful consideration of their potential impact on the patent system altogether.

II. Legal Consequences of the Deceitful Conduct

Whatever the extent of the duties ultimately imposed upon patent applicants, a separate though extremely intertwined question arises as to the legal consequences that may derive from a failure to comply with those duties. Needless to say, the stricter the duties the higher the relevance that this question is likely to have. Yet even with less strict rules like those in place in Europe, the question might still be worth asking. Should courts, eg, refuse to enforce a patent for the sole reason that the owner conducted the patent application proceedings in bad faith?

The inequitable conduct doctrine developed by US courts is habitually considered to have evolved from the unclean hands doctrine—a traditional legal principle according to which plaintiffs may be denied legal redress if it is shown that they have behaved in bad faith with respect to the matter of the complaint. This legal principle, however, is also acknowledged in many other jurisdictions where an inequitable conduct doctrine did not ultimately emerge. This fact seems to suggest that the inequitable conduct doctrine is not an inevitable upshot of that legal principle but rather a discretionary interpretation of it followed by US courts.

Yet even if not required by ethical or traditional legal principles, it is open to question whether adopting a similar approach could be nonetheless advisable from a more utilitarian perspective. Indeed, many scholars in the US have argued that the existence of an inequitable conduct defence induces patent applicants to conduct their proceedings with greater candour—which can thus lead to higher quality of patents. The advantages that may be perceived on the surface, however, are offset when analysing the matter in greater depth.

In the first place, having courts decide on what patent office examiners need appears as a rather oblique and defective way of approaching the patent quality conundrum. Indeed, patent offices are likely to be in a much better position to decide on the kinds of collaboration that they need from patent applicants and court attempts to influence on this issue may configure an inappropriate interference in the administrative process.

Perhaps more importantly, bringing this sort of questions to the table in infringement proceedings is also prone to increase the costs of litigation significantly and to divert the attention from more important issues like the validity of the patent and its infringement. Moreover, in the particular case of the EPC, it has been argued that the hypothetical advantages that an inequitable conduct doctrine could bring may be eclipsed by the post-grant opposition system.

Yet even if there was no post-grant opposition procedure available, a deeper look reveals that the only scenarios in which the inequitable conduct doctrine is qualified to offer additional aid are those where that contribution may not be all that desirable. In arriving at this conclusion, the universe of hypothetical cases should be divided into two categories: (i) cases where the misconduct is tied to an invalid patent (ie, where at least one of the patentability requirements is not met), and (ii) cases where the misconduct is tied to a patent that is nonetheless valid.

In the first scenario, the existence of an inequitable conduct defence appears as clearly superfluous. Challenging the validity of the patent is a much more straightforward defence for the alleged infringer and does not require the court and attorneys to delve into endless subjective questions on what the patent applicants knew or should have known, often many years ago, or what the examiner would have or would have not considered relevant.

In the second scenario, it is not clear whether it is indeed desirable to refuse to enforce a valid patent for the mere fact that the applicant showed a reproachable behaviour. The Federal Circuit in *Therasense* answered in the affirmative, at least with regard to affirmative egregious misconducts, but this approach is debatable at the very least. If an applicant indeed made a worthy invention and a valuable contribution to technological development, refusing to enforce the patent is not necessarily an optimal solution.

That is not to say that reprehensible conducts taking place at the patent office bear no legal significance or that they should go unpunished. If the requirements are met, the patent attorneys involved in the procedure could be subject to sanctions by the corresponding disciplinary boards—and even criminal sanctions could apply in the most severe cases. That, however, does not imply that the question must be brought to every patent infringement case.

2. *The Patent Applicant's Conduct as a Competition Law Concern*

The question on how patent applicants conduct their proceedings before the patent office can also become relevant from a competition law perspective. Indeed, due to the undeniable impact that patents are bound to have on the market, at least potentially, unwarranted conducts during patent prosecution may be perceived as an additional source of antitrust concern.

In this particular area, the scenarios in Europe and the US are also rather different. US case law has long acknowledged that fraudulent conducts before the patent office can constitute antitrust violations and has developed certain standards—although those standards are not always entirely clear and seem to overly focus on the ulterior enforcement of the patent rather than on the antitrust concerns of the fraudulent conduct itself. Under EU law, this area remained for a long time outside the radar of competition law, even though recent developments evidence that the scenario might be changing—particularly after the *AstraZeneca* decision by the CJEU.[1505] It seems important, hence, to determine how competition law ought to tackle this kind of behaviour by identifying the appropriate theory of harm and, on that basis, develop suitable standards for its assessment.

A. *The Experience so far in the US and in the EU*

I. *The Scenario in the US: Walker Process and its Progeny*

The first case in which the US Supreme Court ruled on this specific issue was *Walker Process*,[1506] a case decided in 1965. In its rather succinct decision, the Supreme Court essentially established that the enforcement of a patent procured by fraud may be violative of § 2 Sherman Act. Over time,

1505 Case C-457/10 P *AstraZeneca v Commission* (CJEU, 6 December 2012, ECLI:EU:C:2012:770).

1506 *Walker Process Equipment Inc v Food Machinery & Chemical Corp* 382 US 172 (1965).

Walker Process developed into one of the most often raised antitrust defences during patent litigation, although very rarely in a successful way. On its face, the decision seems to be rather concise and simple, yet its conclusion and the background reasoning opened the door to a number of interesting questions —many of which still remain unanswered to this day.

In the first place, the decision failed to explain how this conclusion fits into the puzzle of the 'antitrust petitioning immunity' doctrine, which had been acknowledged by the same court only a few years before in *Noerr*.[1507] Under this doctrine, the Supreme Court had concluded that, as a principle, no antitrust violation may be derived from mere attempts to influence the passage or enforcement of laws or other governmental acts. Despite the fact that applying for and prosecuting a patent clearly constitute acts of petitioning, the Supreme Court did not even bring up this issue in *Walker Process*. Later on, the Supreme Court did acknowledge it as an open question but expressly declined to solve it. On this basis, some have argued that *Walker Process* is nothing but a variant of sham —the only exception to petitioning immunity expressly recognised in *Noerr*. Others contend that sham and *Walker Process* rather constitute two separate means of stripping a patentee from said immunity.

The Supreme Court decision in *Walker Process* also failed to explain what kind of deceptive conduct is needed in order to trigger antitrust liability. This problem, however, was for the most part unravelled by lower courts, who defined the relevant conduct around the more established standards of common law fraud.

More importantly, neither *Walker Process* nor subsequent decisions from lower courts entirely clarify the theory of harm that underlies this defence. At first glance, antitrust concerns seem to flow from the deceptive conduct taking place at the patent office. The Supreme Court, however, overly concentrated on the enforcement stage and several passages of its reasoning seem to downplay the relevance of the events that take place at the patent office. Indeed, the decision hints that the crucial factor is whether a patentee or assignee enforces a patent knowing of its invalidity, which does not necessarily require a reproachable behaviour during prosecution. A patentee could become aware of the patent's infirmity after grant, eg by discovering an unknown piece of prior art. In any case, the prevailing interpretation today seems to require two essential elements to prove a *Walker Process* antitrust violation: the misleading or fraudulent behaviour before the

1507 *Eastern Railroad Presidents Conference v Noerr Motor Freight Inc* 365 US 127 (1961).

patent office and a subsequent enforcement of the fraudulently obtained patent.

II. The Scenario in the EU: AstraZeneca

In the EU, the first case tackling this issue began with an investigation carried out by the Commission which ultimately concluded with the *AstraZeneca* decision by the CJEU. The case involved a very particular set of facts comprising conducts before the patent office but not referring to ordinary patent applications. Be that as it may, the analysis of the CJEU offers a clear idea of the criteria under which similar conducts may be assessed in the EU in the future.

In *AstraZeneca*, the CJEU decided —among other issues— that a pattern of misleading representations by a firm holding market dominance in order to acquire SPCs to which it was not entitled constitutes an abuse of a dominant position. In general terms, it highlighted that such a conduct constitutes a practice falling outside the scope of competition on the merits and hence a violation of art 102 TFEU.

The CJEU first stressed that dominant firms have a special responsibility that compels them to disclose relevant information in these kinds of situations. In this regard, it is worth pointing out that, as a rule, the SPCs involved in that case were granted without any comprehensive examination, basically relying on the information provided by the applicant. Patent offices had a very limited margin of manoeuvre —which is clearly not the case in ordinary patent applications and hence might speak for a distinct solution in that scenario.

As for the exclusionary effects of the deceptive behaviour, the CJEU emphasised that they derive from the mere existence of the exclusive right which should not have been granted. The General Court expressly highlighted in this regard that the enforcement of the exclusive right was not required. In fact, the CJEU pointed out that it was not even necessary to have obtained the exclusive right, as long as the misleading acts were at least likely to result in their issuance.

Finally, as for the characterisation of the abusive conduct, the General Court interpreted that the pattern of misleading acts configured a case of single and continuous infringement. The CJEU added that the anti-competitive nature of the misleading acts must be evaluated at the time when those acts are committed and, hence, that the fact that a firm does not hold a dominant position any longer by the time the exclusive right is granted does not exonerate it from antitrust liability.

Against this backdrop, the question emerges as to how courts should solve a case of misleading conducts taking place within the context of regular patent application proceedings, where the regime does not necessarily coincide with that of SPCs. On the basis of the case law developed in the US and the guidelines sketched by the CJEU in *AstraZeneca*, the second and final goal of the present work was thus to identify the theory of harm underlying these conducts and develop workable standards for their assessment.

B. Sham or Vexatious Litigation Distinguished

In order to identify the theory of harm underlying these kinds of behaviours, it is important to first distinguish them from cases involving sham or vexatious litigation. Indeed, although similar and often overlapping, sham or vexatious litigation scenarios exhibit particular features which are not necessarily present in the abuses which are the object of this work.

In the US, sham was first acknowledged by the Supreme Court in *Noerr* as an exception to the petitioning antitrust immunity therein established. In fact, sham remains today the sole exception to this immunity expressly recognised by the Supreme Court. In that case, the court established that the act of petitioning the government is immune to antitrust scrutiny unless it is 'a mere sham to cover what is actually nothing more than an attempt to interfere directly with the business relationships of a competitor.'[1508]

Subsequent cases contributed in gradually shaping the boundaries of the sham exception, which was finally defined by the Supreme Court several decades later in *PREI*.[1509] In this decision, the Supreme Court stated that, for a sham conduct to amount to a case of monopolisation, two different elements must be shown: an objectively baseless petition and a specific intent to interfere with competitors through 'the use of the governmental process —as opposed to the outcome of that process— as an antitrust weapon.'[1510]

1508 *Noerr* (n 1507) 144.
1509 *Professional Real Estate Investors Inc v Columbia Pictures Industries Inc* 508 US 49 (1993).
1510 ibid 61; *City of Columbia v Omni Outdoor Advertising Inc* 499 US 365, 380 (1991).

On the EU side, courts developed very similar standards in *ITT Promedia*,[1511] a decision by the General Court which was rendered only a couple of years after *PREI*. In the context of abusive litigation, the General Court interpreted that, in principle, the bringing of an action cannot be characterised as an abuse. In order to qualify as an abuse, the General Court implicitly adopted a test which very much resembles US Supreme Court's test in *PREI*.

Therefore, despite their rather different points of departure, US and EU courts seem to essentially refer to the same conduct when assessing sham or vexatious abuses, ie the use of court and governmental proceedings irrespective of their outcome and with the main purpose of harassing, deterring or hindering competitors. Hence, in order to qualify as an antitrust offence, two separate elements must be shown: an objectively baseless petition and a specific intent to harass competitors through the governmental proceedings. This is, of course, not the exclusive domain of intellectual property rights, as similar abuses are also conceivable with any other act of petitioning to the government. From an economic perspective, it appears to be a variant of the more general strategy of raising rivals' costs, ie a non-price predatory practice.

At this point, the question inescapably emerges as to whether a deceitful conduct before the patent office can be subsumed within the sham tests developed in the US and EU. As for the first element of those tests, it could probably be argued without major hurdles that a misleading conduct, at least if it refers to elements material to patentability, is indeed objectively baseless because the applicant was aware that the patent would not be granted if the examiner became aware of all pertinent facts. But when it comes to the second element, the issue becomes a little thornier. Indeed, if a firm decides to conceal relevant information on patentability, it is very likely that its intent is not to harass or interfere with competitors through the abusive use of the governmental process, but rather to obtain the patent and hence an unwarranted exclusive right to be able to exclude competitors.

Against this background, one may wonder whether this implies that a mischievous conduct before the patent office does not really raise genuine antitrust concerns, or whether the tests developed by US and EU courts are flawed. But the reason why such conducts do not fit the sham criteria is probably different and more connected to the fact that those kinds of conducts are not entirely comparable. This seems to be, in point of fact, the

---

1511 Case T-111/96 *ITT Promedia NV v Commission* [1998] ECR II 2937.

interpretation adopted by the General Court in *AstraZeneca*, which expressly refused to apply the *ITT Promedia* criteria to an abuse consisting of misleading representations. In the US, the FTC advocates for this interpretation as well, arguing that deceitful acts of petitioning the government do not need to be assessed under the light of the sham criteria. Hence, although there might be cases where deceitful conducts take place within a sham strategy, a deceptive conduct before the patent office seems to raise a different type of antitrust concerns: the exclusionary effects appear to flow directly from the governmental act rather than as a collateral effect of the act of petitioning.

C. Deceptive Conduct before the Patent Office as a Case of Inducing Government Action through Improper Means

I. The General Framework in the US and in the EU

In view of the foregoing, it is necessary to look into the question of misleading conducts before the patent office through different lenses, and to that end the standards developed by EU and US courts on the question of improper inducement of government action seem to be an appropriate starting point. At the end of the day, deceptive conducts before the patent office seem to be nothing but a variant of this type of abuses.

As a principle, it should be borne in mind that any government action —be it a law, a regulation, an individual decision— is capable of restraining competition. Those restrictions, however, are often beneath the competition law radar. Yet when the government action imposing those restraints is triggered by a reprehensible private action, competition law intervention may be justified.

In the US, the standards of assessment for these kinds of conducts are not yet entirely clear. As explained earlier, petitioning the government is, as a principle, immune to antitrust laws in this jurisdiction. The only exception expressly acknowledged by the Supreme Court is sham. Admittedly, the Supreme Court also hinted in other decisions that deceptive practices may not always be immunised, yet it never explained whether a separate exception really exists. Be that as it may, lower courts ordinarily interpret that misrepresentations in non-political arenas are not immune and rely on diverse grounds to reach this conclusion. The FTC and several scholars increasingly advocate for a separate exception and *Walker Process* could in fact be invoked as a touchstone to support this view.

In the EU, the scenario was relatively similar until not very long ago, as courts had insinuated different parameters along several cases but had never addressed the question directly. In *AstraZeneca*,[1512] however, the General Court attempted to draw a more general conclusion and expressly stated that the submission of misleading information to the government which is liable to lead to the grant of an exclusive right to which an undertaking is not entitled is a practice that falls outside the scope of competition on the merits.

II. Elements for Competition Assessment

Admitting that a deceptive conduct before the patent office may be considered, at least theoretically, an improper inducement of governmental action capable of harming competition only constitutes the first step in the competition law assessment. As in any other case of monopolisation or abuse of a dominant position, there are different elements that need to be shown, essentially relating to market power, the abusive behaviour and the anticompetitive effects. To that end, and given the singularities of this particular set of conducts, a number of important factors must be taken into account before concluding that a violation of competition law really exists.

a. Causal Link

In the first place, it is indispensable to verify the causal link between the governmental act that imposes restrictions on competition and the deceitful conduct of the private party, so as to determine whether the former is a direct consequence of the latter. In other words, it must be analysed whether the patent has been granted specifically because of the mischievous prosecution by the patent applicant.

The question may seem at first sight simple, yet it is often difficult to deconstruct the mental process of the decision maker —in this case, the patent examiner. Complications may arise, eg, if the false information provided by the patent applicant was not the sole reason why the examiner decided to grant the patent. Moreover, even if a patent is clearly the result of a fraudulent conduct, it could very well happen that the patent would have been nonetheless granted even in the absence of the fraudulent behaviour.

1512 Case T-321/05 *AstraZeneca v Commission* [2010] ECR II-2805.

In that case, it could be argued that the private party's conduct —though reproachable— does not actually amount to a competition law violation, as the restrictions on competition would have been imposed anyway.

Because the question on causal link very much resembles the 'materiality' element of inequitable conduct cases in the US, many of the opinions expressed by the courts in those cases may also be transposed to the antitrust sphere.

b. Conceptualisation of the Misconduct

Additionally, it is important to define what exactly constitutes a deceptive conduct by a private party. Despite the technical nature of the areas that it governs, patent law is no exact science and the fact that a patent is incorrectly granted does not by any means imply that the applicant behaved in a fraudulent way. Even though anticompetitive conducts are ordinarily defined under objective parameters, both EU and US courts seem to acknowledge that cases involving deceptive conducts before the patent office may represent an exceptional scenario where the specific intent of the applicant plays a decisive role. This does not mean that the relevant conduct necessarily entails positive misrepresentations, as omissions may also be deemed deceptive depending on the circumstances of the case. Ultimately, it is crucial that the reproachable conduct is not defined too broadly in order to avoid undermining the integrity of the patent procedure.

c. Discretion of the Patent Office

Particular attention should also be paid to the margin of discretion enjoyed by the public authority when receiving input from private parties. Ordinarily, patent offices have ample room for manoeuvre in order to verify the accuracy or veracity of the information they receive from patent applicants. Yet there are situations where public authorities enjoy less discretion, in which cases the resulting public act is less likely to embrace public policy concerns. In those cases, the potential anticompetitive effects seem to flow directly from the undertakings' own judgment rather than from a governmental decision.

In any event, it seems clear that, as a general rule, the undertakings' duty of transparency becomes stricter in inverse proportion to the government office's margin of discretion and is likely to vary depending on the factual circumstances of each case.

d. Anticompetitive Effects

Even if shown that a patent applicant has deliberately deceived the patent office and that this conduct has been material to the grant of a patent, an infringement of competition rules cannot be found unless anticompetitive effects are also shown.

In the first place, it may be argued that the sole existence of the granted patent is capable of having exclusionary effects, even though US courts seem to require evidence that the patent has been somehow enforced too. The sole existence of the fraudulently obtained patent on the market may increase market entry costs for competitors. And with regard to competition in innovation, there may be cases in which the improper grant of a patent could discourage competitors to invest in R&D on that particular technological area.

In order to assess the anticompetitive effects in practice, it is important to define the relevant market and weigh it against the scope of the patent (ie, its claims). In fact, a patent can have from insignificant to vast effects on the market depending on the specific technology that it aims to protect and the existence or not of alternative non-infringing products.

At least theoretically, it could be argued that even deceitful conducts which do not result in a granted patent may have exclusionary effects. In practice, however, these effects might be very hard to prove and should not be analysed laxly as they could turn in practice into a *per se* violation.

e. Market Power

Last, but certainly not least, unilateral anticompetitive conducts require proof not only of the anticompetitive behaviour but also of an element of market power. This may be particularly interesting in the cases at hand, as a patent applicant may have no market power at all when prosecuting a patent application, yet it may acquire significant market power subsequently —precisely due to the improperly obtained patent.

In the US, the fact that market power is not held at the time of the relevant conduct is not particularly problematic, as § 2 Sherman Act is a rather flexible provision in this regard. Indeed, the figures of monopolisation and attempt to monopolise are able to seize conducts by non-dominant firms which later lead to market power —or even when they do not, provided that there is a dangerous probability of achieving it. In practice, however, US courts deem the enforcement of the fraudulently obtained patent as the relevant conduct, and at that point in time it is more likely that patent holders will hold at least some degree market power.

In the EU, art 102 TFEU shows important differences in comparison to § 2 Sherman Act. As opposed to the latter, art 102 TFEU focuses on what undertakings do once they attain market power, but evidences several problems when facing conducts performed by non-dominant firms —even if they later achieve some degree of market power and even if they become monopolists. Admittedly, some alternatives exist to enable the applicability of art 102 TFEU under certain circumstances, eg by defining the relevant market in narrow terms. Ultimately, however, this seems to be yet another example of the limitations of EU competition law when dealing with the abusive acquisition of market power.

III. Ownership or Enforcement of Fraudulently Obtained Patents

Despite of whether the deceptive prosecution of a patent application may on its own amount to a competition law violation, it is also interesting to consider whether the maintenance and enforcement of a patent so obtained can become relevant conducts from a competition law viewpoint. This question becomes particularly relevant under EU law considering the limitations of art 102 TFEU described above.

From a US law perspective, enforcement is not only a relevant element when assessing fraudulent acquisition of patents: it is an essential one for any *Walker Process* claim to succeed. These claims, however, also require proof of a fraudulent conduct before the patent office, which in practice implies that there are not one but two separate conducts that need to be shown. In other words, this unilateral anticompetitive conduct could very well be performed by different parties, e.g. if the patent is fraudulently obtained by one party, later transferred and ultimately enforced by a different one. In any case, US court decisions make the anticompetitive effect somehow difficult to identify: as they disregard ownership alone and make enforcement an indispensable element, they seem to bring the anticompetitive concerns closer to sham or other predatory conducts.

Under EU law, it could first be considered whether art 102(a) TFEU may become applicable against these particular sets of cases, ie whether the ownership or enforcement of fraudulently obtained patents may be deemed exploitative abuses in the form of excessive selling prices. In the context of patent ambush cases, the Commission seems to have relied on this provision[1513] and a similar reasoning could be made here. The Commission, however, only used this provision as a pretext to evaluate an exclusionary abuse that had taken place before but could not be reached because the undertaking did not hold sufficient market power at that time. In fact, applying art 102(a) may entail significant risks, as it requires competition agencies to become price regulators. Tackling high prices seems to give the idea that the competitive process failed somewhere along the way and that competition law should have intervened earlier.

Additionally, taking into consideration that the owner of an improperly obtained patent is not likely to be willing to license it out, it should also be considered whether the 'refusal to license' case law could offer an alternative course of action by warranting a duty to license. Many of the relevant factors contemplated in the referred case law, however, may pose significant challenges for its transplantation to this other scenario. More importantly, the question of competition law is likely to arise after the patent has been declared invalid and this fact would render any subsequent licensing uncalled for.

Ultimately, what should be considered is whether the ownership or enforcement of patents obtained through deceptive means may be considered as separate exclusionary abuses. The question is certainly worth asking but is beyond the scope of this work. Indeed, the proper question seems to be whether the ownership or enforcement of patents which are known to be invalid can be a violation of competition laws. No significant differences exist from a competition law standpoint if the patent being maintained or enforced has been obtained through fraud or if the owner only later became aware of the cause of invalidity. Posed in these terms, the question raises a myriad of new problems that certainly merit further research, though caution is advised so as to avoid imposing excessive or vague duties upon patent holders and undermining the integrity of the patent system altogether.

1513 *Rambus* (Case COMP/38.636) Commission Decision 2010/C 30/09 [2010] OJ C30/17.

Bibliography

— — *Black's Law Dictionary* (9th edn, 2009).

— — 'Deception as an Antitrust Violation' (2012) 125 Harv L Rev 1235.

— — 'EPO Round up: Part 2' (*IP Kat*, 7 June 2005) <http://ipkitten.blogspot.de/2005/06/epo-round-up-part-2.html>.

— — 'Is the Patent Misuse Doctrine Obsolete?' (1997) 110 Harv L Rev 1922.

— — 'Recent Legislation' (2012) 125 Harv L Rev 1290.

— — *Restatement (2d) of Torts* (1977).

Abramowicz M and Duffy J F, 'Intellectual Property for Market Experimentation' (2008) 83 NYU L Rev 337.

Adelman M J, 'The Relevant Market Paradox: Attempted and Completed Patent Fraud Monopolization' (1977) 38 Ohio St L J 289.

Adelman M J, 'The New World of Patents Created by the Court of Appeals for the Federal Circuit' (1987) 20 U Mich J L Refom 979.

Akers N J, 'The Referencing of Prior Art Documents in European Patents and Applications' (2000) 22 World Patent Information 309.

Akman P, 'Searching for the Long-Lost Soul of Article 82 EC' (2009) 29 Oxford J Leg St 267 (2009).

Akman P, *The Concept of Abuse in EU Competition Law: Law and Economic Approaches* (Hart 2012).

Allison J R and Lemley M A, 'The Growing Complexity of the United States Patent System' (2002) 82 Bost U L Rev 77.

Ampollini D, 'Looking for Sense in the Italian Antitrust Authority Decision in the *Pfizer Xalatan* Case' [2012] Antitrust Chronicle vol 7(2) 1.

Anderman S D, 'The Strategic Use of Patent Enforcement and Acquisition Methods and Competition Law' in Govaere I and Ullrich H (eds), *Intellectual Property, Market Power and the Public Interest* (Peter Lang 2008) 171.

Anderman S D, 'The IP and Competition Interface: New Developments' in Anderman S D and Ezrachi A (eds), *Intellectual Property and Competition Law: New Frontiers* (OUP 2011) 6.

Anderman S D and Kallaugher J, *Technology Transfer and the New EU Competition Rules: Intellectual Property Licensing after Modernisation* (OUP 2006).

Andrews N, 'Abuse of Process in English Civil Litigation' in Taruffo M (ed), *Abuse of Procedural Rights: Comparative Standards of Procedural Fairness* (Kluwer 1999) 65.

Anenson T L, 'Treating Equity Like Law: A Post-Merger Justification of Unclean Hands' (2008) 45 Am Bus L J 455.

Areeda P E and Hovenkamp H, *Antitrust Law: An Analysis of Antitrust Principles and Their Application* (3rd edn, Aspen 2011).

Areeda P E and Hovenkamp H, *Fundamentals of Antitrust Law* (4th edn, Wolters Kluwer 2011).

Arena A, Bergmann B and Himes J L, 'Two Bodies of Law Separated by a Common Mission: Unilateral Conduct by Dominant Firms at the IP/Antitrust Intersection in the EU and the US' (2013) 9 Eur Comp J 623.

Arezzo E, 'Is There a Role for Market Definition and Dominance in an Effects-Based Approach?' in Mackenrodt M O, Conde Gallego B and Enchelmaier S (eds), *Abuse of Dominant Position: New Interpretation, New Enforcement Mechanisms?* (Springer 2008) 21.

Armitage E, 'The New British Patent Legislation' (1978) 9 IIC 207.

Arrow K J, 'Economic Welfare and the Allocation of Resources for Invention' in National Bureau of Economic Research (ed), The Rate and Direction of Inventive Activity: Economic and Social Factors (Princeton Univ Press 1962).

Balmer T A, 'Sham Litigation and the Antitrust Laws' (1980) 209 Buffalo L Rev 39.

Banks K and Marenco G, 'Intellectual Property and the Community Rules on Free Movement: Discrimination Unearthed' (1990) 15 E L Rev 224.

Batchelor B and Healy M, 'CJEU AstraZeneca Judgment: Groping Towards a Test for Patent Office Dealings; (2013) 34 Eur Comp L Rev 171.

Beier F K, 'Die Rechtsbehelfe des Patentanmelders und seiner Wettbewerber im Vergleich: Eine rechtsvergleichende Untersuchung zur Chancengleichheit im Patentverfahren [1989] GRUR Int 1.

Beier F K, 'Industrial Property and the Free Movement of Goods in the Internal European Market (1990) 21 IIC 131.

Benkard G, *Patentgesetz* (Asendorf C D and others eds, 10th edn, Beck 2006).

Bensadon M, *Ley de Patentes Comentada y Concordada con el ADPIC y el Convenio de Paris* (LexisNexis 2007).

Bently L and Sherman B, *Intellectual Property Law* (4th edn, OUP 2014).

Berg W and Brankin S P,'Das AstraZeneca-Urteil des Gerichts der Europäischen Union' [2011] EuZW 91.

Bicknell G M, 'To Disclose or not to Disclose: Duty of Candor Obligations of the United States and Foreign Patent Offices' (2008) 83 Chi-Kent L Rev 425.

Bishop S and Walker M, *The Economics of Competition Law: Concepts, Application and Measurement* (3rd edn, Sweet & Maxwell 2010).

Blanco White T A, *Patents for Inventions and the Protection of Industrial Designs* (5th edn, Stevens & Sons 1983).

Bodenhausen G H C, *Guide to the Application of the Paris Convention* (BIRPI 1968).

Bohannan C, 'IP Misuse as Foreclosure' (2011) 96 Iowa L Rev 475.

Bohannan C, and Hovenkamp H, *Creation without Restraint: Promoting Liberty and Rivalry in Innovation* (OUP 2012).

Bork R H, *The Antitrust Paradox: A Policy at War with Itself* (Basic 1978).

Borrás S, 'The Governance of the European Patent System: Effective and Legitimate?' (2006) 35 Economy and Society 594.

Bostyn S and Petit N, 'Patent=Monopoly: A Legal Fiction' (2013) <http://ssrn.com/abstract=2373471>.

Bowman W S, *Patent and Antitrust Law: A Legal and Economic Appraisal* (Univ of Chicago Press 1973).

Brack H P, 'Patent Infringement Warnings in a Common Law versus a Civil Law Jurisdiction - An Actionable Threat?' (2006) 37 IIC 1.

Brophy D, 'Rule 141 and further EPO obstructions' (*IP Kat*, 12 August 2010) <http://ipkitten.blogspot.de/2010/08/rule-141-and-further-epo-obstructions.html>.

Brown A E L, *Intellectual Property, Human Rights and Competition* (Edward Elgar 2012).

Bushell G, 'AstraZeneca v Commission: Advocate-General Mazak's Opinion of 15 May 2012' (*Kluwer Competition Blog*, 11 June 2012) <http://kluwercompetitionlawblog.com/2012/06/11/astrazeneca-v-commission-advocate-general-mazaks-opinion-of-15-may-2012>.

Caballero R J and Jaffe A B, 'How High Are the Giants' Shoulders: An Empirical Assessment of Knowledge Spillovers and Creative Destruction in a Model of Economic Growth' in Blanchard O and Fischer S (eds), *NBER Macroeconomics Annual 1993: Volume 8* (MIT Press 1993) 15.

Calkins S, 'Developments in Antitrust and the First Amendment: the Disaggregation of Noerr' (1988) 57 Antitrust L J 327.

Castillo de la Torre F, 'State Action Defence in EC Competition Law' (2005) 28 World Competition 407.

Chafee Z Jr, 'Coming into Equity with Clean Hands' (1949) 47 Mich L Rev 877.

Chandra A, 'Antitrust Liability for Attempting to Enforce a Fraudulent Patent' (1999) 81 J Pat & Trademark Off Soc'y 201.

Chiang T J, 'The Upside Down Inequitable Conduct Defense' (2013) 107 Northwest U L Rev 1243.

Chisum D S, *Chisum on Patents* (Lexis Nexis).

Clifford R D, 'Is it Time for a Rule 11 for the Patent Bar?' (2013) 53 IDEA 351.

Cole M, 'Pharmaceuticals and Competition: First Strike to the Commission?' (2013) 34 Eur Comp L Rev 227.

Cole P, 'Patents and Scientific Integrity' [2008(5)] CIPAJ 2.

Conde Gallego B, 'Unilateral Refusal to License Indispensable Intellectual Property Rights – US and EU Approaches' in Drexl J (ed), *Research Handbook on Intellectual Property and Competition Law* (Edward Elgar 2008) 215.

Conley N L, 'Considerations in Patent Litigation Brought About by Walker Process Equipment, Inc v Food Machinery & Chemical Corp' (1966) 9 S Tex L J 9.

Cooper J C and Kovacic W E, 'U.S. Convergence with International Competition Norms: Antitrust Law and Public Restraints on Competition' (2010) 90 Bost U L Rev 1555.

Cotropia C A, 'Modernizing Patent Law's Inequitable Conduct Doctrine' (2009) 24 Berkeley Tech L J 723.

Cotropia C A and Lemley M A and Sampat B N, 'Do Applicant Patent Citations Matter?' (2013) 42 Research Policy 844.

Cotter T F, 'An Economic Analysis of Patent Law's Inequitable Conduct Doctrine' (2011) 53 Az L Rev 735.

Cotter T F, 'Four Questionable Rationales for the Patent Misuse Doctrine' (2011) 12 Minn J L Sci & Tech 457.

Cornish W R, Llewelyn D and Aplin T F, *Intellectual Property: Patents, Copyright, Trade Marks and Allied Rights* (8th edn, Sweet & Maxwell 2013).

Costilo L B, 'Antitrust's Newest Quagmire: The Noerr-Pennington Defense' (1967) 66 Mich L Rev 333.

Crane D A, 'Judicial Review of Anticompetitive State Action: Two Models in Comparative Perspective (2013) 1 J Antitrust Enforcement 418.

Crawford B W and DeGiulio J V, 'New (Limited) Duty of Candor in the EPO (Amended European Rule 141)' (2010) 8[4] MBHB Snippets 13 (2010).

Creighton S A and others, 'Cheap Exclusion' (2005) 72 Antitrust L J 975.

Cremers K and others, 'Invalid But Infringed? An Analysis of Germany's Bifurcated Patent Litigation System' (2014) Max Planck Institute for Innovation & Competition Research Paper 14/14 <http://ssrn.com/abstract=2504507>.

Crew E, 'The Use of Patent Litigation to Violate the Antitrust Laws' (2006) 11 Intell Prop L Bull 69.

Crouch D, 'Supplemental Examination: Inequitable Conduct Amnesty and Beyond' (*Patently-O*, 16 September 2012) <www.patentlyo.com/patent/2012/09/supplemental-examination-inequitable-conduct-amnesty-and-beyond.html>.

Crouch D, 'Is the New Supplemental Examination a Complete Replacement for Owner Initiated Ex Parte Reexamination?' (*Patently-O*, 3 October 2012) <www.patentlyo.com/patent/2012/10/is-the-new-supplemental-examination-a-complete-replacement-for-owner-initiated-ex-parte-reexamination.html>.

Czapracka K, *Intellectual Property and the Limits of Antitrust: A Comparative Study of US and EU Approaches* (Edward Elgar 2010).

Daniel B D, 'Walker Process Proof: The Proper Prescription' (2009) 41 Rutgers L J 105.

Davenport N, *The United Kingdom Patent System: A Brief History* (Mason 1979).

Davidow J, *Patent-Related Misconduct Issues in US Litigation* (OUP 2010).

de Saint-Georges M and van Pottelsberghe de la Potterie B, 'A Quality Index for Patent Systems' (2013) 42 Research Policy 704.

DeSanti S and Cohen W, 'Competition to Innovate: Strategies for Proper Antitrust Assessments' in Dreyfuss R C, Zimmerman D L and First H (eds), *Expanding the Boundaries of Intellectual Property* (OUP 2001) 317.

De Stefano G, 'Tough Enforcement of Unilateral Conduct at the National Level: Italian Antitrust Authority Sanctions Bayer and Pfizer for Abuse of Dominant Position (aka AstraZeneca Ruling and Essential Facility Doctrine in Italian Sauce)' (2012) 3 J Eur Comp L & Prac 396.

Dieny E, 'The Pharmaceutical Industry and Competition Law between the Present and the Future' (2007) 28 Eur Comp L Rev 223.

Dolak L A, 'Inequitable Conduct: A Flawed Doctrine Worth Saving' (2010) 11 Wake Forest Intell Prop L J 1.

Dolak L A, 'America Invents the Supplemental Examination, but Retains the Duty of Candor: Questions and Implications' (2012) 6 Akron Intell Prop J 147.

Drahos P, '"Trust Me": Patent Offices in Developing Countries' (2008) 34 Am J L & Med 151.

Drexl J, 'Intellectual Property and Antitrust Law - IMS Health and Trinko: Antitrust Placebo for Consumers Instead of Sound Economics in Refusal-to-Deal Cases' (2004) 35 IIC 788.

Drexl J, 'Is There a "More Economic Approach" to Intellectual Property and Competition Law?' in Drexl J (ed), *Research Handbook on Intellectual Property and Competition Law* (Edward Elgar 2008) 27.

Drexl J, 'The Relationship Between the Legal Exclusivity and Economic Market Power: Links and Limits' in Govaere I and Ullrich H (eds), *Intellectual Property, Market Power and the Public Interest* (Peter Lang 2008) 13.

Drexl J, 'Deceptive Conduct in the Patent World: A Case for US Antitrust and EU Competition Law?' in Prinz zu Waldeck und Pyrmont W and others (eds), *Patents and Technological Progress in a Globalized World: Liber Amicorum for Joseph Straus* (Springer 2009) 137.

Drexl J, '"Pay-for-Delay" and Blocking Patents: Targeting Pharmaceutical Companies under European Competition Law' (2009) 40 IIC 751.

Drexl J, 'Real Knowledge is to Know the Extent of One's Own Ignorance: On the Consumer Harm Approach in Innovation-Related Competition Cases' (2010) 76 Antitrust L J 677.

Drexl J, 'Anticompetitive Stumbling Stones on the Way to a Cleaner World: Protecting Competition in Innovation Without a Market' (2012) 8 J Comp L & Econ 507.

Drexl J, '*AstraZeneca* and the EU Sector Inquiry: When do Patent Filings Violate Competition Law?' in f Drexl J and Lee N (eds), *Pharmaceutical Innovation, Competition and Patent Law: A Trilateral Perspective* (Edward Elgar 2013) 290.

Dreyfuss R C, 'The Federal Circuit: A Case Study in Specialized Courts' (1989) 64 NYU L Rev 1.

Eilmansberger T, 'How to Distinguish Good From Bad Competition Under Article 82 EC: In Search of Clearer and More Coherent Standards for Anti-competitive Abuses' (2005) 42 CML Rev 129.

Elhauge E, 'Making Sense of Antitrust Petitioning Immunity' (1992) 80 Cal L Rev 1177.

Elhauge E, 'Defining Better Monopolization Standards' (2003) 56 Stan L Rev 253.

Elhauge E and Geradin D, *Global Antitrust Law and Economics*, (2nd edn, Foundation Press 2011).

Erstling J, 'Patent Law and the Duty of Candor: Rethinking The Limits of Disclosure' (2011) 44 Creighton L Rev 329.

European Generic Medicines Association, 'Patent-Related Barriers to Market Entry for Generic Medicines in the European Union: A Review of Weaknesses in the Current European Patent System and their Impact on the Market Access of Generic Medicines' (2008).

Farrell J and Merges R P, 'Incentives to Challenge and Defend Patents: Why Litigation Won't Reliably Fix Patent Office Errors and Why Administrative Patent Review Might Help' (2004) 19 Berkeley Tech L J 943.

Feldman R C, 'The Insufficiency of Antitrust Analysis for Patent Misuse' (2003) 55 Hastings L J 399.

Filmore S, 'Defining the Misrepresentation Exception to the Noerr-Pennington Doctrine' (2001) 49 Univ Kan L Rev 423.

Fischel D R, 'Antitrust Liability for Attempts to Influence Government Action: The Basis and Limits of the *Noerr-Pennington* Doctrine' (1977) 45 U Chi L Rev 80.

Fischmann F, *«Reverse Payments» als Mittel zur Beilegung von Patentstreitigkeiten - Ein Verstoß gegen das Kartellrecht?* (Stämpfli Verlag 2016).

Fisher F M, 'Monopolization versus Abuse of Dominant Position: An Economist's View' in Hawk B (ed), *International Antitrust Law & Policy: Fordham Corporate Law 2003* (Juris Publishing 2004) 157.

Flanagan A, Ghezzi F and Montagnani M L, 'The Search of EU Boundaries: IPR Exercise and Enforcement as "Misuse"' in Flanagan A and Montagnani M L (eds), *Intellectual Property Law: Economic and Social Justice Perspectives* (Edward Elgar 2010) 112.

Flores E S and Warren S E Jr, 'Inequitable Conduct, Fraud, and Your License to Practice before the United States Patent and Trademark Office' (2000) 8 Tex Intell Prop L J 299.

Floyd C D, 'Antitrust Liability for the Anticompetitive Effects of Governmental Action Induced by Fraud' (2001) 69 Antitrust L J 403.

Forrester I S, 'The Interplay Between Standardization, IPR and Competition Law' in Caggiano G, Muscolo G and Tavassi M (eds), *Competition Law and Intellectual Property: A European Perspective* (Wolters Kluwer 2012) 113.

Fox E M, 'Monopolization and Dominance in the United States and the European Community: Efficiency Opportunity and Fairness' (1986) 61 Notre Dame L Rev 981.

Fox E M, 'We Protect Competition, You Protect Competitors' (2003) 26 World Competition 149.

Fox E M and Healey D, 'When the State Harms Competition: the Role for Competition Law' (2014) 79 Antitrust L J 769.

Fuchs A, 'Patent Ambush Strategies and Article 102 TFEU' in Drexl J and others (eds), *More Common Ground for International Competition Law* (Edward Elgar 2011) 177.

Gallasch S, 'AstraZeneca v the Walker Process – A Real EU-US Divergence or Just an Attempt to Compare Apples to Oranges?' (2011) 7 Eur Comp J 505.

Galloway J, 'Driving Innovation: A Case for Targeted Competition Policy in Dynamic Markets' (2011) 34 World Competition 73.

Geradin D, 'Limiting the Scope of Article 82 EC: What can the EU Learn From the US Supreme Court's Judgment in *Trinko* in the Wake of *Microsoft*, *IMS*, and *Deutsche Telekom*?' (2004) 41 CML Rev 1519.

Geradin D and others, 'The Concept of Dominance in EC Competition Law' (2005) GCLC Research Paper on the Modernization of Article 82 EC <http://ssrn.com/abstract=770144>.

Geradin D, 'When Competition Law Analysis Goes Wrong – The Italian Pfizer/Pharmacia Case' (2014) <http://ssrn.com/abstract=2393383>.

Gerber D J, *Law and Competition in Twentieth Century Europe: Protecting Prometheus* (OUP 2003).

Gervais M, *The TRIPS Agreement: Drafting History and Analysis* (4th edn, Sweet & Maxwell 2012).

Ghidini G, *Innovation, Competition and Consumer Welfare in Intellectual Property Law* (Edward Elgar 2010).

Gilbert R J and Sunshine S C, 'Incorporating Dynamic Efficiency Concerns in Merger Analysis: The Use of Innovation Markets' (1994) 63 Antitrust L J 569.

Glader M, *Innovation Markets and Competition Analysis* (Edward Elgar 2006).

Goldman R J, 'Evolution of the Inequitable Conduct Defense in Patent Litigation' (1993) 7 Harv J L & Tech 37.

Govaere I, *The Use and Abuse of Intellectual Property Rights in EC Law* (Sweet & Maxwell 1996).

Govaere I, 'In Pursuit of an Innovation Policy Rationale: Stakes and Limits under Article 82 TEC' (2008) 31 World Competition 541.

Guimarães de Lima e Silva V, 'Sham Litigation in the Pharmaceutical Sector' (2011) 7 Eur Comp J 455.

Gunther J P and Breuvart C, 'Misuse of Patent and Drug Regulatory Approval Systems in the Pharmaceutical Industry: An Analysis of US And EU Converging Approaches' (2005) 26 Eur Comp L Rev 669.

Hacon R, *Concise European Patent Law* (Hacon R and Pagenberg J eds, 2nd edn, Wolters Kluwer 2008).

Hall B H and Harhoff D, 'Post-Grant Reviews in the U.S. Patent System Design Choices and Expected Impact' (2004) 19 Berkeley Tech L J 989.

Hall B H and others, 'Prospects for Improving U.S. Patent Quality via Postgrant Opposition' in Jaffe A B, Lerner J and Stern S (eds), Innovation Policy and the Economy: Volume 4 (National Bureau of Economic Research 2004).

Handler M and De Sevo R A, 'The *Noerr* Doctrine and Its Sham Exception' (1984) 6 Cardozo L Rev 1.

Heald P J, 'A Transaction Costs Theory of Patent Law' (2005) 66 Ohio St L J 473.

Heinemann A, 'The Contestability of IP-Protected Markets' in Drexl J (ed), *Research Handbook on Intellectual Property and Competition Law* (Edward Elgar 2008).

Helsel S D, 'Preventing Predatory Abuses in Litigation between Business Competitors: Focusing on a Litigant's Reasons for Initiating the Litigation to Ensure a Balance between the Constitutional Right to Petition and the Sherman Acts Guarantee of Fair Competition in Business' (1995) 36 Wm & Mary L Rev 1135.

Herper M, 'The Cost of Creating a New Drug Now $5 Billion, Pushing Big Pharma to Change' *Forbes* (New York, 11 August 2013) <www.forbes.com/sites/matthewherper/2013/08/11/how-the-staggering-cost-of-inventing-new-drugs-is-shaping-the-future-of-medicine>.

Herstein O J, 'A Normative Theory of the Clean Hands Defense (2011) 17 Legal Theory 171.

Hess B, 'Abuse of Procedure in Germany and Austria' in Taruffo M (ed), *Abuse of Procedural Rights: Comparative Standards of Procedural Fairness* (Kluwer 1999).

Hricik D, 'Where The Bodies Are: Current Exemplars of Inequitable Conduct and How to Avoid Them' (2004) 12 Tex Intell Prop L J 287.

Hovenkamp H, 'The Monopolization Offence' (2000) 61 Ohio St L J 1035.

Hovenkamp H, *The Antitrust Enterprise: Principle and Execution* (Harvard Univ Press 2005).

Hovenkamp H, 'IP and Antitrust Policy: A Brief Historical Overview' (2005) Univ Iowa Legal Studies Research Paper 05/31 <http://ssrn.com/abstract=869417>.

Hovenkamp H, 'The Walker Process Doctrine: Infringement Lawsuits as Antitrust Violations' (2008) U Iowa Legal Studies Research Paper 08/36 <http://ssrn.com/abstract=1259877>.

Hovenkamp H, 'Patent Exclusions and Antitrust after *Therasense*' (2011) U Iowa Legal Studies Research Paper 11/39 <http://ssrn.com/abstract=1916074>.

Hovenkamp H, 'Antitrust and the Patent System: A Reexamination' (2014) U Iowa Legal Studies Research Paper 14/27 <http://ssrn.com/abstract=2486633>.

Hovenkamp H and others, *IP and Antitrust: An Analysis of Antitrust Principles Applied to Intellectual Property Law* (2nd edn Supp 2013, Wolters Kluwer).

Hughes J, 'The Philosophy of Intellectual Property' (1988) 77 Geo L J 287.

Hull D, 'The AstraZeneca Judgment: Implications for IP and Regulatory Strategies' (2010) 1 J Eur Comp L & Prac 500.

Hull D, 'The Application of EU Competition Law in the Pharmaceutical Sector' (2011) 2 J Eur Comp L & Prac 480.

Hull D, 'The Application of EU Competition Law in the Pharmaceutical Sector' (2012) 3 J Eur Comp L & Prac 473.

Hulme E W, 'History of the Patent System under the Prerogative and at Common Law' (1896) 12 LQR 141.

Institute for Applied Economic Research (IPEA Brasilia), 'Study on the Anti-Competitive Enforcement of Intellectual Property (IP) Rights: Sham Litigation' (Report for the WIPO Committee on Development and Intellectual Property CDIP/9/INF/6 REV, 2012).

Jacob R, 'Patents and Pharmaceuticals: A Paper given on 29th November at the Presentation of the Directorate-General of Competition's Preliminary Report of the Pharma-Sector Inquiry' in Hansen H C (ed), *Intellectual Property Law and Policy: Volume 12* (Hart 2013).

Jacob R, 'Patent Thickets: A Paper for the European Patent Office Economic and Scientific Advisory Board Meeting' (2013) 8 J Intell Prop L & Prac 203.

Janicke P M, 'Do We Really Need So Many Mental and Emotional States in United States Patent Law?' (2000) 8 Tex Intell Prop L J 279.

Janicke P M, 'Overview of the New Patent Law of the United States' (2013) 21 Tex Intell Prop L J 63.

Janis M D, 'Transitions in IP and Antitrust' (2002) 47 Antitrust Bull 253.

Jones A and Sufrin B, *EU Competition Law* (5th edn, OUP 2014).

Jones C A, 'Patent Power and Market Power: Rethinking the Relationship Between Intellectual Property Rights and Market Power in Antitrust Analysis' in Drexl J (ed), *Research Handbook on Intellectual Property and Competition Law* (Edward Elgar 2008).

Joshua J, 'Single Continuous Infringement of Article 81 EC: Has the Commission Stretched the Concept beyond the Limit of its Logic?' (2009) 5 Eur Comp J 451.

Käseberg T, *Intellectual property, Antitrust and Cumulative Innovation in the EU and the US* (Hart 2012).

Kallaugher J and Weitbrecht A, 'Developments under Articles 101 and 102 TFEU in 2010' (2011) 32 Eur Comp L Rev 333.

Kaplow L, 'Why (Ever) Define Markets?' (2010) 124 Harv L Rev 437.

Katz A, 'Making Sense of Nonsense: Intellectual Property, Antitrust, and Market Power' (2007) 49 Ariz L Rev 837.

Keeling D T, *Intellectual Property Rights in EU Law Vol I: Free Movement and Competition Law* (OUP 2003).

Kern B R, 'Innovation Markets, Future Markets, or Potential Competition: How Should Competition Authorities Account for Innovation Competition in Merger Reviews?' (2014) 37 World Competition 173.

Keyte J A and Stoll N R, 'Markets? We Don't Need no Stinking Markets! The FTC and Market Definition' (2004) 49 Antitrust Bull 593.

Khan B Z and Sokoloff K L, 'History Lessons: The Early Development of Intellectual Property Institutions in the United States' (2001) 15 J Econ Perspectives 233.

Kitch E W, 'The Nature and Function of the Patent System' (1977) 20 J L & Econ 265.

Kjølbye L, 'Article 82 EC as Remedy to Patent System Imperfections: Fighting Fire with Fire?' (2009) 32 World Competition 163.

Klein C C, 'Strategic Sham Litigation: Economic Incentives in the Context of the Case Law' (1986) 6 Int'l Rev L & Econ 241.

Klein C C, 'The Economics of Sham Litigation: Theory, Cases, and Policy' (Bureau of Economics Staff Report to the FTC, April 1989) <www.ftc.gov/sites/default/files/documents/reports/economics-sham-litigation-theory-cases-and-policy/232158_0.pdf>.

Klein C C, 'Predation in the Courts: Legal Versus Economic Analysis in Sham Litigation Cases' (1990) 10 Int'l Rev L & Econ 29.

Klein C C, 'Anticompetitive Litigation and Antitrust Liability' (2007) Middle Tennessee State University, Department of Economics and Finance Working Paper 2007/13 <http://capone.mtsu.edu/berc/working/SHAM07WP.pdf>.

Kobak J B Jr, 'Professional Real Estate Investors and the Future of Patent-Antitrust Litigation: *Walker Process* And *Handgards* Meet *Noerr-Pennington*' (1994) 63 Antitrust L J 185.

Kobak J B Jr, 'The Doctrine that Will Not Die: Nobelpharma, Walker Process, and the Patent-Antitrust Counterclaim' (1998) 13 Antitrust 47.

Kobak J B Jr and Reznick R P, 'Antitrust Liability for Statements about Intellectual Property: Unocal, Unitherm and New Uncertainty' (2004) 19 Antitrust 87.

Korah V, 'The Limitation of Copyright and Patents by the Rules for the Free Movement of Goods in the European Common Market' (1982) 14 Case W Res J Int'l L 7.

Korah V, 'The Interface Between Intellectual Property and Antitrust: The European Experience' (2002) 69 Antitrust L J 801.

Korah V, *Intellectual Property Rights and the EC Competition Rules* (Hart 2006).

Korah V, *An Introductory Guide to EC Competition Law and Practice* (9th edn, Hart 2007).

Kovacic W E and Winerman M, 'Competition Policy and the Application of Section 5 of the Federal Trade Commission Act' (2010) 76 Antitrust L J 929.

Kraßer R, 'Verpflichtung des Patentanmelders oder –inhabers zu Angaben über den Stand der Technik' in Bruchhausen K and others (eds), *Festschrift Für Rudolf Nirk zum 70. Geburtstag* (Beck 1992).

Kraßer R and Bernhardt W, *Patentrecht* (6th edn, Beck 2009).

Krattenmaker T G, Lande R H and Salop S C, 'Monopoly Power and Market Power in Antitrust Law' (1987) 76 Geo L J 241.

Krauß J, 'Equitable Doctrines in International Patent Laws' in Toshiki Takenaka (ed), *Intellectual Property in Common Law and Civil Law* (Edward Elgar 2013).

Kuhn J M, 'Information Overload at the U.S. Patent and Trademark Office: Reframing the Duty of Disclosure in Patent Law as a Search and Filter Problem' (2010) 13 Yale J L and Tech 89.

Lande R H, 'A Traditional and Textualist Analysis of the Goals of Antitrust: Efficiency, Preventing Theft from Consumers, and Consumer Choice' (2013) 81 Fordham L Rev 2349.

Landes W M and Posner R A, 'Market Power in Antitrust Cases' (1981) 94 Harv L Rev 937.

Landes W M and Posner R A, *The Economic Structure of Intellectual Property Law* (Harvard Univ Press 2003).

Lao M, 'Reforming the Noerr-Pennington Antitrust Immunity Doctrine' (2003) 55 Rutgers L Rev 965.

Lao M, 'Reclaiming a Role for Intent Evidence in Monopolization Analysis' (2004) 54 Am Univ L Rev 151.

Lawrance S and Treacy P, 'The Commission's AstraZeneca Decision: Delaying Generic Entry is an Abuse of Dominant Position' (2005) 1 J Intell Prop L & Prac 7.

Leaffer M, 'Patent Misuse and Innovation' (2010) 10 J High Tech L 142.

Lemley M A, 'The Economic Irrationality of the Patent Misuse Doctrine' (1990) 78 Cal L Rev 1599.

Lemley M A, 'Antitrust Counterclaims in Patent and Copyright Infringement Cases' (1994) 3 Tex Intell Prop L J 1.

Lemley M A, 'Rational Ignorance at the Patent Office' (2001) 95 Northwest U L Rev 1495.

Lemley M A, 'The Myth of the Sole Inventor' (2012) 110 Mich L Rev 709.

Lemley M A and Shapiro C, 'Probabilistic Patents' (2005) 19 J Econ Perspectives 75.

Lerner A P, 'The Concept of Monopoly and the Measurement of Monopoly Power' (1934) 1 Rev of Econ Stud 157.

Leslie C R, 'The Anticompetitive Effects of Unenforced Invalid Patents' (2006) 91 Minn L Rev 101.

Leslie C R, 'Patents of Damocles' (2008) 83 Ind L J 133.

Leslie C R, 'Antitrust and Patent Law as Component Parts of Innovation Policy' (2009) 34 Iowa J Corp L 1259.

Leslie C R, 'Antitrust, Inequitable Conduct, and the Intent to Deceive the Patent Office' (2011) 1 U C Irvine L Rev 323.

Lim D, *Patent Misuse and Antitrust Law: Empirical, Doctrinal and Policy Perspectives* (Edward Elgar 2013).

Lim D, 'Revisiting the Patent Misuse Doctrine' in Josef Drexl (ed), *The Innovation Society and Intellectual Property* (Edward Elgar, forthcoming).

Lipsky A B Jr, 'Current Antitrust Division Views on Patent Licensing Practices' (1981) 50 Antitrust L J 515.

Luterkort E, 'Vexatious (Patent) Litigation & Art. 82 EC Following *AstraZeneca*: EC and US Converging Approaches?' (Master thesis, University of Lund 2007).

Lynch J F, 'An Argument for Eliminating the Defense of Patent Unenforceability Based on Inequitable Conduct' (1988) 16 Am Intell Prop L Asso Q J 7.

Mabey W K Jr, 'Deconstructing the Patent Application Backlog' (2010) 92 J Pat & Trademark Off Soc'y 208.

Machlup F, 'An Economic Review of the Patent System' (Study No 15 of the Subcommittee on Patents, Trademarks, and Copyright of the Committee on the Judiciary of the US Senate, 85th Congress, 2nd Session, Washington, 1958).

Machlup F and Penrose E, 'The Patent Controversy in the Nineteenth Century' (1950) 10 J Econ Hist 1.

Mack K, 'Reforming Inequitable Conduct to Improve Patent Quality: Cleansing Unclean Hands' (2006) 21 Berkeley Tech L J 147.

Maggiolino M, *Intellectual Property and Antitrust: A Comparative Economic Analysis of US and EU Law* (Edward Elgar 2011).

Maggiolino M and Montagnani M L, 'Astrazeneca's Abuse of IPR-Related Procedures: A Hypothesis of Anti-Trust Offence, Abuse of Rights and IPR Misuse' (2011) 34 World Competition 245.

Mammen C E, 'Controlling the "Plague": Reforming the Doctrine of Inequitable Conduct' (2009) 24 Berkeley Tech L J 1329.

Manley M I and Wray A, 'New Pitfall for the Pharmaceutical Industry' (2006) 1 J Intell Prop L & Prac 266.

McFarland I G, 'In the Wake of *Therasense* & *Nisus Corp.*: How Can Patent Attorneys Defend Themselves against Allegations of Inequitable Conduct?' (2011) 78 Tenn L Rev 487.

McGowan D and Lemley M A, 'Antitrust Immunity: State Action and Federalism, Petitioning and the First Amendment' (1994) 17 Harv J L & Pub Pol'y 293.

Merges R P, 'Reflections on Current Legislation Affecting Patent Misuse' (1988) 70 J Pat & Trademark Off Soc'y 793.

Merges R P, 'As Many as Six Impossible Patents Before Breakfast: Property Rights for Business Concepts and Patent System Reform' (1999) 14 Berkeley Tech L J 577.

Merges R P and Duffy J F, *Patent Law and Policy: Cases and Materials* (6th edn, LexisNexis 2013).

Mes P, *Patentgesetz, Gebrauchmustergesetz* (3rd edn, Beck 2011).

Miege C, Gärtner A and Besen M, 'Missbrauch einer marktbeherrschenden Stellung durch Irreführende Angaben bei Patentanmeldungen: Anmerkung zu EuG, Urt v 01.07.2010 – EUG 01.07.2010 – T-321/05' (2010) 11 PharmR 586.

Monti G, *EC Competition Law* (Cambridge Univ Press 2007).

Motta M, *Competition Policy: Theory and Practice* (Cambridge Univ Press 2004).

Motta M and de Streel A, 'Exploitative and Exclusionary Excessive Prices in EU Law' in Ehlermann C D and Atanasiu I (eds), *European Competition Law Annual 2003: What is an Abuse of a Dominant Position?* (Hart 2006).

Moy R C, 'The Effect of New Rule 56 on the Law of Inequitable Conduct' (1992) 74 J Pat & Trademark Off Soc'y 257.

Mueller J M, *Patent Law* (4th edn, Wolters Kluwer 2013).

Müller-Graff J and Fischmann F, 'Der Fall AstraZeneca: "Tool boxes" in Arzneimittelsektor – Wer hat die Bessere Werkzeuge und Welche sind Erlaubt? Zum Urteil des Gerichts der Europäischen Union vom 1. Juli 2010, Rs. T-321/05' [2010] GRUR Int 2010 792.

Murphy F and Liberatore F, 'Abuse of Regulatory Procedures: The AstraZeneca Case' (2009) 30 Eur Comp L Rev 223.

Murphy N M, 'Inequitable-Conduct Doctrine Reform: Is the Death Penalty for Patents Still Appropriate?' (2009) 93 Minn L Rev 2274.

Myers G, 'Antitrust and First Amendment Implications of Professional Real Estate Investors' (1994) 51 Wash & Lee L Rev 1199.

National Research Council of the National Academies, *A Patent System for the 21st Century* (Merrill S A, Levin R C and Myers M B eds, National Academies Press 2004).

Negrinotti M, 'Abuse of Regulatory Procedures in the Intellectual Property Context: The AstraZeneca Case' in Govaere I and Ullrich H (eds), *Intellectual Property, Market Power and the Public Interest* (Peter Lang 2008).

Niro R P and Wigert J W Jr, 'Patents, Fraud and the Antitrust Laws' (1968) 37 Geo Wash L Rev 168.

Nolan-Stevaux K, 'Inequitable Conduct Claims in the 21st Century: Combating the Plague' (2005) 20 Berkeley Tech L J 147.

O'Connor S M, 'Defusing the Atomic Bomb of Patent Litigation: Avoiding and Defending Against Allegations of Inequitable Conduct after McKesson *Et Al*' (2009) 9 J Marshall Rev Intell Prop L 330.

O'Donnell S W, 'Unified Theory of Antitrust Counterclaims in Patent Litigation' (2004) 9(8) Va J L & Tech 1.

O'Donoghue R and Padilla A J, *The Law and Economics of Article 102 TFEU* (2nd edn, Hart 2013).

Ohlhausen M K, 'Section 5 of the FTC Act: Principles of Navigation' (2013) 1 J Antitrust Enforcement 1.

Ohly A and others, *Gesetz gegen den unlauteren Wettbewerb* (6th edn, Beck 2014).

Ottaviano I, 'Industrial Property and Abuse of Dominant Position in the Pharmaceutical Market: Some Thoughts on the AstraZeneca Judgment of the EU General Court' in Caggiano G, Muscolo G and Tavassi M (eds), *Competition Law and Intellectual Property: A European Perspective* (Wolters Kluwer 2012).

Ortiz Blanco L, *Market Power in EU Antitrust Law* (Hart 2012).

Peeperkorn L, 'IP Licences and Competition Rules: Striking the Right Balance' (2003) 26 World Competition 527.

Peritz R J R, 'Competition Policy and its Implications for Intellectual Property Rights in the United States' in Anderman S D (ed), *The Interface Between Intellectual Property Rights and Competition Policy* (Cambridge Univ Press 2007).

Peritz R J R, 'Competition within Intellectual Property Regimes: the Instance of Patent Rights' in Anderman S D and Ezrachi A (eds), *Intellectual Property and Competition Law: New Frontiers* (OUP 2011).

Petherbridge L, Rantanen J and Mojibi A, 'The Federal Circuit and Inequitable Conduct: An Empirical Assessment' (2011) 84 S Cal L Rev 1293.

Petit N, 'Microsoft v Google – Karate Competition Law?' (*Chillin' Competition*, 7 April 2011) <http://chillingcompetition.com/2011/04/07/microsoft-v-google-karate-competition-law>.

Petrovčič U, 'Patent Hold-Up and the Limits of Competition Law: A Trans-Atlantic Perspective' (2013) 50 CML Rev 1363.

Phillips J, *Charles Dickens and the 'Poor Man's Tale of a Patent'* (ESC 1984).

Picht P, *Strategisches Verhalten bei der Nutzung von Patenten in Standardisierungsverfahren aus der Sicht des Europäischen Kartellrechts* (Springer 2013).

Podszun R, 'Can Competition Law Repair Patent Law and Administrative Procedures? *AstraZeneca* ' (2014) 51 CML Rev 281.

Posner R A, 'The Social Costs of Monopoly and Regulation' (1975) 83 J Pol Econ 807.

Posner R A, *Antitrust Law* (2nd edn, Univ of Chicago Press 2001).

Priddis S and Constantine S, 'The Pharmaceutical Sector, Intellectual Property Rights, and Competition Law in Europe' in Anderman S D and Ezrachi A (eds), *Intellectual Property and Competition Law: New Frontiers* (OUP 2011).

Rai A K, 'Growing Pains in the Administrative State: The Patent Office's Troubled Quest for Managerial Control' (2009) 157 U Pa L Rev 2051.

Rapp R T, 'The Misapplication of the Innovation Market Approach to Merger Analysis' (1995) 64 Antitrust L J 19.

Rato M and Petit N, 'Abuse of Dominance in Technology-Enabled Markets: Established Standards Reconsidered?' (2013) 9 ECJ 1.

Riziotis D, 'Patent Misuse als Schnittstelle zwischen Patentrecht und Kartellrecht: Eine Rechtsvergleichende Darstellung' [2004] GRUR Int 367.

Robinson A T, 'The America Invents Act and the Best Mode Requirement: Where Do We Go From Here? (2012) 20 J Intell Prop L 179.

Röller L H, 'Exploitative Abuses' in Ehlermann C D and Marquis M (eds), *European Competition Law Annual 2007: A Reformed Approach to Article 82 EC* (Hart 2008).

Rousseva E and Marquis M, 'Hell Freezes Over: A Climate Change for Assessing Exclusionary Conduct under Article 102 TFEU' (2013) 4 J Eur Comp L & Prac 32.

Salop S C and Scheffman D T, 'Raising Rivals' Costs' (1983) 73 Am Econ Rev 267.

Sampat B N, 'Examining Patent Examination: An Analysis of Examiner and Applicant Generated Prior Art' (Dphil thesis, University of Michigan 2004).

Sampat B N, 'When Do Applicants Search for Prior Art?' (2010) 53 J L & Econ 399.

Scellato G and others, 'Study on the Quality of the Patent System in Europe' (Report for the European Commission, DG Internal Market, 2011).

Schade J, 'Synergies created by international cooperation in the patent area' in Prinz zu Waldeck und Pyrmont W and others (eds), *Patents and Technological Progress in a Globalized World* (Springer 2009).

Schechter E R and Thomas J R, *Principles of Patent Law* (Thomson/West 2004).

Scherer F M and Ross D, *Industrial Market Structure and Economic Performance* (3rd edn, Houghton Mifflin 1990).

Schneck T, 'The Duty to Search' (2005) 87 J Pat & Trademark Off Soc'y 689.

Schumpeter J, *Capitalism, Socialism and Democracy* (Harper 1942).

Seidel D, *Europäische Missbrauchsaufsicht nach AstraZeneca: Fallrelevante Problemkreise unter besonderer Berücksichtigung des Konfliktfeldes Immaterialgüter-/Wettbewerbsrecht* (Shaker 2008).

Seitz C, 'Klare Grenzlinie und Minenfeld: Die Marktmissbrauchskontrolle im Arzneimittelsektor nach dem AstraZeneca-Urteil des EuGH' [2013] EuZW 377.

Shapiro C, 'Competition and Innovation: Did Arrow Hit the Bull's Eye?' in Lerner J and Stern S (eds), *The Rate and Direction of Inventive Activity Revisited* (Univ of Chicago Press 2012).

Singer M and Stauder D (eds), *The European Patent Convention: A Commentary* (3rd edn, Sweet & Maxwell 2003) vols 1 and 2.

Siragusa M, 'The EU Pharmaceutical Sector Inquiry: New Forms of Abuse and Article 102 TFEU' in Caggiano G, Muscolo G and Tavassi M (eds), *Competition Law and Intellectual Property: A European Perspective* (Wolters Kluwer 2012).

Smith N A, 'Fraud upon the Patent Office as a Violation of the Sherman Antitrust Law' (1970) 14 Pat Trademark & Copyright J Res & Educ 507.

Spillmann A, 'Transparency Obligation for Holders of EU IP Assets in the Pharmaceutical Industry' (2014) 9 J Intell Prop L & Prac 125.

Spulber D F, 'How Patents Provide the Foundation of the Market for Inventions' (2014) Northwest L & Econ Research Paper 14/14 <http://ssrn.com/abstract=2487564>.

Steinman D R and Fitzpatrick D S, 'Antitrust Counterclaims in Patent Infringement Cases: A Guide to Walker Process and Sham-Litigation Claims' (2001) 10 Tex Intell Prop L J 95.

Stothers C and Ramondino M, 'Aftermath of AstraZeneca and the Pharmaceutical Sector Inquiry: the Big Chill?' (2011) 32 Eur Comp L Rev 591.

Strandburg K J, 'What Does the Public Get: Experimental Use and the Patent Bargain' [2004] Wis L Rev 81.

Straus J, 'Patent Application: Obstacle for Innovation and Abuse of Dominant Position under Article 102 TFEU?' (2010) 1 J Eur Comp L & Prac 189.

Straus J, 'Can Antitrust Adequately Assess Patent Settlement Agreements Disconnected from Patent Law Relevant Facts? The Servier Case – Its Public Perception and its Underlying Facts' (2016) 38 EIPR 533.

Taylor D O, 'Patent Fraud' (2010) 83 Temp L Rev 49.

Temple Lang J, 'European Community Antitrust Law: Innovation Markets and High Technology Industries' (1997) 20 Fordham Int'l L J 717.

Temple Lang J, 'Reprisals and Overreaction by Dominant Companies as an Anticompetitive Abuse under Article 82(b)' (2008) 29 Eur Comp L Rev 13.

Tom W K and Newberg J A, 'Antitrust and Intellectual Property: From Separate Spheres to Unified Field' (1997) 66 Antitrust L J 167.

Van Malleghem P A and Devroe W, 'AstraZeneca: Court of Justice Upholds First Decision Fiding Abuse of Dominant Position in Pharmaceutical Sector' (2013) 4 J Eur Comp L & Prac 228.

van Pottelsberghe de la Potterie B, 'The Quality Factor in Patent Systems' (2011) 20 Industrial and Corporate Change 1755.

Vezzoso S, 'Towards an EU Doctrine of Anticompetitive IP-Related Litigation' (2012) 3 J Eur Comp L & Prac 521.

Völcker S B, 'Developments in EC Competition Law in 2005: An Overview' (2006) 43 CML Rev 1409.

Vogelenzang P, 'Abuse of a Dominant Position in Article 86: the Problem of Causality and Some Applications' (1976) 13 CML Rev. 61.

Vossestein A J, 'Corporate Efforts to Influence Public Authorities, and the EC Rules on Competition' (2000) 37 CML Rev 1383.

Waelbroeck D, 'Tough Competition: What is the Relevance of Intention in Article 82 cases?' (2006) 5(8) Comp Law Insight 5.

Wallace J M, 'Rambus v FTC in the Context of Standard-Setting Organizations, Antitrust, and the Patent Hold-Up Problem' (2009) 24 Berkeley Tech L J 661.

Wainwright R and Bouquet A, 'State Intervention and Action in EC Competition Law' in Hawk B (ed), *International Antitrust Law & Policy: Fordham Corporate Law 2003* (Juris Publishing 2004).

Wasserman M F, 'Limiting the Inequitable Conduct Defense' (2008) 13(7) Va J L & Tech 14.

Werden G J, 'The 1982 Merger Guidelines and the Ascent of the Hypothetical Monopolist Paradigm' (2003) 71 Antitrust L J 253.

Westin J, 'Defining Relevant Market in the Pharmaceutical Sector in the Light of the Losec-Case: Just How Different is the Pharmaceutical Market?' (2011) 32 Eur Comp L Rev 57.

Whish R, *Competition Law* (8th edn, OUP 2015).

Wilson B B, 'Patent and Know-How License Agreements: Field of Use, Territorial, Price and Quantity Restrictions' (Remarks Before the Fourth New England Antitrust Conference, 6 November 1970).

Wofford R, 'Considering the "Pattern Litigation" Exception to the *Noerr-Pennington* Antitrust Defense' (2003) 49 Wayne L Rev 95.

Wright J D, 'Proposed Policy Statement Regarding Unfair Methods of Competition Under Section 5 of the FTC Act' (19 June 2013) <www.ftc.gov/sites/default/files/documents/public_statements/statement-commissioner-joshua-d.wright/130619umcpolicystatement.pdf>.

Zbierska K, *Application and Importance of Supplementary Protection Certificates for Medicinal Products in the European Union* (Shaker 2012).

Zimmer D (ed), *The Goals of Competition Law* (Edward Elgar 2012).

Official Documents

Communication from the Commission, Pharmaceutical Sector Inquiry: Final Report (8 July 2009).

Deutsches Patent- und Markenamt, 'Jahresbericht 2013' (Lex Lingua 2014).

European Commission, Econ Advisory Group on Competition Policy, Report on an Economic Approach to Article 82 (July 2005) <http://ec.europa.eu/dgs/competition/economist/eagcp_july_21_05.pdf>.

FTC, 'Enforcement Perspectives on the Noerr-Pennington Doctrine: An FTC Staff Report' (2006) <www.ftc.gov/sites/default/files/documents/reports/ftc-staff-report-concerning-enforcement-perspectives-noerr-pennington-doctrine/p013518enfperspectnoerr-penningtondoctrine.pdf>.

FTC, 'To Promote Innovation: The Proper Balance of Competition and Patent Law and Policy' (October 2003).

London Economics, 'Economic Study on Patent Backlogs and System of Mutual Recognition: Final Report to the Intellectual Property Office' (2010).

Organisation for Economic Co-operation and Development (OECD), 'Competition, Patents and Innovation' (2008, DAF/COMP(2007)40) <www.oecd.org/dataoecd/26/10/39888509.pdf>.

UKIPO, 'Facts and Figures: 2012 and 2013 Calendar Years' (UKIPO 2014).